D0045796

JACK LONDON
117-7

Jack London

A WRITER'S FIGHT FOR A BETTER AMERICA

Jack London

A WRITER'S FIGHT FOR A BETTER AMERICA

Cecelia Tichi

THE UNIVERSITY OF NORTH CAROLINA PRESS

Chapel Hill

Designed by Richard Hendel
Set in Quadraat and Owen types
by Tseng Information Systems, Inc.
Manufactured in the United States of America

This book was published with the assistance of the William R. Kenan Jr. Fund of the University of North Carolina Press.

This book is also available in an enhanced ebook edition that includes video material.

The paper in this book meets the guidelines for permanence and durability of the Committee on Production Guidelines for Book Longevity of the Council on Library Resources.

The University of North Carolina Press has been a member of the Green Press Initiative since 2003.

Jacket illustrations: Jack London, photograph by Arnold Genthe (Courtesy of Library of Congress, Prints and Photographs Division, LC-G4085-0411); USA flag, © Thinkstock.com / Hemera / Harm Kruyshaar; vintage boxing gloves, © Thinkstock.com / iStock / rimglow

Library of Congress Cataloging-in-Publication Data
Tichi, Cecelia, 1942–
Jack London and the fight for America's future / Cecelia Tichi.
— First edition.
pages cm
"Published with the assistance of the William R. Kenan Jr. Fund of the University of North Carolina Press" — Verso title page.
Includes bibliographical references and index.
ISBN 978-1-4696-2266-8 (cloth : alk. paper) —
ISBN 978-1-4696-2267-5 (ebook)
1. London, Jack, 1876–1916. 2. Authors, American—19th century—Biography. 3. Authors, American—20th century—Biography. 4. London, Jack, 1876–1916.—Political and social views. 5. Social problems in literature. 6. Social ethics in literature. 7. United States—In literature. I. Title.
PS3523.O46Z9825 2015
813′.52—dc23

2015010517

MIX
Paper from responsible sources
FSC® C013483

This book is dedicated to

LEV SOLOMON GREZEMKOVSKY

"He also that is valiant, whose heart is as the heart of a lion"

— Samuel 10

ALLEGRA CHAYA GREZEMKOVSKY

"They shall prosper that love thee"

— Psalms 19

If, just by wishing, I could change America and Americans in one way I would change the economic organization of America so that true opportunity would obtain; and service, instead of profits, would be the idea, the ideal, and the ambition animating every citizen. This in itself would effect all minor changes such as doing away with the commercial spirit, with child labor, with graft, with suffering and degradation, with war, and similar barbaric nuisances that exist in our country today.

—Jack London to *Los Angeles Times* reporter, 1914

CONTENTS

ILLUSTRATIONS

Jack London

A WRITER'S FIGHT FOR A BETTER AMERICA

Jack London, American Public Intellectual

AN INTRODUCTION

In all his novels, Mr. London cleverly weaves his theories of social reform.
—"Jack London in New Haven," *Yale News*, January 1906

On the morning of January 26, 1906, the Yale University community awoke to find the trees on the campus blazoned with a poster proclaiming, "JACK LONDON AT WOOLSEY HALL . . . WILL SPEAK ABOUT THE COMING CRISIS." The oversize posters featured London wearing an incendiary "red sweater" against the "lurid glare of a great conflagration." One student predicted that the faculty would be "shocked beyond measure" this evening, and he envisioned "the sons of the rich listening to the thunderbolts of the prophet of the new order." London's lecture, he knew, was an updated version of his "Revolution," the speech that rocked the Berkeley campus of the University of California the previous spring with its indictment of capitalism's failings and its trumpet call to a new social order.[1]

That winter night, hundreds of students, faculty, and workmen overflowed Yale's "million-dollar white marble" Woolsey Hall, with its Corinthian columns and gorgeous massive pipe organ. The student organizers had "bombarded" nearby factories and shops with handout "dodgers" to spread the word, and the young men of Yale sat shoulder to shoulder with immigrant workers from area mills, from nearby brass plants, and from the sprawling Winchester Repeating Arms Company. Yale president Arthur Twining Hadley sat in the gallery, as did the revered conservative political economist Professor William Graham Sumner. All who were present saw the speaker walk to the edge of the stage at the appointed hour. His dark hair was "combed low over one side of his forehead," and he'd renounced the gentleman's starched shirt and stiff collar in favor of an informal "black cheviot suit with a white flannel shirt, rolling flannel collar, a black silk tie and well-worn patent leather pumps." Those seated in the

1. Jack London's lecture was announced on posters that appeared on the Yale University campus on the morning of his presentation. The socialist students who sponsored London's visit feared that advance publicity would prompt cancellation by school officials. (California Department of Parks and Recreation)

YALE UNION

JACK LONDON

—AT—

WOOLSEY HALL, FRIDAY, JAN. 26

AT 8 P. M.

ADDRESS :

"THE COMING CRISIS"

RESERVED SEAT, 25c

2. Ticket for the best seats at Jack London's lecture at Yale University, January 26, 1906. General seating tickets cost ten cents. (Anderson Collection, Sonoma, California)

rear of the auditorium reportedly heard "a clear voice that reached easily to the farthest reaches of the hall."[2]

"I speak tonight on behalf of the Intercollegiate Socialist Society," he began, "for the purpose of starting in the various colleges an intelligent study of socialism." As he explained to the audience, socialism is "a science and a philosophy that deals with the human, and attempts to make a better world for the human." "Its purpose," he went on, is "to get a more rational organization of society than we have to-day." The movement, he asserted, "is clean, noble, and alive."[3]

Listeners heard the famous author pose this challenge to the industrial capitalist order: "Why are there 10,000,000 people in the United States to-day who are not properly sheltered and properly fed?" And "why, to-day, in the United States, are 80,000 children working out their lives in the textile factories alone?" "This is the question the revolutionist asks," said London, "and he asks it of the managing class, the capitalist class." He paused here to repeat the questions so the gravity of the situation could strike home. "The capitalist class," he said, "does not answer it. The capitalist class cannot answer it." America, he asserted, desperately needed the "awakening . . . of its college men" to achieve "a healthier order of things."[4]

The whole country needed to awaken, Jack London knew, and he steeled himself to continue to sound the revolutionary alarm. Backed by facts, the tough political statements of the kind he offered in Woolsey Hall could make their mark, for he never shied away from uttering what he knew to be verifiably true. And Jack London had other potent weaponry in his armament. As one Yale professor remarked, he was a distinguished "literary" man. The "literary" man was far more powerful than many recognized. Lost to the Yale president and his colleagues were the carefully targeted messages in London's novels and short stories, for popular fiction was a megaphone that amplified his voice to millions each day of the week. In athletic terms, London's fiction was a prizefight of many rounds for the cause of social political and economic justice. The fight went to Yale tonight, but the national and international campaign was ongoing, and London's brand-name best-selling fiction was its field of action and its driving force.[5]

In a career spanning the tumultuous years of the late nineteenth and early twentieth centuries, Jack London (1876–1916) has long been hailed as a prolific producer of best-selling fiction; a flamboyant adventurer; a daring sailor; a resourceful war correspondent on the front lines; a travel writer, sports reporter, playwright, socialist essayist, and lecturer. One identity that is fundamental to an understanding of his work and its significance to America's historical development, however, has been lost in successive decades: that is, Jack London, the great American public intellectual. To add London to this pantheon now, nearly a hundred years after his death, is not, however, meant to confer a posthumous award or to shuffle the deck of American luminaries. On the contrary, renewed attention to London's career reveals how a figure of enormous popular appeal and astonishing output in fact exerted great leverage for social change in a critically vital historical moment.

London lived in the first Gilded Age of American material abundance, technological superiority, global prestige, and economic growth—all undershot with stupendous wealth inequality, cycles of joblessness, treacherous workplaces that ravaged adults' and children's lives, farming practices that exhausted the soil, a criminal justice system that rivaled Dante's *Inferno*, and an imperial global presence that brought indigenous populations to heel while exploiting their natural resources. Reformers and investigative journalists of London's day exposed these arrangements as brutal in the present and dangerous for the future, and their names grew familiar as muckrakers and Progressives. Meanwhile, London rocketed to fame as the popular producer of fiction of the exotic Yukon and the South Seas, of the sport of prizefighting and of sailing adventures. A marquee author, the photogenic London was captured by the camera in varied autobiographical identities, from working man to bon vivant, his face commemorated in a sculptural bas-relief and, in the late twentieth century, by a US first-class postage stamp.

Politically an avowed socialist, he held fast to his convictions in published essays and spoke publicly to make the case for a sociable America of material well-being for its expanding population. Some saw two separate identities: the popular writer of adventure stories and novels reaching millions; and the political partisan indulging his personal tastes in a fringe movement that waxed and waned.

Both views had validity—but both miss the larger and far more important point that can be understood in the twenty-first century, when the country is once again experiencing an era of vast disparities of wealth, high unemployment, record-breaking levels of incarceration, the blight of factory farming, and other sociopolitical and economic dislocations. This contemporary sociocultural context sets the stage for the reappraisal of Jack London as a figure who championed progressive reform and did so with a wealth of archival documents to support his extraordinary outreach into the public sphere.

From the late twentieth century, the term "public intellectual" has edged into widespread use in domains ranging from the arts to economics and poli-

3. Photo portrait of Jack London, the rising young author.
(Henry E. Huntington Library, San Marino, California)

tics, all of which were central to Jack London's prolific and versatile career. A debate that he entered—one that still stirs in the twenty-first century—asks what level of expertise defines such intellectuals, to what purposes their efforts are directed, and to what extent the public is moved to act on the ideas they advance. A basic working definition, supplied by the legal scholar Richard Posner, posits a public intellectual as expressing himself or herself on issues of political or ideological import in a way that is readily accessible

to the public, a point that Jack London underscored on numerous occasions. The group or groups that constitute the public were, what's more, on London's mind as fully as they are on those of pollsters and media experts today. In recent decades, we have come to distinguish between the public intellectual as a broad-based generalist able to pronounce on a wide range of the day's pressing issues, and the specialist called upon to illuminate a single strand of knowledge in an increasingly dense web of information and activity. This split arose in London's era when professional training and credentialing surged in US universities even as figures of acknowledged sagacity held forth from podiums and the printed page. Distinct from specialist experts, on the one hand, and from dilettantes, on the other, the public intellectual has been understood to recognize and enter into the zeitgeist or "spirit of the age" in order to reinforce it or to redirect it for the sake of a better common future.[6]

Today's array of social media, in which "thought leaders" bend the digital universe in their direction, were of course unforeseen in London's time, even by the utopian visionary Edward Bellamy, whose best-selling socialist novel *Looking Backward—2000–1887* (1886) London much admired. But while Bellamy forecast the communications technologies of radio and telephone, he could not begin to glimpse the digital revolution that today encourages us to seek out the agent of change whose authority is not official but personal, able to disseminate ideas to an expanding public across the continent and the world. The popular medium of communication in London's day was the printed page, and at frequent intervals he reached millions with both his fiction and personalized accounts of his life and times in books and mass-market magazines that blanketed the country—the *Saturday Evening Post*, *Cosmopolitan*, *The Bookman*, *Ainslee's*, the *Woman's Home Companion*, *McClure's*, *The Independent*. The list goes on and on. Competitive and robust, these periodicals cross-referenced each other with subscription advertising as they sought to build readership by the hundreds of thousands in a US population that topped just over 76 million by 1900. (In 1908 the *Saturday Evening Post* boasted that its weekly sales had reached 1 million copies.) Delivered punctually to homes and newsstands by a national network of reliable railroads and a superefficient postal system, these and hundreds of other magazines were the social media of Jack London's era, the medium through which an impassioned nonexpert sought to influence opinion and, ultimately, policy.

Jack London's fiction and essays put him in a tight-wire act of irresistible entertainment coupled with scalding revelations about the miseries and injustices of the contemporary American scene—and about the urgent need for reform. Ambitious, energetic, and drawn to socialist ideas even as a young man, London prepared himself to expose the depredations of the Gilded Age through the printed word and the speakers' platform even as he answered every letter of the thousands he received from friends and acquaintances, business associates and strangers.

The dawn of London's debut as public intellectual is open to debate. Some might cite the 1903 publication of *The Call of the Wild*, in which the teams of work dogs appear as surrogates for mistreated industrial workers. Others might point to a novel of the following year, *The Sea-Wolf*, in which the dictatorial sea captain stands in for the Gilded Age moguls who held the social order in their collective vise. Still others might call attention to London's essays, such as "What Life Means to Me" (1905), in which he vowed to "set the whole edifice rocking" by laboring "crowbar in hand, shoulder to shoulder, with intellectuals, idealists, and class-conscious workingmen." Whichever texts are cited, however, one point is incontestable: literary skill at a professional level was paramount to his effort.[7]

At the beginning, however, the twenty-two-year-old Jack London simply hoped to avoid a lifetime of crushing manual labor by earning a living with the pen. Already, at that point, he had a checkered history of work and family relationships, arising from an impoverished California boyhood when he'd worked on ranches and farms, done odd jobs for nickels and dimes, and later toiled in a steam laundry, a boiler room, a cannery, and a jute mill—all to earn his keep and help his struggling family, which comprised his mother, stepfather, two stepsisters, and, later on, a nephew. By the time he was in his teens, with grammar school completed, London borrowed three hundred dollars to purchase the small sailboat on which he raided privately owned oyster beds in the San Francisco Bay, sold the booty for cash, then shipped out as a crewman on a seal-hunting schooner in the Bering Sea. After resuming high school in 1895, he entered the University of California at Berkeley for one semester before spending the Klondike gold rush winter of 1897–98 in the Yukon and, upon his return, committing himself to professional writing. He then labored to produce the marketable verses, short stories, and newspaper "storiettes" that he classed as the "hack" work he despised but might be, he hoped, lucrative.

Students of London's career agree that once he failed to find gold in the Yukon, he ever afterward mined a lode of harrowing experiences and memorable campfire and cabin tales for polished narratives. Many of these feature the veteran gold-hunting "sourdoughs" who contended with newly arrived *chechaquos* and Klondike natives during subzero weather in a snowed-in and ice-bound "white silence." These stories—including "To the Man on Trail," "In a Far Country," and the oft-reprinted (and revised) "To Build a Fire"—were the fictional raw gold that Jack London mined and milled for an eager public. Earle Labor, London's biographer and a preeminent scholar of his work, remarks that "London's year in the Northland was the most crucially important experience in his literary career" and that "this experience—a genuine rite of passage—did not merely change the youth into the man: it transformed the man into the author, the amateur into the professional." By the opening years of the twentieth century, with the publication of *The Son of the Wolf* (1900), *The People of the Abyss* (1903), and *The Call of the Wild* (1903), London had soared to fame as America's best-known writer.[8]

Entertaining the public, Jack London also worked from a mandate voiced by one of his contemporaries, journalist and political activist Upton Sinclair, who saw fiction in utilitarian terms, claiming that its "*true purpose . . . is to alter reality*." London's own route to public engagement on the economic and political issues of labor, working conditions, criminal justice, the nation's agricultural crisis, and other topics is a story of an evolving consciousness and of literary maturation as London grew to realize that he must use his fiction to educate the public about the development of a system of wage slavery that, a generation after the Civil War, bound industrial workers to corporate masters.[9]

He recognized, in addition, that he must bolster the public resistance that was mounting against the domination of the corporate monopolies and trusts—a domination that threatened to reduce citizens to subjects. His personal experience and self-guided education drove him to the novel to sound the alarm against the plundering and exhaustion of rich American farmland. His reportage from the frontlines during the Russo-Japanese War in 1904, and again during the Mexican Revolution in 1915, moved him to warn against the carnage and waste of ill-advised warfare. When his arrest for vagrancy resulted in a horrifying month of imprisonment in the Erie County penitentiary in 1894, London knew he must record the experience in autobiography and fiction in order to publicize the dire facts of the American criminal injustice system. These and other campaigns took shape along London's own life journey as he read voraciously and cast his eagle-eyed gaze at conditions directly in his sightline. It was only when traveling to Hawaii and the South Pacific in 1907–8, for instance, that he saw the exploitive nature of capitalist imperialism in operation. In response, London produced fiction and essays that exposed the morally corrosive commercial system that appropriated land, commandeered resources, and subjugated peoples for corporate profit.

Given London's reputation for high-decibel language and extravagant plotting, it is ironic that a certain subtlety was crucial to his campaign to expose intolerable conditions in order to redress them. Unlike Upton Sinclair, who pummeled readers with a constant barrage of industrial society's horrors on nearly every page of fiction, London preferred to pace his reformist messages, to touch down throughout his narrative with graphic exposition that alternated with glancing blows and subtle jabs. Grouped with writers that one late-1800s newspaper called the "savage realists," Jack London also bore in mind the sentiments as expressed in 1886 by William Dean Howells, the contemporary "dean" of American letters, that "the American public does not like to read about the life of toil," the life of "vulgar and commonplace people." As the cultural historian David Shi has put it, "Readers did not want their noses rubbed in the sordid realities of the underclass." London nonetheless found ways to immerse the public's conscience in such realities and, in addition, to expose the sordid hypocrisies of the bourgeoisie, a social stratum that bought his books and read his stories and essays in magazines that reached their homes weekly and monthly from coast to coast.[10]

London's public shows—or publics show—an extraordinary demographic range. His stories and novels captured the attention of the working class of tradesmen, military men, and artisans in such occupations as draymen, stewards, teamsters, stablemen, and metal workers, together with the country's burgeoning middle classes, who held sway in local civic affairs, in churches and synagogues, in fraternal lodges, sewing circles, and garden clubs. These groups had swelled from the later decades of the nineteenth century to include, in historian Andrew Lawson's listing, "a growing professional cadre of lawyers, physicians, dentists, pharmacists, and engineers . . . joined by a newly expanded corps of business managers and corporate employees—accountants, advertisers, wholesalers, insurance agents, traveling salesmen—along with increasing numbers of public-service personnel." This was the new "white-collar" workforce situated, in Lawson's term, "between the capitalist class of financiers, speculators, and railroad barons" on one side and an increasingly wretched industrial workforce on the other. "As the rural and immigrant poor flooded into the central cities," Lawson continues, "many among the well-to-do fled to the new 'street-car' suburbs on the urban periphery," retreating to what Theodore Dreiser called "little islands of propriety" protected from the turmoil and misery of inner-city poverty. This streetcar suburban population, both men and women, was genteel, polite, and somewhat anxious about their status, but also, as Lawson emphasizes, "more at ease with itself" than its stiff Victorian predecessors. It was an America "needing to be entertained" but also "in want of information."[11]

Jack London was not alone in his drive to inform and persuade, for his campaign was part of a larger movement for reforms from the late 1800s and into the opening years of the new twentieth century. The Anti-Imperialist League, whose leaders included Harvard president Charles Eliot Norton, warned against American expansion and the annexation of territory, while the National Consumers' League, headed by activist Florence Kelley, advocated for workplace safety, for workers' health and living wages, and for the rights of children to be educated and freed from wage work. The attorney Louis D. Brandeis (later a justice of the US Supreme Court) worked to secure legal protections along these lines, while the Harvard physician Alice Hamilton helped launch the field of industrial toxicology with research indicating that industrial metals such as lead and copper were poisoning workers. To improve wages, the University of Wisconsin labor economists Richard Ely and John R. Commons brought together the disciplines of sociology and economics to propose alternatives to the prevailing laissez-faire system in business and industry. Established churches became involved too, notably in the Social Gospel movement, led by Protestant ministers such as Washington Gladden and Walter Rauschenbusch, joined by a few Catholic priests, notably Father Edward McGlynn in New York. These groups, too, relied on a social network of magazines, especially *Charities* and *The Survey*, under the superb editorial guidance of the journalist and reformer Paul Kellogg.

Jack London kept close watch on the progress of these reforms and on those who opposed them in public forums and from behind the scenes. In fiction and nonfiction, he could readily have relied on his own experience of Gilded Age brutality, having nearly lost his life when he toiled in treacherous workplaces as a boy laborer who was paid near-starvation wages and pushed to the point of exhaustion and injury. But London was not content solely to exploit his own personal history. In an era of voluminous print culture and mass distribution, he sought the documents that both informed his position and bolstered opposing arguments.

London's encyclopedic files, some fifty thousand documents now housed at the Henry E. Huntington Library in San Marino, California, reveal the astonishing extent of this public intellectual's immersion in the major issues of his day. From his early twenties until his death, London compiled a formidable database of books, pamphlets, and newspaper and magazine articles that he marked, in many instances, with his own commentary and filed under precise headings from politics to religion, race, women's concerns, labor strikes, health, tax policy, and warfare. These files contain the data he relied on to substantiate his arguments in the public sphere and were fundamental to his mission to "mould" public opinion in order to realign the country's political and social priorities. To this campaign he added his personal goal of an incredibly prolific output of a thousand words a day. While scholars, biographers, and other investigators have consulted these documents for closely focused research, the role of these extraordinary files as the foundational basis of London's career as both a writer and public intellectual has never been fully explored.

Considering the fame that enveloped Jack London in his lifetime, together with his continuing prominence over a century and more, we must ask why London's sociopolitical influence has been overlooked in the United States, especially in light of his international reputation as an admired and respected figure in American social and political history. Much of his work remains in print, especially the novel *The Call of the Wild* and his widely anthologized story "To Build a Fire," which regularly appear on students' lists of recommended readings. Literary critics hail his contributions to the realist and naturalist movements of the late 1800s and early 1900s and to modernism, while biographers, hewing strictly to personal facts, map the genealogy and chronology of his life. A few in the academy have called attention to the importance of London's political writings, but London is not numbered among the individuals who have exerted powerful intellectual energy in the public arena. His name is nowhere to be found in such seminal works as Samuel Eliot Morison's *Oxford History of the American People* (1965), Louis Menand's *Metaphysical Club: A Story of Ideas in America* (2001), or Jackson Lears's *Rebirth of a Nation: The Making of Modern America, 1877–1920* (2009), to cite just a few.

Reasons for this oversight are easy to find and deserve attention. The American public intellectual in our own twenty-first century is typically affiliated with an institute or think tank, with the academy, the political establishment, or a prominent journal. So too were London's historical counterparts. For instance, Jane Addams, whose Chicago-based settlement, Hull House, was at the center of the new profession of social work, was a graduate of the collegiate Rockford Female Seminary, while John Dewey, the educational reformer whose name is synonymous with the philosophy of pragmatism, was a member of the faculties of the University of Chicago and later of Columbia University and elected president of the recently formed American Psychological Society (professionalism again!).

London, however, had no such credentials. In his two decades of work in the public sphere—roughly the first twenty years of the twentieth century—

he neither held a university position nor occupied any clerical, editorial, or journalistic post. The newspaper trade struck him as a literary stylist's "suicide." And he spurned editorial positions as desk-bound drudgery often performed by failed creative writers who were enslaved to their business managers and to circulation figures. In the late 1800s and early 1900s, an era that was notable for the intense development of the professions, London's schooling was largely self-guided, while others' expertise developed formally in social, political, or scientific realms. London's single undergraduate semester at the University of California in 1896 kept him far afield of the cohort of the professoriate, the legal profession, or the scientific societies. Lacking the authority that radiates from credentials and institutional affiliations, London has not been numbered in the fellowship of those who exert influence by addressing and responding publicly to the urgent problems of society. Accordingly, like numerous self-taught figures, he can seem less than intellectual, his fame the stuff of celebrity.

London's exclusion can also be traced to skepticism about the social and political authority of literature. Experts best equipped by training to highlight London as an outspoken social critic and agent of change—the historians and political scientists—have not done so, mainly because they do not recognize literary figures as public authorities on matters of public debate. As a rule, they see novels, stories, or personal essays as illustrative fillips, perhaps, but not as documentary data for the work they undertake, while historically literary writing has been subject to derision, from the New England Puritans' denunciation of fiction as "vain romances" to Thomas Jefferson's censure of novels as a "mass of trash" to the shift of historical and governmental study from the humanities into the "social sciences" in the late 1800s. Admittedly, there have been rare, if widely acknowledged, examples of novels—Harriet Beecher Stowe's *Uncle Tom's Cabin* (1852), Upton Sinclair's *The Jungle* (1906), or even Ayn Rand's *The Fountainhead* (1943) and *Atlas Shrugged* (1957)—that have been credited as unique engines of social change, arriving at a moment ripe for the abolition of slavery, the passage of health and safety legislation, or a prime political turning point in the history of conservatism, but their exceptionalism proves the rule. Given this legacy, the notion of a best-selling writer or stories and novels as a politically influential figure may seem like a contradiction in terms, one not likely to yield significant benefits in a utilitarian culture.[12]

In this book, I hope to offer a certain course correction, a summons to realign the kinds of texts that matter in public discourse and an admonition to pay attention to relevant figures and documents that are hiding in plain sight. Jack London's career as a public intellectual is best approached through a bifocal lens that alloys his literary skills with his sociopolitical passions. To do so is to better understand a dynamic, contentious period of US history through the piercing beam of a figure who exposed injustices of human agency and laid the foundation for a refashioned, better world.

1

Napoleon of the Pen

I resolved to make the fight of my life by making my living with my pen. This was precarious, for my assets were nil, and my liabilities legion.
—Jack London, letter to Maitland L. Osborne, March 24, 1900

By 1903, millions knew the name Jack London as a blockbuster entertainer. The author of *The Call of the Wild* and numerous Klondike gold rush stories was a cultural icon, a living legend, an American tall tale of strength and power, fame and success. Born in the Gilded Age and blessed with a "splendid constitution," Jack London boasted a "stomach that would digest scrap-iron." With remarkably delicate hands, he "learned how to fight" in the streets and to spar in the ring. A witness swore that his "brain ran sixty miles a minute." With a stroke of his pen, he could reach millions. His "power of endurance was practically unlimited," said a close friend, believing London to be "endowed with an indomitable spirit" and thereby "invincible." One intimate, Anna Strunsky, called him a "Napoleon of the Pen," a reference that circulated in American culture from Ralph Waldo Emerson's tribute to the exemplary "Man of the World," a premier activist whose name was "wrought into the verbs of language."[1]

Jack London's birth year—1876—coincided with a major milestone in US history, the one hundredth anniversary of the signing of the Declaration of Independence. The infant's mother, Flora Wellman (b. 1843), might have seen an astral linkage of her newborn son with the nation's founding, for Flora earned her living as a spiritualist in the city of San Francisco and took great pride in the old American stock of her ancestry. She had grown up in privileged circumstances in her hometown of Massillon, Ohio, where her father and uncles were successful bankers and merchants. One of five children, Flora suffered the early death of her mother and found her new stepmother to be distant. A severe bout of typhoid fever struck her at age twelve, stunting her growth and damaging her eyes. Schooled as a genteel Christian young lady, taught to play the piano, she nonetheless veered from the Wellman family's liberal Protestantism to embrace the then-popular spiritualism with its "gifts" of communicating with the dead.

Flora's migration to the West Coast began with a rift within her family, prompting her departure with a married sister in 1860. Within a decade she had reached Seattle and in the early 1870s met the astrologer William H. Chaney, a "powerful-looking man" twenty-two years her senior with three ex-wives and a history of shifting religious affiliations. Flora was to be wife number four (of an eventual six), drawn to this man who declared astrology to be "the most precious science ever made known to man." He earned his living lecturing, teaching, and producing astral charts. The two moved south to San Francisco, and though no documentary proof of their marriage exists (the San Francisco earthquake and fire of 1906 having destroyed the city's civil records), Flora identified herself in a countercultural publication in 1875 as "Flora Wellman Chaney, Teacher of Elocution and Instrumental Music." She and Chaney, as their granddaughter Joan London later observed, were among the "hordes of self-appointed enlighteners" who "roamed the country, lecturing, publishing magazines and pamphlets, and making their living out of the eager credulity of the American public."[2]

Flora's pregnancy precipitated the couple's crisis. When she refused to accept Chaney's ultimatum to abort the pregnancy, he sold off the household furnishings and deserted her, whereupon she attempted suicide with a drug overdose and a gunshot that produced only a flesh wound. Her baby's birth announcement appeared in the *San Francisco Bulletin*: "In this city, January 12, wife of W. H. Chaney, a son." Flora's newborn, named John Griffith Chaney, would become the celebrated Jack London. But that was twenty years in the future.[3]

Beyond the melodrama of his parentage, the infant John was ushered into a dizzying age of great capitalists whose industrial and financial might was rapidly remaking the country, a future world that was being lavishly displayed three thousand miles eastward from San Francisco at the 1876 United States International Exhibition in Philadelphia. The city's Fairmount Park fairgrounds mapped the modernity that Jack London was to explore, challenge, critique, and do his utmost to reform with tremendous personal risk and daring. It was a world that he helped to transform even as he himself was transformed into a powerful public figure, the most famous and arguably influential author in the nation.

The Philadelphia Fair provides a rare opportunity to survey the Gilded Age into which Jack London was born, to glimpse the awesome industrial products that proved enticing to Jack—and the dark underside that threatened his survival and fueled his reformist passion. Baby John was just five months of age when the Philadelphia fair proclaimed a century of the new nation's progress. The fairgrounds at the Centennial, as the Philadelphia fair was known, buzzed with excitement and gave no hint that for the past three years the country had been suffering a severe economic depression. The jobless and the desperate were not among the nearly 10 million gentlemen in swallowtail coats and ladies in floor-length bustled skirts who marveled at the exotic pagoda rooflines and Moorish arches. They were not among those who grew silent before the US naval ordnance and the German cannon ("Krupp's killing machine"). Cosmopolitan flavors of "other nations and empires" reached fairgoers through the buildings and products of Germany, Great Britain, France, and elsewhere in the world, representing "37 countries and a number of their colonies."[4]

Through long summer days and evenings the visitors also marveled at state-of-the-art products from thirty-eight states of the Union. Machine manufacture was booming, and consumerism was on the march. Here were Steinway grand pianos and wagon wheels, cameras and clocks and crystal goblets. Most memorable was Machinery Hall, where awed visitors faced the new world of industrial mechanization and corporate power. They gawked at steam-driven farm engines, machine tools, and the thirteen locomotives that reminded some of the "golden spike" celebration marking the completion of the US transcontinental railroad just seven years earlier. Towering over all was the iconic gargantuan Corliss engine, a colossus that thrust some forty feet above every visitor's top hat or bonnet and produced the power of twenty-five hundred horses.

The Women's Pavilion, what's more, suggested even greater changes ahead. It was reassuring to many, on the one hand, to learn of women inventors whose patents for corsets and other undergarments reinforced womanly tradition of the Victorian era. Just inside the pavilion, however, sat "an attractive young woman at the controls of a steam engine running six looms and a printing press." She informed visitors that "a steam engine was much less demanding than children, and less fatiguing than cooking over a kitchen stove." The term "New Woman" was not yet in play, but the woman at the controls of the steam engine, a Miss Emma Allison, heralded radical changes for women's lives—and thus for men's. Thoughtful fairgoers had to agree with the critic and travel writer Bayard Taylor that the Centennial was "not so much a holiday show as a great school of instruction."[5]

Much instruction now reached the nation through print and visual illustration and their widespread distribution by rail. As if awaiting Jack London's

4. The United States of America straddles the continent and proclaims itself a colossus on the world stage in "The Stride of a Century," a poster from the Philadelphia Centennial Exposition 1876. (Library of Congress)

moment, the tools of his own trade were also on exhibit at the Centennial fair in Philadelphia, London's future inscribed in the books and printing presses and in the telegraphy by which reporters eventually broadcast the comings and goings of the famous California author. The fair's photography exhibit, too, anticipated London's zeal for his Kodak and his own darkroom setup, not to mention the rakish and boyishly photogenic self surrendered endlessly to the camera on the decks of sailing craft, on horseback, in swimming or sitting for formal portraits in a photographer's studio.

Esteemed literary voices were jubilant at the exhibition's displays. William Dean Howells, the "dean" of American letters, proclaimed that "the national genius most freely speaks" in "these things of iron and steel." The California poet Joaquin Miller, whom Jack London was to admire for capturing "all the strength, & health, & joy, & beauty of the West," declared that the "American's heart thrills with pride and love of his land as he contemplates the vast exhibition of art and prowess here." Miller foresaw an ever more glorious future. "Great as it seems today," he went on, "it is but the acorn from which shall grow the wide-spreading oak of a century's growth." The "acorn" in question was the Corliss engine, but the poet merged nature and the foundry without a qualm.[6]

Writ large, the entire Centennial was emblematic of John Chaney's—Jack London's—world. The time of handcrafts and small-scale artisanry and agriculture was fast waning. The new era of US global imperial and corporate power had arrived, certified in material terms at the fair's exhibitions. The buildings of the world's nations and colonies, the machinery of industrial production, the agricultural commodities ready to be shipped in bulk and processed—all were manifest at Fairmount Park. The natural world, too, was referenced and admired, as in the Mississippi exhibit, a building roofed with Spanish moss and featuring "curious formations found in Mississippi forests." The ascendency of the press was also in evidence, as the fair was promoted and publicized in the leading media of the time, including popular national magazines such as *Harper's Weekly* and *Frank Leslie's Illustrated Newspaper*.

The exhibits from California, on the other hand—the silk moths, the sheep pelts, the wine barrels and thick grapevines—seemed crude and unfinished, signaling potential that was not yet realized. These raw materials were destined to help make the United States a national and international powerhouse, but it would take time for these industries to rise to importance and recognition. A pelt was transformed into a bolt of cloth; grapes became wine. A destitute child matured into celebrated adulthood.

If the San Francisco spiritualist pondered a visit to the Philadelphia fair with her baby, the stocky and broad-faced Flora would have quickly banished the thought. Cross-country travel to Philadelphia was prohibitively expensive for the cash-strapped new mother. That summer of 1876 she barely eked out a living teaching piano lessons and giving spiritualist consultations. Besides, she was pressed with worries. The Ohio native had no family in California, her recovery from a difficult childbirth was slow, and her doctor advised her to hire a wet nurse for the baby. Having given the newborn the surname of the departed William Chaney, Flora sought out Virginia Prentiss, a black woman who was born into slavery in antebellum Virginia, learned domestic arts and childcare as a house slave in Tennessee, and in the post–Civil War years married a carpenter and made her way west with him. Known as Mammy Jennie, she had lost her own infant and now suckled and cradled the infant John. In the months and years ahead, Flora was to prove herself a cold mother, demanding and stingy with affection. Certain historians of the future would see her as a free spirit, the vanguard of the late twentieth-century hippie or New Age movements. In Victorian terms, however, Flora was a socially disgraced unwed mother, and her present goal was to gain new respectability and financial support through marriage. To Flora, her new baby boy was not necessarily a gift of the heavens or a fulfillment of womanhood; instead he was a badge of shame.

Until his twenties, Jack London knew nothing of the circumstances of his birth. By the close of the Centennial in autumn of 1876, Flora had married John London, a forty-seven-year-old semi-disabled Civil War veteran and widower with two daughters, the eight-year-old Eliza and the six-year-old Ida. (A son, Charles, had died just days after London's arrival in California in 1874.) The courtship was short. The couple married in September, and baby John immediately was renamed John Griffith London.

He faced an unsettled boyhood. The elder London, an experienced farmer from his prewar years in Iowa, now farmed on land he leased (and briefly owned) in the Bay Area and the peninsula south of San Francisco. He was a skilled grower of prized vegetables, and little Johnny became a ranch boy helping with the livestock and fieldwork. At age ten, he posed for a studio photograph with Rollo, a pet dog that perhaps accompanied the boy and his stepfather into the fields. No one at that time, however, saw the black-and-white mongrel as a forerunner of the wolf dogs of London's future fiction. In the London household the boy was sometimes called Jack, and on graduation from grammar school he claimed the name permanently. But the change was no rebuke to the elder London, for the boy enjoyed the affection of the man he knew as his father, and just as Mammy Jennie offset his mother's coldness, so did the maternal warmth of his loving stepsister Eliza.

But the family's fortunes soon declined. A business partner had cheated London, and Flora's restless ambition for the opportunities she ever envisioned "Just Beyond" drove him to expand his operations recklessly, to borrow heavily, and to make several financially disastrous moves. From a series of cramped San Francisco slum apartments that the infant and toddler Jack shared with his mother, stepfather, and stepsisters, the family embarked on an odyssey of incessant moves from 1879 to 1890. They caromed from a spate of cheap Oakland apartments to farm rentals, then to a brief prosperous moment owning a ranch in Livermore, before foreclosure sent them back to the flatlands of Oakland. The words "bungalow" or "cottage" were euphemisms for what a schoolmate of Jack termed the London family's "squalor of an aggravated type." (One dwelling was built of scrap materials from nearby dismantled buildings.) By the time of John London's death in 1897, the family had resided at several West Oakland addresses located in "a poverty-stricken community of immigrant Italians and brutally exploited Chinese."[7]

To London, the domestic life within was relentlessly bleak. Flora's strict frugality struck her son as extreme poverty. The family's mealtime tablecloths were newspapers, and hunger became a searing boyhood memory. The Londons' home meals of potatoes and cheap cuts of beef that were fried in a broken skillet were a high contrast to the occasional "delicious dainties" of the city saloon bar lunches where Jack, accompanied by his stepfather, occasionally feasted on "strange crackers, cheeses, sausages, sardines—wonderful foods that I never saw on our meager home-table." In boyhood he created childhood treasures from the illustrations on discarded cigarette packages because he "never had toys nor playthings like other children." His most prized childhood article of clothing was a single store-bought undershirt that he "insisted on wearing . . . without any outer garment . . . so all the world could see." When the prized shirt was too soiled, he surrendered to the "awful home-made things." Meanwhile, Jack attended Garfield Elementary School and Cole Grammar School, located in one of Oakland's poorest neighborhoods and thought to provide sufficient formal schooling for youngsters destined for wage work as laborers or factory operatives.[8]

The world all the while accelerated into the future displayed at the Centennial fair. The boy of the ranch and waterfront was growing up in industrial and imperial America, and he glimpsed its parameters largely through his insatiable appetite for the printed word. Exotic Moorish arches reached him through a borrowed copy of Washington Irving's *Alhambra*, and he sampled Africa through the travelogues of the anthropologist Paul du Chaillu. From his boyhood, the Oakland library was his fount of learning, where Ina Coolbrith, California's future poet laureate, gave the boy the keys "to the kingdom of the mind" and saw him dive into books with "the glory of youthful passion." By his own admission London read obsessively: "I read mornings, afternoons, and nights. I read in bed, and I read at recess while the other boys were playing." A frequent boyhood guest in the London household was to recall his friend Jack's treasured copy of Shakespeare and of Melville's *Typee*, these and the precious few other titles "soiled and worn by constant use."[9]

History and adventure were London's favorites, but the cosmopolitan world was even closer at hand at the Oakland waterfront and San Francisco Bay, where Jack London could peer through a "forest of masts" to spot sailing vessels' stern flags flying: "English, German, Japanese." A peephole into his future opened at age eight when he read the novel *Signa* by the exotic

5. Flora Wellman London, Jack's mother. Her ambitiousness and instinct for gambling against long odds set the stage for her son's literary success. (Henry E. Huntington Library, San Marino, California)

6. John London, Jack's stepfather, wearing the badge of his late-life employment as a deputized night watchman. (Henry E. Huntington Library, San Marino, California)

7. Studio photo portrait of six-year-old Johnny (Jack) London with dog Rollo. (Henry E. Huntington Library, San Marino, California)

Ouida (Marie Louise de la Ramée), the story of an Italian mountain peasant boy who rises to fame and fortune as an artist. London saw himself as "a little peasant on a poor California ranch" whose "narrow hill-horizon" was "pushed back" by the story. He had a stunning, crystalline insight: that "all the world was made possible if I would dare it."[10]

To "dare it" required stupendous bootstrap effort. London's fiction would later tap the mélange of his life's adventures—his childhood odd jobs, his teenage years pirating (and sometimes policing) the privately owned oyster beds on the San Francisco Bay in a sailboat, the *Razzle-Dazzle*, that he bought with money borrowed from Mammy Jennie. To these he added his voyage on a seal-hunting schooner to East Asia and the Bering Sea in 1893 when he was merely seventeen. His factory toil in a cannery, a jute mill, and a laundry would take its place in his novels and stories too, as would the attempt at a Horatio Alger experience he sought in good faith when London was hired to shovel mountains of coal to feed the steam boiler of the Haywards Electric Railway system. The nineteen-year-old London was assured by the baldfaced lies of the company executive who hired him that entry-level shoveling was the starting gate to "great success," prompting London to imagine that he could work his way to the top and marry the boss's daughter. As the more mature and skeptical London recalled, "I still believed in the old myths which were the heritage of the American boy when I was a boy."[11]

His fiction and nonfiction would expose the "old myths" as seductive lies, but London's readers would also be privy to his cross-country tramping, riding the rails, in 1894. His friends, family, and biographers have shown how ardently he sought advanced formal education, starting with his enrollment in Oakland High School in 1895, when he wrote for the school literary magazine, the *Aegis*. He was determined to hasten his scholastic progress. "I'm striving to go through High School in half the usual time," he confided to friend Frank Atherton. "And then I want to go to College if I possibly can. That's why I'm cramming so prodigiously day and night; why I don't get but about five or six hours sleep any night." Leaving high school, London stepped up his cramming for the entrance examinations at the University of California. His daughter Joan was to convey the monumental task facing her father when the twenty-year-old Jack London began "preparing for examinations in English, history, mathematics and physics." She goes on: "To study physics without a laboratory, to fix precisely facts and dates in a year's course of history, to review elementary algebra and geometry and push ahead as far as possible into advanced algebra, to have grammar and composition at his fingertips, as well as knowledge of the masterpieces of English and American literature—this must be accomplished in a little over three months." Tutored by friends, London did pass, borrowed the forty-dollar tuition from saloonkeeper Johnny Heinold, and spent one semester studying at the Berkeley campus before withdrawing from the university, too broke to continue. He worked as a laundryman just as the Alaskan gold rush beckoned him to the gold fields through the winter of 1897–98.[12]

A luckless miner, London endured a pitch-black subzero winter on a diet of beans, bacon, and sourdough biscuits and, when the ice broke up, shot the rocky Yukon rapids during the spring of 1898 in a homemade boat and navigated fifteen hundred miles downriver to port. There he hired out on a steamer, heaving coal as a fireman to earn his way back south to Oakland. In years to come the public would learn the quality of the rich fictional ore London mined during the Yukon months observing and listening to the prospectors, to the merchants and whisky runners, and to the Inuit natives in and around the gold camps, with their omnipresent snarling sled dogs. He was to mill all these and more into such popular stories as "The White Silence," "The Son of the Wolf," "An Odyssey of the North," and his best-known novels, *The Call of the Wild* and *White Fang*.[13]

The characters London met inevitably spiced up his stories and novels, from the old salts in the forecastle of the seal-hunting schooner to the wharf rats on the Oakland waterfront, the tramps and hoboes in the boxcars and rail yards, the gold hunters in the Yukon, the indigenous *kanakas* of Hawaii, and the natives of Oceania. He would exploit his relation to alcohol, too, praising the camaraderie he found in Johnny Heinold's Oakland waterfront bar but critiquing America's pervasive saloon culture. Initiated into the world of "John Barleycorn," London was whipsawed in periodic bouts of binge drinking and finally succumbed to chronic dependence on alcohol even as he was admired as a man who could hold his liquor. All these experiences would tumble out in popular works that made Jack London the first American author to earn a million dollars.

Biographers have tracked London's grueling apprenticeship from 1898 at borrowed and rented typewriters where he pounded out fiction and verse, essays and jokes that boomeranged with rejection slips. The rumor that publishers paid ten cents per word triggered his resolve, but mastering the formula for marketable writing proved excruciating. "I am groping, groping, groping for my own particular style," London confessed in 1899 to a fellow writer, admitting it to be a style that he had "not yet found." Troublesome circumstances pressed at every turn. His stepfather's death in 1897 meant that Jack became the male head of household, and Flora saw to it that he took financial responsibilities seriously. His possessions at the time were three: a bicycle for transportation, a respectable suit for paying visits, and his stepfather's mackintosh for protection from the rain. By 1898, when he struggled to produce publishable writing, his beloved stepsister Eliza was no longer in the London home, having married Captain J. H. Shepard, a Civil War veteran and widower with three children of his own. The London domicile, however, added another mouth to feed, for Jack's other stepsister, Ida, like London's mother, had been deserted by her husband and now brought her own young son, Johnny Miller, to live with the Londons. To Jack's dismay, Flora doted on Johnny, lavishing on him the warmth and affection denied to her own son.[14]

Flora, however, aided Jack in one crucial way: she encouraged his ambition to become a marketable writer. Offered a job as a postal worker in 1899, Jack turned it down with Flora's backing. The attic room of the Londons' Oakland residence at 962 East Sixteenth Street (now Foothill Boulevard) was Jack London's literary boiler room. He clipped notes and vocabulary words to strings that resembled tiny clotheslines, and he pounded out his thousand-word daily quota as though his space was itself an industrial plant. A major cost of production was postage, and he aimed high, dispatching such typescripts as "From Dawson to the Sea" and "The Clondyker's Dream" to leading national magazines such as *Cosmopolitan*, *Munsey's*, and *Lippincott's*. Thick-skinned and businesslike, London viewed a rejected story as an opportunity to try once again. When a story came back with a rejection slip, he slid it into a fresh envelope and posted it elsewhere. Yet he confided to a friend, "You know that we are living hand to mouth . . . [and] much of my stuff is in pawn and bills running galore." As London tested his fortunes in the world, he nonetheless clung to the idea that his effort saved and sanctified, his work ethic a driving force as he committed himself to the task of writing full time.[15]

Meanwhile, his fledgling manuscripts "made amazing round-trip records between the Pacific and the Atlantic." His break finally came in 1899 with the publication of a story based on his gold rush adventure, "To the Man on Trail," in the highly regarded *Overland Monthly* and the acceptance of "An Odyssey of the North" by the prestigious *Atlantic Monthly*.[16]

By the turn of the century, London's last-ditch effort at an economic lifeline—writing—had finally paid off. Prestigious magazines began publishing his stories regularly, and by 1900 his first book appeared: *The Son of the Wolf*, a collection of stories. That inaugural volume was followed by a battery of titles that established his reputation in the United States and abroad between 1902 and 1903: *A Daughter of the Snows*, *Children of the Frost*, *The Cruise of the Dazzler*,

8. The world-famous author Jack London is surrounded by translations of his books. London was the first American author to earn $1 million. (Henry E. Huntington Library, San Marino, California)

together with *The People of the Abyss*, the coauthored *Kempton-Wace Letters*, and the book that made him famous, *The Call of the Wild*.

Despite London's enduring celebrity, relatively few knew the man who fought against black melancholy and ravaging injury and sickness throughout his life. He'd nearly died of diphtheria in infancy, his brown hair turning so white that Mammy Jennie called him "cottonball." Twice he'd nearly drowned, once as a crewman in East Asia when he was seventeen, and another time in the waters of the San Francisco Bay near Benicia. His instinct for survival had kept him alive in the penitentiary where he was sentenced for vagrancy in 1984. It might have proved his death camp. Indeed, by that time the old waterfront friends of his youth were headed for prison or an early grave. London had fought hunger and subfreezing temperatures through the pitch-black Yukon winter, and in years to come it became clear that the price he'd paid to mine the gold rushers' and native peoples' lore and legends for his fiction was exorbitant, for scurvy ravaged his teeth and severely taxed his constitution. The years-long audit of Jack London's health reads like a ledger of medical afflictions: kidney stones, pleurisy, shingles, rheumatism, ills of the gastrointestinal tract, and the uremia which hastened London's early death at age forty, for the medicine dosed to him for tropical maladies in 1908 contained the ultimately fatal mercury that his kidneys could not expel. The public persona of the famed author was all athletic robust health: London typically boasted to a news reporter, "I swim every day about two hours. . . . I ride horseback . . . [and] put on the gloves for a boxing bout." "On the mend" was his favored affirmation of good health on the upswing, a phrase readily penned to his New York editor. Accounts of his illness and injury, including severe sprains and ruptures, were reserved mainly for intimates. London's aversion to walking due to chronic pain was sometimes mistaken for indolence. Few knew the real story, and he preferred it that way.[17]

Mental health, too, was a taboo topic for the celebrity writer, though the adult London was dealt severe blows to the psyche, from his relationship with a mother who was cold and rigid to the shocking discovery at age twenty-one that his father was not John London but probably a footloose astrologer ("probably" because Chaney sowed confusion in his response to Jack's inquiry letter by implying that at the time of Jack's conception he was impotent and Flora unfaithful). London also suffered a painful estrangement from his two daughters, Joan (b. 1901) and Becky (b. 1902), both of whom sided lifelong with their mother, Bess Maddern London, whom London divorced in 1905, having wed Bess in 1900 from friendship, not love. The athletic middle-class young Oakland woman with blue-black hair and hazel eyes had tutored London in mathematics when he prepared for college study, and she shared his enthusiasm for bicycling and photography. She seemed appropriate as the spouse of the twenty-four-year-old author, who was focused on settling down. In time Bess evidently resented having to compete for Jack's attention with his growing circle of bohemian friends and admirers. Jack, in turn, found the domestic Bess prim and prudish, a version of the Victorian stereotype, Miss Grundy, whom he castigated repeatedly in print. His successful second marriage, to Charmian Kittredge in 1905, was sorely tested when the couple lost two children, one to a miscarriage and the other, named Joy, due to a medical error during birth. Another devastating blow was the August 1913 conflagration that destroyed the Londons' dream house, Wolf House. The embers smoked as London grieved the loss of "so much beauty" even as the fire was suspected at the time (later disproven) to be a crime of arson.[18]

The melancholy that struck London intermittently also came with the realization that financial and literary success did not ensure happiness. Poet George Sterling reminded his famous friend that "the recognition of your fame, and the amusements that are planned everywhere for you" were surely ample compensation for any "discomfort." In 1904–5, however, London borrowed Nietzsche's phrase the "Long Sickness" to characterize his own state of ennui and depression. To pal Frank Atherton he confided the "utter despondency" that drove him toward suicide, and Charmian was to recall his "nerve-racked look" at the time, his eyes "haunted with a hopeless weariness, and glassy as from fever." He talked, she recalled, "very hard, as if . . . in fear of silence." Exploiting every aspect of his life in his writing, London did not flinch from descriptions of the dual psychic poles of the "white logic . . . soul sickness" at one extreme, and darkness at the other. While he portrayed his own near-death by drowning in the San Francisco Bay as a result of a drunken swim in a high tide, he reprised his own state of hopelessness in the suicide of the protagonist of his quasi-autobiographical novel, *Martin Eden* (1909). At the end of the novel Eden swims inexorably to a point of no return and dies by drowning, as if "falling down a vast and interminable stairway" that ends in "darkness."[19]

London knew, too, how idealized was "clean" living in his contemporary moment. Hygiene meant a convergence of public health and sexual morality in the late nineteenth and early twentieth centuries. The term was especially applicable to boys and men, and a man who lived "clean" was a figure of irreproachable character. Sexual desires and practices were coded or otherwise concealed in the writings of London's contemporaries, and his works were no exception. Recently his close friendship with the California poet George Sterling has been cast as a homosexual attraction, for Sterling called London by his intimate nickname "Wolf," and London reciprocated with "Greek," a presumed tribute to the poet's knowledge of the ancient language and to his sculptural body (and perhaps to the open practice of homosexuality in ancient Greece). (The two men posed for photos side by side in swim trunks at Carmel-by-the-Sea.) Male homoerotic dimensions of London's life at sea and in prison have also been cause for surmise by some commentators, as have London's sexual relations in and out of wedlock. Approaching his first marriage in 1900, London foresaw the salutary effect of his life with his then wife-to-be, Bess Maddern. "I shall be a cleaner, wholesomer man because of the restraint being laid upon me in place of being free to drift wheresoever I listed," London stated in a letter shortly before his marriage to Bess. To Charmian, his "Mate Woman" whom he wed when his divorce from Bess was finalized in 1905, London vowed, "I have always wanted to live clean all my life. And I have always felt, with rare exceptions, that I was living clean."[20]

The "rare exceptions" have tantalized scholars and critics of London's life and letters, as in his reference to his photograph with a shady Joro girl in Japan and the sexual initiation that came with his purchase of the *Razzle-Dazzle*, when the lover of the previous owner, French Frank, gave her favors to young Jack. The drama critic Blanche Partington also may well have been one of London's extramarital lovers, and he was apparently tempted by the New York City prostitutes, as some biographers have indicated. Charmian recalled the moment when Jack confessed, "There *may* come times when the temptation to 'drift'—for an hour, or a day, will stick up its head; and I may follow." The "clean" life was nonetheless important to him, even if it meant an unacknowledged double standard that dodged the vexatious term "hypocrisy."[21]

The virulent racism of his era has also come to stigmatize Jack London, whose writings largely endorsed the racial hierarchies of his time, although recent investigation by Jeanne Reesman proves that London's ideas about race underwent major revision later in his life, especially as of his Pacific ventures in 1907–8. Yet the racialized world of his upbringing was itself powerful. At the 1876 Philadelphia Centennial, the US Government Building exhibited artifacts of the "Red Man" alongside taxidermied mammals, and the Restaurant of the South on the exhibition grounds featured an "Old Plantation Darky Band." The adult Jack London was to accuse his mother of inordinate "pride" in her "old American stock" at the expense of the immigrant Irish and Italians, but much of London's published writing played its part in perpetuating the racial codes and vernacular of the era. He cherished his identity as a racially superior Anglo-Saxon and clung to that lineage even after learning that John London was not his true father, and he punctuated his novels and stories with racial slang and slurs, unacceptable yet common in his day.[22]

Lest Jack London bear the full brunt of the label "racist," however, it is worth noting that his allegiance with life's underdogs often moved him to portray minority characters empathetically and heroically in his fiction, for instance in the stories of the Melanesian "plum-black" Mauki and of Koolau in "Koolau the Leper." London's racial views, what's more, were prevalent in contemporary science and pseudoscience, from phrenology to eugenics, all relentlessly propagating racist hierarchies well into the twentieth century. For years he admired the views of the president of Stanford University, David Starr Jordan, an ichthyologist by training, who declared in 1907 that "the survival of the fittest in the struggle for existence is the primal cause of race-progress" while warning that "the survival of the unfittest is the primal cause of the downfall of nations." On his visits to the famed plant nurseries of Luther Burbank in Santa Rosa, California, Jack London probably heard the distinguished plant breeder speak in racial terms, for Burbank saw "unsuspected racial tendencies" in plants as in human beings and stated his intention to breed "a new race of potatoes," together with "races of plums," "races of corn," and "races of sugar cane." Whether reading, writing, or strolling the Santa Rosa orchards, Jack London was not exempted from the racial taxonomies that ran thc gamut from thc soil to the academy.[23]

Borrowed as it was, London's Anglo-Saxon identity boosted the self-confidence of a young man who determined to be a player on the national and world stage. Indeed, it was Jack's "bigness" that struck one of his closest college-age friends. Bigness, said the friend, was young Jack's "dominating quality." "Merely a boy," he seemed "yet a man of the world." A high school classmate sensed in him a "super-egoist," and an acquaintance thought him "all steel and dew . . . as though to him life were a constant battlefield." No one mistook the adult London for a physical giant, but self-styled grandeur was another matter. Convinced that "playing the game in a small way was the losing way," London was "full of gigantic plans." "All he did was in a large way." Half in jest he confided in a letter, "I love power, to dominate my fellows."[24]

In numerous ways "big" Jack London was a perfect fit for this America, which struck commentators at the 1876 Centennial as "big," "bold," and "powerful." Materially, too, London was in sync with the country when his financial success was secured. In a term widely used a century later, Jack London lived large. Proclaiming that "money's only good for what it can buy," he spent freely for others' pleasures as well as his own. The cornucopia of consumer products at the Centennial fair and thereafter became his for the asking. The china and crystal featured at the fair graced his own table, and his wife honored his musical requests at the keyboard of the household Steinway grand. Hard work deserved "compensation of living," he was to exclaim, listing the material rewards for an individual as smart and successful as he became through his bootstrap efforts, including prime "porterhouse" beefsteaks and thick table "cream," plus "saddle horses, bicycles, and automobiles; cameras, shot guns," watercraft of various sorts, tents and camping gear, and the cash for all these and a host of other items.[25]

Genial, courteous, and sociable, London was a hail-fellow-well-met, a man of "sympathy and understanding." He hobnobbed easily with the Bay Area artists and the political and business elites who welcomed him to membership in the Bohemian Club, with its annual retreats in the redwoods of the male-only Bohemian Grove. He was as sociable with business nabobs as with disenfranchised Hawaiians and the Solomon Islands cannibals whom he lived with and photographed. Yet he developed powers of critical insight that others denied themselves. He had earned these powers—at once his burden and his gift—during a childhood and youth that threatened to turn him into a self-styled "work beast" of the modern industrial system. Jack London was to know from personal experience, for a start, the depressing months-long futility "looking for work in the ranks of the unemployed." Yet he also learned how treacherous and "degrading" industrial work could be. Behind the marvelous steam engines were the coal bunkers, meaning that the engine of the engines was human muscle shoveling mountains of black rocks until hands and wrists swelled and throbbed. The jute carpets that were lauded at the Centennial for "excellence of design, construction, and . . . economy" were produced, as London understood, by child laborers toiling for ten or more hours at a stretch in jute mills for mere pennies. The foodstuffs on display from various states—the apples and the vegetables from Iowa or New Jersey—looked as innocent as they were abundant. But he knew the cannery workers were children operating treacherous machines that sliced off fingers in the blink of an eye. He knew these things because in boyhood and youth he had shoveled the coal, toiled in the jute mill, and survived the cannery with his fingers intact only by dint of his lightning-fast reflexes. He knew to his marrow the extreme exhaustion of these labors and also how mind numbing they were. The electricity that powered businesses and brightened homes, Jack realized, meant the "damned drudgery" of coal heaving that nearly made him a "slave." Firsthand experience taught him that many of the vagrant boys and men riding the rails as tramps sought freedom from the work that stole their minds, crushed their spirits, and wrecked their bodies. Not until his contact with East Asia did London encounter Buddhism, but he sensed its teachings instinctively. "The body feels what the mind knows, and the mind knows what the body feels."[26]

Body and mind, London grasped the hidden meanings of Centennial and post-Centennial America. The wondrous locomotives signified a railroad system whose chiefs denied the workers living wages and crippled the farmers who were forced to ship their harvests at extortionist rates. The stacked barrels of cane sugar crystals at the Hawaii exhibit cheered many as sweeteners for food and drink. To London, however, they also meant the takeover of the Pacific island kingdom by hypocritical missionaries, greedy sugar barons, and the iron hand of the military. Ever afterward he shoved back the curtain to expose the fair behind the fair, the horrific modern Centennial America—Gilded Age America—that its sponsors, promoters, and visitors never let themselves glimpse. As he put it, "I do not propose to live in the front parlor with the blinds drawn. I want to see the kitchen and the scullery. . . . We are no cleaner because we have someone else to do our dirty work for us."[27]

Where did this put him? Weren't the chewy taffy and cannonball hard candies that he loved all his life sweetened with sugar from island plantations, and the rope lines of the boats he sailed on the bay and ocean seas twisted or braided from jute? And the trains that he rode as a vagabond or ticketed passenger, weren't they stoked by coal that an exhausted fireman shoveled into the firebox? He accused the rail magnate Collis P. Huntington of supporting child labor, but London eagerly accepted the rail passes that allowed him and Charmian to travel free on Huntington's Southern Pacific line, even as he published fiction in the Southern Pacific's promotional magazine, *Sunset*. What's more, his chosen occupation—professional writer—catered explicitly to an expanding middle class with sufficient leisure and material comfort to read his stories and books. His own productions were shipped to readers by modern rail and sold to consumers in a marketplace economy. He relied on the comfort of Pullman cars and the swift modern trains to send him all over the country on lecture tours and appearances to promote his books and make deals with publishers. In short, he was deeply enmeshed in the very culture he critiqued and vowed to reform. London was always aware of these ambiguities and contradictions. As a writer and talented photographer, his gaze was both close-up and wide-angle. He knew that his livelihood—and later his wealth—came from social, political, and economic arrangements he both relied on and loathed.

The economic system that served him, further, was largely created by "big men" whose own "Big Interests" were the fundamental structures of modernity. Andrew Carnegie meant steel; Edison signaled electricity. The Standard Oil Corporation denoted one name only—John D. Rockefeller. Synonymous with the industrial system and imperial power, these names connoted authority and achievement. Few of these tycoons paused for self-reflection, but all would confirm their "fierce business ambition and massive talent." They "personified the unlimited entrepreneurial opportunities suddenly opened by America's vast resources and its freedom from constraints of class and caste." True, they "cut brutally through any conventions, competitors, or ordinary people who stood in their way." Yet the jobs they created put food on the tables of the skilled and the unskilled alike, from talented engineers and managers to illiterate immigrant laborers who spoke no English. Their railroads crossed deserts and snaked through mountain passes to become the arterial supply line for the continent. Their talents shrank time and space across three thousand miles and ensured steady supplies of the products that alleviated household drudgery, from tedious soap making with fireplace ashes to spinning and weaving cloth to nighttime lighting by dreary tallow candles. The comforts and pleasures of modern life were of their making. "The captains of industry," London was to write, "are doing, moulding, achieving, building the house humanity lives in and is to live in." Like everybody else, Jack London lived in that house.[28]

To London, however, it was also a house of shame. He judged its masters, the "supermen" of industry, as fatally flawed sociopaths who were so dangerously "aloof" that they were "hostile" to the very society they created. To him, the walls of this "house" were blackened with the verified "misdeeds" of Rockefeller and Huntington. London heard hypocrisy and double dealing in the western capitalist's very name. Collis P. Huntington cared nothing, for instance, for the rights of workers. Having spent his long life "buying the aid of countless legislatures," the railroad tycoon now waxed "virtuously wrathful" in condemning "the dangerous tendency of crying out to the Government for aid' in the way of labor legislation." To London, Huntington typified the reigning industrialists who ran "tens of thousands of child laborers through life-destroying cotton factories," who routinely forced workers to accept compulsory " 'take it or leave it' contracts" that offered "starvation wages," "knowing that to leave it meant to die of hunger." This house of capital left an outrageous number of empty pantries and empty bellies.[29]

Some thought the house well protected from afar by its expansive military, especially the Pacific fleet, which was commanded by Admiral of the Navy George Dewey, a man lionized for defeating the Spanish in the Battle of Manila Bay in the Philippines in 1898. It was the beginning of a war that was to cost some two hundred thousand Filipino lives. A historian of US foreign relations, George C. Herring, has written that "in a smashing victory that set the tone for and came to symbolize the war, Dewey's six new warships crushed the decrepit Spanish Squadron in Manila Bay, setting off wild celebrations at home . . . and creating an opportunity for and enthusiasm about expansionism." The American public was reportedly "electrified" at the news of Dewey's "overwhelming victory" and made him "the hero of the hour." Congress awarded him a jewel-encrusted ceremonial sword and elevated him to the rank of admiral of the entire US Navy. At the time, Jack applauded the defeat of the Spanish as a "stroke against monarchy" and thus a forward step in the long march toward "industrial and political democracy." However, London sneered at the self-delusional fantasy that was exposed in Dewey's reported declaration that "God superintended the fight in Manila Bay." As those close to him knew, London could not "countenance . . . religion, as the average man knows religion." The very young might succumb to such "superstition," but life was too short "to fly against gods and devils." In his terms, Dewey was either a fool or a cynic.[30]

Either way, the admiral foretold a future of wasteful war, "'the whole / Dark butchery without a soul,'" as London put it, quoting from the American poet Richard Le Gallienne's *Illusion of War*. London knew the self-deluding "peace lovers" who said that "war is past" ignored "the forty millions of [dollars for] new warships the U.S. ordered" in the year 1900. He understood the need for a nation to protect itself militarily, lest it confront another nation's hostility, and he recognized the crowd psychology at work as "the people of the United States signified their overwhelming approval of the political and geographical expansion of the United States." Yet he tasted the bitter irony of US expansionism that was "stamped democratically with the seal of [public] approval [that] the U.S. hold all territory gained by her since '98," meaning Cuba, the Philippines, Puerto Rico, and, ultimately, Hawaii. Democracy, London said, thus betrayed itself, for "control of the tropics by the dominant white races from their seats in the temperate zone [was] a latter-day slavery" that coincided with the neoslavery of "the negro of the South" in the post-Reconstruction era of Jim Crow laws.[31]

On land and at sea, nonetheless, Dewey and Huntington were the architects and builders of the dwelling that Americans occupied. Certain others were complicit, like the public relations men, preeminent among them Ivy Ledbetter Lee, a behind-the-scenes apologist for corporations that turned employees into "work beasts" and promoted blind faith in their opaque machinations. Not all these enablers were male. The strait-laced, self-appointed guardians of female propriety and genteel respectability virtually imprisoned generations of women, numbing their minds and blocking active female involvement in the smart, good, and humane things of life. The new modern house would banish these housekeepers, whom London distilled in the Victorian stereotype, Miss Grundy. Her signature room, the parlor, would be banished and the modern woman liberated from physical and mental bondage.

Bondage in the literal meaning of imprisonment was also much on London's mind, for the newspapers were filled with accounts of years-long prison sentences meted out to hapless individuals whose petty crimes prompted judges to make public examples of them. Men's and women's lives were ruined because of the theft of a few dollars or trinkets. Hidden behind the prison walls, London knew, were helpless prisoners subjected to torture at its most barbarous extremes. A serious writer must confront the wretched prison system, bring it to public attention, and help mount reforms through law and law enforcement.

The environment, too, cried out for attention. Those who were heedlessly ravaging nature must be checked, lest the landscape become a ledger of relentless destructive greed. The torn hillsides of the picked and shoveled gold fields of the California placer country were themselves a reproach to the rush of the forty-niners and the corporate mining companies that blasted whole mountainsides away with water cannon so powerful they could kill a man in an instant. The onetime ranch boy whose father grew the best row crops and cared well for livestock also saw the assault on the rich agricultural lands: too many farmers, London learned, were marauders whose heedless farming techniques devastated excellent California soil and wasted the precious gift of water—and thus threatened the nation's future food supply. In the "great economic problems of the present age," London saw the long-term solution in "a return to the soil." The issue was personal to the best-selling writer who doubled as a committed farmer-rancher.[32]

Detesting hypocrisy, London was nonetheless face to face with incriminating facts. The "house humanity lives in and is to live in" was cursed. It had a fatal flaw: it was not a home. He must work to raze it, his very prose a wrecking ball and a blueprint for the new structure in which material abundance did not sacrifice bodies and minds and leave the earth ravaged and barren. Surely he had it in his power to smash "the slippery rock wall that reared before a man who submitted everlastingly to manual labor." Surely "economic or material conditions" generated ideas whose expression changed minds and prompted action. "Some day," London observed, "we'll cleanse the cellar and build a new habitation for mankind, in which . . . all the rooms will be bright and airy, and where the air that is breathed will be clean, noble, and alive."[33]

For the long campaign, the written word was to be his armament, principally the fiction that was his best bet for earning a living for himself and his family, for London always took these responsibilities seriously. He had necessity at his back and life's mission driving his future. "To work and work, and to work with the greatest care . . . to hammer out in sweat and blood"—this was his mandate, for Jack London was as much an individualist as the "big men" in his sights, and he never saw conflict between the individual and his social activism. His signature style was crafted for a reading public that was excited, charmed, amazed, tantalized, eager for every title that bannered the Jack London brand. Over decades, he was to have his critics, from President Theodore Roosevelt, who accused him of "faking" an animal encounter in the novel *White Fang*, to the charge by Hawaiian officials that he had libeled the Territory with his story of a leper under assault by greedy Anglos, not to mention various others who accused him of "savage realism" or of plagiarizing newspaper stories. London answered all of his contemporary critics, though in the long run readers will decide for themselves, for instance, whether the prominent California historian Kevin Starr has accurately charged that London mythologized his life and his home state in an act of grand egotism and self-delusion.[34]

London's popularity signaled a world hungry for the "action" that he provided. While his political writing was a no-holds-barred demolition of the corporate state and a rally for its overthrow, most readers relished his rousing fictional adventures of exotic life in faraway extremes of tropic heat and the frozen North. And he knew better than to turn his stories and novels into relentless polemics against the injustices of the capitalist system. Political ranting and foaming from page 1 to "The End" would gain nothing. As his fellow writer Stephen Crane said, "Preaching is fatal to art in literature." London's campaign for social reform was instruction sheathed in irresistible entertainment.[35]

Was it art? Was he an artist? That was for the public to decide, a public he courted with fiction that shied away from sociology in favor of "atmosphere" and characters "who live and breathe . . . and cause reading lamps to burn overtime." London was well aware that some sneered at him as a "rough, savage fellow . . . who likes prizefights and brutalities, who has a clever turn of pen, a charlatan's smattering of art, and the inevitable deficiencies of the untrained, unrefined, self-made man." It was impossible to persuade them otherwise. It was "so much easier to leave their convictions alone."[36]

Could he win? He was an optimist. An avid fan of—and writer about—prizefighting, London put himself in the ring against the established heavyweights of his era. Win or lose, the punches, jabs, uppercuts and "short-arm jolts" in every round of his prose were meant to bring the fans, the very public, to his corner. Spectators today, they were tomorrow's citizen activists.

Otherwise, the cause was lost. Would he be battered? Bloodied? Probably. He had to fight. He had no other way. "Trust thyself," said the writer of an earlier generation, Ralph Waldo Emerson. Jack London gave the command a practical new twist that he garnered from Stanford University president David Starr Jordan and made it his mantra: "*Will it work—will you trust your life to it!*" With pen and typewriter, he came out swinging.[37]

2 The Fight for Public Opinion

To stand up is the point of the game, to stay on one's feet, to not lie down, to not run away. This is the point of it, and the spirit.
—Jack London, "The Jeffries-Ruhlin Fight," 1901

The "springlike" break in the mid-January weather in early 1906 did not fool Jack London. To the Californian, New York was always cold, even on that "scorching" hot summer day back in the depression year of 1894 when he first ventured into the city to sightsee as a jobless teenage tramp and got cracked on the skull by a bull cop's billy club. No matter how much money poured in from his writing or how great his fame, the cop's blow never faded into from memory. London saw the billy club, along with the batons and guns of the Pinkertons and the state militias, as versions of the overseers' whips in this era of industrial slavery. Its overthrow was his life's mission, and public support was vital to success. The stakes of the game were never higher than on this January evening, when four thousand New Yorkers gathered in the midtown Grand Central Palace Exhibition Hall to hear a rousing political speech by the famous author of *The Call of the Wild*.

Spirits ran high as the 8:15 P.M. hour of London's speech approached. A reporter in the audience noted the many "red dresses or red hats or red ribbons" of the women, each one a political hurrah for the revolutionary spirit that enveloped the name Jack London. Women naturally flocked to him, and from the newspapers many of them knew of his controversial recent divorce and remarriage to a woman named Charmian Kittredge—both headlines conveying the hint of scandal, especially since the papers repeatedly published rumors of his illicit amours. His publicity photographs fed those notions. They showed a rakish figure in various soft wool caps, loose neckties, and silk crepe shirts. His "burning eyes" were boyish and smoldering, alluring and a bit dangerous. One observer thought him "all sweetness and ferocity."[1]

The audience eagerly anticipated a larger-than-life figure, a novelist, journalist, sailor, war correspondent, exponent of modern marriage, sportswriter, and, most recently, a gentleman farmer-rancher. His audience reached from the workers with "hard hands and strong arms" to the affluent bourgeoisie of "placid . . . sedentary existence." Awaiting his appearance in the hall, many in the audience opened purses or dug into trouser pockets to snap up the ten-cent " 'genuine' blood red flags, the 'Jack London souvenirs of a great and momentous occasion.' " The fiery female union organizer from the coalfields, Mother Jones, was in the hall, and her shout-out later in the evening was to be memorable for its typical "crisp" and "clipped speech." The atmosphere was amiable, though the speaker was overdue because his train was late. When London finally took the stage at 9:15 P.M., no one in the audience (not even the *New York Times* reporter) guessed that the celebrated Jack London was half-sick from lingering effects of the flulike grippe. This was America's epicenter of capitalism, and Gotham could flatten a man who didn't show himself fit in body and mind. Such a man wouldn't last one round.[2]

London held forth this January night with a fiery lecture titled "The Coming Crisis." Slightly edited, it was the speech he'd delivered all over the Midwest these past weeks, a reprise of a talk entitled "Revolution" that he had first delivered to students at the University of California in Berkeley last April. In New York's Grand Central Palace, the famous author embodied entrepreneurial success but spoke on behalf of growing numbers of Americans who knew to the bone that the captains of industry and finance had failed millions with their exploitative economic system. The titans' names were American bywords of the era: Rockefeller, Carnegie, Vanderbilt, J. P. Morgan, Collis P. Huntington, and others. Historians later called them "The Tycoons" and the "American Colossus." But many Americans, including Jack London, agreed with the caustic economist Thorstein Veblen, whose bestselling *Theory of the Leisure Class* (1899) profiled them in terms of their "outlawry," "barbarian temperament," and "spectacular quasi-predatory careers of fraud." Their success in a "pecuniary culture," Veblen wrote, depended on their "freedom from scruple, from sympathy, honesty and regard for life."[3]

An admirer of Veblen, London had brought the economist's words to life in his popular recent novel, *The Sea-Wolf* (1904). Audience members in the Grand Central Palace doubtless linked the "blind and greedy" capitalists London denounced in his speech with the amoral, monstrous ship captain in the novel. The tycoons were flesh-and-blood versions of the fictional Wolf Larson, a lone predator who ravaged others and was motivated solely by self-interest.

It was not the tycoons' wealth as such that rankled, London insisted in his speech, but their spectacular failure at managing the social world they had made. They had "organized the machinery of life and made possible a wonderful era for all mankind," an era that ought to provide plentiful food, opportunities for "education, for intellectual and spiritual uplift," an era "wherein no creature should cry aloud because it had not enough to eat."[4]

Instead, London charged, their system produced shocking periods of joblessness, chronic hunger, and misery nationwide. Materially, the great capitalists had triumphed, London acknowledged, but socially they had failed "deplorably, ignobly, horribly." London never relied on flamboyant rhetoric or hearsay; instead he marshaled a barrage of numerical facts to seal his indictment. In a national census of over 80 million, 10 million Americans' bodies were weakened for lack of sufficient food, London reported, and "all over this broad, prosperous, enlightened land, are men, women, and children who are living miserably." The system that enabled his own success, he argued, had lost its legitimacy. Even in prosperous times, "the bottom of the social pit" awaits "a hearty, well-fed workingman . . . [who] sees the shambles waiting for him and his children and recoils from the descent." Surrounded by the largely admiring, politically sympathetic audience, London issued this threatening challenge to the regime of the tycoons: "The workers of the world, as a class, are fighting the capitalists of the world, as a class. . . . It is the world's workers that are in revolt." He pulled no punches. "We of the revolution which is at hand want all you possess. We want the power of Government in our own strong hands. We are going to take all you have away from you."[5]

The fight for America's future had taken a fierce turn at the start of the twentieth century, and Jack London prepared to do battle. Over his lifetime, the captains of industry had transformed America into an economic system that was the marvel of the modern world. A country that was formerly dotted with small farms and artisans' shops was now an industrial powerhouse welded by railroads that carried raw materials and finished manufactured products everywhere. The last quarter of the nineteenth century—the years of Jack London's life—was aptly branded as the era of Big Business, which is to say the era of triumphant laissez-faire capitalism, and the names of its founding fathers veined London's writings. Their achievement, London knew, brought unprecedented bounty and convenience to homes and workplaces, and their enterprises provided jobs for millions and radically revamped the nation's economy. In the new twentieth century, the corporations and trusts were the legacy of the last decade's tycoons, and, in effect, these institutions now governed the country. The whole period has been termed the era of "the incorporation of America."[6]

Another famous American, however, viewed the era more critically and much more in line with London's own experience. *The Gilded Age*, the 1873 novel written by Mark Twain (and coauthor Charles Dudley Warner), became an enduring indictment of the era by pointing to a hidden dark underside of the emerging capitalist order. Beneath the shining surface were unconscionable atrocities: child labor, tenement housing, cycles of joblessness, starvation wages, political corruption. The modern regime had come at a horrendous social cost, and by 1900 reformers were sounding alarms and campaigning for corrective measures. Unlike most reformers, London personally knew the miseries that lurked just beneath the golden façade because he had suffered them for most of his impoverished lifetime. These indelible memories fueled his righteous anger on behalf of all those who lived as he had. No one, he swore, should so suffer in this rich land of plenty.

Jack London laced on his gloves to join the battle against this brutal economic system by drawing liberally on the popularity of a blood sport—boxing—that had moved out of saloons and smoky backrooms in the late 1800s. A boyhood brawler who knew saloons, Jack learned boxing from his friend Jim Whitaker, an athletic British army veteran and socialist who earned his living as a grocery store worker in Oakland. After hours, Jim closed the store blinds and taught Jack to box. No more would he "windmill" his arms and flail at opponents in vacant lots; rather, he would fight "scientifically," as his friend Cloudesley Johns remarked. His writing displayed a keen understanding of the "new kinetic" style of boxing "in keeping with the up-tempo spirit of the age." It "rewarded footwork, defensive skills, and counterpunching"—all abilities crucial for this combative writer and public intellectual.[7]

The sport and its terms suited the times. The "manly art" of bare knuckles and glove boxing had surged in popularity by the late nineteenth century, a development the historian Elliott Gorn ascribes to "a burst of upper- and middle-class . . . glorification of male prowess." Some ten years before Jack London was born, the bare-knuckle era had given way to gloved fights under the 1866–67 rules set down by the eighth Marquess of Queensbury. The new rules "specified the size of a boxing ring, the use of turf, the role of seconds and umpires." Outlawed were "head butting, kicking, and biting." By the turn of the new century, the standardized rules and professional referees lent new respectability and prestige to prizefighting as bouts moved indoors. Fights were now staged throughout the United States under the artificial suns of blazing electric lights in venues that seated thousands. "Under the Queensbury rules, there would be a set number of rounds . . . limited to three minutes each, with one minute between rounds. A man who was knocked down was allowed ten seconds to get to his feet or lose the fight by a knockout." Gloves were compulsory, and the retailer Sears, Roebuck & Co. offered a free instruction book with every pair of the "finest" kid leather boxing gloves in its famous mail-order catalogue.[8]

Artists were tracking all this. Whereas the Currier and Ives lithographic prints had featured the bare-knuckle contests in the open air, as in *The Championship Slugger / "Knocking 'Em Out,"* such artists as Philadelphia's Thomas Eakins and New York's George Bellows now applied oil to canvas to capture the sheer combative muscularity of the indoor bouts where zealous male fans cheered and jeered at ringside. Jack London witnessed prizefights of the sort that Eakins portrayed in *Between Rounds* (1898–99), in which a corner man tries to cool the seated, weary fighter who regroups for the next go-round. Jack London was to report, in addition, on the 1910 championship bout that Bellows uncannily anticipated in his racially charged *Both Members of This Club* (1909), a painting that draws viewers' eyes to the bloodied lower jaw of the white boxer being overpowered by his black opponent—a reality that London was to concede in his reporting on the 1910 triumph of the black Jack Johnson over the white Jim Jeffries and in his 1901 coverage of the Jeffries–Gus Ruhlen match in a sweltering indoor arena in which each fighter was fanned with towels between heated rounds.

Social status and executive power also played their part in the zest for pugilism, for college men of the Ivy League now learned the basics of proper stance and "scientific" punching. Along with other competitive sports, boxing was thought to be the tonic for the debilitating modern syndrome of "overcivilization" and thus young men's best preparation for the "strenuous life" of business and battlefield leadership—or, as Oliver Wendell Holmes Jr. put it, "for headship and command."[9]

Its attraction for Jack London, an aspirant front-rank figure on the national scene, included both leadership and, as London's daughter Joan noted, the opportunity to gain "suppleness and grace." Books in London's personal library underscored the exquisite moment "when stoutness of heart and soundness of limb are tested . . . with padded gloves in a padded ring." The "noble art," Jack was assured, let a boxer "inflict damage" on opponents without a blemish to his own character. London thrust pugilistic figures everywhere in his writing and kept sets of gloves for sparring on land and on decks while at sea. In 1905, the first of his two novellas about boxing, *The Game*, was published, just as several years later he was to write another novella about a

9. Jack and Charmian London lace up boxing gloves for sparring, believing the punches and feints to be a healthful exercise. Charmian's diary regularly recorded her progress in the sport, just as Jack also cast himself as a sociopolitical prizefighter. (Henry E. Huntington Library, San Marino, California)

boxer, *The Abysmal Brute* (1913), and to feature prizefighters in the short stories "A Piece of Steak" and "The Mexican."[10]

The arena that Jack London entered, however, stretched from the Atlantic Seaboard and into the far Pacific and overrode partisan sparring between the two major parties, the Republicans and Democrats. Entering the political ring at five foot seven, weighing 165 pounds, the best-selling author cut an appealing manly figure with his whorls of dark curly hair, sparkling gray eyes, ready smile, and the rolling gait of a sailor. A self-identified underdog who grew up "pinched by poverty," London saw whole populations sacrificed to the depths of the "Social Pit." In his teens he tramped the country with "sailor-men, soldier-men, labor-men," whose bodies and minds were now "wrenched and distorted and twisted out of shape by toil and hardship and accident, and cast adrift by their masters like so many old horses." In freezing cold weather, his teeth chattering, London had "bedded in pools of water" and also drew close to "the woman of the streets and the man of the gutter." Seized with "terror" lest their lives become his own, London swore to climb up the slick and slimy pit walls through sheer strength of brain and mind and will.[11]

In fighting trim and famous, London now prepared for combat against the unbridled capitalism that he saw as the root cause of the pandemic of human misery and degradation that had nearly claimed his own life in knockabout years of tramping, brawling, boozing, and ducking cops' billy clubs. Given the tremendous popularity of the sport and his own frequent sparring with male friends—and with wife Charmian too—it is understandable that for his writing and speeches Jack London would draw heavily and continuously on its terms, both its figures of speech and its ideology of blows exchanged over many rounds, the winners of the contest standing tall, the defeated visibly flattened on the canvas or collapsed in the arms of allies.

By 1900, the US census numbered some 80 million people, and the term "public" had new weight and valence. Reformers of every stripe made efforts to sway attitudes toward progressive social change. The corporations and trusts, too, were awakening to the need for public approval, which is to say they began to see the advantage of favorable public relations. London was convinced that a vast American citizenry that was roused to outrage against the dominant and brutal economic regime could marshal its energy, exert revolutionary power, and usher in the new and better era for the future. The prize in this main event was common support for an "equal chance for all men," and especially "equality of opportunity in industrial life" as a basic tenet of "simple justice." The ultimate prize, however, could be awarded only by the public, and the American future be secured by the weight of its driving force.[12]

People must be made to understand, for starters, that the cardinal term for the capitalist Gilded Age regime—"laissez faire"—was not simply a catchphrase for individual freedom or a "doctrine of liberty." In this age of social Darwinism some equated it with the "survival of the fittest" or considered it simply shorthand for "mind your own business." None of the above, London argued. To him, "laissez faire" was the frenchified linguistic trick that let a cunning few grab the lion's share of the wealth and power of the nation—indeed, of the world. A public that grasped this point could exert its force to defeat the system that London cast in terms of the Satanic. "*Laissez faire*," he said, means "everybody for himself and devil take the hindmost." Setting the public right on this matter was a top priority. After all, the country's most cherished public document, the Declaration of Independence, proclaimed the principle of "a decent respect for the opinions of mankind." One of London's heroes, Abraham Lincoln, had famously said that with the "public support, nothing can fail" but "without it, nothing can succeed." When he signed his letters "Yours for the Revolution," London knew to his marrow that the revolution was a fight that could be won only with the public on his side.[13]

The topic of public opinion was much debated during Jack London's boyhood years, for the collective viewpoint of millions of Americans was a subject roiling intellectual circles while London struggled to earn money and to find his voice. He was just ten years old when his family moved back to Oakland from their foreclosed Livermore ranch, and he knew nothing of the launch in 1886 of a new American weekly, *Public Opinion*, that would continue publication for the next twenty years. All the while that the ten-year-old Jack swept out Oakland saloons, set pins in a bowling alley, and earned a few nickels and dimes "as boy-helper on an ice-wagon," a nationally prominent professor, William Graham Sumner of Yale University, was expressing deep misgivings about civic leaders' failure to discipline an unruly American populace. A social Darwinist, Sumner feared that those responsible for "the body of public opinion" were unwitting contributors to social disorder of labor strikes. The "people of standing," he charged, were a Babel of "contradictory and heterogeneous doctrines about life and society."[14]

Entering his turbulent teens, London remained unaware of the growing conviction among the nation's leading intellectuals that public opinion was vitally important to every area of American culture and society. The sometime teenage oyster pirate "Sailor Jack" London revered such Oakland waterfront celebrities as "French Frank" and "Whisky Bob." Center stage in his thoughts was occupied by these men, not the goateed Yale University political economist (and soon to be president) Arthur Twining Hadley, who taught and wrote about the triumphs and perils of fluctuating public attitudes. London was dazzled by a daring Bay Area skipper named Nelson, a "reckless maniac . . . with the body of a Hercules," but he knew nothing of Edward Alsworth Ross, a younger political economist who arrived in California in 1893 to teach at Stanford University just as London was toiling in an Oakland jute mill for ten-hour shifts for ten cents an hour. Within a few years Ross was to publish *Social Control* (1901), a detailed analysis of the dynamics of public opinion, many of his insights later reinforcing London's mission to school the public and guide the nation's future direction.[15]

Soon after Ross's arrival on the West Coast, the Anglo-Irish Viscount (James) Bryce's two-volume *American Commonwealth* (1894), with its lengthy discussion of "The Nature of Public Opinion," took its place on the library shelves of affluent Americans. At that time, London was serving a hellish stint as a coal shoveler in Oakland and would soon ride the rails cross-country to chase a contingent of an army of jobless men en route to Washington to petition the federal government for help. In that depression year, London was convicted of vagrancy and served his one-month sentence in the Erie County Penitentiary. The feudal conditions of incarceration would soon open him to the work of a socialist, W. J. (William James) Ghent, who argued that capitalist modernity was actually a veiled neomedieval state. In the 1890s, however, London had no inkling that Ghent's reflections on the promise and pitfalls of public opinion were to prove invaluable and that his book, *Our Benevolent Feudalism* (1902), would occupy prime space in London's own library.

For all of them, the notion that public opinion was crucial for success was no mere political piety but a true statement of paramount importance. To Bryce, it constituted "the chief and ultimate power" in the United States. Yale's Hadley agreed that the nation "must accept the principle of public sentiment," which is "all-powerful." The socialist Ghent allowed that "public opinion in these United States" might be "more potent than ever," Ross, for his part, relied on public opinion to "guard the social peace," apply pressure to prevent misdeeds, and exert itself with prompt immediacy. ("The mills of Justice grind slowly," he observed, "but the mills of the public grind promptly.") Ross foresaw the emergence of wise "leaders" and "influencers" who would become the "rallying points of public opinion."[16]

But who were these "leaders" and what, exactly, was public opinion? And how could it be shaped? London himself would later find that most men (and women) were "a tangled mass of contradictions, paradoxes, and lies." Though the leading intellectuals proclaimed public opinion to be the summa of authority, they also hedged the term with caveats and provisos. Gone and "never to return" was "the day of the sturdy backwoodsman, settler, flatboatman, or prospector" who defied "law and public opinion as well." But whose opinion now mattered? How could it be won—and kept? And at what point did public opinion degenerate into mob rule?[17]

The experts agreed that the public could be disturbingly impressionable, could turn fickle or credulous, or succumb to violent emotion unchecked by reason. In *Social Control*, Stanford University's Ross spoke sharply of the public's blurred aims, rash leaps to judgment, contradictory goals, confusion of purpose, and scattered energies. "The public has a short wrath and a poor memory," he said, and is given to "mere impotent rage." Its "frown is capricious," and "its favor is fitful." It operates on an amoral plane, for "its pains are not inflicted to deter from evil, nor are its prizes given to promote virtue." The socialist Ghent pointed out other treacheries. He warned about the public's inertia, its "acquiescence in the existing regime" as reformers wearied and ceased their efforts and ordinary Americans betrayed their own interests in the Gilded Age of the tycoons. "False consciousness" was not yet a term in fashion, but Ghent pinpointed its meaning. "The imaginations of most men are fired by the spectacle of the few achieving great fortunes," he observed, for "each believes that a like fortune lies somewhere within his own reach." Bowing to a social order that "he instinctively feels to be inequitable," said Ghent, the ordinary American wallows in "blind fatuity."[18]

Bryce, too, had his say. A self-styled heir to Alexis de Tocqueville, he offered a critique of American culture and politics in the tradition of the early nineteenth-century French traveler and social observer who penned the classic *Democracy in America* (1840). Bryce's *American Commonwealth* (revised and updated in 1905) cautioned that the notion of an unbiased public was a pipe dream. "No event, no speech or article ever falls on a perfectly virgin soil," he said, "since "the reader or listener is always more or less biased already." Bias, he explained, was a mix of "previous education, habits of mind, accepted dogmas, religious or social affinities, [and] notions of personal interest." Despite American tributes to individualist thought, Bryce found that "among all classes" Americans' public opinion was reducible to "two or three prejudices and aversions." It was "two or three phrases or catchwords" that passed for analytical depth of thought. No matter how crucial the questions before the public, Bryce concluded, the ruling motivation was not "thought" but "sentiment."[19]

Sentiment? Yale's Hadley shuddered at the very notion. Promoted to the university presidency in 1899, this "slight, wiry figure" mesmerized generations of students with his "fists clenched in pugilistic fashion" and an intellect of "nervous force," inveighing against the mindless "unreasoning emotion" that promoted the swelling socialist scourge of recent years. Hadley warned against the dangers posed by human emotion, whether "admiration or abhorrence, respect or derision." The Yale president's trepidation was politically and economically focused. Above all, he feared that runaway feelings, positive or negative, could stampede a shortsighted public toward revolution. Christian sympathy for the plight of those less fortunate was understandable and commendable, Hadley acknowledged, but the "existence of certain evils in industrial society" reduced the public to a dangerous state of mindless "unreasoning emotion." Politically that meant the scourge of socialism. To keep it in check, the public needed reminders of the French social psychologist Gustave Le Bon, whose jeremiad *The Crowd* (1895), then in wide circulation in America, telegraphed the dangers of social groups run amok. The infamous Paris Commune of 1871, in which tens of thousands were killed in months of street fighting, set the stage for Le Bon's pathbreaking work. The "sentiments" of a crowd, wrote Le Bon in medical terms, are intensified by "suggestion and contagion." Absent all sense of "responsibility," the crowd grows increasingly violent, having completely lost the faculty of "reason." So much for the downward spiral of "sentiment."[20]

Sumner, Hadley, Ross, Bryce, Ghent were ciphers to the young Jack London, but they would soon be his familiars. And by 1898, after his stepfather's death following a life spent in backbreaking toil, London knew that a laborer's life was nothing less than disastrous, so he renounced the manual labor that threatened to destroy him. He realized that brains paid, not brawn, and he determined never again to subject his body to manual labor. ("*I shall do no more hard work, and may God strike me dead if I do another day's hard work with my body more than I have to do.*") In a cramped attic room provided by his widowed mother, London plunged into a strict regimen of intense intellectual and literary self-schooling, scheduling his day so tightly that he had no free time whatsoever. At age twenty, when he graduated from Oakland High School and crammed for the entrance exams for the University of California, London saw the irony in his situation. "I was working to get away from work," he reflected, "and I buckled down to it with the grim realization of the paradox." Hammering at a crude typewriting machine, apprenticed to himself and to the editors who stood between him and the reading public, he managed to thrust himself into national prominence in the first years of the new twentieth century. By then the names of Sumner and Ghent et al. threaded through his letters and essays, for London understood the profound importance of public opinion, the topic they had debated for more than a decade.[21]

When Jack London began his own campaign to swing public opinion to his side in the late 1890s, his aim was local—and predictably provocative. He first garnered his public reputation with his incendiary speeches in a city park at the Chabot Observatory in Oakland, delivered in "a terrible diatribe" of " 'fire and sword.' " One genteel Oakland High School acquaintance noticed his "mental ruthlessness for pursuing his ideas" and spoke in trepidation of London's "eloquence and force," which served as a "Revolutionary means . . . to destroy what some people had in order that others should be relieved of many distresses of life." She added that "many good people were frightened," that the police were called and "arrested him but there was no punishment" because "Jack London was under age." The nineteen-year-old London struck this same acquaintance as "strong and rugged," his face suddenly alight when the topic of conversation turned to socialism, though he was dismayingly "uncouth" and "unbelievably shabby," his face "ruddy and sunburned" and his "disheveled hair" obviously raked with grimy fingers. London's first in-print efforts to sway the larger public to his side came via the Letters to the Editor section of the *Oakland Times*. Identifying himself as an "assiduous reader" who had so far "failed to see the Socialist represented," he warned that business competition was a shell game and a sure path to monopoly and that "small fry capitalists" might therefore soon find themselves collapsing into the dreaded sinkhole of the laboring class. (He also proposed the notion of municipal ownership of the local water system, a somewhat radical proposition at the time.)[22]

London's political education gained momentum when, in his twenty-first year, serendipity brought him a mentor. An assistant reference librarian in Oakland, Frederick Irons Bamford, was a temperamentally gentle, scholarly Canadian-born Christian socialist who steered the reading choices of the rough questing London, who had ventured once again into the free public library by the old Oakland city hall and asked about the most important books in order that he could grapple with them. The two seemed an odd couple. Across the desk, the scruffy young London saw a slim bespectacled figure with carefully combed silver hair and a trim moustache, his desktop adorned with a vase of fresh flowers, a small sculpture, and a selection of new books. A former classroom teacher, Bamford was engaged in the study of socialism when he met and befriended London, who was then enrolled for his single semester as a university student on the eucalyptus-fringed Berkeley campus. The librarian had been drawn to Christian socialism, and while London never believed in the divinity of Jesus of Nazareth, he understood the Nazarene as a socialist in thought and deed, as in the pamphlet *The Socialism of Jesus*, which profiled "a working-class man, animated by the same feelings and judging from the same point of view as the free-minded man of the working-class of all ages, including our own." Bamford pointed to the good work of the British Christian socialists, Charles Kingsley and Frederick Denison Maurice, two blunt British theologians who exhorted the well-off public to confront its complicity with a system that perpetuated poverty and child labor.[23]

Bamford steeped himself in the socialism of other British literary Victorians, "Ruskin, Carlyle, Mill, Arnold, Morris, and others." In addition, the librarian was "strongly enthusiastic about Karl Marx." According to his widow, he "was first impressed with Jack London's great eagerness for knowledge," especially of "economics and sociology." The librarian was also struck by the young man's "great powers of assimilation." Mrs. Bamford sensed that her husband "felt the enthusiasm of a co-worker in his dreams for the betterment and uplift of humanity." The mentor and his protégé occasionally lunched together, attended Ruskin Club dinners in San Francisco, and kept up their friendship for years to come. London cherished his copy of Bamford's 1903 compilation *The Passion of Socialism*, a miscellany of voices chorusing aspirations for human liberation: for "the noble work of liberating the working people," for a reformation to set mankind "free in the sphere of economics," for "the training and development of the human race to freedom."[24]

At the time of London's tutelage, socialists in America were a diverse lot, ranging from West Coast syndicalists and western miners to the tenant farmers of Oklahoma, the stolid German immigrants in Wisconsin, and the Yiddish-speaking Jewish immigrant workers in New York's Lower East Side. Many supporters, including the young and impressionable Jack London, were drawn to what the historian Irving Howe has called the movement's "most indigenous voice," the pulp newsprint *Appeal to Reason*, which "spoke in rich homespun accents," expressing "both an unspoiled idealism and the naivete of a poorly-digested Marxism." In addition, Howe observed, "a torrent of pamphlets poured out of the socialist national office in Chicago," while "speakers, organizers, part-time volunteers toured and tramped across the country" even as "socialist lyceums sprang up" and "the socialist hall . . . became a familiar landmark in hundreds of cities and towns." American-born socialists were especially attuned to the linkage with the earlier nineteenth-century abolitionist movement, for they fought against a new system of enslavement—wage slavery—in an industrial era in which American capitalism "clung to a brutal system of domination" of legions of workers.[25]

London, however, craved the factual, historical and theoretical knowledge that toned him for the long fight. To him, socialism was a program to enact, not a saloon whiskey dream or airy bourgeois fantasy. The omnipresent machine technology of London's era inevitably played its part in his outlook. Everywhere, it seemed, meshing gears and interlocking girders were open to public view as machines and structures took command of space, from the moving rods and wheels of rail locomotives to the steel-framed bridges and buildings that rose in every American city and town. Contemporary life meant an "omnipresent and masterful and intimate" relation to "cogs and wheels and belts," proclaimed Gerald Stanley Lee, a Protestant minister who inscribed a copy of his *The Voice of the Machine* (1906) to Jack London, his overview of modern life breathtakingly mechanistic. ("Modern government is a machine. . . . Modern trade is a machine. . . . Modern charity is a machine for getting people to help each other. . . . Modern literature is a machine for supplying ideas. Modern journalism is a machine for distributing them.") In sync with the age, London demanded to know the mechanics of the social order, its motor and its workings. The lingo of the age became his own. In the social pit, he first "saw the wheels of the social machine go around" and "watch[ed] the machinery work." Later in life he came to understand "the cogs and springs of men's actions." Socialism likewise demanded scrutiny of its inner workings. London sought operational knowledge of its complex history and of varied theoretical positions on its aims and goals.[26]

Americans, London knew, usually encountered socialism in print and public speech allied with communism, nihilism, and anarchism—all isms that were dreaded and feared by the very middle classes that London campaigned to win to his side. In a short essay in 1895 in the *San Francisco Examiner*, "What Socialism Is," he cast aside these other isms as dark extremes (anarchism, for example, which rejects all law in favor of individual supremacy without restraints). London pivoted from the warmest idea of fellow feeling: "A socialist is of necessity social—hence the name." He reinforced the point, saying that the socialist "wishes to be social—that is, to live in a society formed of social beings like himself." Encompassing the groupings of the "family, community or State," London insisted that the socialist "must conform to the laws," including those that were yet "perhaps unwritten." He showed the mentality of the socialist to be progressive, for "all he wishes is to better such laws." The future was really part of an evolutionary cycle, London explained, graphing steady historical human enlightenment from an ancient era of slavery to one of feudalism, thereafter to the present of capitalism—and onward toward the imminently better future. "Socialism," said London, "means a reconstruction of society with a more just application of labor and distribution of the returns thereof." He challenged readers to ponder the limitations of the present socio-legal order of things and to consider the crying need for corrective action.[27]

In London's terms, finally, a socialist was "any man who strives for a better form of Government than the one he is living under." Surely every reader of the young writer-activist's newspaper article could imagine a "better form of Government," especially when political cronyism was much on the public mind, as London knew. His home state's history of "general corruption of politicians and bad conduct of [the] State, county, and city government" were common knowledge, as was "the tyranny of corporations, especially railroads."[28]

By the turn of the twentieth century, London had trained for the rounds ahead with a formidable list of books, tracts, and pamphlets that gave him knowledge of the movement and its history, both in the United States and abroad. Grueling personal struggles had ignited his political passion, but London wrote and spoke from a deepened knowledge of socialist history and theory; myriad titles had become the tools of his trade, including Marx's *Das Kapital* and Friedrich Engels's *Landmarks of Scientific Socialism*. He admired Edward Bellamy's blockbuster socialist utopian novel of 1887, *Looking Backward*, and he knew Henry George's *Progress and Poverty* (1879), with its innovative tax proposal and its quintessential dark conundrum of modern life, namely, that the jobless tramp somehow accompanied the technologically advanced railroad locomotive. London read and filed the work of contemporary socialists such as Richard Ely, Robert Hunter, George Herron, John Spargo, and Daniel DeLeon, and he penciled comments in the margins of his many books, among them *Patriotism and Socialism*, *Women under Socialism*, *Socialism as the Sociological Ideal*, *The Social Unrest: Studies in Labor and Socialist Movements*, and *An Exposition of Socialism and Collectivism*. The fight against wage slavery, the capitalist exploitation of slaves before the Civil War, the use of blacks to weaken trade unions, the labor statistics that were generated by the prominent statistician Carroll D. Wright—all these and more proved literally noteworthy as the young writer and speaker prepared for his bouts. Reflecting years later on her father's socialism, London's daughter Joan concluded that it lacked depth, that London had taken a crash course in socialism, socialism on the fly. In practical terms, it sufficed. "The time for Utopias and dreamers is past," London said flatly in a letter early in the summer of 1899, amplifying the point the following December when he identified himself as "a scientific socialist" and "economic man," definitely not a "utopian."[29]

Sentiment, nevertheless, was about to become a powerful armament in London's writing. The popular sentimental novels of the nineteenth century were passé, most of them authored by women and thick with emotional appeals on behalf of orphans, waifs, wronged maidens, and so on. Still, London believed that skillfully stoked sentiment could stir the public to action in the new twentieth century. Just as Yale's Hadley feared, strong feelings ignited the engine of social change. Readers' sympathies and their sense of righteous anger would be roused and shaped on behalf of workers whose brutal treatment London was to feature repeatedly in his work. Feelings of moral outrage would surely rise as readers empathized with the work beast, the tormented dog Buck in *The Call of the Wild*, and with the hapless crewmen who were terrorized by the sadistic captain—a coded captain of industry—in *The Sea-Wolf* (1904). The plight of the poor working-class striver in the quasi-autobiographical *Martin Eden* would surely touch heartstrings, as would the portrait of the mill boy laborer in "The Apostate." And London's journalism could also enlist activist sympathies. His *The People of the Abyss* (1903) unblinkingly exposed the disgraceful, deadly slums that were woven into the social fabric of England, the nation supposedly at the apex of human civilization. The equally deadly practice of torture inside US prison walls must also be made known, arousing horror at this barbaric reproach to civilization. His novel *The Star Rover* must expose atrocities in prisons in order to help put a stop to them. As a scholar remarked in a 1909 treatise on US newspapers, "Reading affects habits of thought and habits of thought give rise to habits of action." Every Jack London story, novel, essay, or nonfiction narrative could be a round fought for the socialist future.[30]

The socialist side, in fact, was winning its share of bouts. To be sure, the movement had a mixed history in nineteenth-century America, arguably because of the country's aggregate immigrant ethnicities, its surplus of workers, its hostility toward politics, and its sheer continental vastness. In addition, the infamous Haymarket riot in Chicago in 1886, where a deadly explosion at a rally in support of the eight-hour workday had killed seven policemen, had proven disastrous. The rebirth of the movement in the 1900s and 1910s, however, thrilled Jack London and countless others. The circulation of one American socialist publication had reached three hundred thousand, and the formerly outlying trade unions were on board, recognizing the class struggle in the cycles of unemployment.

Other groups leaned in the socialist direction, since "a large number of brilliant journalists and university men are sympathetic." Socialist officials, moreover, had been elected to office in some state legislatures, notably in Wisconsin. The Intercollegiate Socialist Society, of which London was a founding member, trusted that it "exercised a considerable influence in a quiet way in the universities." What's more, the charismatic former railway union leader Eugene Victor Debs had risen to leadership nationally under the US Socialist Party. One historian remarked that Debs was "an orator able to establish a rapport with the American people such as no other radical in this country has ever had." Each new election cycle showed major advances, and the socialist Declaration of Principles endorsed by Debs in 1897 mapped the specifics of public ownership of the resources of the United States, from its water works, telegraphs, and telephones to its minerals and precious metals.[31]

"How we are growing!" Jack London exclaimed in a letter to a literary-political friend in 1899. He remembered when the few socialists in Oakland could be counted "on one's great toes." In the 1904 presidential election, over four hundred thousand US voters supported the Socialist candidate, Debs, an increase of nearly 400 percent in the party's showing in four years' time. The momentum was undeniable. Viscount Bryce knew that "ten men who care are a match for a hundred who do not," and he understood the power of an energized minority to "leaven and convince" the majority. Bryce's grasp of public opinion at the ballot box was inspiring: "When a man has voted, he is committed"; one view has been "vanquished" while another has "triumphed." By 1907 Professor Woodrow Wilson of Princeton University included a sympathetic section on socialism in his college textbook, *The State*. The future US president argued that the socialists were justified in their "revolt" against "selfish, misguided individualism" and the tyranny of "distorted competition." Though they erred, he cautioned, in their quest to abolish all marketplace competition, the socialists were correct "to seek to bring the individual with his special interests, personal to himself, into complete harmony with society with its general interests, common to all."[32]

Socialism was buoyed, it seemed, by a foundering opponent, for the capitalist industrial regime appeared to be rapidly falling from public favor at the approach of the twentieth century. The new gargantuan size of corporations was itself becoming a major source of public anxiety. One political cartoon captured the new public mood in its rendering of "THE TRUST" as a muscle-bound Goliath that was belted with trophy skulls representing the slain "Small Grocer," the "Small Merchant," and "Honest Labor." In his depiction, the cartoonist may have been making reference to a landmark 1886 Supreme Court ruling, *Santa Clara County v. Southern Pacific Railroad*, in which the court conferred all the legal rights, privileges, and status of a "person" on the business corporation.[33]

Person or not, the huge corporations and trusts provoked widespread distrust, and public opinion toward these institutions had chilled—a reversal from the previous century, when hundreds of thousands of business corporations had met with general approval. Following the Civil War, the captains of industry were largely acclaimed, admired, and celebrated figures. They laid an amazing network of rail and produced every conceivable modern convenience, from fountain pens to home sewing machines. (Somewhat tongue-in-cheek, Jack London called himself a "small-fry capitalist" who borrowed three hundred dollars to buy the skiff *Razzle-Dazzle* in 1891, hired a crew of one, and profited from the sale of pillaged oysters from privately owned beds in the San Francisco Bay until the boat, his capital, was wrecked, whereupon he sold the hulk for scrap for a mere twenty dollars.)

The sheer scale of the business transformation that occurred by 1900 had changed all that. As one historian has argued, "Many companies, through mergers and other forms of vertical integration and horizontal consolidation, so dominated their industries that they now controlled the market as much as they were ruled by it." As a result, "the traditional potency of the family, the church, and the local community suddenly seemed dwarfed by the sway of the giant corporations." The outcome of this "momentous shift in the balance of social forces" was "a crisis of legitimacy for the large corporations." To Jack London, the crisis was a moment of truth and a revolutionist's prime opportunity.[34]

Big Business also aroused public suspicion because of its penchant for secrecy. The mining companies, the manufacturers, and the railroads could trace their habits of extreme confidentiality to customs of the medieval guilds, but their secrecy was now the source of self-inflicted injury. According to one public relations historian, "The greater the potential public interest in an industry, the more attention it was likely to give to keeping its operations secret." The senior John D. Rockefeller voiced the quintessential attitude in his maxim "Silence is golden."[35]

If silence roused suspicion, public remarks by captains of industry and finance sometimes inflicted serious damage, particularly with heedless statements of apparent callous disregard for tens of millions of their fellow citizens. In 1882, the railroad giant William Henry Vanderbilt, mindful that his principal responsibility was to his companies' stockholders, ignited a firestorm with his crack "The public be damned," as did financier J. P. Morgan, who remarked, "I owe the public nothing." A similar galling statement surfaced in 1902 in the midst of an anthracite coal miners' strike that threatened winter shortages of heating fuel in the populous Northeast. The railroad president George F. Baer was outraged by the audacity of the emboldened miners and adamantly refused to negotiate with their union. The "Christian men of property," Baer stated arrogantly, are in "control of the property rights of the country," and they alone are thus entitled to determine "the rights and interests of the laboring man."[36]

Though Baer's comment was expressed privately in a letter, that made no difference once it was leaked to the press, and a public that rarely sided with organized labor now threw its support behind the workers' cause. Newspapers nationwide ridiculed "Divine Right Baer," and in New York City's own Cooper Union hall, one speaker quoted the railroad executive's statement and cracked that "if God did that, it was one of the most ill-advised acts of which the Almighty ever was guilty." The laissez-faire system suffered another political and economic blow when President Theodore Roosevelt and the press weighed in on the side of the United Mine Workers, who were awarded a 10 percent pay increase and a workday reduced from ten hours to eight.[37]

Not that London fooled himself about the magnitude of the work ahead. "I know that socialism is not the very next step," he confessed to one correspondent in 1901. "I should much prefer to wake to-morrow in a smoothly running socialist state; but I know I shall not." But the Californian had good reason to be optimistic. He was the author of five books, a rising literary star on the national scene, and a dues-paying member of the Socialist Labor Party. The capitalist side, it seemed, was losing round after round, and soon would be forced to forfeit the fight.[38]

Meanwhile, across the country in New York City, another combatant was likely to take note of Jack London's upward career trajectory and find it alarming. Mr. Ivy Ledbetter Lee was no admirer of socialist literature of any kind. Quite the opposite. From his vantage point, it was an attack from the enemy camp. With his "dark hair, keen blue eyes, and robust, well-knit frame," the six-foot-tall Lee had the "lean physique and carriage of an ambitious man." Quite close in age to London, Ivy Lee (b. 1874) was just now launching a career in a new field called public relations and sought his clientele among the very captains of industry that Jack London and his allies reviled. For strategic reasons of his own, Lee tracked such public statements as London's in order to repudiate and nullify them in public regard. Lee vowed, what's more, to replace the socialist agenda with a glowing vision of the capitalist era just ahead. It came down to this: as forcefully as Jack London and his ilk advanced the cause of a socialist future, Ivy Ledbetter Lee would strive to put a stop to it.[39]

An aspirant journalist from his college days, Lee became a stringer for New York newspapers before reporting full time for the *New York Times* and Joseph Pulitzer's *New York World*. His career turned sharply upward when he became the publicist for the political campaign to reelect New York City mayor Seth Low. A former merchant and president of Columbia University,

Low had successfully reduced the rampant graft of the city's entrenched Tammany political machine by hiring municipal employees through a merit-based civil service system.

The year that London's *Call of the Wild* was published, 1903, saw Lee's own first book in print, a 160-page campaign manifesto extolling Low's political gifts, entitled *The City for the People: The Best Administration New York Ever Had*. Lee's biographer notes that it "contained many of the features that were to be common to [his] publicity efforts in the years to come," meaning that each opponent was discredited (the Tammany crowd was dismissed as "a dismal failure and hot-bed of 'graft' "), while the favored side was celebrated for unstinting service to a broad spectrum of society (notably the "good horses" the Low administration provided for fire brigades, and its cost-efficient wintertime removal of snow). As a partner in the fledgling public relations firm of Parker and Lee, Ivy Lee staked his career on the very corporate system that Jack London fought to overturn.[40]

While London had grown up penniless in California, Lee's life had begun on the opposite side of the Continental Divide, in the rubble of the post–Civil War South, where his boyhood featured a prestigious round of visitors to the family parsonage in Atlanta presided over by his father, the Reverend James W. Lee. The young Jack London saw "reporters, editors, lawyers, judges" in the Oakland saloons, where, he later realized, these civic leaders "sought forgetfulness of jaded toil and stale grief." The young Ivy Lee, however, observed these same sorts of figures at their most publicly presentable as he overheard the high-minded conversations of the prominent businessmen, politicians, bishops, and journalists that the Lees entertained in the 1880s and 1890s. While young Jack London helped his farmer stepfather with livestock and field crops on the "bleak sad coast . . . south of San Francisco," Ivy Lee listened to the parlor voices that served as his prep school. Young London spent endless hours atop "heavy potato wagons" listening to the dull thudding hooves of "plodding horses," while Ivy Lee absorbed his father's silvery rhetoric at the pulpit and in the parlor. Known for bridging differences over doctrine and across denominations, the Reverend Lee allied with an industrial business culture. "Commerce," he wrote, "to be permanent and healthy and progressive, must fall into line with the purpose nature has put upon its perilous course to subserve." If his phrasing sounds lofty and awkward, the elder Lee's success at smoothing over discord nonetheless signaled to his son that rhetoric was the best lubricant for human relations.[41]

Throughout this period, a series of influential mentors shaped young Ivy Lee's outlook, most notably Henry W. Grady, the prominent and nationally influential editor of the *Atlanta Constitution* who has been termed "the most respected apologist for the [post–Civil War] New South." Grady had cemented his reputation in a speech in December 1886 to the New England Society in the banquet hall of Delmonico's restaurant in New York City, where he offered a vision of modern southern agricultural diversity and especially of a New South of railroads and industry in league with those of the North. His speech was reprinted in newspapers nationwide and judged to be a masterpiece of rhetoric that promoted progressive North–South reconciliation through business and finance. Before Grady met an untimely death from illness in 1889 at thirty-nine years of age, the young Lee had "absorbed all of Grady's interests: Wall Street, the stock market, banking and investments." Ivy Lee idolized him.[42]

The young southerner's intellect would also soon be stamped with the worldview of the recently deceased president of Princeton University, James McCosh, when he transferred to the Ivy League campus in 1896 after two years of study at Emory in Atlanta. Like most college and university leaders of the time, James McCosh promoted a doctrine of divinely sanctioned rights to wealth, property, and freedom from interference by government. Under the McCosh mantle, Lee learned that the "hand of God" directed the human quest for the qualities that produced "wealth" and "the powers which wealth puts in operation." "God has bestowed upon us certain powers and gifts," wrote Princeton's late president, assuring those who enjoyed wealth and power that God himself sanctified their privileged lives, a sermon echoed in Protestant pulpits across the country each week. (As one Protestant church publication of the time declared, "God has need of rich Christians, and He makes them.")[43]

The Steel King, Andrew Carnegie, authored his own secular credo, "Wealth," which appeared in 1889 in the august *North American Review* and was reissued in 1900 as "The Gospel of Wealth" in the collection *Other Timely Essays*. Carnegie's essay justified great fortunes and doubled as an instruction manual for the few who amassed them. The "man of wealth," Carnegie insisted, must first "set an example of modest, unostentatious living" and, second, provide adequately for his dependents. All other revenues must be considered "trust funds . . . for the community," with the ultrarich philanthropist "doing for them better than they would or could do for themselves." In harmony with McCosh, Carnegie proclaimed a "Law of Competition" that justified a social Darwinist view of human life: "sometimes hard for the individual" but "best for the race because it insures the survival of the fittest in every department."[44]

Ivy Lee took this code as his own, convinced, as his biographer remarks, that it "provided the true antidote for social ills." Jack London had learned firsthand the miseries of life deep in the "social Pit," where industrial workers were scrapped like old horses that stumbled "through merciless servitude to the hide-house [and] glue-rendering works." Lee's outlook, however, was aerial—as if gazing down from a new flying machine at the panorama of industrial modernity. For him, the scene was like a creation story out of Genesis. As if peering over the shoulder of the tycoons—the Big Men—Lee saw what laissez-faire capitalism and finance had wrought, and he saw that it was good.[45]

Like London, Lee knew something about prizefighting. From the gentlemanly sidelines as a student staff member of the *Daily Princetonian* in the late 1890s, Lee had helped publicize his college boxing club and the course of pugilist instruction at Princeton. Lee's passion for the game was sparked when, as a young reporter, he covered the training of the Irish-born boxer Tom Sharkey, a heavyweight whose career (1893–1904) was notable for its thirty-seven knockouts in forty winning fights and a smattering of draws and losses. Lee "worked out with him in the ring" while Sharkey prepared for his world championship bout with Jim Jeffries. "The experience made him a fight fan for the rest of his life." Like Jack London, Lee understood and embraced the ethos of the sport: "Boxers exhibited composure under pressure, unflinching fortitude, and heroic stoicism, all in the name of masculine prowess."[46]

The source of the rising public fear and loathing of Big Business, as Lee understood it, was public perception—or, rather, misperception. The solution, however, was at hand. If the public could be persuaded to see things through a different, favorable lens, then its collective sense of threat and anger would evaporate. A new appreciation for business, industry, and finance would arise—all for the mutual benefit of God's own capitalist order and of his public as well. This was Lee's sterling insight: that public opinion could be altered to favor the institutions of modern capitalism. It remained only for capitalists to recognize and grasp their opportunity to channel new messages to the public. Just as Jack London was socialism's champion, Lee was in training to become capitalism's "courtier."

But by 1902, the year of the anthracite coal strike, Ivy Lee had yet to win a round. Capitalism, he knew, was losing in the all-important court of public opinion. To Lee, the responsibility for the crisis indeed lay at the feet of Big Business—but not because of the huge size of the monopolies and trusts. From Lee's outlook, the business habit of compulsive secrecy soured

10. Ivy Ledbetter Lee, a public relations founding figure whose clients included industrial corporations from railroads to mines, steel, and petroleum, notably Standard Oil and its founding family, the Rockefellers. Like Jack London, Lee amassed an extensive research library. (Princeton University Library)

its reputation nationwide. Business, he thought, had become its own worst enemy. Its obsessive secrecy, together with its distorted gargantuan image and the maladroit outbursts of its big men, were gross errors and mistakes of stewardship of the public. The financial and corporate leaders had neglected the "decent respect for the opinions of mankind."

By then Lee had a wife and child to support, plus his share of the Parker and Lee partnership office expenses. Eking out a living in press agentry, his clients included politicians, a scandalous insurance heir named Thomas Fortune Ryan, and a circus. But the office of Parker and Lee at 20 Broad Street nonetheless proclaimed ambition, for it was located in a building adjacent to the New York Stock Exchange. Lee's allegiances were clear, and he'd shown a knack for meeting important men from his Princeton days. Back then, he'd snagged a quote from the recently retired US president Grover Cleveland, who took a fancy to the young Lee and gave him an exclusive on several stories. In these first years of the twentieth century Lee met as many top businessmen as possible and reportedly gave this advice to a young colleague: "Seek the right people. Flatter them. Play the games they play, and if they don't like to lose let them win." Healthy and vigorous, Lee prepared for a long campaign, awaiting his moment to serve the lords of modern business.[47]

In terms of the ring, Ivy Lee became a superb coach and corner man for the titans of industry and finance. Both he and Jack London and Lee knew that they fought in the arena that mattered most, battling the biggest fighters and commanding the most public attention: by the early 1900s, weight categories were established in boxing, and Jack London and Ivy Lee agreed with the pundits that theirs was the epoch of the Big Men, the heavyweights. Neither needed coaching on the definition of the term, and both were virtually obsessed by it, for they grew up in decades when the nation boasted towering skyscrapers, giant corporations, and massive industrial complexes—all comprising, as one historian put it, "a culture of size"—no less in business than in the public's appetite for its own outsized figures, from the lumberjack Paul Bunyan to the steel-driving John Henry. To claim Big Man status, London toned up with nationwide publicity until the word "famous" was a standard prefix of his name, for he consistently saw the world as populated by "big people and little people" and felt convinced that it was the "big people" alone who "live and think and know and act" and accomplish the world's "big things."[48]

The fight was set. The terms of the London-Lee matchup might have been voiced by Viscount Bryce, who wrote that public opinion "does not merely grow" but "is also made," meaning crafted and manufactured. To London and Lee, the point was as true as it was energizing. Crafting the ordinary person's thought, Bryce said, were the activists who "aspire to create and lead public opinion," who deliberately mold the "faint" and "shapeless" opinions of "ordinary . . . fluid" minds and "crystallize" them into "definiteness and strength." In America, the average man, the so-called "man in the [street]-cars," was told "what to think and why to think it." Ivy Lee reportedly understood this perfectly and prepared to pitch the corporations' messages in "the language of the man who rides the trolley car and goes to ball games, who chews gum and spits tobacco juice." Jack London called this figure "the common man" and expected him to show his clout in the new century. Speech and published writing, argued Bryce, would be the requisite weapons "in developing and moulding the judgment of the people." "Moulding"—the very term both London and Lee used in reference to the support that each must win to secure the American future.[49]

• • •

Odds makers might have anticipated a bout between two evenly matched contestants. Lee's advantage appeared to be his newspaper background, but London also knew the press trade. As a newsboy toting "a big load of newspapers . . . in a canvas bag with a wide shoulder strap," London had loafed a bit in the Oakland newsrooms and observed the doings of reporters and editors in the saloons. His first publication had appeared in 1893 in the *San Francisco Morning Call* when he won twenty-five dollars in a contest with his descriptive "Typhoon Off the Coast of Japan." A decade later, in 1904, the outbreak of the Russo-Japanese War prompted the Hearst newspapers to hire him as its war correspondent. Working as a full-time hireling of a newspaper mogul was not for London, who had seen his friend and fellow fiction writer Cloudesley Johns lose far too much of his own precious writing time while working as a beat reporter for papers in Los Angeles and San Francisco. London kept a close watch on his public image, however, and shaped it in quotes and quips for newspapers and magazines. The publication of his first short stories in the late 1890s prompted his subscription to the "Authors' Clipping Service," and he closely monitored publicity about himself in a wide range of US periodicals, from the hometown *Oakland Enquirer* to the *Seattle Post-Intelligencer*, the *South Bend (IN) Daily Times*, the *Minneapolis Tribune*, the *Salt Lake City Herald*, the *San Francisco Examiner*, the *Albany (NY) Press-Knickerbocker*, the *Boston Herald*, the *Springfield (MA) Republican*, and a host of others.[50]

Relishing the boxer's "wonderful play of muscle, joint, and nerve," London sprang forward to promote socialism whenever a lectern or a newspaper, magazine, or book contract afforded the opportunity. Socialist publications such as *Wilshire's Magazine* or the *Internationalist Socialist Review* called him "Comrade Jack London," but he made certain that journalists elsewhere saw the genial human face of his politics. He literally had cleaned up his act. Renouncing starched collars, he donned shirts and ties of high-quality crepe silk. An appealing "interval of wit and humor" was said to punctuate a London-led hotel dinner roundtable discussion of socialist issues. Reporters' euphemisms sometimes made his politics palatable (and doubtless shielded them from attack). London reportedly spoke in disarming terms on "the industrial and commercial struggle of corporations" or simply on "present-day thought" as expressed in his "breezy and clever comments." He was also portrayed as a devoted son who cared for his mother even as he took an "interest in economics and sociology." The well-known reviewer Mrs. Humphry Ward emphasized that he was no sloth, earning his own living from the age of sixteen. (One reporter wrote forgivingly that London, a "deep thinker," was nonetheless "a socialist—but what eminent writer has not had his own peculiar eccentricity.")[51]

The promotion and cross-promotion of upcoming stories, novels, and journalism, meanwhile, kept the brand-name author's face and name constantly before the public, as did feature stories on his comings and goings. Readers of the *New York Sun* found this quarter-page ad on December 28, 1903: "If you want to read a story that will tingle your nerves and make you smell salt water, read *The Sea Wolf*." Subscribers to *Scribner's* were likewise alerted that "Jack London's Great Novel *The Sea Wolf* begins in the January 1904 issue of the *Century*." Such taglines as "Great New Story," "His Greatest Novel," the "best story he ever wrote," and "A Great Author's Greatest Story" were as customary in periodicals as the oversize photographs, etchings, or charcoal portraits of the photogenic author.[52]

Assignments for Hearst and other newspapers likewise ginned up publicity. The January 1904 *Denver Daily News* headlined "Jack London, the great writer who has gone to the Orient to handle the Japan-Russia crisis," while the *New York Herald* of June 1910 announced, "Jack London Will Report Great Prize Fight for *Herald*." Various feature stories kept the publicity mills turning: "Jack London Catches Fish with Diamond," "Author London Reaches Town for Operation," "Woman Circles Globe to Win $5,000 Bet for Jack London," "Jack London Writes a Libretto. Novelist Tries Musical Comedy." The *New York Herald* dubbed him a "Literary Knight Errant."[53]

The summa of glowing portraits appeared in 1903, when a notable woman of letters, Fannie K. Hamilton, interviewed London in an "open-air sitting room" at his California family bungalow "high up in the Piedmont hills." She rhapsodized in print about the boyish "genius" and "literary giant" whose "face lights up [as] he becomes animated" on the topic of possibly founding and editing a socialist magazine at some future point in his career. The London she profiled was no revolutionary zealot ready to storm the mansions of the capitalist tycoons, but "boyish, noble, lovable . . . most approachable of men . . . with a warmth of hospitality which places the visitor on the immediate footing of a friend," yet who "radiates courage and intensity of purpose." Brilliant at his own public relations, London thoroughly understood that the bare-knuckles era had given way to a time of padded gloves of supple kid leather. He told his hardest truths with a fierce directness that was mediated, though never softened, by extraordinary personal charm.[54]

For the socialist cause, London knew he needed all the favorable press he could get. The fact was, the media was governed by a network of Ivy Lee's idols, the capitalist owners of newspapers and magazines. The newspaper chains—whether Hearst in San Francisco, Chicago, and New York, or Ochs, who was dominant in New York and Philadelphia, or the Belo syndicate in Texas—all either thrived or shriveled depending on the disposition of their advertisers, meaning other capitalist enterprises. One analyst referred flatly to newspapers molding public opinion and controlling it as "a giant force." Jack London, as a socialist, repeatedly drew the wrath of probusiness southern California press lord Harrison Gray Otis, whose *Los Angeles Times* lambasted him as an "enemy of peace" and sneered that "no man has made so much money as Mr. London through reviling society and sympathizing with the poor." "Ole Man Otis" reamed one of his reporters "most awfully" for writing favorably about London. "*Times* nasty, saying Jack is in . . . with the insurrectionists," Charmian noted in her diary of February 1911. Paging through Charmian's scrapbook of her husband's press clippings, the socialist writer Upton Sinclair, whose best-selling novel *The Jungle* (1906) had indicted the meatpacking industry for horrific brutality and abysmal health standards, found a raft of scurrilous newspaper attacks on London. They came from Chicago, upstate New York, the Middle Atlantic states, the Midwest. London was denounced variously as "a pestilential agitator," a traitor to the US Constitution, and a "literary anarchist" who found "joy" in political assassination. Charmian noticed that her husband's book sales slumped whenever the press attacked him for expressing his prosocialist views. Newspapers that previously celebrated the "brilliant young author," she found, suddenly condemned him as a pathological "neurasthenic" or smeared the "socialist sensation-monger who calls himself Jack London."[55]

From Ivy Lee's perspective, business was ill served by any newspaper publicity that lent legitimacy, and occasional approval, to socialist heresy. One dreadful example was London's glowing 1902 *San Francisco Examiner* account of a "millionaire-socialist" manufacturer who instituted an employee profit-sharing plan as a first step toward the socialist "inevitable public ownership" of capital. To Lee, a mainstream paper like Hearst's *Examiner* ought to know better. Its editor surely had dozed.[56]

Jack London was not the only figure hammering at starvation wages and human misery that he blamed on Big Business and its very biggest captains and kings. London's bruising punches now landed in rhythm with those of a cadre of investigative journalists known as muckrakers. While London pounded the great corporations and their socially pathologic leaders in speeches, essays, stories, and novels like *The Sea-Wolf*, a woman named Ida Tarbell pummeled Rockefeller's Standard Oil in the popular *McClure's Magazine*. The newspaperman Ray Stannard Baker had drawn public sympathy to a striker's family as victims of the dictatorial George Pullman, a big man who invented and manufactured the passenger rail cars that bore his name and gave unprecedented comfort to travelers nationwide—and who built a model town with parks and flower beds and spacious living quarters for workers who thanked him by walking out on strike when their wages were cut (even though, admittedly, Pullman insisted on full rental payment by the workers whose incomes had nearly collapsed). Still worse to Lee's way of thinking, a dangerous contradiction had gained legitimacy in public discussion of a brand of "Christian Socialism," two concepts that Lee believed ought never to be coupled.

To Lee, Big Business was overdue for new, favorable publicity, and when he got his break in 1906, his opening involved the very coal and rail executive whose outburst about the ruling Christian "men of property" had backfired in the anthracite strike of 1902. George F. Baer now saw the light, and Ivy Lee was put under contract as the Pennsylvania Railroad's director of communication. Against long-term and deeply ingrained business practice, Baer and his fellow executives signed an authorized statement, composed by Lee, vowing to shatter the wall of secrecy and silence that roused so much public suspicion against business. "The anthracite coal operators," the statement began, "realizing the general public interest in conditions in the mining regions, have arranged to supply the press with all possible information."[57]

This was the moment Ivy Lee had waited for, and he seized the opportunity to send all newspaper city editors a "Declaration of Principles" regarding the role of his colleagues in the flow of information to the media. The document had the ring of a term that corporations were to trumpet a century hence: "transparency." "This is not a secret press bureau," Lee proclaimed. "All our work is done in the open. We aim to supply news. This is not an advertising agency. . . . Our matter is accurate. Further details on any subject treated will be supplied promptly, and any editor will be assisted most cheerfully in verifying directly any statement of fact." Lee swore to give the "press and public of the United States prompt and accurate information concerning subjects which it is of value and interest to the public to know about."[58]

Lee was on the offensive, and in that same year, 1906, executives like Baer learned the value of their new and untried public relations man. No sooner had Ivy Lee signed his contract as the Pennsylvania Railroad's director of communication than an accident occurred on its line at Gap, Pennsylvania, a speck of a town with a copper mine and the historical distinction of a visit in colonial days by the state's namesake, William Penn. In keeping with the long-term tradition of secrecy, rail officials moved immediately to hush up the news of the accident. Lee, however, stepped in to invite reporters to travel to the scene at the railroad's expense. On site, he arranged for photographs and helpfully provided factual information to the newsmen. As one historian has observed, "Angry protests came from some of the road's highest executives, but when the commotion settled down, the Pennsylvania found itself basking in one of the few good presses it had enjoyed since the turn of the century."[59]

Lee, no less than Jack London, knew a secret that had eluded leading businessmen: that no one need fear the role of human emotion in swaying public opinion. On the contrary, properly guided emotion was an invaluable asset. The corporations had a "story" to tell, said Lee, one that rightly "produces an effect upon the people's imagination and emotions." In the years ahead Lee's client list was to include internationally famous banks and numerous corporations engaged in the production of coal, oil, iron, steel, and copper, together with railroads, textile mills, and meatpacking companies, and one notable father-and-son team, the senior and junior John D. Rockefeller. Lee's mission for this roster of clients was one and the same: to persuade the public that big business was not a murderous Goliath but a "benevolent Giant" with a generous "soul."[60]

Jack London could scoff at the notion of benevolent corporate souls, but he harbored no illusions about his adversary's strength or the timeline for this battle. By 1900, some twenty-six hundred newspapers were published in the United States, with a combined readership of over 24 million. Each was a forum for the gain or loss of public opinion. In addition, London knew that modern America was a world of "market-places" and that battles would be fought for "dollars and cents and for marts and exchanges." He was not naive about the schedule for major reform. It is likely that London knew of the legendary heavyweight John L. Sullivan–Jake Kilrain fight of 1889. It lasted seventy-five rounds. Let that be a benchmark. A knockout would be glorious, but more likely was a slugfest for years and decades to come.[61]

Jack London and Ivy Lee never met in person; they waged their battle in the court—on the canvas—of public opinion, just as other such fierce debates have been similarly conducted, including several at that time. For instance, Chicago's Philip D. Armour and Augustus Swift, the titans of industrial meat processing, defended their businesses through favorable newspaper accounts and advertising but never made the acquaintance of Upton Sinclair, the novelist whose best-selling *The Jungle* (1906) charged the packers with the contamination and adulteration of food products on America's tables. The founder of the American Federation of Labor, Samuel Gompers, never faced off directly against Henry Clay Frick, the coke baron who partnered with Andrew Carnegie to defy unionized labor in the 1892 Homestead steel strike. The rail car mogul, George Pullman, was not in the audience to reproach Jane Addams for portraying him in public as "a modern Lear" whose stubborn resistance to the economic plight of his employees triggered the infamous Pullman strike of 1894. The investigative journalist, Ida M. Tarbell never met the Standard Oil magnate John D. Rockefeller in a face-to-face encounter; instead she made her case against the petroleum monopolist in her *History of the Standard Oil Company* (1905), even as Rockefeller hired Ivy Lee to counter Tarbell's muckraking and burnish the Rockefeller name in public.[62]

The London v. Lee contest was fought, then, in the court of public opinion. In print, London's art was "sketched in blood," and it would go as many rounds as he had strength to throw a punch. For his part, Lee deliberately operated behind the scenes, where he could work the channels of the corporate-owned newspapers on behalf of his clients. Public relations expertise, he knew, must be exercised out of sight of the very public it fought to win. The corporations themselves must be front and center in the public eye, as if their benevolent goodwill were self-evident, not generated by the machinations of their communications counsel. Lee was not shadowboxing, but he fought hard from the shadows. Upton Sinclair gave the so-called "dean" of public relations the nickname that stuck in socialists' circles: "Poison Ivy." London reserved one choice word for these apologists: "parasites." With the benefit of national name recognition, London usually bypassed newspapers to reach the public in books and magazines. His readers thought they got stories about dogs and wolves and gold miners and ships and cannibals. What they really got was a mandate for a necessary revolution.[63]

In 1905–6, London took the fight directly to one group whose backing would be crucial in years to come: college students across the nation. In the fall of 1904, a Chicago-based agency, the Slayton Lyceum Lecture Bureau, approached the celebrated author of *The Call of the Wild* to propose an extensive speaking tour. "The college lecture course is very valuable to a literary man," wrote the Slayton agent, "and we are sure you would enjoy your trip"—adding, if further inducement were wanted, that he was sure "it will increase your royalties."[64]

Far from enjoyable, the tour took London to Kansas, Wisconsin, Illinois, and elsewhere through the Midwest in a grueling months-long series of one-nighters in autumn of 1905. As the leaves turned and the temperature plunged, he zigzagged through the region week after week, changed trains at ungodly hours, and coped with broken sleep, mainly for the opportunity to publicize the socialist "Cause" in dozens of remote college towns. The campus appearance that would attract the most attention, however, was not one on the Lyceum schedule but an invitation from the student socialist club at Yale.[65]

The Yale speech was a capstone of the college tour, but the performance that brought reporters and an audience of thousands to see and hear London had taken place a few days earlier in New York City, where, on January 19, 1906, he spoke at the midtown Grand Central Palace Exhibition Hall.

"THEY ALL WEAR RED TO HEAR JACK LONDON," headlined the next day's *New York Times*. The audience saw the redoubtable Mother Jones walk the length of the great hall to embrace Jack at the close of the speech. Passages from his speech were quoted in the paper, and Charmian surely clipped the story for one of her many scrapbooks, though London never mistook a triumphant speech for a victory. He was well aware that New York was the center of corporate power even as he and his new bride Charmian boarded the Twentieth Century Limited a few days later to begin "gliding homeward." They stopped in Chicago, where they met the renowned Jane Addams of Hull House and enjoyed dinner with her in its dining room. He and Charmian were given a tour of the stockyards and "slaughtering" plants, which Charmian termed "an unpleasant but instructive sight." Jack lectured on "the social revolution" to an overflow audience at the University of Chicago—the "intellectual stronghold of Standard Oil," as Charmian called it, and soon to be on Ivy Lee's client list for the lubrication of the public. On they went to St. Paul and to Grand Forks, North Dakota, where Jack again lectured and was honored at dinners. Back in Glen Ellen at last, the newlyweds seemed ready to settle in to their new life in the Sonoma hills of Northern California.[66]

But not for long. Within weeks, London commissioned a costly sailboat for a seven-year round-the-world voyage. His daily thousand-word quota could be penned on the deck in midocean, and if some scorned him for seeming rootless, his rebuttal was at hand. A new book by a young British literary critic, Arthur Compton-Rickett, spoke directly to Jack London in terms that were uncannily apt and had arrived at the most propitious moment. The bulk of the book was devoted to various major writers (Henry David Thoreau, Walt Whitman, Robert Louis Stevenson, and a few others), but *The Vagabond in Literature* (1906) framed its subject in terms that fit Jack London to a T. Years earlier London had identified "vagabondage" as central to his very nature, so he took up Compton-Rickett's book with interest. "There are some men born with a vagrant strain in the blood," its opening pages proclaimed, men with "an insatiable inquisitiveness about the world beyond their doors," men "with an ingrained distaste for the routine of ordinary life and the conventions of civilization." Particular vagabonds, went the opening salvo, are the world's "natural revolutionaries."[67]

"Natural revolutionaries"—how Jack London needed this benediction just as he was delivering his speech on revolution all over the United States and when the forces mounted against him proved unrelenting. London pasted one of his personal wolf bookplates on the inside cover of *The Vagabond in Literature*, packed it aboard his boat, the *Snark*, and kept it close at hand it on the next episode of his life journey.

3

War and Empire

THE WHOLE DARK BUTCHERY WITHOUT A SOUL

Come now, . . . from the United States, the white-skinned armed men with an inherited genius for government.
—Jack London, "The Trouble Makers of Mexico," 1914

At his Glen Ellen home, Jack London lighted an Imperiale cigarette, reached for his ink pencil, and began an important—and jolting—letter to the editor of *Cosmopolitan* magazine. It was February 18, 1906, and his opening sentence was as simple as it was stunning: "The keel is laid." The nautical term fractured the pastoral moment, for London seemed rooted in residence in the Sonoma hills of his 130-acre California Beauty Ranch. He'd lost no time getting back to writing since arriving back home from his lecture tour the previous fall and early winter in the Midwest and East Coast. Charmian blamed the rigorous tour for the "dark shadows lurking about his eyes," but Jack relied on the healing powers of his "Blessed Ranch," as he called his Glen Ellen farm acreage. He hummed to himself while filing letters and sorting his "mountain" of books, and he scanned the newspapers for possible story ideas, convinced that the daily papers represented "life" in its raw essentials. He and Charmian bought a "two-seated rig and a runabout" to bring guests to Glen Ellen from the railroad station, and he ordered fruit trees and dozens of varieties of table grapes for the ranch. When their dog, Brown Wolf, surprised them with a litter of puppies, Jack selected the best one for his daughters in Oakland. At work each morning, he often paused to read his latest manuscript pages aloud to Charmian before the ink was dry. She later typed them and tallied the word count. To all appearances, the Londons were at home at Glen Ellen for the foreseeable future.[1]

Jack's pronouncement—"the keel is laid"—shattered that notion. The "keel" in question was the wood spine of a beam that ran from the bow to the stern of the forty-five-foot sailboat that he'd had ordered from Anderson Ways, a San Francisco boatyard located at Hunter's Point, across the bay from Oakland. The boat under construction was custom-designed by Jack with two equally vital goals in mind, beauty and strength, qualities that he prized in every realm of life, including a favorite recreation, sailing. Just as he stabled handsome saddle horses and laced up boxing gloves for fitness, so Jack London always kept a sloop moored on the bay for solitude or a quick escape with friends. Year-round sailing the inland waters of the San Francisco Bay was his passion, as his friends and readers knew, and while he enjoyed the summer's gale-force "sea-breeze" off the Pacific, he reveled in the defiant wintry "howling northers." Whether the *Spray* or *Roamer*, his sailboats were unbeatable for "hard work and excitement," he said, because small boats tested a man's ability to take "wood and iron and rope and canvas and compel it to obey his will on the surface of the sea."[2]

The announcement of the new keel in the letter to the editor, however, signaled momentous change. It meant that Jack London was staking his claim to worldwide sailing adventures to begin next autumn. Ever restless, defying borders and boundaries, he planned to devote the next seven years of his life to a personal era of global exploration. With Charmian and a small crew he intended to sail the wide world and to encounter its lands and peoples first-hand on his terms and under his command. The boatyard listed his boat as "recreational," but to Jack London "the trip around the world" meant one thing: "personal achievement" and "big moments of living."[3]

Fearing for his safety, his friends voiced alarm even as they socialized with Jack in the city or at Glen Ellen. Some were puzzled. They thought their friend had surely learned nature's deadly lessons, for the adventure stories Jack mined from his savage 1897–98 gold rush winter in the Yukon were also a written record of disasters that befall human beings in hostile environs. Hapless characters drowned in icy currents in his Yukon fiction, just as individuals actually died in tropical salt seas. The oceans swallowed huge ships, never mind a forty-five-foot boat. Jack's close friend, the poet George Sterling, was deathly afraid ("O Jack, but it makes me sick to think of you going out on this ocean!"). Jack's former mentor, the librarian Frederick Bamford, was also concerned, as were the various artists and writers who took the train to Glen Ellen to enjoy the Londons' hospitality, including visits to nearby redwood groves and bathing in the "warm mineral tanks" of the local "valley resorts." Dinnertime, followed by evenings of music, card games, and conversation, let well-meaning friends express their doubts about his oceanic sailing plans, but their host's response was firm. Jack sought "the achievement of a difficult feat" that could be measured in the "successful adjustment to a sternly exacting environment." And "the more difficult the feat, the greater the satisfaction in its accomplishment." He put his case in literary, metaphorical terms: the "life that lives is life successful, and success is the breath of its nostrils."[4]

Adamant in the face of well-meant objections, Jack welcomed opportunities for social pleasures in this months-long interlude while his boat was being built. His days were also filled with hard work on fiction, on book reviews that he'd promised, and on careful planning for the trip. Photographs, for instance, would be de rigueur, and London decided on a second camera to supplement his "one good camera with a splendid Goertz lens" that was ideal for large-format photos. Music, too, could be a heartening feature of seaborne life, and he was thinking of a phonograph and a hundred or more recordings, mainly operas, for the long evenings when the wind died and the seas were calm.

At this time, war and empire were the furthest things from Jack London's thoughts. True, he'd grown up with a stepfather whose damaged lungs were directly traceable to Civil War soldiering, and in boyhood Jack "read of the Civil War," the only US war that school textbooks presented with an "aura of tragedy" instead of "the buoyancy and easy optimism so evident in descriptions of other American wars." Grade school pupils of Jack's era, what's more, were often assigned to read and memorize selections from the ubiquitous *McGuffey's* readers, and the essay on war might well have chilled the sixth-grade Jack, with its phrases on "mangled" bodies and "spattering brains." (Indeed, when Jack turned to a Civil War setting in 1910 for a short story, "War," he was unable to find a mainstream US magazine to publish it, the editors perhaps deciding that John W. DeForest's *Miss Ravenel's Conversion from Secession to Loyalty* [1867] and Stephen Crane's *Red Badge of Courage* [1895], though not schoolbooks, had given the public its fill of grisly moments in that lamentable episode in American history.)[5]

The upcoming round-the-world sailing voyage, however, had no apparent link to war or to the imperial ambitions of nations. It seemed unimportant, at the time, that Jack London's new boat was being built virtually in the shadow of the nearby Union Iron Works, the builders of the US Navy's battleships, including the *Olympia*, the flagship of Admiral George Dewey, who commanded the triumphant fleet in the imperial 1898 Spanish-American War. Besides, the public already had a taste of Jack London's views on war. His boyhood friend Frank Atherton recalled that Jack had "always spoken against wars," and in 1900, he'd argued in print that the carnage of modern warfare made war untenable and thus most probably extinct. "The Impossibility of War," his review-essay published in the *Overland Monthly*, endorsed the views of the

Polish economist Jean De Bloch, whose *The Future of War* (1899) argued that among the major powers, "war is no longer possible."[6]

London saw the wisdom of Bloch's observation that "whichever side advances, advances to its own destruction," based on the Boer War against the British in South Africa. Jack expanded on the point in a letter to his good friend Cloudesley Johns, emphasizing that modern war simply defied all logic. It was nothing short of mass suicide. Nowadays, he wrote, "men would not go up against each other to be exterminated."[7]

Yet Jack London's stance in 1900 had proven premature. In the winter of 1904, rivalry between imperial Russia and Japan for control of Manchuria and Korea prompted the czarist government to threaten armed conflict against Japan, confident of easy victory over the Asian foe. With hostilities imminent, the Hearst newspapers offered Jack a lucrative contract as its war correspondent covering this upcoming Russo-Japanese War.

An imperial war? What did Jack think about imperialism?—essentially, that the British Empire became "great" by "minding the business of the world" through "the force of arms, the force of trade, and the force of law," as he'd emphasized to Cloudesley in a letter in 1899. To Jack, England's exemplary imperial conduct was evident in its worldwide colonial showroom of military posts and nationlike protectorates. He had read *Imperial Democracy*, by the Stanford University president David Starr Jordan, and concluded that "it is the English brain and English muscle which hold the world together" and that the United States must stand with its former "Mother Country" in "obligations of blood, and thought, and language, and character," all of these distilled in one word—"Saxon"—that was synonymous with racial superiority.[8]

London had witnessed imperial pageantry firsthand when he stood in London's Trafalgar Square on August 9, 1902, amid a jubilant crowd celebrating the coronation of King Edward VII. By that time his view of empire, expressed in *The People of the Abyss* (1903), was decidedly mixed. In the city of London, this "uttermost heart of the empire," he beheld the "superb display of armed power," of "myriads" of uniformed men "whose sole function in life is blindly to obey, and blindly to kill and stamp out life." He photographed the royal coach and the imperial procession of "the pomp and certitude of power" as upheld by "these men of steel, these war lords and world harnessers." More recently, he'd read a sobering, skeptical essay by an English socialist, J. A. Hobson, who argued that imperialism was driven by overproductive capitalism that "needs foreign markets for goods and for investment."[9]

Hearst's offer of a three-month contract to cover a war between two non-Saxon adversaries prompted Jack to sign up. The battlefield never enticed him, but his marriage to Bess was faltering at the time, and a few months spent far away from California sounded like a good bet. Along with other war correspondents, notably the dashing Richard Harding Davis, he'd set off in mid-January 1904 aboard the SS *Siberia* to thrust himself into the midst of a war between two modern imperial powers, unaware that he was about to cover what historians later called the first great war of the twentieth century. Despite the Russians' confidence, the Japanese proved militarily superior and were victorious in several battles, most memorably the triumphant siege of Port Arthur. Though "84,000 Japanese were killed (and 143,000 wounded)," the war was a humiliating defeat for Russia in which "the Japanese established their status as a great power."[10]

Jack London's wartime dispatches, first sent from Japan, were initially jaunty accounts of "ludicrous" misadventures, such as his first ride on a bucking bronco of a saddle horse and his detention on suspicion that his snapshots of "coolies carrying cotton" were acts of espionage for the Russians. Later that winter in Korea, however, he reported on modern war's "hellish business," its modern "machines of destruction" and the wastefulness visible in the harbor choked with "the masts and funnels of sunken ships."[11]

Two such ships were the Russian *Petropaylovst* and Japanese *Hatsuse*, both battleships reportedly sunk in minutes at Port Arthur when their steel-plate sides "tore open" from a mere "bump against underwater explosive mines." In 1905, back in California, Jack learned the cost in dollars—"$10,000,000 of the fighting capital of Russia and Japan"—when he read an article on modern battleships in the colorful *Booklovers Magazine* and was intrigued by the statement that the modern battleship was "the frailest thing man has evolved."[12]

Wartime, however, seemed a thing of Jack's past in early 1906. In Glen Ellen, he routinely filed magazine clippings on armaments and the military as part of his effort to keep abreast of a full range of current events. Building his boat and preparing to sail around the world, he couldn't guess that twinned issues of war and empire were about to erupt once again and become a constant in his life and his writing. He had no inkling that his iron resolve to keep his face windward to the future soon would be undercut by a disaster that rolled the bellicose past into the contemporary moment and kept it there, both personally and politically. The early spring of 1906 proved to be a prelude to a near-term catastrophe that reshaped Jack London's thought and his urgent message to the world. At home in Glen Ellen, committed to his daily goal of a thousand-word output and with his "plans for . . . the building of his deep-sea boat," he busily charted his and Charmian's route around the globe, unaware that cataclysmic change was in the offing.[13]

His current plan called for the Londons to sail in October from San Francisco's Golden Gate across the Pacific to Hawaii, then into the South Seas, to Samoa, New Zealand, and Tasmania and on to Australia, New Guinea, Borneo, and Sumatra. The Philippines would be next, then northward to Japan, Korea, and China, followed by India, the Red Sea, and the Mediterranean. "We expect to spend from one to several months in every country in Europe," London proclaimed, adding, "We expect to do a lot of inland work," meaning they'd ship or lower the mast and cruise the Nile, the great rivers of Europe, and the canals of China. Jack's excitement was captured in a reporter's remark that "when Jack London talks of his purposed voyage, he is all boy, all enthusiasm." For her part, Charmian yearned for "the glamour of Romance," with its flight from boredom and "the commonplace." As his forefinger traced the atlas maps on their Glen Ellen table, London doubtless recalled the far-off harbors alive with the exotic watercraft that he'd seen in his younger days as a crewman in the Pacific. In due course his new boat would drop anchor amid the sampans and junks. Standing on deck at the rail, the Londons would spy shoreline beaches fringed with outrigger canoes.[14]

Other vessels, however, might well loom largest in the high seas and at the Londons' cosmopolitan ports of call. The oceans where London planned to sail were well-traveled roadways of the imperial nations' merchant ships and were patrolled by these nations' armed naval vessels. Jack needed only to reach into his files to retrieve his copy of a 1902 *Cosmopolitan* article, "The Naval Strength of Nations," to refresh his pictorial memory of the gargantuan modern battleships and cruisers that commanded the deepwater harbors and would silhouette the horizons of the Londons' journey. Perhaps they'd spot the German *Kaiser Barbarossa* or the British *Hannibal*, the Russian *Retsivan*, the French *Jeanne D'Arc*, or the United States' *Kentucky* or numerous others. In oceanic terms, the age of empire expressed itself in these behemoths bristling with big guns whose explosive "shriek," as London later was to write, killed by "the shock of the explosion" or by "flying splinters of iron." Indeed, in August 1895, the battleship *Olympia*, the battleship that became Admiral Dewey's US flagship in the Battle of Manila, had sailed from San Francisco to Honolulu—more or less the route of the *Snark* a dozen years later. Water left no trail, but water routes, the sea lanes, were charted like roads.[15]

At Glen Ellen in the early spring of 1906, Jack made plans to equip and provision the yet-unnamed boat and select one or two new crew members from the hundreds of competing applicants who deluged him with letters pleading for a berth once the voyage was publicized in magazines and newspapers nationwide. Offers to crew for Jack London poured in from schoolteachers, a photographer, typists, a dentist, a valet, an electrician, a surgeon, and numerous other "men and women of every imaginable trade, professions or inclination." Women offered to be "lady companions" for Mrs. London, and a Philadelphia chef offered his services free, while others offered to pay for the privilege of a seven-year-long global voyage with the renowned author.[16]

As amusing as some letters were, selecting the right crew was crucial, for London learned from hard experience that sailing was no lark. The most placid seas could suddenly swirl into "cyclones and tornadoes," while favorable breezes metamorphosed into "lightning flashes and cloud-bursts." Add to these the treacherous "rip-tides and tidal waves, undertows and waterspouts, great whirls and sucks and eddies," not to mention the "surfs that thunder on rock-ribbed coasts." For the sake of survival, London's boat must be built for maximal buoyancy and maneuverability, its seaworthiness matched by the maritime skills of the navigator, the helmsman, and anyone who manned the sails. Jack London modestly could say that he'd "followed the sea a bit," having sailed the tricky tidal waters of the San Francisco Bay since his early teens and having crewed as an able-bodied seaman on the *Sophia Sutherland* on the Pacific Ocean and Behring Sea in 1893. Charmian's youth, however, was devoted to mastering the piano keyboard and horsemanship, not sailing. And what about her uncle, Roscoe Eames, who pronounced himself a yachtsman?[17]

Uncle Roscoe, in fact, put this globe-girdling sailing adventure in play with his direct question "When do we start?" The pivotal moment when Jack London's dream became a plan of action could be traced back to casual banter among Jack, Charmian, and Uncle Roscoe as they all dried off in the hot Sonoma sun after a swim in the summer of 1905. They had recently read Captain Joshua Slocum's *Sailing Alone around the World* (1899), an account of Slocum's solo journey in a thirty-foot sloop. Slocum regaled readers with accounts of towering waves, slashing sleet, and days-long gales, but he also wooed them with descriptions of the restful trade winds and the notion that "to cruise the Pacific brings you close to nature . . . and the vastness of the sea." And Slocum was hosted by the widow of Robert Louis Stevenson. Imagine!—the possibility of evenings in the company of the widow of the writer whom Jack had hailed as "a storyteller" and "essayist" who was "without equal" and never once "turned out a foot of polished trash." Slocum's book spurred the Londons' and Uncle Roscoe's "inevitable talk about boats" and raised the tantalizing possibility of their own round-the-world journey "in a small boat, say forty feet long."[18]

Not so fast, Jack said at first. At Glen Ellen he "had a house to build on the ranch, also an orchard, a vineyard, and several hedges to plant," plus livestock. In principle he liked the idea but put the optimal launch ahead by four or five years.[19]

Charmian countered with her irresistible "Why wait?" Beauty Ranch needn't suffer neglect during their absence, she pointed out. Its upkeep and improvement could be supervised by the foreman, Mr. Werner Wigot. And her Aunt Ninetta, Roscoe's wife, could keep an eye on the mail and tend to Jack's stateside business. Jack could keep in touch by letter and wire, for the whole civilized world was linked by shipping and undersea cable. Besides, they weren't getting any younger, Charmian also emphasized. Jack would turn thirty on his next birthday, and she was going on thirty-five. Roscoe, who was approaching sixty years of age, chimed in: "When do we start?"[20]

They'd start next October, London and the boatyard now agreed, as did Roscoe, who was put in charge of overseeing the boat construction at Anderson Ways. Two young men won prized berths as crewmen, one of them an athletic Stanford student named Herbert Stolz who was admittedly Jack's "after-thought," since he realized that he "could not do [his] full share of sailorizing and at the same time do the writing and keep the pot boiling." The other successful applicant was a young Kansan, Martin Johnson, whose letter of application showed gumption and who promised that he could cook (and who was to distinguish himself as a prominent world adventurer in years to come). Martin's main task was to be meal preparation, "plain cooking" with a "minimum of grease" and no lard, since Jack and Charmian preferred olive oil. "You will merely have to pass the food to the cabin-boy," London explained, "a Japanese boy of your own age [who is] the soul of gentleness [yet] brave as a lion." Most of the voyage was planned for "hot weather," and London advised Martin to pack a small wardrobe of lightweight clothing.[21]

"All of us will be crew," London emphasized in a letter to his newly hired cook. "There is my wife, and myself. We will stand our watches and do our trick at the wheel." In "moments of danger," he cautioned, all hands must turn to. "I will not be a writer, but a sailor," he wrote. "The same with my wife. The cabin-boy will be a sailor, and so also, the cook. In fact, when it's a case of all hands, all hands it will be." He also promised his new crewman and cook ample "shore-liberty" and "lots of good times together. . . . Boxing, swimming, fishing, adventuring." Reading Jack London's letter of acceptance, Martin Johnson could hardly believe his luck.[22]

The *Wolf*—as Jack tentatively named his boat—was a ketch, which he chose as a compromise between a yawl and a schooner to promote the best sailing and cruising. It was to measure forty feet at the waterline, with maximum fifteen feet abeam and six feet of headroom below decks. Jack called it a "yacht," and it was, but the word was elastic in meaning. The public might think of William K. Vanderbilt's steam-driven, 285-foot *Alva*, or financier J. P. Morgan's steam yacht *Corsair*, which the US Navy bought and renamed the USS *Gloucester* for service in the Spanish-American War. The Londons' yacht, one-sixth the length of these floating palaces, would operate under sail but boast the most modern equipment. Plans specified an auxiliary gasoline "seventy-horsepower engine, a dynamo, storage batteries, . . . tanks of water to last long weeks at sea; space for fifteen hundred gallons of gasoline, fire extinguishers, and life-preservers." The boat would have water-tight compartments, and its "great store-room" would hold "food, spare sails, anchors, hawsers, tackles, and a thousand and one other things." "It is the strongest boat ever built in San Francisco," Jack boasted to the newly recruited Martin. "We could go through a typhoon that would wreck a 15,000-ton steamer."[23]

Comfort was not a luxury but a necessity for so lengthy a voyage, and Jack's design called for a combination living room, library and smoking room, a dining area, galley, modern bathroom, electrical lighting, and private sleeping quarters for the owners. For serving meals, his personal valet, Paul Tochigi, would be aboard as a sixth crew member. "To make our rough-weather days and nights more comfortable," said Jack, the "large and roomy cockpit" was to be "sunk beneath the deck." Other design features were meant to guard against the "colossal menaces," meaning the "seas that leap aboard the largest crafts that float, crushing humans to a pulp or licking them off into the sea and to death." "Titans of destruction," London pronounced them. His boat would thus have no treacherous "[wheel]house and no hold," Jack explained, for "the fact that there is no house to break the strength of the deck will make us feel safer in case great seas thunder their tons of water down on board." No expense was spared for top quality. The plans called for superior woods and fittings of the very best. The total cost was estimated at seven thousand dollars.[24]

As with most Jack London enterprises, financing must come from his writing, his self-styled "marketable goods." Thus his February letter to *Cosmopolitan* editor Bailey Millard promoted the project and sought a high-dollar contract to generate revenue from writing and from photographs. ("It is granted, always, that I deliver the goods," wrote London. "No writer of prominence, in the days of his prominence, has ever gone sailing around the world. . . . We expect lots of action, and my strong point as a writer is that I am a writer of action.") He reminded Millard of his "graphic, reportorial" skills, his efficiency and thoroughness in research, the uniqueness of the venture, and his track record as a photographer when he covered the Russo-Japanese War. Knowing he'd be paid by the word, London put his business question squarely to the *Cosmopolitan* editor: "How much space will *The Cosmopolitan* be able to give me?"[25]

As negotiations with *Cosmopolitan* and with other magazines proceeded that spring, he also dealt with his book editor, George Brett, at Macmillan, and by late March he looked ahead to the publication of two short story collections, *Moon-Face* and *Love of Life*. His novel *White Fang*, currently serialized in *Outing* magazine, was also scheduled for book publication, though it irritated Jack when reviewers called it a formulaic reversal of the storyline of *The Call of the Wild*, a point he firmly rejected. He was busy writing new fiction, as always, and reading too, including the German professor August Weismann's *Essays upon Heredity*, which postulated the transmission of traits passed on through millennia at the molecular level of the cell. The book gave London an idea for a rather long story of prehistoric humans, and he got to work on it. Everybody, it seemed, was interested in evolution, and a story that tapped the current zeitgeist was surely marketable, especially if based on the scientific principles set forth by the authoritative Weismann. Jack would call his story *Before Adam*. He also launched a dystopian political novel to be called *The Iron Heel*.

As spring advanced, life at Glen Ellen was pleasant. When the weather permitted, Charmian set the table outdoors for open-air dining while "butter and cream cooled in the ripples" of a nearby brook. At all times, but especially in advance of the sailing adventure, Jack London tried to be honest about human strengths and frailty. He despised suffocating self-protection as much as he shunned the delusion of false pride. "Here am I," he said in tones verging on self-mockery, "a little animal called a man—a bit of vitalized matter . . . fallible and frail, a bit of pulsating, jelly-like life—it is all I am." He named the forces that could snuff him out in an instant—a sharp blow, a snakebite, a fall or a fatal plunge into watery depths, "a splinter of lead from a rifle." Scorching heat was on the list, as was the lethal hypothermia that was soon to become the plot of a story he'd rewrite next year, thereby transforming a forgettable juvenile moralistic tale into an adult story of fatal hubris in subzero weather. Readers would know the latter version, the rewrite, by the title of the original, "To Build a Fire."[26]

Despite the perils, Jack proclaimed himself "a sailor" who could "thread" his "precarious way" through this "maze and chaos of the sea . . . vast and draughty Titans." He felt confident, "having spent years on the water and before the mast." "The bit of life that is I will exult over them," he boasted and added, "It is good to feel godlike and ride the tempest."[27]

Tempest?—the very word became an understatement in a traumatic predawn moment in April 1906, when, without warning, the world itself cracked apart. At home in Glen Ellen on the evening of Tuesday, April 17, Jack and Charmian were hosting the Norwegian landscapist Johannes Reimer and his wife. Offering advice on "trees and vines," Reimer also ordered "a hedge of Japanese hawthorne" for the Londons' ranch. Perhaps Jack mentioned that tomorrow at the boatyard at San Francisco's Hunter's Point, the five-ton iron weight was scheduled for installation on the keel of his boat. The guests and their hosts turned in for the night—Charmian and Jack in separate rooms, as usual, because of her insomnia and his restlessness. Fifty-two miles away in late-night San Francisco, meanwhile, liverymen and firemen noticed the draft horses' state of high agitation. "Restless tonight," remarked a stable boy. "Don't know why." The caged animals at the city's Chutes Animal Park also exhibited "queer behavior" that night, especially the elephant. It wasn't the first time that animal behavior signaled an imminent natural disaster.[28]

Charmian was to recall the very instant a few minutes before five Wednesday morning when her eyes "flew open inexplicably . . . when suddenly the earth began to heave, with a sickening onrush of motion for an eternity of seconds." The havoc began in San Francisco at exactly 5:12 A.M., April 18. From her bedroom window at Glen Ellen, Charmian saw the treetops thrashing "crazily," and when the "sharp undulations" stopped, she and Jack regrouped with the Reimers in the living room, each of the four recounting an individual experience of the catastrophic San Francisco earthquake of 1906.[29]

Within the hour the Londons were at the stable, where their own saddle horses "were still quivering and skittish." Riding to their ranch, they saw "the smoke of San Francisco's burning," a "lurid tower visible a hundred miles away." Miraculously, the trains were running, and by afternoon Jack and Charmian were en route to the city's earthquake epicenter, where they "started afoot up old Broadway, and all night roamed the city of hills." Jack took his camera to record the scene as light permitted. They looked for the last time, as Charmian later recalled, at "one or another familiar haunt, soon

11. The Call Building aflame in the 1906 San Francisco earthquake. A landmark high-rise structure housing business tenants, the building withstood the quake, though fire gutted the interior. (Henry E. Huntington Library, San Marino, California)

to be obliterated by the ravaging flames," and they heard "the muffled detonations of dynamite, as one proud commercial palace after another sank on its steel knees, in the desperate attempt of the city fathers to stay the wholesale conflagration." Indeed, the National Board of Fire Underwriters had recently warned that San Francisco was a veritable tinderbox with its flammable structures, its lack of water supply, and its inadequate firefighting services. To London, the scene literally defied description, and Charmian heard her husband vow, "I'll never write a word about it. What use trying? One could only string words together, and curse the futility of them."[30]

London balked at writing about it despite the flurry of "frantic telegrams" from *Collier's Weekly* that implored him for "twenty-five hundred words . . . descriptive of San Francisco." Twenty-five hundred words on unutterable death and devastation? He had no taste for it. He was no mercenary. Yet the new boat rising on its cradle at Hunter's Point was costly, and the new stone barn at the ranch must be rebuilt because the quake reduced it to rubble. Compounding the shock, the collapsed barn exposed corruption on Jack London's doorstep. The "solid" and "honest" barn that Jack had ordered, the barn whose plans called for stout "two-foot-thick stone walls" no matter what the cost, was actually hollow, two "mere shells of rock" filled in with "the flimsiest . . . debris." His contractor was cheating him. When Jack murmured, "Jerry-built," Charmian heard the "hurt in his voice," though he'd immediately "turned his back upon the swindle" to focus on the catastrophic big picture. Now *Collier's* offered twenty-five cents per word, and for reasons of utility London could not turn down the highest rate he was ever to command. He "jumped" into the article and wrote furiously to produce the "scribbled sheets" that Charmian "snatched . . . hot from his hand" and "swiftly typed" for dispatch "over the wires." London thought his effort was merely "the best stagger I can make at an impossible thing." He and Charmian were puzzled, however, by the daily barrage of telegrams from *Collier's* over the next week—"Why doesn't your story arrive?" "Must have your story immediately." "Holding presses at enormous expense." "Must have story for May Fifth number." Unknown to the Londons or the *Collier's* editors, the damage to the telegraph system blocked messages sent west to east, but Jack London had also sent a copy through the trusty US Postal system as an extra safeguard, and that copy met the deadline.[31]

The *Collier's Weekly* issue of May 5, 1906, offered America the traumatic earthquake and fire through the lens of Jack London's "The Story of an Eye-Witness." He gave readers a vicarious tour of San Francisco streets that were "humped into ridges and depressions, and piled with the debris of fallen walls." Through his eyes Americans saw steel rails that were twisted at right angles and water mains that had burst but were dry. His readers conjured visions of "factories and warehouses, the great stores and newspaper buildings, the hotels and palaces of the nabobs"—all "gone." London conveyed the feeling of the "dead calm" of a "doomed" and "deserted" city consumed in a "vast conflagration." And his readers heard the dynamite blasts by which the firefighters, in a futile attempt to create firebreaks, deliberately "crumbled" San Francisco's "proudest structures . . . into ruins."[32]

Collier's readers, however, were not privy to the deeper meanings that flared from the depths of Jack London's being. The shattered and burning San Francisco so eerily resembled a war zone that the sight of it drove London into a wartime mentality he surely thought was a thing of his past. The scene before him became a déjà vu of his work as a war correspondent in the early spring of 1904. The ravages of the Russo-Japanese War now came home to Kearney and Market Streets, to Union Square, to Nob and Russian Hills. Suddenly, the war zone of London's past became the reality of the present, for the panorama of a destroyed San Francisco reenacted the destruction he had witnessed in wartime East Asia on the Korean peninsula, where the Russo-Japanese War was largely fought.

It was probably inevitable that London's "The Story of an Eye-Witness" echoed his war dispatches for Hearst. Then, as now, he was an eyewitness to martial order, violence, and civilian chaos. On the Korean peninsula in 1904, London had reported on two clashing empires, Japan's and Russia's, and now the destruction of San Francisco struck him as the collapse of "a modern imperial city." In the aftermath of the quake, an incongruous "perfect order" and "courtesy" prevailed in the city, as it had in the Korean war zone, where London had observed that the Japanese soldiers kept "perfect order" as they prepared to march into battle from Seoul to Ping Yang and farther north.[33]

Other parallels were inescapable as the two catastrophic worlds merged in a shifting cross-fade of past and present, one scene a mirror of the other. London's glimpse of "two United States cavalrymen sitting their horses, calmly watching" the devastation of San Francisco, was a reprise of the moment when he pressed the shutter of his camera to photograph the proud implacable Russian Cossack astride his stallion in Seoul, Korea in 1904. He saw thousands of refugees evacuate San Francisco on foot, just as they had fled the wartime Korean villages. "Wrapped in blankets," the suddenly "homeless" San Franciscans "carried bundles of bedding and dear household treasures," just like the robed Korean family London had photographed crossing a field with "household goods on their backs." Once abandoned, the San Francisco neighborhoods were reminiscent of the Korean villages where "houses appeared blank and sightless, mutely protesting against the general devastation" of war. The flames consuming San Francisco, what's more, were reminders of the tactical arson of the Russian army that "set fire to the customs house and various villages and farm houses" in Manchuria. Just as two years earlier Jack London had found himself in a racial mix of Japanese, Koreans, Russians, and a few American war correspondents like himself, so now he "sat on the steps of a small residence on Nob Hill with "Japanese, Italians, Chinese, and Negroes."[34]

Embedded with the military in the Russo-Japanese War, London once again reported on "picket-lines of soldiers" who stirred the San Francisco civilians with their "menace of bayonets." "There was no water," he wrote. Therefore, "surrender was complete."[35]

A more personally moving spectacle drove London further into mindfulness of what he called "the chaos of war." In Korea, he had seen human beings reduced to "draught animal and packhorse": the Koreans in the service of the Japanese carried staggeringly heavy backpacks of weapons, ammunition, and foodstuffs, as did the Japanese foot soldiers. "Their shoulders were stooped forward," London wrote at the time, "their faces bent toward the ground, their backs burdened with rice and fish, soy and saki, and all the food supplies of an Oriental army." London had scorned the Korean "coolies" as a cowardly and weak race. Yet their suffering had troubled his conscience, for the Koreans, with their feet "lacerated" from marching, were forced relentlessly onward in "freezing mud" or forced to charge "across the paddy fields and up to the crest of mountains" while enduring "excruciating pain."[36]

Those dreadful scenes resounded here and now in the destroyed US city, for the lack of horses forced the San Francisco evacuees to become their own draft animals. Families harnessed themselves "to a carriage or delivery wagon," and every other San Franciscan, it seemed, was "dragging a trunk." "The hills of San Francisco are steep," said London, "and up these hills, mile after mile, were the trunks dragged." "Everywhere were trunks, and across them lying their exhausted owners, men and women." The soldiers' task "was to keep the trunk pullers moving." "Over these trunks," Jack saw, "many a strong man broke his heart that night." And death, of course, was everywhere. Back on the Russo-Japanese frontlines, he had written of "death-dealing missiles" and casualties numbering one thousand. Here in San Francisco, London wrote, "An enumeration of the dead will never be known."[37]

The earthquake and fire of 1906 made an indelible mark on Jack London. On one level, it triggered a black comedy of frustration and delay, as if the boat he designed to propel him thousands of watery leagues from the devastation was star-crossed the instant he named it *Snark* (for Lewis Carroll's nonsensical *Hunting of the Snark* [1874]). At the boatyard, crewman Martin Johnson helped watch over the project, and the young Kansan chronicled "the trouble . . . getting the *Snark* ready for her long sea-bath," including shortages of urgently needed carpenters in a city that was just "beginning to rise anew from wreck and ashes." Workers' wages "soared skyward," and shipments (including a freight car of oak ribs for the boat) disappeared for weeks at a time in a "terrible tangle" of mixed-up logistics. In capital letters Jack trumpeted a certain consolation: "THE PARTIALLY-BUILT BOAT IS SAFE." Martin noticed, however, that Roscoe Eames was "spending money freely," as "the *Snark*'s bills came pouring in faster than [Mr. London] could earn money to pay them." In May *Cosmopolitan* editor Bailey Millard requested a photograph of Jack "alongside the hull" for publicity purposes, forcing the author's surprising reply from Glen Ellen. "There ain't no hull," Jack confessed, but only an "iron keel, wooden keel, and stem and a few ribs." He had "not been near the boat," he admitted, and did "not expect to go until it

12. Photographed by Jack London when he covered the Russo-Japanese War in 1904, this Korean family carries all their possessions as they flee the fighting between Russia and Japan. The battles largely took place on the Korean peninsula. (Henry E. Huntington Library, San Marino, California)

is practically finished." His work schedule, he explained, was too jammed. "I am too busy. It would mean the loss of two entire days for me merely to go down and look."[38]

Despite his heavy workload, Jack and Charmian enjoyed the following summer as best they could. On horseback they treated themselves to a two-week holiday camping trip in Northern California that was rattled by after-shocks from the quake. At home they swam, fenced, flew kites, and enjoyed "moonlight romps and games." The novelty of "blowing soap bubbles" was popular at the moment, and Jack furnished the pipes from his Korean souvenirs. They enjoyed stocking up on trinkets for trade with natives in the South Seas, the beads and the "gay neckerchiefs and calicoes and ribbons."[39]

The October sailing date passed, however, as did November's and also December's as editors pressed Jack for the contracted-for magazine installments and friends wagered on the eventual sailing dates of the *Snark* while newspapers ridiculed the venture in satirical rhymes. Jack successfully petitioned the Victor Talking Machine Company for a free phonograph for the trip. ("Countless people of social and financial standing . . . will hear this

13. San Franciscans drag their salvaged household goods along city streets amid ruins of 1906 earthquake and fire, the scene reminiscent of a war zone in which civilians must fend for themselves. (San Francisco History Center, San Francisco Public Library)

phonograph on my yacht; and . . . you can readily comprehend the immense advertising the phonograph will receive.") By December, he and Charmian had relocated to Oakland, continuing their preparations as Jack worked at his fiction amid "all manner of oars, odd assortments of clothing, books, papers, charts, guns, cameras, and folding canoes, piled in great stacks upon the floor." "I have taken no exercise," he complained late in January. "I am seven pounds and a half over-weight . . . and am so disgusted with the delay that I can't summon the resolution to take any exercise."[40]

"Nothing went right," said Martin. "The *Snark*," he concluded, "seemed indeed born into trouble." In all, the boat cost London thirty thousand dollars and was to remain unfinished when at last he set sail on April 23, 1907, determined to have *Snark* completed by shipwrights in Honolulu. "Inconceivable and monstrous," London was to dub the whole enterprise, his term a seriocomic gloss that took its cue from Lewis Carroll's promised tone of

14. Jack London and the "skeleton" of his ketch, *Snark*, whose construction was delayed by disrupted supplies and labor shortages in the aftermath of the San Francisco earthquake. (Henry E. Huntington Library, San Marino, California)

"infinite humour" in his nonsense narrative of "the impossible voyage of an improbable crew to find an inconceivable creature." London's *Cruise of the* Snark (1911) was to become a narrative whose humor was based on a marine comedy of errors.[41]

The San Francisco earthquake and fire, however, made a deep, profound, and lasting impact on London once he had walked and photographed the devastated city and relived it in terms of the Russo-Japanese War. The earthquake and fire and their linkage to war were now too deep in his mind to be left ashore. Indeed, that trauma reshaped Jack London's consciousness despite his proud "habit of looking ahead" and his boast to Charmian that "retrospect" was for "old men and women." His motto was "The world is all before me now," but the world before him was ever afterward colored by the war that he'd relived when walking the rubble and dodging the conflagration of San Francisco.[42]

Creativity had its therapeutic uses for Jack. The horrors he saw as he angled his way through the city's flaming wreckage immediately put their stamp on the two novels he'd launched in Glen Ellen and Oakland before the quake. As the *Snark*'s sailing date was repeatedly delayed, Jack vacationed and joined in lighthearted frolics with Charmian and their friends. With his ink pencil, however, he turned to the new fiction as a psychological necessity, desperate to make sense of what he'd seen in the Russo-Japanese War and then relived in San Francisco—the violence and destruction, the suffering, the cruelty and indifference, the wanton aggression, the futile gestures, the intermixed kindness and compassion and fortitude and courage and death.

Fortunately, the two novels on his drawing board gave Jack the private space he needed, and he wisely set them in centuries distant from the fractured moment of these 1900s. Jack London's craftsmanship could mask the direct connection of his fiction to the personal anguish of April 1906 and its reprise of the Russo-Japanese War. A close reader, however, could see the burn marks of Jack's experience in both the futuristic *The Iron Heel* and the prehistoric *Before Adam*.

Just two days before *Collier's* published his twenty-five-hundred-word "Story of an Eye-Witness" on the San Francisco devastation, Jack alerted his book editor, George Brett, to the "new 40,000-word story" that was under way. He added, "I have decided to call it *Before Adam*."[43]

In terms of the market, Jack was confident of sales success for a story set in prebiblical—specifically, in "Mid-Pleistocene"—times, and his copy of the German Weisman's *Essays upon Heredity* gave him the scientific grounding that his story needed. In Weisman's pages Jack saw detailed diagrams and evolutionary examples from birds to fleas, all driving a major point about human development: that "the substance of the reproductive cells potentially contain the somatic substance with all its characteristic properties." In other words, traits embedded in cells that lived eons ago were brought into the world of today by the evolutionary processes of reproduction. Civilization might obscure those traits but could not efface them. This idea, which gained considerable currency in the late 1800s and early 1900s, was known as racial memory.[44]

Jack used the theory to play a double game in writing *Before Adam*. His readers could venture into the primeval jungles, swamps, and forests to imagine the lives of their Darwinian protohuman ancestors. The postquake Jack, meanwhile, explored and explained to his satisfaction the basis of peace—and of war. The characters he summoned to occupy this world—"half man, and half ape"—gave Jack his opportunity to ponder human minds and behaviors at their most basic. The interplay of his proto-human beings could shed light on the human traits that millennia of evolution had disgorged into the modern world. Jack needed a plausible fictional time-travel device, and he found it in a nighttime "falling-through-space dream." Nightly, his chosen narrator, a young college student, finds his prehistoric self and lives out his "racial memory" as a protagonist whose Pleistocene-era name is Big Tooth.[45]

The adventures that readers expected in trademark Jack London fiction were amply present in *Before Adam*. The young Big Tooth is acrobatically skilled at treetop "aerial paths and forest flights." He fends off wild pigs and a saber-toothed tiger, learns to hunt and to endure hunger and painful bloody injury, and shows resourcefulness as he invents, for instance, a "primitive catamaran." Other compatible characters round out the cast (Lop Ear, the Chatterer, Broken Tooth), and Jack London knew readers would warm to the budding romance between Big Tooth and girlfriend Swift One. Readers ally with Big Tooth and his people who are known as the Tree People or Folk. They develop language, learn to cooperate, form a communal government, discover ways to provide food and shelter for everyone, and find consolation in art. Their evolutionary journey is foundational for the best of civilization. Socialists at heart, they represent peace.[46]

Before Adam, however, is no idyll. The dread figure of Red Eye—"so called because of his inflamed eyes" that "advertise the terrible savagery of him"—threatens destruction at every point. Physically a "giant," he "was a monster in all ways." From beginning to end, the unregenerate Red Eye signifies boundless rage, hostility, rapacity, aggression, and greed. The chief of the fierce Fire People, Red Eye is bent solely on destruction and territorial conquest. Writ large, he is war and empire incarnate.[47]

Before Adam is a bipolar world of war and peace, but the odds favor the genocidal Fire People, for the Folk are repeatedly attacked and driven from their lands by Red Eye's marauders, who kill indiscriminately and compulsively. By the end of the story, the Folk are exhausted from incessant flight and shrunk to a small band of survivors. They take refuge in a swamp and forest, only to be invaded yet again. As Big Tooth recounts, "We lived through a day of terror . . . and all day hunting parties of the Fire People ranged the forest, killing us wherever they found us," in a "deliberately executed plan." The plan is a campaign of "slaughter, indiscriminate slaughter . . . sparing none, killing old and young, ridding the land of our presence." Big Tooth sees clearly that he is powerless to stop the Fire People from "increasing beyond the limits of their own territory" when they "had decided on making a conquest of ours." Here was the fundamental principle of imperial warfare, with

Red Eye as its avatar. Big Tooth speaks the bitter, tragic eulogy: "It was like the end of the world to us." Thus concludes the story, at which point Jack's time-traveling readers saw their best evolutionary future hang by a thread in the vestige of the Folk who live on at the mouth of a remote, inaccessible cave.[48]

Before Adam was a great commercial success. Appearing first in *Everybody's Magazine* in 1906, it was published the following year as a book in a lavish format with color plates and a profusion of drawings. Reviews were glowing, the *Cleveland Plain Dealer* praising Jack's literary "audacity," his "success" from an "artistic standpoint," and "no less a success from the standpoint of the reader who seeks to be entertained." Jack London's personal quest for the elemental truth about peace and war was also successful, though disturbing. Readers were implicitly asked to see what he had seen: that evolution favored the Fire People, that the contemporary landscape of the 1900s had its share of imperialistic Red Eye tyrants, and that the best of the human race, best by every standard of morality and ethics, is at all times vulnerable, its gains fragile, its jeopardy a constant throughout history into the present and the future too. Critics might praise the novel as a tour de force, but to London it was a warning issued as a literary aftershock of war.[49]

Jack was afloat on the *Snark* in the azure but treacherous waters of the South Seas in 1908 when the companion to *Before Adam* saw print, though *The Iron Heel* was also well under way before he set sail. Those who were enthusiastic about *Before Adam* could turn to its kindred volume, unaware that this book, too, was scorched by the author's trauma of war.

Readers of *The Iron Heel* entered an apocalyptic world to find an updated version of *Before Adam*. This time, Jack plucked his framing device from the distant future, a cache of documents supposedly unearthed nine centuries hence to reveal a tumultuous historical moment in the US 1910s (the very point at which the *Snark* was expected to return from its round-the-world journey). Jack's new Fire People are the authoritarian regime of the ruling corporate oligarchs, and his readers were invited to ponder the extremes to which, say, US Steel or Standard Oil might go to maintain their power, abetted by public relations experts like Ivy Lee who gulled the public into a blind faith in corporate beneficence. In the novel, the "strength" of the corporate oligarchy is signified in the decibels of the new brute force, the "roar of shell and shrapnel and in whine of machine guns." A modern Red Eye regime, the Iron Heel steadily crushes the Folk, who are industrial workers and the middle classes. The regime has targeted the hero-protagonist, Ernest Everhard, who bears a remarkable physical and intellectual resemblance to

Jack London. Everhard, as the story goes, awakens cadres of 1910s resisters, and they make valiant but doomed efforts to stop the juggernaut of the Iron Heel.[50]

"Power is certainly the keynote of this book," said one reviewer in the *Indianapolis News*. "It contains a mighty lesson and a most impressive warning." As an overt warning to the complacent middle class, *The Iron Heel* cautioned that imperial fascism, manifest in the trusts, not only imperils the working class but threatens to engulf and enslave every segment of American society. In the novel, the entire population is held in bondage to industrial-era masters whose rule is enforced by a fawning media, an obsequious clergy, the military, and the "Mercenaries." Jack London links *Before Adam* to *The Iron Heel* in his remarks that the "cool captains or industry and lords of society" are really the "snarling, growling savages in evening clothes" and that "we had not changed much from primitive man, despite the war automobiles that were sliding by."[51]

The concluding scenes of *The Iron Heel* bear the brunt of London's revulsion against imperial war, as Everhard, his lover, and their allies fight to the finish in Chicago. The city's history as a cauldron of labor strife sets the scene for the apocalyptic conclusion of the novel, and readers' memories are refreshed by references to widely publicized actual strikes and hints of the nationally notorious 1886 Chicago Haymarket Riot, when a bomb was thrown at a labor rally and policemen killed. London also saw an advantage in Upton Sinclair's bestselling *The Jungle* (1906), which lashed Chicago's meatpackers as an iron-heeled, monopolistic cabal, a point that Jack underscored with a fictional climax featuring Chicago as the "storm-centre" and "city of blood." Jack's readers were likely to recall that Chicago was leveled by a spectacular fire in 1871, and some probably recalled that a writer he admired, Frank Norris, called Chicago the seat of "Empire."[52]

Jack's final chapter, "Nightmare," reprises the San Francisco war zone in a panorama of Chicago reduced to smoking ruins. The city's calm before the storm is broken in a rerun of the destruction that was fresh in Jack London's mind from the Russo-Japanese War as replayed in San Francisco. The oligarch's mercenaries have blown up water mains, detonated bombs, and cratered the streets with "holes" as their blasts bring "a mass of wreckage and death." "Panic" seizes groups on the streets, and the "iron" girders of a building are exposed when the stone facing is "torn away." On the pavement lies a woman "in a pool of blood." Each day the destruction intensifies with the "rattle" of firearms as civil society collapses while the "people of the abyss"—those at the very bottom of the social order—become a vengeful "snarling and growling" mob with "nothing to lose but the misery and pain of living." The hero-protagonist, Everhard, escapes to fight another day, but the signature feature of Chicago, its vast stockyards, is left a "smouldering ruins." As a closing fillip, Jack lets Everhard and his lover (now spouse) flee to a "green country" and thereafter to New York to assess the damage and regroup, though he ended the novel with a sentence broken off midway and added a footnote referencing Everhard's "execution." The Iron Heel has triumphed, but its victory is the pyrrhic victory of rampant demolition. Whether critical or approving, readers found Jack's political convictions and apprehensions underscored in every line of the novel. Few, if any, recognized what his skill successfully concealed—that the futuristic *Iron Heel* was more than a dystopian novel, that it was also Jack London's personal war-zone journal.[53]

Both novels, *The Iron Heel* and *Before Adam*, show a fundamental fact about Jack London. In the aftermath of the Russo-Japanese War and the San Francisco earthquake and fire, he was ever afterward a war correspondent. He could not be otherwise. Officially, he was not to accept such an assignment until 1914, when he covered the US intervention in the Mexican Revolution. But as of 1906, London always was at the ready to tell the public—directly or subtly, flagrantly or in nuance—that war and its corollary, empire, were inglorious, wasteful, corruptive, and inhumane.

If Jack needed relief from war's trauma, the *Snark* voyage promised to be the perfect tonic—or distraction. "We have been out only three days, but there is so much to tell," enthused Charmian in her log entry of April 25, 1907. The London party was at last on course across the Pacific toward Hawaii, the gilt letters on the stern transom proclaiming

SNARK
San Francisco

"The water is purple, and such purple!" Charmian exclaimed. "Jack and I took a trip out to the end of the bowsprit this afternoon, and sat for a long time watching our little white ship cleave the amethyst flood."[54]

Jack bypassed Charmian's lyrical "amethyst flood" to speak, instead, of leakage. Indeed, damage control was evidently a main mission from the moment the *Snark* set sail in April to the unanticipated abandonment of the voyage in the South Pacific by December 1908, at which point everyone on board had fallen ill with malarial fevers and infections, Jack most of all, his body blistered with bacterial yaws (Solomon sores) and the skin of his swollen hands peeled so badly that he could not grip a rope line.

15. At sea in 1907-8, the *Snark* had neither a wheelhouse nor a hold. As London said, "The strength of the deck will make us feel safer in case great seas thunder their tons of water down on board." (Henry E. Huntington Library, San Marino, California)

Trouble stalked them from the beginning. No sooner had the *Snark* cleared the Golden Gate than the designated navigator, Roscoe, revealed his complete ignorance of navigation. To turn back? Out of the question. Jack fetched a sextant and a stash of manuals and began the self-study of celestial navigation. Filled with the "thrill and tickle of pride" each time he shot the sun with the sextant and calculated the *Snark*'s position by the stars, he also kept faith in his new skill. The test would be the volcanic peaks of the Hawaiian Islands appearing on the horizon after weeks afloat on the northern Pacific.[55]

Meanwhile, other urgent problems demanded attention. The *Snark*'s deck "leaked, and it leaked badly," as did the lifeboat. The salt brine swamped Roscoe's bunk and ruined the tools in the engine room, "to say nothing of the provisions it ruined in the galley." Jack chronicled the daily pumping required to "keep her afloat" because the hull also leaked. ("I have stood on the floor of the galley, trying to catch a cold bite," he lamented, "and been wet to the knees by the water churning around inside four hours after the pumping.")[56]

The troubles multiplied. The "magnificent" watertight compartments "that cost so much time and money—well, they weren't water-tight at all." Odors of gasoline meant the gas tanks also leaked, ruining more of the food, even as the wrought iron fittings "snapped like macaroni" and the custom-built engine died and proved unreliable despite Martin's tinkering and several mechanics' efforts to repair it in various ports of call throughout their journey. Worse yet, the *Snark* refused to answer the helm and "heave-to" in high wind and waves. Instead of riding "bow-on to wind and sea," it wallowed in the troughs of the waves, "the most dangerous position of all in which to lay a vessel" because the hull can turn turtle and sink the craft. The sea anchors proved useless and so, at first, did the young crewmen. In genteel terms Charmian called the cabin boy's illness "*mal de mer*," but Jack's terms hit hard when he admitted he'd "forgotten to calculate on seasick youth" as "the cook and cabin-boy lay like dead men in their bunks." [57]

More hardship was to strike in the months ahead, as if the US newspapers were prophetic when reporting that the *Snark* and all hands were lost at sea—this before the London party reached the Honolulu harbor on May 21, 1907. In her log Charmian bluntly wrote, "The sea is not a lovable monster. And monster it is." Roscoe evidently agreed, for he exited the *Snark* in Honolulu, returning unlamented to California, whereupon Jack hired the first of three captains whose temperaments, competence, and honesty varied widely. Jack, however, was the man in charge, the man welcoming a "sternly exacting environment" and never more exacting than in the fall of 1907, when the Londons and crew sailed—or, more accurately, drifted—from Hawaii south to the Marquesas. Becalmed, its engine disabled, the *Snark* idled in a sixty-day traverse along "one of the loneliest of the Pacific solitudes" with no other boat or ship in sight and the grim fact that "a disabled vessel could drift in this deserted expanse for a dozen generations, and there would be no rescue." Late in the following November, their fresh water ran dangerously low because the tap on the deck tanks had somehow been left open. As Martin reported, "Not a drop of water was left in any of the tanks, and only about ten gallons below." Jack immediately ordered the remaining gallons "put under lock and key" and restricted everyone to one quart daily. Charmian noted the "water-famine" in her log entry of November 25, and Martin recalled, "Our thirst raged. . . . We spoke of nothing but water. We dreamed of water. . . . Twelve hundred miles from land, and no water!" Said Jack, "I had never been so thirsty in my life." Finally, by the first of December they spread an awning to catch the "bucketfuls and tubfulls" of a "heavy, soaking tropical rain" and replenished the tanks. Still they drifted.[58]

Climaxing this endless "stark calm," however, was "something ominous and menacing up there to windward," the sudden gust of a squall that "rose up, covering half the heavens" in the nighttime on Jack's watch. "The *Snark*," as Jack reported in the immediacy of the present tense, "goes over and down until her lee-rail is buried and the whole Pacific Ocean is pouring in." Should he call Martin and Stolz topside to shorten sail? Tempted, he hesitates, admitting that it is "lonely there at the wheel, steering a little world through howling blackness." The responsibility for that world, however, is his alone. "After all," Jack admits, "it is my intellect, behind everything, procrastinating, measuring its knowledge of what the *Snark* can endure against the blows being struck at her, and waiting the call of all hands against the striking of still severer blows." Through months upon months of blows, however, through doldrums, squalls and gales, through the rotation of the captains and the tantrums of the engine and departure of Stolz, who returned to college, the *Snark* proved buoyant and somehow beloved in all weathers as a "dear old tub" and was affectionately dubbed by Jack "the old girl."[59]

The dual purposes of the voyage were never out of mind. Adventure was topmost, but so was the search for new material for Jack's fiction and journalism. His Klondike fiction sold steadily, but he now sought exotic South Seas local color. As the *Snark* sailed into Polynesia and Melanesia in 1907–8, Jack collected and shaped dramatic new materials for fiction and reportage, and soon US and British magazines began to publish such stories as "The House of Mapuhi," "Mauki," "The Chinago," "The Terrible Solomons," "Yah! Yah! Yah!," and "The Inevitable White Man." Readers accustomed to London's tales of the snow-blanketed "white silence" of the Yukon now entered the tropical South Pacific islands. They found archipelagos with their atolls, reefs, lagoons, and inland jungles, their "crashing sunrises of raw colours spread with lawless cunning," their "palm-tufted islets set in turquoise deeps," and their "flower-garlanded, golden-glowing men and maids." They found villages of grass houses, war canoes, and pigs, and they heard much of "long pigs," the last term meaning edible human flesh, for this was the world of "head-hunters and man-eaters, half-devil and all beast."[60]

The place-names in Jack's new stories surely sent US and British readers to their globes and atlases: Hikueru, Fiji, Tahiti, Fakarava, Huru-Huru, Viti Levu, Bora Bora, and the like, even as readers encountered "chiefs . . . who had literally eaten hundreds of their fellow men" and islanders "with a hearty appetite for human flesh and a fad for collecting human heads." The indigenous characters in London's fiction of the "primordial . . . North" wore moccasins of "red-tanned moosehide" and parkas of "squirrel-skin" and other furs, but those of the South Seas bore fantastic inflections of the Western world that encroached upon them. Readers of Jack's story "The Terrible Solo-

16. South Pacific islanders, photographed by Jack London. (Henry E. Huntington Library, San Marino, California)

mons," for instance, encountered a native helmsman whose nose "sported a ten-penny nail, stuck screwdriverwise through his nose," while "thrust through holes in his ears were a can-opener, the broken handle of a toothbrush, a clay pipe, the brass wheel of an alarm clock, and several Winchester rifle cartridges." London also gave readers samplings of the polyglot lingo of the South Seas, the serviceable *bêche-de-mer* or pidgin English that crossed cultures between English and various island dialects. ("This fella trader he one fella. You fella kanaka plenty too much. You fella kanaka just like m' dog—plenty fright along that fella trader.")[61]

Economics and human exertion spiraled like a double helix in these new stories, for the characters' quests for the riches of Yukon gold and timber now shifted to the South Seas hunts for the pearls, pearl shell, coconuts, ivory nuts, and especially copra, the dried coconut meat so invaluable for the extractable oil used as a foaming agent in the manufacture of soaps. (Lever Brothers was one customer.)

The plots of Jack's new stories often centered on conflict between white island traders, their brigand mates, and their rebellious black native boat crews ("niggers" in the dialogue and narrative), and on the contentious coconut plantation system, which was steeped in resentment, fear, anger, and brutality. In that arrangement, land must be cleared, roads and bridges built, groves of coconut palms planted, and harvests of nuts cracked open by hand to expose and release the white flesh, which was then sun-dried to become copra, which in turn must be packed and stowed for shipping.

Jack's fiction exploited the tensions rife in this system, for labor recruitment for the plantations was undergirded by a vile practice called "blackbirding." Two twenty-first-century editors of Jack London's South Sea stories explain that "blackbirding was carried out by small bands of generally ruthless rascals in small vessels, cruising the coastal shores throughout the South Pacific and seeking recruits. Over the decades, tens of thousands of Solomon Islanders were gathered, sometimes kidnapped, sometimes sold by their own kin, sometimes terrorized into 'volunteering' to work on the . . . copra plantations." Blackbirding, the editors add, "could be forceful, violent, and coercive. . . . However the recruits were obtained, blackbirders would sell their labor contracts to a plantation. The recruits would typically serve an indenture for a sum of six [British] pounds per year," roughly thirty US dollars. Not surprisingly, European absentee owners of plantations found it nearly impossible to hire competent managers because of "low pay, extreme isolation, and primitive living conditions," and therefore such employees were at times drunkards and cruel sadists with no incentive to treat the laborers decently.[62]

These extremes were ideal for Jack London's adventure fiction. His Klondike tales of desperados, naifs, outlaws, exotic natives, and dogs were now transposed to the South Pacific where danger and treachery abounded. Here were whites and blacks, bushmen and saltwater men, heathens and Christians, including missionaries—all with clashing agendas. The islands' natives were armed with poison-tipped spears and Snider rifles, and the Western traders countered them with superior Mauser rifles, "ammunition, dynamite," and "detonators." Death was meted out to the guilty and the innocent alike, often casually. In this world of lawlessness and degeneracy, Jack also introduced a hero whom he projected as the protagonist of a series of "Sun Tales." "David Grief will be the hero of all the tales," London explained in 1911 to the editor of the *Saturday Evening Post*. Grief's scene was to be "the real South Seas—the *sailor's* South Seas." A wealthy adventurer and entrepreneur, the blond and deeply tanned Grief is a paragon of athletic strength and ethical dealings. Jack's various other white male characters physically and morally rot in these tropics, but the robust and physically fit Grief is the benevolent patriarch, peace-maker, and bringer of justice, a true "son of the sun."[63]

"Funny way to make a living, isn't it, Mate-Woman?" Jack mused to Charmian in late December 1907, when the Londons were ashore in Papeete,

Tahiti. At that moment Charmian wondered at her husband's ability to "hang his writing elbow on any old table," to spread his "little note-pads," slant his "manuscript tablet," select an ink pencil and get down to work. How many men, she asked, could "carry their business around with them . . . living romance and creating romance at the same time."[64]

For Jack, romantic adventure fell far short of the whole story. The *Snark* voyage was pushing him smack against roiling geopolitics in the Pacific. In boyhood, he had seen the flags of distant nations flying from the masts along the Oakland waterfront and learned the word for that scene: "cosmopolitan." Now in the South Pacific and a veteran war correspondent, he understood that term to be a facile gloss over a deeper, more complex and troubling reality. Many of those flags signified political, corporate, and military power, and the word for that nexus was "imperialism."

Many readers, it was true, would relish Jack's South Seas stories solely for gripping exotic adventure. Others, however, would see that these tales were freighted with the author's sober discovery of the turbulent and destructive geopolitics of imperialism. Several years earlier Jack had equated that ism with Britain's rightful domination of the world and upheld America's allegiance to the British system. At that time, he had brashly backed the imperialist US Spanish-American War of 1898 as "the Yanko-Spanko War" that gave the United States possession of Puerto Rico, Guam, the Philippines, and a stake in Cuban territory. "As to the war," he wrote to his friend Ted Applegarth in 1898, "I was in favor of it." Back then, he saw the defeat of Spain as a "stroke against monarchy" and thus a forward step in the best long-term interests of "industrial and political democracy," that is, "Socialism." Now things were not so clear-cut. The Russo-Japanese War, the scenes of "imperial" San Francisco in ruins, and the Pacific venture all prompted rethinking—and rewriting.[65]

Looming over the imperial system, for one thing, was the continuous threat of war. Jack set one David Grief story, "The Feathers of the Sun," on the remote Polynesian island of Fitu-Iva, whose freedom depended mainly on the militarized imperial powers holding one another in check. Readers learn that "Japan, France, Great Britain, Germany, and the United States discovered its desirableness simultaneously" but "got in one another's way." "The war vessels of the five Powers cluttered Fitu-Iva's one small harbour," and "there were rumours of war and threats of war."[66]

War is averted, but the image of cruisers and battleships clogging the tiny harbor sets the tone of cheerful satire as Jack shows how one rogue Irish trader cozies up to the local king and corrupts the island as fully as any single imperial power could do. The island's economy is monetized, an army is raised to keep gun-barrel order, and paper money is issued with wildly fluctuant values. Native food and fiber crops become exports and disappear as commodity prices go sky-high, whereupon food (most now imported) becomes unaffordable, tariffs and duties are imposed, and the island is subjected to a legal system whose terms are opaque to all but the Irish rogue, the king, and the inner circle. The scheme collapses at the story's end, but Jack has compressed into one tale his critique of imperialism, a critique that he thrust into a veritable years-long archipelago of South Pacific fiction.

The first of the David Grief stories, "A Son of the Sun," offers a thread to tug to loosen the dark geopolitical skein of modern imperialism. The heroic Grief relies on a "crumpled official-looking paper," a document identified as "an admiralty warrant." The admiralty in question is British, a reference to Britain's claim to legal imperial dominion over the South Pacific. From the mid-1800s, as one early twentieth-century analyst reflected, "Great Britain . . . annexed or otherwise asserted sway over . . . numerous islands in the Pacific." Readers of Jack's previously published story "Mauki" may have noticed the corporate business that is protected by Britain's governmental and military claim. The title character, a "plum-black" son of a Melanesian chief and thus a prince, has been blackbirded into a cruel multiyear indenture on the copra plantations owned by the "ubiquitous Moongleam Soap Company." The Moongleam soap, presumably displayed halfway around the globe behind the sparkling plate glass of the modern department store, was a Western consumer's lunar luminescent delight. But Jack exposed the brutality of the faraway supply chain that enchained its workers and was legalized by British governmental authority and enforced by military power. In "punishment for murders" in Mauki's Solomons, for instance, Jack personally "encountered English war vessels burning and shelling villages." Empire, in these terms, meant a tight bonding of business, government, and the military. Other broad hints of Britain's imperial claims appear in the familiar but strangely anglicized place-names of ports and islands of the plantations. Readers who stumbled over the syllables of the indigenous names might be eased, yet disconcerted, by those that supplanted them in the imperial moment: Port Adams, Lord Howe Atoll, New Georgia, New Caledonia, New Britain.[67]

Britain, however, was not alone in claiming vast swaths of the South Seas, as Jack had learned from an essay on imperialism in a volume titled *The Heart of the Empire* (1902). It defined the term as "hunger for territory, whether in the temperate zones or the tropics, whether already occupied by settled governments or no." The essay named "England, France, Germany, Belgium, Italy, and the United States" as having "joined in the scramble" to control "over five million square miles of tropical territory," and it cued Jack about imperial rhetoric ("England 'expands,' but Russia 'encroaches'"). The imperial drive, the essay stated, is a cold fact of power: "The notion of territorial expansion of the dominant races is not a matter to which considerations of morality apply."[68]

The *Snark* voyage renewed these lessons, and Jack cycled them into stories that tagged characters or money or job categories with imperial inflections. The "German plantations on Samoa," the "German New Guinea," and the "German Solomons" were facts relayed into Jack's fiction. He also scattered phrases such as "French dollars" and "francs" in his story "The House of Mapuhi" and put American and German pearl buyers on a vessel named *Petite Jeanne* in "The Heathen." Charmian glibly referred to Tahiti's Papeete as the "Paris of the Pacific," but Jack wove the deeper meaning of the French presence into his fiction. Readers of "The Chinago" surely noticed the plantation of the "English Company" that "imported into Tahiti, at great expense, five hundred coolies" in the hope that the company's stockholders might at last reap dividends from the Chinese coolies' contract labor in the Tahitian cotton fields. No reader could miss the outrageous crime of the story: that the innocent coolie worker, Ah Cho, is wrongfully convicted of murder in a trial conducted in the French language, which is to him so much "explosive . . . gabble," and is then executed by a seasoned colonial French sergeant in collaboration with a brutal German overseer. Both men realize the French chief justice has erred in the case but nonetheless bow to the established French judicial authority, which the story bitterly satirizes by commenting on "the virtues and excellences of French law."[69]

Britain, Germany, France—the *Snark* sailed the colonial waters of three of the world's leading empires that bid to carve the planet into nationalist domains. Jack's grasp of, and distaste for, the system etched his stories in acid. When the heroic blond David Grief confronts a foe over a campfire meal in "The Devils of Fuatino," he hears this tribute: "We are both strong men. . . . We might have been fighting for empires a hundred years ago." Grief responds with his own view of history's irony. "As it is," he says, "we are scrapping over the enforcement of the colonial laws of those empires whose destinies we might possibly have determined a hundred years ago." Despite his enormous wealth and power, this heroic "son of the sun" sees himself as a pawn of decades-long imperial geopolitics. In effect, he is trapped in an era which the late twentieth-century historian Eric Hobsbawm termed *The Age of*

Empire (1986) but which a contemporary of Jack's, the British public intellectual J. A. Hobson, scrutinized and flayed in *Imperialism: A Study* (1902). Jack kept a magazine excerpt of Hobson's book in his files back in California. Whether he knew more of Hobson's work is uncertain, but his South Seas stories were fiction's validation of Hobson's point that the "occupation" of these territories was achieved by "a small minority of white men, officials, traders, and industrial organizers, exercising political and economic sway over great hordes of populations regarded as inferior and as incapable of exercising any considerable rights of self-government in politics or industry." In an argument that came alive in Jack's fiction, Hobson wrote that imperialism constitutes an "attack upon the liberties and the existence of weaker or lower races," that is, on indigenous groups who were bereft of the manufacturing and technological firepower of the West. Imperialism, added Hobson, is a regime that incites a counternationalism that "bristles with resentment" even as the system thwarts a broad-based internationalism by "fostering animosities among competing empires."[70]

Jack's South Seas stories throbbed with these conflicts. The nonwhite characters who are virtually enslaved, such as Ah Cho and Mauki, denounce the imperial occupiers variously as "French devils," "ferocious creatures," and agents of "hell." What's more, the lash of the overseer and crack of the blackbirder's rifle seemed to be at work at the level of the microorganism, for when the *Snark* reached the Marquesas, Jack eagerly sought the 1840s "garden" paradise of Herman Melville's classic *Typee*. A boyhood favorite from the Oakland public library, Melville's travel narrative had inspired Jack one day to visit the "wonderful" Solomon Islands. In dismay, he found that garden was now a foul "wilderness" in which "life has rotted away" from diseases introduced by the "white race." "One is almost driven to the conclusion," Jack conceded, "that the white race flourishes on impurity and corruption."[71]

Not that the imperial project guaranteed an everlasting future for what Jack's narrator calls the "inevitable white man, who, with Bible, bullet, or rum bottle, has confronted the amazed savage in his every stronghold." Mauki triumphs at last by literally skinning his tormentor alive, and the microbes that decimated the Marquesans equally ravage the whites. Jack himself suffered tropical afflictions so severe that he sought treatment in Australia and aborted the *Snark* voyage by December 1908, and he reflected on the "terrible Solomons," where "fever and dysentery are perpetually on the walk-about," where "loathsome skin diseases abound" and "the air is saturated with a poison that bites into every pore, cut, or abrasion" and proves fatal to "many strong men."[72]

The eighteen months on the *Snark* and various islands of the Pacific netted Jack a tropical cornucopia for fiction and nonfiction. Once treated for his tropical maladies in Australia, he sold the *Snark* at a loss and returned to Glen Ellen to restore his health and tap his storehouse of South Seas material for new work. Never again was he tempted to return to the South Pacific. Among his mementos was a trove of publishable photographs, including several of Charmian in the notorious Solomons with her Smith and Wesson .32 holstered at her hip. He and Charmian had traded calico and sticks of tobacco for calabashes, carvings, tapa cloth, and other "curios" of their adventure, and they planned to display them decoratively in the mansion they were soon to build among the redwoods on their Beauty Ranch property. The income for this and other projects was to come in part from Jack's South Seas stories, which appeared first in such magazines as the *Century*, *Hampton's*, *Harper's Monthly*, the *Saturday Evening Post*, the *Illustrated London News*, and *Sunset*. Later gathered in books that generated additional income, collections of the stories were published as *When God Laughs* (1911), *South Sea Tales* (1911), and *The Son of the Sun* (1912). The episodes of the sailing venture, first published in *Cosmopolitan*, appeared as *The Cruise of the* Snark (1911), and Jack mined his South Seas experience for two novels, *Adventure* (1911) and the posthumously published *Jerry of the Islands* (1917).

As he absorbed and wrote about the imperial geopolitics of the Pacific, Jack reached a US public that was somewhat conflicted about the unforeseen consequences of America's Spanish-American War of 1898. In the Philippines, the triumphant Battle of Manila Bay had raised false hopes of easy victory, but the subjugation of the Philippines required an invasion by the US Army, a guerrilla war that continued from 1898 into 1902, an occupation, and finally an annexation that did little to satisfy the newly subjugated Filipinos or appease ardent opponents of US imperial expansion and domination, including William James and Andrew Carnegie.

Jack, however, had yet another, quite different story of American imperialism to tell the American public, a story centered in the North Pacific islands of Hawaii'Nei. This volcanic island chain had its own deeper history of conquest and unification by a powerful Polynesian chief, Kamehameha, who ruled the island kingdom with a strict hand from 1795 until his death in 1819. Spanish adventurers may have visited the islands, but it was the arrival of the British captain James Cook in Oahu in 1778 that presaged imperial designs from the Western powers. Initially welcomed, Cook was murdered on the Hawaiian island of Maui the following year, though the Islands' sandalwood was regularly transported to China on ships owned by white men. By the close of the eighteenth century, cattle were a significant part of the Hawaiian economy, having been introduced by the British captain George Vancouver as a gift to the Hawaiian king. The Islands' rulers through the 1800s adopted the names of the great chief Kamehameha, and though Britain and the Unites States contended for favor and influence, their rivalry did not erupt into armed conflict.

All this is to say that Hawaii as Jack London encountered it was an archipelago unmarked by the bombardment of modern battleships or the invasion of nations' armies fighting to the death. The peaceable harbor at the mouth of the Pearl River in Honolulu bore no resemblance to the roiling waters of the Battle of Port Arthur in the Russo-Japanese War. The hills of Oahu showed no scars of a cannonade as had those of Korea in that war. From the spring of 1907, when London's *Snark* sailed into Pearl Harbor, to his 1915–16 return visits by ocean liner, Jack was in love with these apparently serene and peaceable islands that showed no ravage of wars.

His love, however, was not blind. In Hawaii, Jack found a "wonderful green land" whose verdure and hospitality could be seductive—until one saw, as he did, that these islands indeed had been invaded and conquered through the decades of the nineteenth century. The fought-for prize was not pearl or dried coconut, as in the South Pacific, but sugar and, more recently, pineapple. The conquest had largely played out in economic and political terms, and the consequences were profound. The Polynesian Hawaiian people had become refugees in their own land. Though no battlefields marked their defeat nor cemeteries their victimization, they were the dispossessed. Jack London came to see that Hawaii had been conquered as surely as if by guns and battalions of troops. As with the South Seas, he would speak his mind about Hawaii.[73]

Like "awakened Rip Van Winkles"—this was Jack's snapshot of all aboard the *Snark* at landfall in the US Territory of Hawaii on May 21, 1907. He had briefly visited Honolulu as a young sailor, but he now saw Hawaii with fresh eyes. The colors of the island of Oahu were ravishing, from the "azure" sea and sky to the "emerald" waves that "fell in a snowy smother upon a white coral beach." Beyond were "green plantations of sugar-cane" that "undulated gently upward" toward the "jagged volcanic crests, drenched with tropic showers and capped by stupendous masses of trade-wind clouds." "It was all so beautiful and strange," Jack concluded, "that we could not accept it as real." As they dropped anchor, he dubbed Pearl Harbor his "Dream Harbor" "It seemed to us," he said, "that we were dreaming."[74]

Jack's sweet dream continued when a delegation from the Hawaiian Yacht Club motored to the *Snark* in a white launch to welcome the celebrity author and Mrs. London with a resounding "Aloha" and take them ashore, while arrangements were made for Martin and the others to remain on board to begin scheduling repairs of the *Snark*. Weeks of constant rocking and buffeting at sea made Jack and Charmian comically wobbly reclaiming their land legs, but at last the shark-infested "restless, salty sea" yielded to the "rich, soft grass" of the languid Paradise of the Pacific.[75]

To Jack, Hawaii stood for hospitality, for he and Charmian were swept into a "house of coolness" with a broad veranda or lanai, their hostess "a beautiful Madonna, clad in flowing white and shod with sandals." This was Mrs. Albert Waterhouse—Gretchen—who greeted them, as Jack said, "as though she had known us always" and treated them to exotic foods, iced tea, and "a nectar called poi." The Hawaiian "dream" was so inclusive that wordsmith Jack repeated that term, "dream," eleven times in his first description of "Aloha Land."[76]

Entranced, Jack had no reason to be suspicious, no reason to be guarded—no reason to think he was about to be shanghaied. From the moment the *Snark* dropped anchor, however, Jack was targeted for capture. Under the guise of hospitality, he was a marked man. His captor, Lorrin Andrews Thurston (b. 1858), was tall and "heavy-set," with a "leonine head," "keen black eyes," and a body that was "quick to steal into action." For the moment, Thurston wisely stayed out of sight while Jack got his land legs after a harrowing month at sea. He was thus not aboard the yacht club motor launch that greeted the Londons, nor was he a party guest on Gretchen and Albert Waterhouse's lanai. Nor was he among the "throng of reporters" attempting to interview Jack at first landing at the harbor, although a number of the newsmen were his employees, for the forty-nine-year-old Lorrin Thurston was the publisher of Honolulu's leading morning newspaper, the *Pacific Commercial Advertiser*.[77]

As a premier newspaperman with numerous business interests, Thurston knew the power of print to generate favorable publicity. To him, it was providence that made Jack London a virtual castaway on the islands while his battered *Snark* underwent repair. To Thurston, London's mass-market appeal on the US mainland and worldwide was a potential mother lode of publicity for the Islands—that is, publicity on terms favorable to himself and his allies.

Soon enough, Jack would learn that Thurston's Hawaiian roots ran deep, that his paternal grandparents were among the first Christian missionaries to the Islands in 1820 when, as Thurston had written, the archipelago formed "little more than a breech-clouted nation of savages." A graduate of Columbia University's law school and longtime Honolulu attorney and political figure in the Islands, Thurston was a prominent annexationist. With like-minded friends and associates, he'd worked tirelessly to weaken, discredit, and abolish the monarchy and gain Hawaii its official status in 1898 as a Territory of the United States of America.[78]

The annexation project, however, had been long and turbulent for the Thurston faction, and perhaps Jack London had heard rumors or read something about it. Delegations to Washington, DC, were necessary during the Harrison, Cleveland, and McKinley administrations, together with political maneuvers in Honolulu, the rewriting of Hawaii's constitution, and muscular dealings with two monarchs of the archipelago, King David Kalakaua (1836–91) and his now-dethroned successor, his sister Queen Liliuokalani (b. 1838). In Kalakaua's case, an unfortunate catchphrase had lingered—Bayonet Constitution—referring to the 1887 moment when the king's power was reduced to ceremonial status. His majesty's acceptance of the new constitution was achieved under duress and with a certain public antipathy directed against Thurston's so-called "missionary party," a term often uttered in scorn.[79]

The Bayonet Constitution had its own regrettable sequel, for it augured the charge of treason against Queen Liliuokalani. When she failed to restore the powerful monarchy with yet another constitution and a militia of Honolulu Rifles, she was arrested, tried, convicted, and imprisoned for months in the Iolani Palace in Honolulu in 1895, during which she abdicated her throne. Released into house arrest, she was granted a full pardon in 1896, when her civil rights were restored.

Fortunately, from Thurston's vantage point, that time of turmoil was past. Annexation was achieved with fortifying pressure from units of the US military, though not without lingering rancor on the part of significant segments of the Island population, mainly loyalists of the dethroned queen who had peppered her published memoir, *Hawaii's Story by Hawaii's Queen* (1898), with denunciations of Thurston and his colleagues as a "missionary oligarchy" while eulogizing her own people as "strangers on their native soil." Admittedly, the decades-long decline of the Hawaiian population by diseases introduced by whites and others was lamentable. No Christian could feel otherwise. Smallpox and syphilis were particular culprits. But the problem of a declining native population was not new, as Thurston could attest. In the mid-1800s one observer remarked that "the Hawaiians, as a race, are physically and morally doomed to pass away," and another warned in 1875 that native Hawaiians were "*decreasing* at the rate of 1,200 to 2,000 a year." (One of

17. Lorrin Andrews Thurston, businessman, newspaper publisher, and a leader of the US annexation of the Hawaiian Islands, a movement in which Hawaii's governing Queen Liliuokalani was deposed to make way for the US Territory of Hawaii. (Henry E. Huntington Library, San Marino, California)

Hawaii's first native historians, David Malo, had conceded in 1837 that the "Great Countries" of the "whitemen" were certain to "eat" up Hawaii just as "large fishes" devour the small ones.) Somehow, in these opening years of the twentieth century the dethroned Liliuokalani signified the passing of the Hawaiian race. To some on the Islands, she was both a poignant figure and a reproach to modern Hawaiians like Thurston, whose pride and politics were anchored in what he termed the "prosperous, progressive American community, which is no less American because it is across the ocean and under a tropical sky."[80]

With this acrid residue of recent history lingering on, the arrival of Jack London in Hawaii was a godsend to Thurston and his friends. As their potential propagandist, the famous writer was worth his weight in gold. London, however, must be carefully cultivated and drawn toward the correct viewpoint. When he set pen to paper to write about Hawaii, it was crucial that he do so through the territorial lens of the Thurston alliance. The newspaper publisher knew better than to crowd in on the newcomer prematurely. Let him first settle himself and Mrs. London on Waikiki and get his bearings in this late spring of 1907. For the moment, Lorrin Thurston would bide his time.

Jack and Charmian's Hawaiian dreamscape thus continued. Within days they had settled into a temporary, beachfront, three-room canvas-sided cottage on Waikiki, which Charmian called "the seaside resort of the world." At night, with the "salt night-airs wafting through the mosquito canopies," she and Jack were lulled by the "steady boom and splash of the surf," and they slept "like babies." Each new day began with an ocean "dip," and Jack gave Charmian pointers on "diving through the mild breakers." They breakfasted on fresh papaya, and before starting the workday—his on fiction, Charmian's on a "diary" of their current life and times in Hawaii—they "lingered at table reading aloud snatches of books on Hawaii." Soon they found a bungalow for a few months' rental. For the next weeks and months they would revel in the sights of the Islands—the harbor at Honolulu; the outrigger canoes and kanaka fishermen; the Waikiki beachfront, where ladies and gentlemen strolled in finery against the silhouette of Diamond Head while surf riders coasted on the combing waves. They would marvel at the sight of horned cattle driven through the surf by native Hawaiian *paniolos* (cowboys) and delight at the women *pa-u* riders, with their flowing skirts and garlands of flowers. They would shop along the commercial King Street, where Charmian eyed fashions of the tropics.[81]

They also continued reading about the Islands, as Jack was to do after they

18. Against the background of the volcanic Diamond Head, Jack and Charmian London enjoy the beach at Waikiki on the Hawaiian island of Oahu. (Henry E. Huntington Library, San Marino, California)

returned to Glen Ellen. One older book, George Bates's *Sandwich Island Notes* (1854), sounded quaint, for its title referred to the patron of the English adventurer Captain James Cook, who named the islands in honor of the fourth Earl of Sandwich. This was just one of several volumes on Islands travel, history, and lore that Jack had stowed on the *Snark* and bought at Thrum's bookstore on Fort Street in Honolulu, where he also got his copy of Thomas G. Thrum's *Hawaiian Almanac and Annual*, a trove of statistics and useful miscellaneous information.

Jack's self-study of Hawaii was, as always, vocational, in direct service to his writing. He learned from William Ellis's *Polynesian Researches* (1842) that the Hawaiians' ancestors "wore skins of beasts for clothing, painted their bodies with various colours, and worshipped with inhuman rites their cruel gods," including the volcano goddess, Pele, whose "burning torrent" of lava was detailed in Bates's *Sandwich Island Notes* (1854) and H. H. Gowen's *The Paradise of the Pacific* (1892). The non-native visitor, or haole, knows, said Bates, that the Islands are "a land where battles have been fought, and human victims offered to imaginary gods," whose priests were known as kahunas. Piecing together the political and economic history of the Islands, Jack learned that Kamehameha the Great (ca. 1758–1819), aided by the British mariner John Young, defeated rival chiefs and unified the Islands—Oahu, Maui, Molokai, Lanai, Kahoolawe, and Hawaii—to create the Kingdom of Hawaii in 1810. A series of Hawaiian monarchs of the aristocratic *alii* class had ruled thereafter, each adopting the name Kamehameha, and the "first Constitution of the Hawaiian kingdom," a landmark document of 1840, was celebrated for promoting "the consolidation of . . . king, nobles, and representatives of the people." Meanwhile, missionaries from New England had arrived in 1820 and had largely succeeded in Christianizing Hawaii. In more modern times, according to *The Hawaiian Archipelago* (1875) by the intrepid Scots traveler Isabella Bird, the "natives" were "on the whole a quiet, courteous, orderly, harmless Christian community," neither "cannibals" nor "savages," but "all clothed." Ordinary Hawaiians, said Bird, could enjoy "a nice grass house, with very fine mats," and she was fascinated by the outrigger "canoes . . . hollowed out of the trunk of a single tree" and able to "shoot over the water with great rapidity," sometimes assisted by a "spritsail."[82]

Isabella Bird also described a marvelous ocean sport that Jack saw in action when he glanced seaward at the "'wave-sliding boards,' each one "a tough plank shaped like a coffin lid, about two feet broad, and from six to nine feet long." A few "daring riders," said Bird, "knelt and even stood on their surfboards, . . . always apparently on the verge of engulfment by the fierce breakers."[83]

In the Waikiki surf Jack saw this very sight, each upright surf rider "flying through the air, flying forward. . . . a brown Mercury" with "winged" heels. Jack crowned it the "royal sport for the natural kings of earth." He must try it. Luckily, he found the perfect coach in his new Island friend Alexander Hume Ford, a tireless promoter of all things Hawaiian. Ford taught him technique and timing, and Jack rode the surf through trial and error while lying prone on a bulky seventy-five-pound board, at times sledding smoothly on a foamy crest, but at others "tossed through the air like a chip and buried ignominiously under the downfalling breaker." In *The Cruise of the* Snark (1911), he was to devote an entire chapter to the physics of waves, to the glory of surf riding, to Ford's help initiating him into the sport—and to warning "an invalid or delicate person" that surf riding meant the assault of "smashing blows" of "driven water . . . like a sand blast." The account of severe sunburn that blistered what Charmian called his "supersensitive white skin" became Jack's coda. He promised himself nonetheless that before the *Snark* left Honolulu, he would ride a surfboard standing upright as a "sun-burned, skin-peeling Mercury."[84]

Swimming, surfing, reading, writing, after-hours rounds of hospitality and sightseeing—these were the rhythms Jack's dream Island until June, when he and Charmian accepted the surfing coach Ford's invitation to an automobile outing on Oahu with what Charmian called "the best of Hawaii's white citizenship." Sightseeing, Jack and Charmian saw the palisades, "the wonderful mountains and valleys." Their hosts were the marquee businessmen, financiers, and philanthropists of the Islands, men whose names meant banking, industrial agriculture, and the patronage of the Royal School, which educated the native princes and princesses of Hawaii in accordance with a curriculum approved by the white trustees. One member of the automobile excursion was Judge Sanford B. Dole, a former Territorial governor whose name, thanks to the career of his agriculturalist cousin James B. Dole, was synonymous with the pineapple industry. Another was the publisher of the *Pacific Commercial Advertiser*, Lorrin A. Thurston.[85]

Charmian's diary was soon awash with the name "Mr. Thurston." She identified him as the Londons' guide, host, traveling companion, and "good genius." He no longer held political office but was an influential politico as well as a newspaper mogul; a promoter of the Hawaiian sugar, pineapple, and rubber industries; and a developer of Island railroads and of the Honolulu electric streetcar system. As the Londons' self-appointed guide and host, the solicitous Thurston struck Charmian as a man whose "hair greyed in service to his islands," though she also saw "something imperious in his carriage and backward fling of head," a gesture, she decided, that "savours of courts and kings and halls of statesmanship."[86]

Thurston saw to it that Jack was enticed and Charmian charmed and that the couple enjoyed adventures, great and small, on the itinerary he planned. Charmian's diary, first published as *Our Hawaii* (1917) and recently as *Jack London in Aloha-Land*, traced their comings and goings. From an overlook on Oahu, "Mr. Thurston" declared the Londons "lucky" to hear the "strange, savage chanting" of an "old Hawaiian" who was unaware of the haoles who listened from above. While en route with the Londons from one island to another, it was "Mr. Thurston" who secured a "capital luncheon" and an "ideal" breakfast for the couple, including the "good coffee" that Jack loved. Otherwise, the Londons "nooned on a rubber plantation in which Mr. Thurston is financially interested," and by August it was "Mr. and Mrs. Thurston, and their family of one daughter and two sons, who have lifted us, bag and baggage . . . to the cooler site" of their "big house" in the mountains. "Mr. and Mrs Thurston have blossomed," wrote Charmian, "into the most cordial and witty of comrades, ready for anything." Thurston's fluency in the Hawaiian language was also impressive, and it seemed endearing that he'd nicknamed himself "Kakina" and "moved and gestured in the large sweeping way of Hawaiians."[87]

The Londons' sightseeing was thus both tactical and strategic on Thurston's part. His son, Robert, escorted Jack and Charmian to the celebrated Bishop Museum, a visit meant to inspire the couple with the "exhaustively" exhibited "Pacific Ocean" history exhibited in a sumptuous stone edifice that was ornamented with island koa wood "in all its glory." Charmian rhapsodized about the "treasures behind glass," including the feather cloak "that fell upon the god-like shoulders of the great Kamehameha." "All this royal regalia," she added, came from "Mrs. Pauahi Bishop."[88]

The honoree's name—the High Chiefess Bernice Pauahi Bishop (1831–84)—surely caught Jack's attention, since naming was his daily task as a writer of fiction. Known also as Princess Pauahi, Bernice Bishop was an heiress whose estate "totaled approximately eleven percent of Hawaii's land area." Upon her death, her husband, Charles Reed Bishop (1822–1915), a trustee of her estate, built the museum that bore his name as well as hers. A native New Yorker and astute businessman, Bishop had opened a bank under the name Bishop and Company, the forerunner of the First Hawaiian Bank. His profitable interests in currency and finance spanned the period of the monarchy to the modern Territory and included the 1848 Great Mahele, the moment of land division when Hawaiian lands, formerly held by the king, were now opened for outright purchase by others, whether kanakas or white haoles. Or acquired through marriage. His marriage to Princess Pauahi enriched Bishop immeasurably, as did similar marriages of Anglo men to Hawaiian landowning women of the aristocratic *alii* class. If the impact on land ownership by such marriages impressed Jack, he didn't mention it on this visit. The fact was that by 1890, "three out of four privately held acres were owned by white *haoles* or their corporations."[89]

From Oahu, Thurston and his wife took Jack and Charmian for an extended visit to just such acreage, a vast corporate Alexander & Baldwin cattle ranch on the island of Maui (in which Thurston held one-third financial interest). Managed by one of Thurston's good friends, the rugged and wiry Louis von Tempski, the ranch lay within sight of the volcanic peak of Haleakala, known as the House of the Sun. The grandeur of Maui thus surrounded Jack and Charmian. Hosted by Von, as Thurston called the ranch manager, they saw the hearty native Hawaiian paniolos, whose skill at roping made the Buffalo Bill showmen seem "tame." The Londons rode horseback up the slope of Haleakala, camped overnight in the pure crystalline air, descended into the crater of the extinct volcano, and, still on horseback, wended their way north for heart-stopping adventures in the wet "jungle" of gorges where "a mere excuse for a bridge" spanned "a roaring torrent."[90]

Thurston had still other plans for the Londons. Outside Honolulu, they had toured the Ewa sugar plantation thanks to Alexander Hume Ford, and on Maui they enjoyed "a private-car trip over the Hawaii Commercial and Kihei Sugar Companies' vast plantations." The main economic engine of Hawaii from the mid-1800s, as Jack knew from his background reading, was sugar. *Sandwich Island Notes* mentioned "several fine sugar plantations" in the mid-1850s, and a quarter century later Isabella Bird found Hawaiian "sugar" to be "the great interest," the major topic of conversation, and the basis of "a prospective Utopia." Like others, Bird noted that market volatility previously had made sugar growing a "disastrous speculation," since in certain years the price dropped and planters could "barely keep their heads above water." In 1876, however, a Reciprocity Treaty approved by the US Congress and signed into law gave the American navy the rights to a coaling and repair station at Pearl Harbor—and gave the Hawaiian sugar planters an unprecedented price advantage, for their sugar, and theirs alone, was now shipped to the United States duty-free. In reality, Hawaiian sugar had a monopoly in the US market.[91]

Raising sugar required more than trade agreements, and Thurston made certain that Jack understood the chronic problem of securing cane field workers. Native Hawaiians simply refused to do the work, and companies were obliged to import contract workers from China, Japan, the Azores, Puerto Rico, the Philippines, and elsewhere. The workers lived in camp housing the plantations provided for them, many with their families, and the companies worked closely with the representatives of their home governments to persuade the workers to perform their tasks "obediently" from a sense of "national pride." Thurston also insisted that Jack and Charmian tour the industry's Ditch Country, a major achievement of the white ruling business elite of the Territory. If Jack should question why "Americans constitute the ruling and the monied class" of Hawaii, as Isabella Bird had declared, a quick tutorial on the ingenious Ditch Country ought to settle that question. Charmian called the ditches on Maui "unpoetical" and "unimaginative," for the irrigation channels crisscrossing the green cane fields of the island's central plains looked dull to the untutored eye. Thurston might mention the Spreckels Ditch, the irrigation ditch of his former political adversary, the German-born Claus Spreckels, who made a fortune in California beet sugar before starting operations in Hawaii's cane lands in the early 1870s. And Jack might have recalled comments about Spreckelville in *Paradise of the Pacific*, which boasted of the cane field irrigation "from miles away by means of a forty-inch pipe."[92]

It is most likely, however, that to impress upon Jack the importance of the Ditch Country and its origins, Thurston hailed the heroics of his contemporary Henry Baldwin, a founder of Alexander and Baldwin, one of the Big Five companies comprising Hawaii's sugar industry. Jack saw the company's full-page advertisement on the *Hawaiian Almanac and Annual* of 1906 and probably noticed the annual Alexander and Baldwin wall calendar in "Von" von Tempski's ranch house office. Baldwin's story was sure to appeal to Jack London's admiration for courage and ingenuity, for it was a compelling personal account of the founding of the modern sugar industry and cast the Territory in a halo of light. Thurston could remember that as a young man, Henry Perrine Baldwin (1842–1911) risked his life and future to grow and mill sugarcane on a dry, windswept plain on Maui. The "shining landscape" of green cane that delighted Jack and Charmian traced its origin to the achievement of the risky, innovative engineering that Henry Baldwin envisioned and set in motion with his partner, Samuel T. Alexander, in 1870, six years before Jack's birth. The two former boyhood friends, both sons of missionaries, formed the Alexander and Baldwin Company, bought 559 acres, and started their Maui sugar plantation.[93]

Success required dependable irrigation; as the owner of the Glen Ellen Beauty Ranch, Jack understood this. To survive against drought, Baldwin and Alexander must somehow channel the plentiful rainwater that dashed down deep gorges on the windward slopes of the island's scenic mountains and splashed uselessly into the sea. "The partners conceived the idea of carrying this water through tunnel and ditch from the gorges of East Maui to the potentially fertile but dry lands of Central Maui." It was a major engineering challenge, seventeen miles through "dense forest, . . . large ravines and innumerable small valleys and gulches." In 1876, the partners secured a short two-year lease and, against great odds, secured financing.[94]

Henry Baldwin had a special challenge, for a gruesome accident at the plantation's sugar mill forced the amputation of his right arm just below the shoulder, though he quickly "plunged" back into work and reportedly spoke the following words when he reentered the mill for the first time after his accident: "You have handicapped me for life. Now I am going to make you support me." Support meant laying water pipe along the "greatest obstacle," "the deep gorge of Maliko," which required "the workmen to lower themselves over the cliffs by rope, hand over hand." They refused. An illustration on display at the Alexander & Baldwin Sugar Museum shows Baldwin performing the act of physical courage that Jack London always admired. Here was "Mr. Baldwin . . . sliding down the rope, using his legs and one arm, with which he alternately gripped and released the rope to take a fresh hold lower down. This was done before his injured arm had healed and with a straight fall of two hundred feet to the rocks below." Reportedly "shamed by this exhibition of courage on the part of their one armed manager," the workers "did not hesitate to follow him down the rope." Finished in the nick of time, the Hamakua Ditch began watering the Alexander and Baldwin fields on July 4, 1877, and became the model for numerous other ditches throughout the Islands. "Central Maui, which was once a bare waste, [was] now one of the most productive spots on the globe." In this light, the Ditch Country testified to the pioneering courage and ingenuity of men descended from the American missionary stock, men who made modern Hawaii possible.[95]

Thurston had yet another venture in mind for Jack, once again to gin up the chances of favorable publicity. The newspaper publisher intended to accompany Jack and Charmian to another island, Molokai, whose very name cast a dark shadow on the reputation of Hawaii, for its leper colony was a notorious blot and blight on the Paradise of the Pacific. Back in 1866, mindful of previous outbreaks of fatal smallpox and the ravages of venereal diseases that sailors introduced into the Islands, the government of Hawaii feared yet another decimation of the population, this time by a disease that progressively disfigured its victims by the loss of tissue and by damage to the skin, eyes, nerves, and limbs. To contain the spread of leprosy, which was thought to have arrived from China, Island officials began to quarantine lepers on Molokai. Seven years later, in 1873, Belgium's saintly Catholic priest Father Damien arrived to turn a squalid encampment of diseased evacuees into a village with housing, a church, and medical care. In that same year, 1873, the Norwegian physician Gerhard A. Hansen discovered the bacterial cause of leprosy (*Micobacterium leprae*), but treatment was not to be available for another half century, and the means of transmission were frightfully mysterious. Numerous family members might seem immune to the affliction that could strike one or more of the children, or a parent, a sibling, an aunt or uncle—or a fiancée, a lover, a neighbor, a coworker, or one's closest friend. The only solution remained the mandatory quarantine on Molokai, though in recent years the Territorial government had made great strides in its conduct toward residents of the settlement, providing a modern clinic and furnishing material comforts and support.

At the turn of the twentieth century, author G. Waldo Browne nonetheless proclaimed the leper colony to be the "skeleton" in Hawaii's closet. His chapter, titled "Grim Molokai," included the heart-wrenching tale of a leprous infant who wastes away and dies in its mother's arms as if anticipating its dreaded exile. To Browne's readers, the lepers were "banished victims" who met their "fate" in "melancholy."[96]

A fresh new view to be broadcast to the world in a magazine or book by Jack London was precisely the plan hatched by Thurston and enthusiastically endorsed by the president of the Board of Health of the Territory, Lucius E. Pinkham, who facilitated the visit in the belief, as Charmian put it, "that Jack will write a fair picture." Perhaps the stigma of Molokai could at last be erased. Despite his lifelong chronic seasickness, Thurston and his wife, Harriet, boarded the inter-island steamer, the *Noeau*, with the Londons in July 1907, bound for Molokai. Jack cocked an ear when an American marine engineer for the Inter-Island Steamship Company urged him to reject the "chamber-of-horrors rot" about the island and instead to "write us up straight" and "tell the world how we really are."[97]

In reality, Jack was able to boast of his "disgracefully good time along with eight hundred of the lepers who were likewise having a good time," for during a visit of five days he found the leper settlement on Molokai's Kalaupapa to be a cosmopolitan mix of Hawaiians, Chinese, Portuguese, and others who gathered for recreation and business in harmonious communities. He and Charmian jumped in to enjoy the holiday horse races and shooting contests sponsored by a rifle club, and Jack borrowed a rifle from a resident to try his own luck at target shooting, even as he and Charmian heartily shook hands with any number of the residents, all lepers. There were several churches in the settlement, a YMCA, and organized instrumental and vocal music, and Jack found that lepers kept order as policemen, operated retail shops and service businesses, raised livestock, and ran dairies. The settlement, he emphasized, "enjoys a far more delightful climate than . . . Honolulu" and has "magnificent" scenery. On one side is "the blue sea, on the other the wonderful wall of the *pali* [the cliff], receding here and there into beautiful mountain valleys." Everywhere, he added, "are grassy pastures over which roam hundreds of horses which are owned by the lepers," some of whom "have their own carts, rigs, and traps." In the harbor he saw "fishing boats and a steam launch, all of which are privately owned and operated by lepers.[98]

As for the so-called peremptory sentencing of hapless individuals to exile on Molokai, Jack took care to discredit the "*yellow*" journalism that fed on rotten lies and to describe the careful, professional modern screening of patients by physicians' boards and to note that he had verified all facts with the president of the Board of Health, with several on-site physicians, and with Superintendent J. D. McVeigh. Writing his account, Jack proclaimed that he would prefer to dwell in the settlement on Molokai than amid the desperate "people of the abyss" in the East End of London. He closed his articlc on Molokai with a call for philanthropic donations for research into treatment to dispatch leprosy "swiftly from the earth."[99]

London's "The Lepers of Molokai" appeared in the *Woman's Home Companion* in January 1908, and three years later was reprinted as a chapter in *The Cruise of the* Snark. Lorrin Thurston could not have been more pleased. As Charmian wrote, "Mr. Lorrin A. Thurston avers it is the best and fairest that has ever been written." Indeed, Thurston was convinced that *his* Jack London was poised to produce essays and popular fiction that were certain to redound to the great credit of the Territory. He and Mrs. Thurston and their family had extended their hospitality to the maximum to ensure the very outcome that was heralded in the glowing account of the leper settlement.[100]

There was yet more. The guests at brunch one Sunday morning in August saw Jack London in raptures as he heard Thurston and Sanford Dole reminisce about their youthful raucous old days of the monarchy. It was a brilliant stroke to have Jack and Mrs. London at the "New England breakfast at the Diamond Head seaside residence of Judge and Mrs. Dole." Over tropical fruit, eggs, and bacon, Jack London got a mental action shot of the young Dole and Lorrin Thurston "holding the Palace doors against an infuriated mob during an uprising." It raised Jack's heart rate. "Can't you just see them?" he cried afterward to Charmian. "Can't you see the two of them—the glorious youth of them risking its hot blood to do what had to be done!" Thurston could take satisfaction in his shepherding of Jack London. Whatever scurrilous rumors Jack might hear about Territorial affairs, he surely would consult the right people to set the record straight. The famous author was obviously in love with Hawaii and would celebrate it in publications for years to come.[101]

How could it be otherwise? Jack London's convictions surely meshed with Thurston's, or so the newspaper publisher and his allies evidently thought. They made certain that Jack was given a copy of *The Making of Hawaii: A Study in Social Evolution*, by William Fremont Blackman, a Yale University professor who argued that the last two Hawaiian monarchs, David Kalakaua and Liliuokalani, had dragged the Islands backward into barbarism and reactionary politics. Hawaii, asserted the professor, is the "'child' of America" and of "its free constitutional ideas and government," and he commended the enlightened work of the "Honourable S. B. Dole and L. A. Thurston" in his acknowledgments.[102]

What the Thurston group failed to consider was Jack's individual outlook. Jack London saw things through his own lens, not Thurston's and not Charmian's. She delighted, for instance, in the "high green cane . . . rustling and waving like corn of our Middle West," and she mentioned "the labor element" in the pretty villages peopled by "imported human breeds." Jack, however, saw the actual workers in those sun-baked fields, among them women and children who were far from what Charmian dubbed "picturesque" or what Thurston viewed in terms of a labor supply. Jack saw the workers on the Islands plantations at close range, men and women and children who toiled in the brutal sun, their stifling head-to-foot clothing necessary for "protection against the tropical sun and against the field dust that entered the nostrils, lungs, eyes, ears, and hair." Swathed in heavy denim and cotton wraps, they sought protection from the sharp serrated sawblade edges of the cane leaves and from the stinging fat centipedes or hidden hives of bees in the thickets. In the fields Jack probably caught sight of "the tiny figures of young mothers with their babies tied to their backs, a denim bag over one shoulder, another large bag filled with . . . diapers over the other shoulder, and a hoe in one hand." These mothers "practically had to drag themselves across the fields" for the income of "seventy-five cents for a ten-hour day." On the Ewa plantation tour hosted by Alexander Hume Ford, he saw the "arduous manual labor of cutting [cane] by machete and loading it by hand" onto wagons and rail cars. Jack, in short, saw the people. To him, it was personal. If his geniality was mistaken for agreement by others, that was not his problem. His political views were widely known, and he refused to sugarcoat the Hawaii of the sugarcane.[103]

To be sure, certain accents in Jack's Hawaiian fiction were charming curios, from the ukulele and the hula dance to the *luna* or field boss. Landmarks in his stories included the "statue of Kamehameha I in front of the Judiciary Building" in Honolulu and the "Bishop Museum." Readers of "Shin-Bones" got Jack's virtual museum tour, from the colorful feathered royal symbols, the *kahilis* of the royal *alii*, to the "Taboo poi bowls and finger bowls, left-handed adzes of the canoe gods, lava-cup lamps, stone mortars

19. Multinational and multiethnic sugarcane field workers in Hawaii. Natives of Japan, China, the Azores, the Philippines, and other lands, these contract workers labored year-round for ten to twelve hours daily in torrid heat. (Henry E. Huntington Library, San Marino, California)

and pestles and poi-pounders." Fiction, in addition, let Jack salute the skillful Hawaiian "cow-boys" and his friend and host, "Von Tempsky" [*sic*] of the "Haleakala Ranch" on Maui, and gesture toward Hawaii's history, such as the 1881 round-the-world voyage of King Kalakaua. His stories also tapped the "imaginative" folklore of the Islands as compiled in the 1910s by the Rev. W. D. Westervelt. Jack's "The Water-Baby," which was published posthumously, relied openly on the exploits of Maui, the god whose name is memorialized in the Hawaiian island chain.[104]

Jack's fiction, however, dug deeper to plumb the gnarled politics, economics, and social arrangements of the Paradise of the Pacific. In brief, Jack found a double Hawaii, one that was indeed a paradise, a "dream" world of beauty, hospitality, and nature's abundance to be joyously celebrated. Tempers erupted in Honolulu, however, when he violated a taboo to expose the other Hawaii. When Jack's "Koolau the Leper" appeared in the *Pacific Monthly* in December 1909, readers found vivid descriptions of men and women who were "hideously maimed and distorted" by the disease. No adjective was spared in this fictional revival of the old stereotype of leprosy. From facial disfigurement to the deformity of "rotted" limbs, Jack's literary powers were a full cannonade—and he felt the volcanic blast of Thurston's *Honolulu Advertiser* all the way to Glen Ellen. In a newspaper column signed Bystander, Thurston attacked Jack as a "sneak of the first order, a thoroughly untrustworthy man, and an ungrateful and untruthful bounder." Jack London, charged Bystander, had been treated as a royal "lion" but bit the generous Hawaiian hands that fed and feted him. The betrayal that blindsided Thurston and his associates was surely aggravated as Jack reintroduced the topic of leprosy twice again to explore certain human relationships. "The Sheriff of Kona" (1909) focused on masculine bonding, while "Goodby, Jack" (1909) touched on cross-racial romance.[105]

"Koolau the Leper" was the story of Hawaii stolen from the Hawaiians. Thurston and his cohorts seethed at a betrayal of their interests, believing the benefit to the Islands—*their* Islands—was business and tourism. Somehow they failed to foresee Jack's explosive charge that their power and privilege rested on a criminal history of subterfuge, hypocrisy, and greed. Their revered, pious missionary forebears, Jack charged in "Koolau," had committed grand theft of the Paradise of the Pacific while they themselves continued that larcenous tradition in the present. It was as though Jack London sided with the ex-queen Liliuokalani.

"Koolau," in short, used leprosy to alert readers to sociopolitical realities underlying modern Hawaii. Jack developed his story from an actual historical event that furnished his plot. According to historian Gavin Daws, the leper Koolau, a "native of Kauai," refused resettlement on Molokai and "fled with his family and a small group of diseased Hawaiians into the almost inaccessible valley of Kalalau, and for months stood off the law with his rifle." As Daws recounts, "He killed several deputies and outlasted the sheriffs' posses, and he died a free man, but still a leper." Thus the bare bones plot of Jack's story, which opens with Koolau rallying his people with a roster of the injustices they have endured for generations. From oral folk tradition, Koolau recounts the onset of the era of traders and missionaries in a long-ago time before whites' diseases diminished their numbers, a time when native Hawaiians were "many and strong." Back then, says Koolau, "they," the outsiders, "came like lambs, speaking softly." One group asked "gracious permission to trade with us," the other "to preach to us the word of God." That, he says, "was the beginning." But as time passed, "they that preached the word of God and they that preached the word of Rum have . . . become great chiefs" who "live like kings in houses of many rooms with multitudes of servants." They "who had nothing have everything." Today, Koolau says, "all the islands are theirs, all the land, all the cattle—everything is theirs." As for the native Hawaiians, if "any Kanaka be hungry, they sneer and say, " 'Well, why don't you work? There are the plantations.' " This last word, "plantations," was freighted for any American reader, for its reference to fields of sugarcane or pineapple harked back to the US Civil War, with its basis in human bondage.[106]

Once upon a time in history, however, all of Hawaii was generous to its native Kanakas and to those allied with them in spirit. Old Hawaii, Jack's story showed, was the authentic Paradise of the Pacific, an Eden that was found presently in such spots as the remote Kalalau Valley, where Koolau leads his people to make a stand against their armed pursuers. A "sea of vegetation" greets them, "green billows . . . dripping from the cliff-lips in great vine masses, and flinging a spray of ferns and air-plants," and all so lush that clearings must be cut to make way for the flourishing wild "bananas, oranges, and mangoes" and the easy cultivation of "*taro* patches and melons." "In every open space where sunshine penetrated were *papaia* trees burdened with this golden fruit."[107]

This, then, is the authentic paradise, a space where Koolau's afflicted band of refugees share calabashes of a "fierce distillation of the ti-plant" and, transported in spirit (and by spirits), briefly reenter the glorious life they have lost to the disease, but in a larger sense to the marauding traders and missionaries who are driving them to extinction. Jack gives readers the moving picture of "a woman [who is] apulse with life as she plucked the strings of an *ukulele* and lifted her voice in a barbaric love-call." A man, "timing his rhythm to the woman's song," dances in response, for "love danced in all his movements." This, the story asserts, is "an earthly paradise" that "alien powers" have corrupted and usurped.[108]

Koolau asks, "Who are these white men?" Jack answered that question in another story of Hawaii, "The House of Pride," whose protagonist, Percival Ford, is a bloodless, self-righteous, repressed, thirty-five-year-old white prude of a banker and sugar baron who owns plantations and a railroad but is temperamentally cold and spiteful. Pedigreed as the son of a religiously "zealous" woman and a politically preeminent, deceased missionary, Percival is heir to the fortune that was realized when his father "stepped in between the trading crowd and its prey and [took] possession of fat, vast holdings." This man of "enormous wealth" is a modern philanthropist who supports "schools and hospitals and churches" and is "one of the big men" of the Islands. Representing the powerful missionary elite, he is the antithesis of charity. "You are pure New England stock," a physician remarks to him, adding, "Your blood is thin [and] you go through life like a perambulating prayer-wheel, a friend of nobody but the righteous, and the righteous are those who agree with you as to what is right."[109]

Against a backdrop of an evening dance attended by uniformed US military officers and their bare-shouldered ladies, Jack pivoted his plot on Percival's confrontation with a hard truth that the sugar baron has thus far avoided. An employee whom Percival has repeatedly tormented, an employee who bears a remarkable resemblance to him and to his late missionary father is, in fact, his own half-brother. Employee Joe Garland is the proof of the patriarchal Reverend Isaac Ford's extramarital affair with Eliza Kunilio, a woman of kanaka lineage. And Jack took care to emphasize that Joe is his mother's son, for his kanaka heritage is expressed in Joe's love of music, his surfing, "his *hula* dancing." Joe has what the physician in the story calls (in a classic Jack London line) the "cosmic sap and smoke of life"—unbearable to Percival, who harries his brother off the Islands and renews his filiopiety.[110]

Readers of "The House of Pride" are not marooned with the desiccated Percival. Those who appreciated Jack's story when it appeared in *The Pacific Monthly* (1910) or in *The House of Pride, and Other Tales of Hawaii* (1912) were also treated to the Hawaii that Jack so loved, a scene of misty moonlight with Diamond Head "silhouetted . . . against the stars," of a woman's laughter and "love-cry" in the darkness," of the beached "outrigger canoes" where the kanaka men and women were "reclining languorously, like lotus-eaters," and of the beach where a couple stroll arm in arm while on a nearby lanai "the voices of singers [break] softly and meltingly into a Hawaiian love song."[111]

In a series of letters, Jack London and Lorrin Thurston more or less reconciled. Whether Thurston saw himself shadowed in the fictional portrait of the missionary progeny is an open question, but the nonsmoking, abstemious, teetotaling Thurston, whose "firm-lipped smile" caught Charmian's attention, implied a stark contrast to Jack's broad and ready grin, his omnipresent lighted Imperiale, and his reputation as a man who enjoyed his liquor. From the *Snark* voyage of 1907–8 to his final visits to Hawaii in 1915–16, Jack turned repeatedly to the Islands as a wellspring for fiction and a balm to his body and spirit, and Hawaiian stories were to flow from his pen to the end of his life, as would a final testament to the Islands.[112]

Jack's Hawaiian paradise continued to be, for him, a living reality from the moment he and Charmian stepped down the gangplank of the Matson Line steamship, the gleaming white *Matsonia*, in 1915 and again in 1916. His final statement on Hawaii was to be a love letter of sorts in the form of three nonfiction articles (all 1916) titled "My Hawaiian Aloha." They sketched modern Hawaiian history and surveyed the Islands' cosmopolitan mix of East Asians and numerous others in a "great experimental laboratory . . . in ethnology and sociology." Jack's "My Hawaiian Aloha" noted the diversity of those "shanghaied . . . by love" of the Islands, and he celebrated the climate, the recreational opportunities, the flora and fauna, and the wondrous new unifying "Pan-Pacific" movement that promised to promote interracial and multiethnic understanding and peace. He had entered exuberantly into Islands customs, from swimming and surfing to the outrigger canoe ride, to the ukulele musicale, the luau feasts, the plantation excursions, the visit to the grade school classrooms, the hula dance performance, the evening reception at the Queen's Gardens where the Royal Hawaiian Band serenaded the guests and the deposed Queen Liliuokalani smiled pleasantly and extended her hand to all who were presented to her. "With Hawaii," Jack wrote, "it seems always to be love at first sight," and he expressed his fervent wish to become a naturalized adoptee certified in the honorific word *kamaaina*.[113]

The other Hawaii, however, the Hawaii ruled by what the dethroned Liliuokalani called the "missionary oligarchy," was more potent than ever, and Jack must broadcast that brutal fact. Politically and economically speaking, he was yet again explicit: "Hawaii is a paradise—and I can never cease proclaiming it; but I must append one word of qualification: *Hawaii is a paradise for the well-to-do.*"[114]

As an honored guest, Jack London enjoyed the privileges of the well-to-do. He was ever alert, however, for social, economic, and political complexities and constraints, and he waved red warning flags in "My Hawaiian Aloha." No laborer ought to seek work in Hawaii, he warned, nor should a homesteader or anyone of modest capital try his hand, for all were doomed to fail. By now, Jack had the documentation to support this stance, for his files in Glen Ellen held detailed analyses of the Islands' monopolistic sugar industry, which "strenuously" exploited the small landholder. A cane planters' association circular of 1915 exposed what it termed the "real" issue in Hawaii, meaning the plight of the independent sugarcane producer, who toiled seven days a week, working "longer hours than the plantation laborer." With his spouse and children as field hands, he lived at a bare subsistence level, for he was in reality in bondage to the corporate sugar trust "to which he must

20. Jack London reads newspaper to keep abreast of current events and glean ideas for new stories. (Henry E. Huntington Library, San Marino, California)

sell his produce." This so-called freeholder, Jack learned, was a version of the post–Civil War southern sharecropper.[115]

Jack's files also held the extensive, explosive 1911 exposé of the Hawaiian sugar industry by a well-known investigative reporter, the muckraker Ray Stannard Baker. His fact-filled dissection of the sugar trust, titled "Wonderful Hawaii" and published in the *American Magazine*, corroborated Jack's years-long firsthand observations. Baker found that three of the Big Five sugar companies were "dominated by the old missionary families and missionary interests," and he opened his report with the assertion that the Hawaiian sugar industry was now unique in its predominance in the United States and presented "a vivid illustration of the way in which private business organization . . . permeates, influences, and controls the life of a country." Baker compared modern Hawaii to the pre–Civil War South, with sugar and pineapple as the new plantation cotton and the multinational fieldworkers as the present-day serfs, if not slaves. "These great sugar estates of Hawaii are without exception owned by corporations," Baker wrote, and their major landholders constitute a "modern aristocracy."[116]

Perhaps emboldened by Baker's thoroughgoing analysis, Jack's "My Hawaiian Aloha" issued a no-holds-barred attack on the "invading whites who dispossessed the native Hawaiians of their land." "The *haoles*, or whites," he said, "overthrew the Hawaiian Monarchy, formed the Dole Republic, and shortly thereafter brought their loot in under the sheltering folds of the Stars and Stripes." The "white man," he added, "is a born looter," and the inevitable upshot is that "the land and industries of Hawaii are owned by old families and large corporations."[117]

One word—"feudalism"—conveyed Jack's outrage to the public at large. For him, feudalism conjured images not of beautiful stained glass, soaring Gothic cathedrals, or fluid Gregorian chant, but of patriarchal rule undergirded by populations of the disenfranchised, the powerless and oppressed. In terms of workers, feudalism meant serfdom, a point of supersensitivity to a former jute mill and cannery worker who feared becoming a "work beast." For Jack, "feudalism" was a loaded word, a weaponized word from the early 1900s when he'd admired W. J. Ghent's caustic *Our Benevolent Feudalism*. Ray Stannard Baker, he saw, invoked "feudal" repeatedly to describe Hawaii's political and economic hierarchy and declared the sugar industry elites to be a "feudal aristocracy." Well into the new twentieth century, Jack knew no word more damning than "feudal" to label modern-day Hawaii. "Be it understood," he announced, "that Hawaii is patriarchal rather than democratic," that its ownership combines modern machinery and "medieval feudal methods." Philanthropy was flourishing in the Islands, he said, but under a system "distinctly feudal."[118]

Jack London's discovery of feudal Hawaii began when he met Lorrin Thurston, Sanford Dole, and others on the automobile outing on Oahu in the summer of 1907. The Ewa sugar plantation on Oahu and the expansive cane fields he saw on Maui were not only marvels of industrial agriculture and hydraulic engineering, but also reminders of his early life in the farm fields of Northern California. From the automobile and the private rail car of his Islands excursions, he saw the toiling figures in the ubiquitous cane and pineapple fields, low-wage toilers who echoed London's boyhood in his stepfather's farm fields and signified the monumental effort to escape the life of a manual laborer. It was at this time that Jack rewrote "To Build a Fire," converting the tale from moralistic juvenile fiction to a stark account of death that awaits a man who is oblivious of his peril.

That same summer of 1907, Charmian noted that Jack was working in a "shady corner . . . out of range of the distracting landscape." With a working title of "Success," he was "swinging along," she said, "on that autobiographical novel he has so long contemplated." The surname of the main character, Martin Eden, struck the chord of the island paradise, but the launch of the novel can be traced to the mirror Jack looked into when he gazed at the cane and pineapple fields. Few would link the controversial *Martin Eden* (1909) to the scene of hundreds and thousands of workers cutting, stripping, and lifting heavy bundles of sugarcane or bending to tend the rows of prickly fruit. But Jack's past was inscribed in what he saw, and he felt driven to tell his story without delay. He pressed on with it as the *Snark* sailed into the South Pacific and continued to work on the novel even as he produced short stories of Hawaii and the Solomon Islands. It was not easy for him. Charmian "could sense the strain he was under" as he pressed on with the autobiographical *Martin Eden*, and she "ached to see drawn lines around his mouth and a blue wanness, like shadows on snow, beneath his eyes." Jack "is always teaching," she had remarked. "It is the breath of his body." *Martin Eden* was to be Jack London's breath of life—and to bring down a storm of public wrath that fueled the next episode of his unrelenting campaign for a progressive American future.[119]

4

House of Progress, House of Shame

I was Martin Eden.
—Jack London,
John Barleycorn,
1913

Life seemed on the upswing in 1909 as Jack and Charmian began the homeward voyage from Hawaii and the South Seas. As in the lull before the storm, all seemed well. Nearly completed, *Martin Eden* was to be published in the fall, and Jack thought the new novel was the "best" he had "ever written." The *Pacific Monthly* had secured serial rights to the book, promising advertisers a huge boost in circulation from "Jack London's latest and greatest novel."[1]

That May he and Charmian boarded the SS *Tymeric*, a "rusty leviathan" of a collier bound from Australia to Ecuador, the first leg of their homeward journey from the South Pacific to California. They had put the *Snark* up for sale at a fraction of its cost and abandoned their round-the-world trip. Recovering from his South Seas afflictions after hospital treatment in Australia, Jack had lingered in Sydney to review the Tommy Burns–Jack Johnson fight for the Hearst newspaper syndicate. Aboard the *Tymeric* he bragged in a letter to poet George Sterling ("Greek," as he called his close friend) that he was "boxing every day now" and had pummeled three of the *Tymeric* officers, "husky young Englishmen" who dealt Jack mere bruises and minor sprains. "I get cramps in my legs while fighting," he admitted, but "am now getting into condition."[2]

The Glen Ellen ranch beckoned, but the three-month-long homeward journey must not be rushed. As the *Tymeric* bucked the gale winds and heavy seas that invigorated Jack (he "'who lived with storms . . . like a kinsman'"), Charmian struggled with seasickness and malarial fevers. However, once in Central America, they were both enthusiastic tourists. From the Ecuadorian port of Guayaquil, they took a train over the Andes for a fortnight in Quito, then went alligator hunting on the Guayas River. Back in Guayaquil, Jack joined Charmian in "a blanket-haggling revel in an old plaza—brilliant dyes of hand-loom weaves from llama wool." The couple proceeded to the Panama Canal Zone, where they saw the "great canal" and "shopped at the Chinese stores." From there they sailed to New Orleans to catch the train trip to Oakland. At every stop Jack's return was "hailed by the newspapers," whose reporters "boarded the train at a number of towns." En route home, Jack wrote two new stories and a novel, *Adventure*, to be published in 1911.[3]

In a brilliant move, Jack hired his capable, dear stepsister Eliza Shepard to be the business manager and superintendent of Beauty Ranch, where he intended to "remain . . . for several years." Cordially he invited friends and business associates to visit, among them his New York book editor, George Brett. "I should like . . . to have you come and loaf for a few weeks," he wrote to Brett. "I can tell you that there will be a string of horses . . . and that I'd like nothing better than to turn you loose among them." As autumn 1909 neared, some nine books were in the Jack London pipeline awaiting publication.[4]

By the winter of 1910, however, Jack London was on the ropes. In California, he "lay sick in Oakland for several weeks, then got up to the ranch to convalesce." No sooner had the year 1910 opened than a horse cart accident on the ranch lamed him. ("I can't trust my weight on my ankle more than a dozen steps at a time.") It was the reaction to *Martin Eden*, however, that dealt the hardest blows. He was blindsided by his critics' pummeling. In the span of a few months he found himself squarely on the defensive.[5]

A certain measure of hostility accompanied the arrival of each new Jack London title. Some reviewers censured his very output. The aim of this "young man in a hurry," grumbled a reviewer of London's *Cruise of the Dazzler* (1902), was "to turn out as many pages of fiction each year as he is physically capable of writing," thus sacrificing "the best literary workmanship." Others took offense at his word choices. "Coarse and cruel," railed a reviewer of London's short story collection *Love of Life* (1907), while his autobiographical *The Road* (1907) had been pronounced "sordid" and "altogether disreputable."[6]

Martin Eden, however, drew blood on a visceral, gut level. Jack's physical and mental stress while drafting it in Hawaii was no casual observation on Charmian's part. She noted in her diary that Jack was "sick . . . mentally" as he completed the novel aboard the ship en route to California. For him, the personal demands of the novel were unprecedented. In its pages London once again insisted that readers confront America's outrageously cruel social conditions. This time, in addition, he explicitly offered his own life story as a case study. In an era in which the medical dissection of the human anatomy was controversial and when religion was invoked on behalf of the inviolable human body, Jack London's story put his dissected life on public display.[7]

What's more, *Martin Eden* combined his life story with a frontal attack on a major sector of his readers, the bourgeoisie. He had personal scores to settle. The critic Eric Miles Williamson is correct that Jack London has been "a curiosity to upper-class folks who can't really understand poverty." More than a curiosity, in his lifetime Jack had often been the butt of smug condescension cloaked as concern and friendship. He launched *Martin Eden* just as he'd got his fill of bourgeois hypocrisies. The recent sojourn in the Hawaiian Islands tipped the scales, in large part because Jack witnessed the horrific labor conditions in the sugarcane and pineapple fields while also gasping for air in the stifling atmosphere of the social scene. As a celebrated author, he had had quite enough of the "hotels and clubs and homes and Pullmans and steamer-chairs" where the captains of industry moralized about peace while hiring Pinkerton gunmen to shoot down their striking factory workers. He'd seen more than his share of their "beautifully gowned, beautiful women" who "prattled sweet little ideals and dear little moralities" and "assisted in sweet little charities" but raged against the poor when reminded that their material comfort was provided by child labor and sweatshops.[8]

His grievance along these lines was no secret. In 1906 he'd denounced the elites' hypocrisy in the mainstream magazine *Cosmopolitan* in an essay titled "What Life Means to Me." That essay basically outlined the plot of *Martin Eden*, for the famous author sketched his climb from "crude and rough and raw" beginnings to the social heights where "men wore black clothes and boiled shirts, and women dressed in beautiful gowns." At first he believed their couture and sartorial splendor had signaled "unselfishness of the spirit, clean and noble thinking, keen intellectual living." Instead, upon reaching their bourgeois "parlor," Jack found brutal hypocrisies masked as good manners. "It was a torment," Jack said, "to listen to the insipidities and stupidities of women [and] to the pompous, arrogant sayings of the little half-baked men," so many of them "cold of heart and cold of head." In Hawaii, the circle of the prominent Lorrin A. Thurston typified those he'd critiqued. The cattle ranch manager, Von Tempsky, "Von," was his kindred spirit; his and Jack's soft-collared shirts signified a "bond of outlawry." There were too few Vons, too many of the others.[9]

Samplings of what London endured from one year to the next remain like sediment in the memoirs of his genteel acquaintances. To sound the depths of the rage that fueled his autobiographical novel, we can listen to his genteel upper-middle-class contemporaries speak from the printed page. For instance, in *The Mystery of Jack London* (1931), Jack's former schoolmate Georgia Maude Loring (later Mrs. Frederick Bamford) recalled the day she first set eyes on Jack. The former Miss Loring made it clear that although she and Jack London attended the same school, they inhabited vastly different worlds, hers without question the superior sort. Seated in high school French class with the "neatly dressed" boys who wore respectable "short trousers," the genteel Miss Loring was aghast at Jack's appearance on the first school day in autumn of 1895. She remembered his "wrinkled and ill-fitting" old suit with "long and baggy" trousers, which marked him as an uncouth young man of the San Francisco slum district "south of the slot."[10]

Housing, too, marked the chasm separating her world from London's. Her family, the bourgeois Lorings, resided among "the most prominent and influential people," meaning those "who were interested in the political and cultural welfare of [the] city and state" and who lived accordingly in "residential" Oakland, with "attractive houses and gardens."[11]

The London "domicile," as she put it, was by contrast little more than a "shack." She inspected it for herself, venturing to the estuary area formerly called Brooklyn Station, where she located the London family "'cottage,'" her euphemism for squalor. Like the surrounding dwellings, it was "of an indescribable ramshackle character." Lacking any "element of modern sanitation," it was built of scrap materials, its "crevices stuffed with old carpets and rags" to "keep out the wind and the weather." Miss Loring conceded that Bay Area artists found the area "picturesque," but her words dripped with condescension when she wrote, "It is small wonder that the sixteen-year-old boy, Jack London, looked toward the stars for hope. There was no other place for him to look." She contrasted the "civilization" of her world with the "ferocious primitive" instinct of Jack London's.[12]

Another, far more potent figure in Jack's life agreed that the writer's "venturesome soul" came with a "repellant touch of the cynical and brutal." This caustic swipe came from David Starr Jordan (1851–1931), a leading scientist and the first president of Stanford University. London and Jordan met in Oakland when the fledgling writer audited Jordan's university extension course on evolution. Preceding Jack by a generation, Jordan had key points in common with his student. Both he and Jack had been reluctant but dutiful farm boys, Jordan admitting to a "distinct dislike" of work in the fields and dairy barn of his upstate New York boyhood. Both, however, had mothers who prized and instilled values of literacy in their sons at an early age. Both roamed nearby hills in search of wildlife—Jordan in the Catskills, London in Oakland's wooded Alameda County. Both enjoyed the fiction of Bret Harte, and both were ardent admirers of Abraham Lincoln. Champions of California, both were outdoorsmen who embraced the physical culture that was bannered in Theodore Roosevelt's celebration of "the strenuous life." Like Jack, Jordan despised the waste of higher education as "a social ornament" that gave "the elect few" a "well-dressed feeling." Both men, what's more, feared the political and economic control of a monopolistic "educated oligarchy," and both used the corrosive term "feudal" to express distaste for the benighted past. Both, in addition, were frustrated in their initial attempts to launch their careers. Jack was snubbed by editors and publishers, while the Cornell-educated Jordan struggled unsuccessfully to secure a university post in the depression years of the 1870s. By the time they met, however, Jordan was an eminent figure in higher education. Having studied under the august Louis Agassiz and served as the president of Indiana University, he was now the first president of newly founded Stanford University. From his classroom seat the young London saw a personage standing six foot two, tall with a high forehead and close-cropped, curly hair that framed a long face with a sensuous mouth, a brushy moustache, and a gaze sharpened by experience. In turn, young Jack struck Jordan as "a stocky young fellow of great physical strength" and "decided individuality."[13]

Lectures on evolution given by Jordan, a eugenicist and ichthyologist, introduced Jack to the work of the British pioneering eugenicist Francis Galton and also to the German eugenicist August Weismann, whose *Essays upon Heredity* so strongly influenced London's novel *Before Adam*. The senior man's sway over Jack London is also evident in London's epistolary novel *The Kempton-Wace Letters* (coauthored with Anna Strunsky). In addition, Jack kept a file of personally inspiring quotations from the eugenicist (e.g., "The Anglo-Saxon race, with its strength and virtues, was born of hard times"). The revered name of David Starr Jordan, he confided to a correspondent, had replaced Alexander the Great in his youthful pantheon of intellectual stars. And he gave Jordan a bit part, of sorts, in his novel *The Sea-Wolf* (1904). The stalwart female character, Maud Brewster, recalls Jordan's scientific expertise on seal colonies and lauds the Stanford president's brilliance as a pragmatist when she asks her soulmate, Humphrey (Hump) Van Weyden, "Do you know Dr. Jordan's final test of truth? . . . Can we make it work? Can we trust your lives to it?" Maud proclaims Jordan "a modern hero."[14]

Jack's outlook meshed with Jordan's in an apparent bond across two generations. When Jordan invited Jack to the Stanford campus "to read from his Alaskan stories," he recalled that the young writer's "manner was both modest and effective, and awakened the kindly personal interest of his hearers." Jordan cited Jack as a "master of trenchant English" whose stories stood as "recognized masterpieces." The university president saw enough evidence of

21. David Starr Jordan, the first president of Stanford University. Jack London audited Jordan's extension course on evolution and accepted the Stanford president's invitation to read his fiction on the Stanford campus. London's respect for Jordan waned in years to come. (From Jordan's autobiography, *The Days of a Man* [vol. 1], 1922)

eugenic science undergirding *The Call of the Wild* and London's other "tales" that he claimed the young writer as his intellectual disciple.[15]

Jordan, however, retreated into bourgeois nostrums and smug slogans that flew in the face of Jack London's hard facts. In 1901 he proclaimed that "for more than a century now the common man has ruled America," when actually the titans of industry and their legatees had ruled the country for decades. The muckraking journalists exposed cutthroat practices of the monopoly trusts in such popular weekly and monthly magazines as *McClure's* and *Collier's*, but Jordan opined that "business morality is on a higher plane in these days of vast combinations." The battles of capital and labor raged over his lifetime, but Jordan insisted that labor strife would simply vanish if only workers were loyal to their employers (and vice versa) in a spirit of "voluntary cooperation"—a notion that echoed his patron and university founder Leland Stanford, who loathed labor unions.[16]

There was more. When Jordan spoke of "the sad plight of the factory children of the South," he emphasized hookworm, merely touching on the children's "overwork" in a single word: "abominable." When he toured Hawaii six years before Jack's first visit, Jordan saw that the native Hawaiians were "wholly controlled by the small white minority," among them Jack London's future host and a foremost figure in that minority, Lorrin A. Thurston. While Jack blasted the sugar barons' greed in his stories of Hawaii, Jordan concluded that "the problem will adjust itself in time" through "conciliation" and "the Anglo-Saxon instinct for fair play." This sort of bourgeois temporizing revolted Jack. To him, conventional society brimmed with soft-focus nostrums, evasions, banalities, and treacherous lies. Progressive social change depended on facing the fact-based truth of things.[17]

David Starr Jordan's impact on Jack London was tremendous—but it spiraled far beyond the orbit of the extension course syllabus. Scientific expertise was the bedrock of his influence, but in directions that Jordan never anticipated. The Stanford president never guessed how he turned his disciple into his antagonist.

Jack's quarrel with Jordan—the very fight he was to pick with the bourgeoisie in *Martin Eden*—traced back to a newspaper poem, "The Man with a Hoe," a five-stanza verse that appeared in the *San Francisco Examiner* on January 15, 1899, the very month that young Jack's first breakthrough story, "To the Man on Trail," was published in the prestigious *Overland Monthly*.

The poet, an Oakland, California, schoolteacher named Edwin Markham, had seen *Man with a Hoe* (1862), by the French artist Jean-François Millet, at an exhibition in San Francisco. Millet's painting depicts a French peasant momentarily pausing from his labors in a muddy farm field. The image of the farm laborer leaning forward against the shaft of his hoe stunned and haunted Markham, who "sat for an hour before the painting" and realized that the image before him "was no mere peasant" but "a symbol of the toiler, brutalized through long ages of industrial oppression." The hoe-man's "brutal jaw" and "slanted brow" testify to "the world's blind greed," said Markham, and to the failure of the "masters, lords and rulers in all lands" to provide resources to nourish the human mind and spirit. No picturesque rustic, the man with the hoe is a stupefied industrial-era "brother to the ox."[18]

Markham's poem became an overnight sensation nationwide. Reprinted, it spread like a California brushfire up and down the Pacific coast and across the country, to "the Mississippi Valley, on into New York and New England, over the line into Canada." It was a topic of feverish parlor conversation and grist for the mills of public debate. The early twentieth-century historian Mark Sullivan quipped that "the newspapers . . . gave as much space to 'The Man with the Hoe' as to prize-fights and police stories." He added that "the

22. Jean-François Millet, *Man with a Hoe*, 1860-62. This French painting of the Barbizon school prompted a fierce nationwide US debate in 1899 when the West Coast poet Edwin Markham interpreted the painting as an indictment of the brutality of the modern industrial system. (J. Paul Getty Museum, Los Angeles)

clergy made the poem their text, platform orators dilated upon it, college professors lectured upon it, debating societies discussed it, schools took it up for study." Postal cards crossed the country showing a brown-shingled house with a cutaway photo of the poet, the caption reading "The Edwin Markham Home. *The Man with the Hoe* was written here."[19]

Jack London celebrated the poem as a profound statement about the crushing reality of modern industrial work. He quoted lines from it in a letter to Cloudesley Johns and referred to the "richly deserved . . . boom" the poem was receiving nationwide. In 1901, when Jack's name as a rising young writer brought him opportunities to write book reviews, he singled out "The Man with the Hoe" in his glowing review of Markham's *Lincoln and Other Poems*. Those who had branded Markham a pessimist, Jack insisted, had failed to recognize that the poet's words were "warm with faith and hope." Markham's "discontent," Jack said, was "a noble discontent, which is the secret of progress."[20]

Jack also learned that the eminent David Starr Jordan took Markham's poem in a starkly different direction in a lecture that he "delivered in many places." Jordan gave the title his own twist, calling it "The Man Who Was Left Behind." Jack heard the Stanford president's lecture on a Sunday night in April 1899, as did Edwin Markham, whom Jack described in a letter to Cloudesley as "a noble-looking man, snow white hair and beard, and very close to sixty."[21]

The twenty-three-year-old London doubtless expected to hear Jordan endorse Markham's view that the painting represented the toiler who was brutalized through long ages of industrial oppression. But he was in for a shock. Instead, Jordan argued that eugenics was the key to the hoe-man's wretched state of life. This man, insisted Jordan, was by no means the "slave of the wheel of labor" in the modern industrial age. Quite the reverse. As the eugenicist explained, the French peasant was regrettably born "oppressed." Quite simply, Jordan argued, many centuries of warfare had wiped out the genetically superior Frenchmen, most recently in the Napoleonic wars that killed off the best, bravest, and most courageous specimens of French manhood. Jordan dismissed Markham's poem as a naive misreading of Millet's painting. "In dealing with [the hoe-man]," Jordan concluded, "we are far from the 'labor problem' of to-day." And far, too, "from all the wrongs of the poor as set forth in the conventional literature of sympathy."[22]

The Stanford president's remarks surely comforted many hearers. Cloaked in the mantle of scientific authority, he ferried the hoe-man to his native soil on the European continent and to the century that was fast closing. Jordan absolved contemporary social, religious, and political leaders—the titans of industry and finance and their bourgeois enablers—of all responsibility for abysmal present conditions.

The reassurance that Jordan's audiences sought, however, required a certain suspension of disbelief, especially in regard to the decade of the US 1890s. Jordan's scientific claims required the avoidance of stark facts that linked Markham's poem directly to recent dreadful events in the industrial United States. From 1893, the country had experienced a severe, years-long economic depression, with unprecedented high rates of business and bank failures and soaring unemployment. At one point, over 15 percent of the workforce was jobless, and the decade saw populations of young male US workers roam the country as day laborers, known as hoboes, the term itself shortened from "hoe-boys."

Jack London, of course, had been such a hoe-boy, a hobo who sought work and handouts of food as he as he rode the rails eastward from California across the country and through Canada in 1894. Readers of his *The Road* were to learn that at eighteen years of age, the now-famous Jack London was a jobless, hungry "hoe-boy" facing hard-hearted men who taunted him for laziness and a few kindly women who furnished a meal if he fabricated a touching, baroque tale of misfortune.

Hearing David Starr Jordan's talk on "The Man Who Was Left Behind" that April evening in 1899, Jack might have drawn on his reading of Marxist literature to challenge the Stanford president's argument. What's more, the young London had an archive of personal experience to refute the Stanford president's eugenics argument. Not only could he recount his and numerous others' ravaging hunger and his futile efforts to get paying work, but he also had a vivid recollection of his "work-beast" stints in the Oakland jute mill and cannery, in the steam laundry and the boiler room of the electric company.

Jack could not bring himself to challenge Jordan in 1899, but he did join the public debate over the poetic quality of "The Man with the Hoe," avoiding a direct confrontation with the Stanford president, a prominent public intellectual on the national stage who lunched regularly with the president at the White House and lectured and published widely on general-interest topics, offering titles such as *The Philosophy of Hope* (1902), *The Care and Culture of Men* (1903), and *The Call of the Twentieth Century* (1904).

Jack London was nonetheless forming his own ideas on the new century, on what terms hope could realistically be based, and on the social arrangements that helped or hindered the care and culture of human beings. He had learned for a certainty that the "upper-class folks," the bourgeoisie, lacked any real grasp of the wretched conditions of the work that provided the material furnishings of their lives, from their Sunday roast beef to their bedsprings. Endured by multitudes of men, women, and children, the working conditions of their industrial era were, as he knew, a killing ground for body and soul even as joblessness murdered by starvation. His mission was to make the affluent public understand this—not only to understand it but to do something about it. His success would depend on public outreach and acceptance. The first few years of the new century were, for him, experimental. His socialist tracts, such as *The War of the Classes* (1905), alarmed middle-class readers. He frightened them with bellicose forecasts of the creative destruction that would ultimately, he believed, rid the Gilded Age capitalists' "house" of its pathological greed and monopolistic power and open the way for a better life for multitudes. His fiction, on the other hand, could cloak his reproaches and admonitions. The techniques of the storyteller and novelist let the public think mainly of entertainment, not social reform. Fiction, moreover, was vitally important because it tapped reservoirs of public empathy that London knew to be foundational for social change.

Jack London's path to *Martin Eden* wove its way through fiction that showed affluent Americans the dark underside of their modern culture of products and services. In a critical barb tucked into his memoir, *The Days of a Man* (1922), Stanford's David Starr Jordan noted Jack's "defiant attitude toward conventional society." To Jack, defiance was necessary. Defiant, he could denounce the incorrigible captains of industry and expose the conventional social arrangement that insulated the bourgeoisie from their own unwitting barbarity. Defiant, he could show the affluent that their material comforts came at the exorbitant cost of backbreaking toil by wretchedly paid workers. Defiant, then, he could prick the conscience of affluent America and lay the groundwork for reform.[23]

With the cover illustration of the 1903 *The Call of the Wild* we see a reminder of Jack London's successful tactics for the education of the public. It shows three rows of sled dogs in the snow, for London used canine creatures to tell a story fundamental to industrial-era Americans. The young writer's ingenuity was serendipitous. Drafting the novel, Jack had found that this very guise, or disguise, could let him touch readers' conscience by showing, at a distance, the miseries of the average worker under the brutal industrial conditions he himself had endured in his youth.

With a dog as protagonist, London gave voice to the plight of the human "work beast." In the novel, a St. Bernard and Scotch shepherd mix named Buck is stolen from his luxurious California home, sold, crated, and shipped to the North Country of the Klondike gold hunters. Beaten repeatedly, he is strapped into the harness or traces with other team dogs to pull sleds in "driving snow" and "wind that cut like a white-hot knife." Serving a variety of masters who seldom spare the whip, Buck suffers neglect and abuse by indifferent and incompetent drivers and by fellow dogs in the sled team pack of comrades and rivals. He learns survival tactics, including fighting skills, and he triumphs in a social Darwinist world to hear, at last, that "deep in the forest a call was sounding," the call of the arctic wild that proves irresistible. After one powerful and moving interlude with a kindly human master whose murder Buck avenges, the dog-hero ultimately becomes a supreme individualist as well as pack leader of wolves—and free at last from human bondage.[24]

Before sending Buck into wilderness freedom, however, Jack London released a cache of information about industrial work and workers, a cache that was stored in his muscle memory. Through the dogs and their masters he was prepared to teach readers the facts of life about the industrial-era "Man with a Hoe." Having been that man in the jute mill, the cannery, the steam laundry, and the electric company boiler room, with its shovel and towering heaps of coal, he was poised to teach what he'd learned. Well taught by experience, London now had the strategy for a counterargument against David Starr Jordan. He would reach the public through Buck, his canine workmates, and the human masters who literally wield the whip. In political terms, Jack called it "class struggle . . . a class inequality, a superior class and an inferior class (as measured by power)."[25]

At close range London had seen the pathologies that crippled those who were trapped in the "inferior" class. His undercover journalism in London's East End in 1902 immersed him in their world, and he knew its American version all too well. He now transposed what he knew from the human to the canine. The work dogs' wages (i.e. rations) are so minimal that they, Buck included, "suffered from perpetual hunger" unless they stole one another's food, meaning that the survival of each individual was dependent on the deprivation of others, the whole brutal system defined by a chapter title, "The Law of Club and Fang." London had other points to chisel into his text, having seen (and nearly become) like the dogs that he portrayed "on their last legs" in the "dead-tiredness that comes through the slow and prolonged drainage of months of toil." When at last "there was no power of recuperation left, no reserve of strength to call upon," the worthless dogs were to be "got rid of" like workers whose muscles, their only capital, were depleted.[26]

Not all readers would see the linkage of the dogs to the plight of industrial workers. Jack London, what's more, was no flagrant allegorist. He did not pointedly invite readers to recognize his critique of industrial-era labor in the story of the work dogs in the Yukon. Some, however, surely noticed the alignment of *The Call of the Wild* with Aesop's fables, the animal tales that taught stringent and clear moral lessons, for the fables were widely available in numerous editions in America and Britain throughout the nineteenth century and were incorporated into America's grade school textbooks, the ubiquitous *McGuffey's* readers. By the time *The Call of the Wild* became a byword for best-selling fiction, countless middle-class American readers knew that animal stories carried thinly veiled messages about human moral conduct, whether fair, unfair, enlightened, or unforgivably cruel. As London's daughter Joan remarked, "Reviewers and friends alike pounced enthusiastically on the human allegory inherent in the dog's life-and-death struggle to adapt itself to a hostile environment."[27]

London put another instructional narrative of egregious labor conditions on the public record, rejecting David Starr Jordan's notion that it was mainly hookworm, not toil, that crippled the children who labored in the mills. In Jack's short story "The Apostate," published in a mass-market magazine, the *Woman's Companion*, in the spring of 1906, he sent a message to its middle- and upper-middle-class readers. "The Apostate" reinforced a certain reform initiative that had been recently gaining steam. In effect, Jack joined a reformist chorus when, as a public intellectual, he used fiction to chronicle the harrowing life of a boy laborer in the industrial Gilded Age.

As Jack well knew, the early-1900s magazines featured essays that were intended to stir the middle-class public conscience and prompt reform by exposing the horrific conditions of the modern industrial workplace. His own files swelled with pamphlets and articles on exploitive working conditions, all aimed at the bourgeois public ("The Diary of a Domestic Drudge," "Ten Weeks in a Kitchen"). For the *San Francisco Examiner* he reviewed *The Long Day: The True Story of a New York Working Girl as Told by Herself* (1905), a harrowing first-person account of work that Jack knew personally, steam laundry work in which crippling injury was "commonplace." Especially wrenching was the subgenre on child labor, including such magazine essays as "Turning Children into Dollars" (1906) and "Children of the Coal Shadow" (1902). By the turn of the twentieth century the perilous state of childhood and the urgency of reform were under continuous discussion among Progressives, most notably Jane Addams and the Hull House children's activist Florence Kelley, who coined the phrase "the right to childhood." Kelley was joining with others across the country to advocate for the creation of a federal agency of the US government to be devoted solely to the interests of the nation's children. Nonfiction essays energized this movement, as did illustrations and photographs such as those of Jacob Riis and Lewis Hine, who showed the plight of ragged, hollow-eyed children toiling in fields and factories. The new multireel motion pictures also joined the campaign against treacherous workplaces in which children labored and sometimes lost their lives. The catastrophic Triangle shirtwaist factory fire of 1911, in which 123 women and 23 men died, was echoed three years later in the film *Children of Eve*, featuring teenage girl workers who succumb to a workplace conflagration.

Jack London cared profoundly about children's vulnerability. His files thickened with magazine articles and newspaper clippings on the horrors of child labor. He marked and filed poet Edwin Markham's 1906 article "The Hoe-Man in the Making" on child laborers in US glass factories. In soft red covers, he carefully bound a set of 1902–3 magazine pieces: "Children of Labor," "Child Labor in Factories," "Child Labor: A Social Waste," "Child Labor in Shops and Homes."[28]

This handmade book was made up entirely of nonfiction journalism. Yet a well-crafted story, as London knew, could summon great powers of emotion and resonate in memory long after its pages were closed. Monetizing his youthful misery wouldn't heal psychic scars but might help move the public to grasp the horrors of child labor and to support laws to ban it. When the editor of the *Woman's Home Companion* wrote to solicit "a child labor short story," the famous name of Jack London entered into the literature of child labor. The September 1906 issue featured Jack's unexpurgated "The Apostate," with the magazine tagline "A Child Labor Parable." Jack's scalding memory of jute mill toil in lengthy mind-numbing shifts for an hourly wage of ten cents became the fictional record of child labor in one of Oakland's most important industries in the closing decades of the nineteenth century. By 1893, there were five hundred workers at the Pacific Jute Manufacturing Company, which occupied an entire block on Second Avenue near East Tenth Street and "boasted 135 jute looms, 3,000 spindles and 115 miscellaneous machines" that produced twine, jute matting, horse blankets, and upward of 4 million yards of burlap that was stitched into sacks for potatoes, grain, and numerous other commodities. The workforce, at first Chinese, was "gradually replaced by American labor," doubtless a consequence of the US Chinese Exclusion Act of 1882, which barred further Chinese immigration to the United States.[29]

"The Apostate" profitably coined Jack's memory of a hellish true-life episode, and he tunneled into the dark shaft of his memory to quarry the tale. "The Apostate" put the child labor crisis into the middle-class parlors of those who would never dream of sending their own daughters or sons into the mills. The central character, the wraith-thin teenage Johnny, began work as a bobbin boy at seven years of age. Hired at first to wind "the jute-twine" at a bank of machines, he has become "a work-beast" whose nighttime dreams are infested with "the shrieking, pounding, crashing, roaring of a million looms."[30]

The turning point of "The Apostate" is Johnny's realization that his mother sacrifices him in order to preserve bright prospects for her favorite younger son, Will, who is "well-built, fairly rugged," and tall, "spilling over with exuberance." In personal terms, "The Apostate" pulses with Jack London's resentment toward the mother who denied him the affection she later showered on Johnny Miller, his stepsister Ida's son. In terms of the wider social scene, the rugged Will represents childhood free of wage slavery, childhood for those who were better off by the accident of birth and favorable circumstance. In the story, Johnny's apostasy mirrors Jack's own, for just as Jack escaped to the rails as the hobo known as the Frisco Kid, so Johnny awakens to the facts of his situation, vows never again to toil his life away, makes his way to the railroad track, clambers aboard an empty boxcar, closes its door and, as the engine whistles, lies down "and in the darkness he smiled."[31]

The ending is no sentimental sop, for Johnny's chronic cough and physical frailty augur the onset of a fatal disease all too familiar in the 1900s: tuberculosis. The boy's solace is simply the cessation of grinding toil. To Jack London, the nation's legions of sacrificial Johnnys were proof positive of industrial criminality. The jute and the myriad other products need not consume the lives of generations of children, and the rich and powerful industrial elites who authorized such unspeakable conditions and normalized them became Jack London's gallery of shame—and his target. He kept a dossier on them. Gathering the articles on child labor, Jack also compiled a series of 1902–3 magazine articles from *Cosmopolitan* titled "Captains of Industry." "To-day," the editorial lead-in announced, "he has the greatest power who commands the most dollars" and "he who wins financial duels is a great potential hero." The warriors of the past, the magazine insisted, were today's businessmen, and Jack's file swelled with *Cosmopolitan* profiles of the current capitalist titans, such as Henry Clay Frick, Charles Yerkes, Henry Flagler, Cyrus Curtis, William Andrews Clark, and others—the kings of copper, oil, munitions, coffee, steel, rubber, railroads, and publishing.[32]

These figures were, in the main, the second generation of the great capitalists who were America's industrial-era Founding Fathers—Andrew Carnegie, John D. Rockefeller, Collis P. Huntington. Added to the list is David Starr Jordan's patron, Leland Stanford, in whose name a modern university had been established. Stanford was one of the four "Associates," the founding figures in the building of the transcontinental Central Pacific Railroad, including Huntington and also Charles Crocker and Mark Hopkins. Their names were synonymous with the steel, oil, and shipping that undergirded modern industry and determined the material conditions of life nationwide. As London said, they had built the "house" that America lived in. They created its paradigms. They dictated its terms. "We are a commercial people," the investigative journalist Ida Tarbell said of Americans in 1904. "Our boast is in the wealth we produce. As a consequence, business is sanctified." The *Cosmopolitan* editors underscored the point in their series "Captains of Industry" and their claim that "he who wins financial duels is a great potential hero." London himself was soon to accept *Cosmopolitan*'s invitation to inaugurate a series of personal essays on famous successful men.[33]

But the sanctification of the "Captains of Industry" infuriated him—just as it angered significant sectors of the public. Free US citizens felt betrayed and overwhelmed by the rise of the monopolies, the holding companies, and the trusts. Their lives seemed no longer to be their own. The press at times underscored the point with personal attacks on these industrial-era "Captains." The steel magnate Andrew Carnegie was cartooned in the *Philadelphia Press* as a two-headed monster who slashed his workers' wages and gave philanthropic gifts of "tainted money." The *San Francisco Examiner* flayed the railroader and shipping mogul Huntington as "a hard and cheery man with no more soul than a shark." The popular *McClure's* charged Rockefeller with "the most gigantic and daring conspiracy a free country had ever seen." The public relations business, spearheaded by Ivy Lee and his colleagues, bent their efforts to nullify these horrific caricatures and to soothe the public with benign portraits of these titans and their corporations as entities committed to the greatest good, all in the name of truthfulness and superior judgment.[34]

The novelists, however, worked toward different purposes. Their mission was the scrutiny of the psychology of the Captains of Industry. The early twentieth-century US novelists included Jack's contemporaries Frank Norris and Theodore Dreiser, together with those whose fiction was to fade from view in the years ahead (Charles K. Lush, Winston Churchill, Henry Adams, Robert Grant, and Davis Graham Phillips, among others). The machinations of the chieftains of rail and wheat were put on display in Norris's *The Octopus* (1901) and *The Pit* (1903), and Dreiser was soon to explore the mentality of the financier in his fictional Cowperwood trilogy based loosely on the career of the transit mogul Charles Yerkes, beginning with the aptly titled *The Financier* (1912), followed by *The Titan* (1914) and the much-delayed *The Stoic* (1947). The success of these and other books in the marketplace indicated that the public was eager to understand the mental and sociopolitical mechanisms at work behind the facial façades of power—the smooth-shaven Rockefeller; the genial bearded Carnegie, who was thought to resemble St. Nicholas; the hulking Huntington, who wore skullcaps indoors to conceal his baldness.

Jack London joined his contemporaries in plumbing the psyche of the Gilded Age "Captain of Industry." He framed this outsized figure in terms of Friedrich Nietzsche's "Super-Man," the *Übermensch* to whom social codes of ethics and morality did not apply. He considered the relation of the Nietzschean Super-Man—in this case John D. Rockefeller—to the social body and found him woefully wanting. "The superman is anti-social in his tendencies," London wrote. "In these days of our complex society and sociology he cannot be successful in his hostile aloofness. Hence the unpopularity of the financial superman like Rockefeller; he acts like an irritant on the social body." As the historian Sean Cashman later put it, "It was Rockefeller who became the symbol of inhumanity in business."[35]

London offered the superman, the titan, to the public in a clarion call for a necessary revolution supported by the bourgeoisie, lest the regime of deathly monopolistic power prevail in the new century and beyond. Once again, he had a message for high-ranking officials who served their Gilded Age masters, obediently dissembling to the point of obsequiousness. One such instance involved David Starr Jordan's struggles with Leland Stanford and, later on, with his widow, who in 1900 forced the university president to fire the brilliant sociologist Edward Ross, whom Jordan had publicly praised as an excellent teacher and "the most effective worker in the country in his field of social science." The sociologist, however, had angered the widow Stanford, who judged Ross "erratic" and "unsound" for supporting railroad unionist Eugene Debs in the strike of 1894. At Mrs. Stanford's insistence (and in the name of her husband, the railroader and former California governor), Dr. Jordan reversed himself, declared Ross "unfit," and fired him. No thanks to Jordan, this professor was, as Jack put it, "broken on the wheel of subservience to the ruling class."[36]

Such Gilded Age surrender to tyranny, in Jack London's view, meant that feudalism still held the modern world in a hammerlock. Its kings, the kings of industry, must be dethroned, and London once again used the novel to show how it must be done. Once again, he successfully fine-tuned the book for the cultural sensitivities of his audience. The bourgeois readers who enjoyed *The Call of the Wild*, "The Apostate," and other Jack London titles now applauded his handling of the characters and plot in *The Sea-Wolf* (1904). Gripped by the story in their parlors and dens, they found a novel that gave them, at close range, a demonic industrial-era captain of their contemporary moment.

They found, in addition, characters with whom they could ally, a man and a woman who shared their values and lifestyles and who, when courage was asked of them, rose to the occasion. The readers rewarded London. *The Sea-Wolf* became a bestseller that distilled the industrial "Captains" into the one figure who actually is a captain and thus by law the supreme dictator of a world entirely at his command, a world whose course of action is his alone to determine, a world in which all others are held in subjugation.

London's audience encountered this captain through the eyes of a character much like themselves, a respectable if overly fastidious bourgeois literary gentleman named Humphrey Van Weyden who nearly drowns in the collision of two ferries in the fogbound San Francisco Bay. Pulled from the frigid waters at the last moment by crewmen of the seal-hunting schooner *Ghost*, Van Weyden expects to be put ashore or transferred to an inbound vessel (and offers a handsome sum for the courtesy). Instead, he is impressed into service as a cabin boy at the command of the *Ghost*'s captain, Wolf Larsen. His rescue, Van Weyden realizes, was no humanitarian act but the strategy of a commander who is short-handed and exploits the maritime catastrophe in the Bay to gain a bonus crewman. No swimmer, Van Weyden is held captive as the vessel speeds under sail from the Golden Gate to the Pacific and the seal-hunting grounds in the Bering Sea.

As the plot unfolds, the narrator, who has been mocked as "Sissy" Van Weyden from boyhood and is cushioned by inherited wealth, toughens up to transform himself into a muscled, calloused, and knowledgeable mariner known as "Hump." The written and spoken word are already his métier, and readers now followed his hands-on struggle as a manual laborer who rises from the galley where he peels potatoes to the bridge from which, late in the story, he issues orders as an officer ("I was 'Mr. Van Weyden' fore and aft, and it was only unofficially that Wolf Larsen himself addressed me as 'Hump'"). Readers also follow the account of Van Weyden's effort to secure his place amid a crew of rogues roiling with "feuds, quarrels, and grudges." He provides medical aid for their injuries even as he verbally spars in Nietzschean philosophic terms with the canny and cunning Wolf Larsen.[37]

London's readers were rewarded with high-stakes adventures ranging from furious sea storms to the shocking onboard arrival of a ladylike literary woman, Maud Brewster. Her presence inevitably creates a triangle involving predation and protection, chivalry and savagery centered on Hump and Wolf Larsen. *The Sea-Wolf* gave its audience oceanic adventure, romance, and an exotic geography in the era when leisure reading included *National Geographic* as well as current fiction.

Wolf Larsen, however, towers over all else in the novel as an oversize, cinematic, terrifying industrial-era titan. He is not the awesome and benevolent "big man" as conjured by the public relations counsel, but a self-centered brain and body. Jack's notes on *The Sea Wolf* directly linked his "superman,"

Larsen, to the financial-industrial titans signified in the name "Rockefeller." He is an "anti-social" figure of "hostile aloofness" and "an irritant on the social body." Finally, "he cannot be successful."[38]

Like the Gilded Age tycoons, Larsen lacks formal education, but he has invented an ingenious navigation instrument that he plans to patent "to make money from it, to revel in piggishness . . . while other men do the work." London feints and thrusts in his physical description of a commander who is "probably five feet ten inches . . . of massive build, with broad shoulders and deep chest" that signals one trait above all: "strength." Images of "wild" and "primitive" animals follow, from the "enlarged gorilla" to the writhing "snake." Larsen, writes London, represents one "extreme end of the ladder of evolution . . . the culmination of all savagery," like "some great tiger, a beast of prowess and prey." Readers see Van Weyden—or is it London?—struggle to convey the sheer power of the man ("What I am striving to express is this strength . . . as a thing apart from his physical semblance"). "This man is a monster," Van Weyden says to Maud. "He is without conscience. Nothing is sacred to him, nothing is too terrible for him to do."[39]

Larsen is "a man so primitive that . . . he was not immoral, but merely unmoral." For the crew—that is, the workforce—the *Ghost* is "a hell-ship" that affords not one "moment's rest or peace." A failed mutiny—a labor strike—prompts no humane reform of the brutal conditions but instead incites Larsen "to making life unlivable" for all. Like Milton's Satan in *Paradise Lost*, he proudly reigns in the hell of his own creation and represents "heartlessly indifferent" power in the age of "industrial organization."[40]

Students of Jack London's sources have pointed out that Wolf Larsen was based on an actual mariner, Alexander McLean, a legendary and notorious Canadian seal-hunting schooner captain who skirted the law in a late nineteenth-century career in the North and South Pacific. London confirmed that he "never personally met Alexander McLean" but that his "wild exploits" opened opportunities for much "imaginative development."[41]

That development amplified the topic of ruthless, monopolistic power in a world of capitalist enterprise. Van Weyden insists to Maud Brewster that his only role is "the role of the weak" and that the two of them must "remain silent and suffer ignominy" in order to stay alive under the tyrannical Larsen. Craftiness and dissembling are their best strategy, he explains, since they "have not the strength with which to fight the man." He adds, "The battle is not always to the strong."[42]

The story proves otherwise—and broadcasts a tutorial to its audience. Van Weyden and Maud are indeed sly in their determination to survive. Both, nonetheless, face the hard fact that their survival depends on neutralizing the tyrant. Their predictable love story intensifies with episodes in which Maud, like her lover, gains skills that demand physical courage (as when the couple escapes in a small boat, fights stormy seas, and lands on a North Pacific island where they become Robinson Crusoe–like survivalists). As Van Weyden puts it, "There was something heroic about this gently bred woman enduring our terrible hardship and with her pittance of strength bending to the tasks of a peasant woman." In Maud, Jack London was profiling the necessary modern New Woman, a figure to supplant the genteel and sentimental flower of nineteenth-century feminine true womanhood. Maud, moreover, supersedes the prim and proper Miss Grundy, the Victorian personification of pious respectability. Maud, in short, is the woman the modern moment of crisis demands.[43]

Reverse the gender, and the same is true of the gently bred Humphrey Van Weyden, who has earned his identity as hands-on Hump. Many twists and turns of plot sustain the story, at the end of which Larsen is imprisoned by Hump and Maud on the *Ghost*. At last physically frail, weakened by strokes, blind and tottering, Larsen is yet bent on sabotage and havoc. He is unrepentant and is spared execution only because his captors are repulsed by the notion of committing murder. They bury his shrouded body at sea, and Maud whispers a Miltonic farewell to "Lucifer, proud spirit," though Hump understands that the "fierce intelligence" of Wolf Larsen "burned on in silence and darkness."[44]

The Sea-Wolf rewarded readers who were eager solely for a tale of adventure, but London thrust a stark social challenge to those who were prepared to grasp its deeper significance. The Wolf Larsens of the world constitute "heartlessly indifferent" power in the age of "industrial organization." For the sake of humanity, their regime must be toppled. Who can stop these Captains of Industry? Not those roiling in society's "pit." Represented by the motley crew of the *Ghost*, this population exists in "a state of unstable equilibrium" where their dark passions "flame like prairie grass." Conspicuous by their absence are the robust and stable crewmen of the working class, who might be shown to combat Larsen in alliance with Van Weyden (Hump). They appear in other Jack London stories and novels, notably "The Dream of Debs," "South of the Slot," and *The Valley of the Moon*. Except for one lone stalwart (and doomed) figure named Johnson, readers of *The Sea-Wolf* must look elsewhere in London's fiction and essays to find strong and brainy working-class figures, for in *The Sea-Wolf* London cleared the decks and fo'c'sle of such crewmen. Those decks, instead, are the stage on which London presents the potential-in-action for the bourgeoisie—that is, for his middle- and upper-middle-class readers to become major players in the country's necessary revolution. In combat against the captain, it is they, and they alone, who occupy the main stage in this novel.[45]

Nationally, then, it is the likes of Humphrey (Hump) Van Weyden and Maud Brewster who are charged with constraining and neutralizing the industrial-era tyrants. As *The Sea Wolf* makes clear, it is they who have the intellectual heft, the social savvy, the cultural capital, and the willpower that can and must be summoned for this monumental challenge. Not, of course, in their former lives of cosseted gentility, for they must undergo a rite of passage in life's rough-and-tumble.

The bourgeoisie must thus stiffen their spines and confront the incorrigible, intractable "Captains of Industry." Doing so, the bourgeoisie can be saved from themselves. This was Jack London's message even before he sailed the North and South Pacific on the *Snark* and began the homeward journey to California, penning new novels and stories on improvised desktops under Hawaiian shade trees, on the decks of the *Snark* and of steamships, in hotels and passenger train car compartments and, as a houseguest, in the makeshift private studios that his hosts arranged from their furnishings. These were the manuscripts that Charmian typed (and sometimes edited) as Jack produced them, fueled by his Imperiale cigarettes and his ample supply of ink pencils, all a flurry of high-volume publications reaching the public as Jack relished life at home once again in Glen Ellen and the ranch.

And then, much to his shock and dismay, the reviews of *Martin Eden* rolled in to hammer him in a barrage of blows.

He didn't see it coming. Determined to settle old scores, Jack neglected to woo his audience as he worked—toiled—on his autobiographical novel. In *The Sea-Wolf*, Humphrey (Hump) Van Weyden and Maud Brewster represent the possibility that bourgeois men and women of America might bend their efforts for vitally needed social change. *The Sea-Wolf* was their instruction manual. *Martin Eden*, on the contrary, was the textbook of their pathologies.

Class-based critiques were nothing new in American culture at the turn of the twentieth century, but they usually were top-down, the educated elite commenting on the foibles and failings of those in the lower realms of society. In the mid-1880s, the prominent Anglo-Saxon Protestant minister Josiah Strong had warned that the typical immigrant "peasant" imperiled the US future by "debauching popular morals." In the 1890s, a Princeton University professor of sociology, Walter Wyckoff, posed as a laborer to travel the country and report on the lives of the working class in two volumes titled *The Workers* (1899, 1901). At about the same time, Josiah Flynt, the university-educated nephew of the Temperance leader Frances Willard, published *The Powers That Prey* (1900), a study of the criminal underworld based on Flynt's underground fieldwork and his alias as "Cigarette." When novelist Edith Wharton published *The House of Mirth* (1905), the social critique went lateral, for Edith Newbold Jones Wharton was of the elite lineage that her novel exposed as superficial, cruel, and cunning. Wharton operated, it was understood, from the entitlement of her class.[46]

In *Martin Eden*, Jack turned the tables on the privileged. He had, of course, already investigated those who were sunk irretrievably in the most wretched slum of England's capital city. There he went underground in 1902 as a participant-observer who posed as a luckless sailor in London's East End and reported on its occupants in terms captured in his title: *The People of the Abyss* (1903). At that time, his challenge was to make the lives of the "abyss" meaningful to readers for whom slum conditions were utterly alien. Well-fed and healthy, his readers enjoyed "white beds and airy rooms," and London pulled out all stops to make a morally indelible impression, lest readers merely browse his pages for amusement and neglect the obligations of social action. That book was set in England, its focus three thousand miles from American shores.[47]

In *Martin Eden*, it was time to bring the story home. He would not approach it from his status as Mr. Jack London, the rich and successful man of property, the owner of a custom-built yacht and member of the elite Bohemian Club of San Francisco. On the contrary, his point of view hearkened to the poor working-class Jack London, a fellow with a working-class outlook. From that vantage point, he was prepared to report on those who lived in the upper reaches of society, the affluent class that was a subject worthy of critical scrutiny in its own right. In this autobiographical novel, the bourgeoisie would get the treatment he felt they deserved. This time, the critique was bottom-up.

Drafting chapters of the novel in the remote South Seas, anguished by the painful memories they stirred, Jack struck out against the class that routinely offered him hospitality in their homes and honored him as a guest in their clubs. Once on the attack, his restraint fell away. "Have just finished a 145,000 [word] novel that is an attack on the bourgeoisie & all that the bourgeoisie stands for," he told his friend Cloudesley Johns in a letter from Tahiti in February 1908, adding that "it will not make me any friends." Such an understatement, but still he continued to bruise and batter scene by scene.

Gloves off, he mounted a bare-knuckle attack that continued to the ending, an ending that the readers and reviewers uniformly detested, fixing their hostile attention on the conclusion in order to deflect the cultural, political, and economic blows that he struck against them.[48]

Jack opened *Martin Eden* in a well-furnished home that could belong to Humphrey Van Weyden, to Maud Brewster, to the novel's affluent readers, or, for that matter, to the newly wealthy Jack London of the twentieth century. The opening, however, echoes Jack's days as a young merchant marine sailor when, as Martin Eden, he arrives for dinner at the Oakland home of the upper-middle-class Morse family. Martin's invitation is a thank-you for shielding the young gentleman Arthur Morse from an attack by toughs on a ferryboat earlier in the day. Arthur has forewarned his mother, his brother Norman, and his college-age sister Ruth that he has invited to dinner a man of the waterfront, "a wild man."[49]

Though Martin has traveled the world, his most foreign port of call is indisputably the Morse home. Its grand piano, its objets d'art, and its table piled with books all terrify him, as does the dining table, set with a "frightening array of knives and forks" that "bristled with unknown perils," a stark contrast to his shipboard meals downed with "battered iron spoons," "sheath-knives and fingers." Sweating and anxious in an ill-fitting suit and stiff shirt collar that chafes his suntanned neck, Martin is suddenly awash in "shame that he should walk so uncouthly." The Morse code of conduct baffles him, and the space itself is agony for the broad-shouldered sailor with gangly arms, a "rolling gait," and eyes "such as wild animals betray when they fear the trap."[50]

The family takes no interest in Martin Eden's store of knowledge, but readers quickly infer his sensitivity and keen powers of observation. He knows of "stokeholes and forecastles, camps and beaches, jails and boozing-kens, fever-hospitals and slum streets." Onshore in Hawaii and the South Pacific, he has seen a "volcano crater . . . silhouetted against the stars" on "sensuous nights" when he lay on "a coral beach where the coconuts grew down the mellow-sounding surf." He remembers the hula dancers keeping rhythm to the "love-calls" of singers "who chanted to tinkling *ukuleles* and rumbling tomtoms." He knows that the kanaka or native Hawaiian word for a finish or completion is *p-a-u*, though when he says the word aloud, the Morse family mistakes it for the barbaric outburst "Pow!"[51]

Martin also knows about life in the US working class, his class and Jack London's too. Its household is redolent of "stale vegetables" and acrid "soapsuds," its breakfast staple a bowl of "half-cooked oatmeal mush," its interior

23. The sailor and workingman Jack London resembles his fictional but autobiographical Martin Eden. (Henry E. Huntington Library, San Marino, California)

walls fouled with water stains from leaks in the roof. He is an expert on the term that so often signifies the workers themselves—*hands*. His late mother's calloused "hard" palms "as she lay in her coffin" are a burning memory, as is his father, who "worked to the last fading gasp, the horned growth on his hands . . . half an inch thick when he died."[52]

The tradition continues. His sister Marian's work with sharp knives in a cannery left her formerly "pretty hands. . . . all scarred," and "the tips of her two fingers had been left in the cutting machine at the paper-box factory the preceding winter." His other sister, Gertrude, hugs him with hands that are either hardened from endless housework or "swollen and red like boiled beef" from laundering with caustic soaps. He remembers when, as a girl, "she would dance . . . all night, after a hard day's work . . . and think nothing of leaving the dance to do another day's hard work" at the laundry. All that was before "the weakness of chronic overwork" made her a drudge.[53]

These thoughts swirl in the gracious Morse ménage, with its "atmosphere of beauty and repose"—and the sight of hands that so deftly manipulate the sterling flatware at the dinner table. They astonish him, for Ruth's are "soft," as are her mother's and her brothers' too. The softness is a revelation. Martin realizes that he is suddenly among "the aristocracy of the people who did not labor."[54]

Thus far in *Martin Eden*, the readers of 1909 found the values of their world to be upheld and intact. The overwhelmed young Martin is to be pitied, his gauche manners duly noted but tolerated, his "cheap" wrinkled coat a sad commentary, his grammar as bemusing as the dialect in the stories of Bret Harte or Mark Twain ("I guess your fam'ly ain't hankerin' to see me"). Martin is also linked to the readers by his attractive temperament, for the young sailor is *of* his class but not fully *in* it. A seaman whose own hands are calloused, he is no lout; he is "keenly sensitive," sharply observant, and "irresistibly. . . . responsive to beauty." He has "discipline" and "the gift of sympathy," meaning the gift of "understanding." He is drawn to a volume of Swinburne in the Morse parlor and intrigued by a seascape in oils. His gaze expresses the wistful "yearning" of a starving man desperate for food.[55]

At the first sight of Ruth Morse, he is thunderstruck—as Jack London himself had been entranced by Mabel Applegarth, the genteel older sister of his friend Ted (Edward), whom he'd met at the Oakland library in 1898 and who introduced Jack to his family. (The Applegarths, in turn, became the prototypes for the Morses.) In Ruth, Martin measures the incalculable distance from his working-class squalor to the aerie of the bourgeois high "caste." The dazzled young sailor beholds a "pale, ethereal creature," a "spirit, a divinity, a goddess" whose "sublimated beauty was not of the earth." Learning that she attends the university, he feels "a million miles" of separation from his world to hers but vows somehow to make her class his own. She is "a world to conquer," and he exalts her in a capitalized pronoun: Her.[56]

For her part, Ruth is erotically drawn to Martin, whose bronzed neck and muscles arouse her despite the warnings of "peril" and "wrong" telegraphed by her genteel upbringing. His "intense virility" surges, however, and she soon becomes his Pygmalion, tutoring Martin in grammar, pronunciation, and vocabulary, and introducing him to the "critical phrases and thought-processes that were foreign to his mind." Her parents agree, for the time being, to tolerate their daughter's attachment to the sailor as "protégé and friend," all a prelude to what they understand to be a proper courtship in due course with a young man of their own class. In good faith, Martin stops drinking, withdraws from working-class outings, attends to personal grooming, and seeks an etiquette guidebook in the public library. For the sake of a future with Ruth, he ponders his life's work: soon he will seek to become professional writer.[57]

First, however, he must somehow educate himself in Western thought from the very rudiments to the level of modern sophistication. His intellect awakened, he haunts the public library, his reading voracious but spotty. A library shelf holds "Karl Marx, Ricardo, Adam Smith, and Mill," but offers no clue on their currency or obsolescence. "He was bewildered, and yet he wanted to know." The synthesizing philosophy of Herbert Spencer ultimately becomes key to the ordering of his thought, and politically he will ally with the socialists while proclaiming himself an individualist. But the arts prove to be his forte. Like music, poetry stirs him profoundly and points to his eventual commitment to write. Through it all, he is Ruth Morse's pilgrim, she his saintly shrine.[58]

That first Morse evening dinner, however, signals the critique that Jack London will level at the bourgeoisie, for he shows readers a hairline crack that the infatuated and terrified Martin cannot possibly glimpse. While he listens raptly to Ruth's recital of university lecture hall doctrines on aesthetics, her tone of voice signals trouble ahead for Martin, who fails to notice that Ruth's voice is "primly firm and dogmatic." Committing himself in due course to a career as a writer, Martin shows her his poems and stories and seeks her educated opinion, but the prim Ruth can see only the mechanics of "sentence-structure and semicolons," censuring as "degrading" and "nasty" any content that violates the Morse standards of gentility.[59]

London eviscerated bourgeois America in three stories played in counterpoint in *Martin Eden*. The template of the Horatio Alger formula hovers over them all. Martin's career is one such, and another is familial, for during his home port stays, sailor Martin is a paying boarder in the household of his sister Gertrude and her working-class striver husband. Brother-in-law Bernard Higginbotham is a penny-pinching grocer who is ambitious to ascend into the middle class by dint of miserly habits that pass for discipline at work and home. Dissembling in his grocery during the day, he is "himself" in the evenings, attacking Martin as a sloth and wastrel and exercising the marital right to be his wife's brutal taskmaster. The exhausted Gertrude measures the human folly of life driven by unstinting miserliness in the name of social betterment.[60]

The upper-middle-class Morse family, however, bears the brunt of London's main attack. They are typical, London insists, not unique. By the 1900s the Oakland and Berkeley hills were indeed stippled with such families, as were the streetcar suburbs and the mosaics of city townhouse blocks throughout the United States. Such cities and counties celebrated their progress and prosperity in promotional publications like the one boasting of "delightful roads," electric and rail lines, "diversified manufacturing," and the "happy homes of thousands" throughout Oakland and greater Alameda County. "Here is everything that modern power, wealth, culture, refinement, and ingenuity can give," exalted one such promotional gazette of 1900, breathlessly adding a "bright, active business and commercial life, splendid business organizations, social and industrial, fraternal and religious societies." That year saw the publication of a colorful bird's-eye view map of the city. Its panoramic grid of Oakland's homes, commercial buildings, and outlying green fields was bordered with symbols of modernity—bank buildings, churches, the county courthouse and hall of records. The pictorial border featured factories whose smokestacks billowed the proof of industrial prosperity, and a real estate agency promising "Homes Built on Easy Terms," together with architected mansions of distinguished citizens. The mills of promotion boosted this self-proclaimed Paris of the Pacific mightily and incessantly to produce an ideal stereopticon view of the Morse family's larger world.[61]

Jack London lunged at all this with a dissecting blade. What he found at the core of the Morse home was meant to apply to their real-life counterparts nationwide. Ruth typifies this class—"conservative by nature and upbringing, and already crystallized into the cranny of life where she had been born and formed." In short order Martin surpasses her intellectually (and by extension her brothers and parents too), for he grasps political realities and enjoys artistic revelations that are "beyond her plumb-line."[62]

No surprise, then, that Ruth's "proprietary" goal is to "rethumb the clay of [Martin] into a likeness of her father's image." The "remodeling" of his life becomes her "passion." Prodding him toward financial success and social respectability, she glorifies a Morse family friend, a Mr. Charles Butler who fits firmly in the Horatio Alger mold. "He had comparatively no advantages at first," Ruth begins, laying siege to Martin with accounts of Butler's self-denial, the scrimping and saving that have crowned him with a law and business career that nets "at least thirty thousand" dollars per annum. "He was honest, and faithful, and industrious, and economical," gushes Ruth. "He wanted a career, not a livelihood." She confirms Martin's surmise that Butler leads a joyless existence and suffers from a gastric disorder traceable to the regimen of extreme self-denial and overwork. Nonetheless, Butler is her gold standard for Martin's future. ("Mr. Butler is a noted public speaker," she says. "Why, you would make a good public speaker. You can go far—if you want to.") Mr. Butler, the novel tells us, is but a well-heeled version of Martin's skinflint grocer brother-in-law.[63]

As *Martin Eden* progresses, Martin befriends a socialist poet and his bohemian circle of questing intellectuals who plunge into free-wheeling debate. In his own knockabout travels Jack had met such "keen-flashing intellects" in the working class and found them also in individuals who were ousted from the clergy and the academy for nonconventional thinking. The figure of poet Brissendon is thought to be modeled on the poet George Sterling, and the confreres include the itinerant socialist Frank Strawn-Hamilton and the free-thinking George Speed. To Jack, these were the "great souls who exalted flesh and spirit over dollars and cents." They are not to be found among the college- and university-educated bankers, professors, lawyers, judges, and businessmen who socialize at the Morse home, where Martin hears only idle chatter and pompous platitudes. Their thoughts, like Ruth's, are but recycled stale knowledge and settled opinion that reinforces the arrangements beneficial to their class. Martin has "discovered that his brain went beyond Ruth's, just as it went beyond the brains of her brothers, or the brain of her father . . . in spite of every advantage of university training." Declaring himself to be "an individualist," young Martin arraigns Mr. Morse and his ilk for their complicity with business corporations which are "the masters of society" and which, in turn, define the Morse circle as mere vassals of their corporate masters. Martin says bluntly to Ruth, "You worship at the shrine of the established," by which point discomfited readers can protest but hardly disagree.[64]

"Why weren't you born with an income?" Ruth snaps in a revealing moment. The novel proceeds to test the bourgeois temperament in personal terms—and shows it to be blind, deaf, and spiritually calloused. Predictably, Martin's journeyman work in poetry and fiction carries no weight with the Morse parents or with Ruth, even when he rents a drafty garret room, lives a spartan existence, and labors to the point of exhaustion at his writing. Lying sick in bed, he gratefully spoons the hot soup his hard-working landlady sends upstairs, while Ruth's bedside visit is memorable for her advice that he give up cigarettes.[65]

Deep in *Martin Eden*, London embedded the scene that posed a clear class-based test of its bourgeois readers, a sort of "Whose side are you on?" Ruth, once again, is to be the conscience of her class on learning that her swain has endured terrible hardship while she and her family, like their actual US counterparts, spent the summer at a vacation resort. The Morses have escaped to Lake Tahoe in the cool Sierras. Martin, too, goes to the mountains. Having given up "sailorizing" and flat broke, he takes the first available job that can pay his bills. Suspending writing, he hires out for the summer as a laundryman at a resort hotel.

Martin's experience was pure autobiography for Jack London, for his laundry work in the Belmont Academy in 1897 remained so vivid that he recorded it first in *Martin Eden* and again in his memoir *John Barleycorn* (1913). London's longtime friend Frank Atherton once visited the laundry and found Jack and his partner at work "amidst dense clouds of steam, plying every muscle to keep with the 'set-speed' of the machinery." Atherton was horrified: "Verily they had ceased to be human beings; they had become robots." He declared that Jack "had virtually hired out as a slave."[66]

The laundry scenes in *Martin Eden* forced readers to see the reality behind their "great heaps of soiled clothes" that magically become freshly laundered bed linens and towels; pressed and folded underclothing; starched collars, cuffs, and shirts. In the laundry Martin and his boss, Joe Dawson, toil for fourteen-hour stretches with mangles, flatirons, caustic chemicals, and vats of scorching-hot starch, while "out on the broad verandas of the hotel, men and women, in cool white, sipped iced drinks and kept their circulation down." The laundry air is stifling. "The huge stove roared red hot and white hot, while the irons . . . sent up clouds of steam." In the "hot California night," the laundry, "with its red-hot ironing stove, was a furnace." For Martin, the worst of it is the utter fatigue. The books that he has brought to the hotel workers' quarters mock his efforts to read. "All you can do is work an' sleep"—and in off-hours find a saloon and drink until the brain crawls with "the maggots of intoxication."[67]

"Some day I will write it up," Martin vows to Ruth when they reunite at summer's end. True to her bourgeois self, she shows a thick hide beneath her creamy complexion, oblivious when Martin says the laundry toil turned him into a "beast." Horrified that liquor has touched his lips, she is impervious to the desperation that drove him to the shot glass.[68]

Readers may feel that Martin Eden's love for Ruth Morse outlives plausibility, that Jack London sustained his protagonist's devotion long after he exposed her to Martin as a prime specimen of her class at its worst. Moreover, the closing sequences of the novel are dense with events—and a conclusion that gave indignant reviewers and readers their perfect target for a counterattack on Jack London. Late in the story, Ruth breaks off her engagement to Martin when a scurrilous newspaper article depicts him as a sworn enemy of society—this just before his writing is published, bringing him great public acclaim and financial success as his formerly rejected manuscripts are suddenly prized and bought up by publishers. The celebrated author is deluged with dinner invitations, leaving him to ask where were the eager hosts when, penniless and hungry, he needed dinners. Liberally he now dispenses the new royalty money to his deserving landlady, to his laundry boss Joe, even to his grocer brother-in-law on the condition that his sister be freed from drudgery. Ruth reappears to try wooing the now-successful Martin back, but he rebuffs her.

Above all, Martin Eden, like Jack London, feels the severe alienation of a displaced person, no longer "Mart" Eden of the working class, much less a clamant to the ranks of the despised upper middle class. Deciding on impulse to relocate to Tahiti, Martin boards a ship but slips out of his porthole to swim deliberately into the depths of the sea. This final scene is one of the most powerful in all Jack London's writing, evocative of his two near-drownings in Japan and in the San Francisco Bay waters of Benicia. Blind to the upcoming firestorm of critical reaction to the novel, London gave his critics their ammunition in Martin's suicide. They seized it. *Martin Eden* was roundly attacked for its hero's self-murder. From the autumn of 1909 and well into 1910 Jack repeatedly argued in print and in letters that Martin's death was caused by his failure, as an individualist, to ally with his fellow human beings in a socialist cause. In effect, said London, Martin Eden's willful isolation killed him. "He was an individualist" and "unaware of the needs of others," London wrote repeatedly, insisting that once his protagonist's illusions vanished, "there was nothing to live for," and "ergo, he died." Neither the critics nor his correspondents were persuaded. As he'd predicted, *Martin Eden* won him no friends. In high dudgeon they vented their fury, focusing on the suicide and keeping silent on Jack London's day of reckoning on them, the bourgeoisie. Ever defiant, London fought back immediately in a volume titled *Revolution* (1910), a cluster of his boldest, most pugnacious political stories and essays, including a reprint of "What Life Means to Me," the quintessential plot of *Martin Eden*.[69]

Jack London had another score to settle, not with the middle classes per se but with his own conscience. To all appearances he was a fearless public intellectual, skewering the upper middle class and flaying the captains of industry. He delivered his lecture "Revolution" on numerous public stages, and he even reproved the president of the United States in print when Theodore Roosevelt accused him of "animal faking" in his fiction.[70]

Yet for years he had stayed uncharacteristically silent about the lecture in which David Starr Jordan put his scientific expertise on the wrong side of the industrial system, absolving its financiers and business leaders from all their wrongs. Jack perhaps shied away from direct confrontation with a university president who doubled as his mentor. He had countered Jordan in a blitz of fiction and in an essay, "The Human Drift," that refuted the Stanford president's theory that war depleted genetically superior men. Years would pass, however, before London came forward to take the stance that he knew to be true to industrial social conditions and to his deepest convictions.

The memory of the Stanford president's lecture called "The Man Who Was Left Behind," so long dormant, came alive when Jack agreed to write the introduction to Upton Sinclair's *Cry for Justice* (1915), a compilation of worldwide prose and poetry of social protest from ancient times to the present. Inside its prepublication pages, Jack found a multitude of short selections (including passages from his own *People of the Abyss*).

The poem that opened the book, however, surely triggered the flashback of the evening of April 1899 when Jordan sidestepped the social crisis and betrayed the public trust. *The Cry for Justice* opened with a poem that Jack knew to be as fresh and true as it was in the first moment of its publication. In Jack's words, this gateway poem trumpeted "the needs of groping, yearning humans who seek to discern truth and justice amid the dazzle and murk of the thought-chaos of the present-day world." The sentiments it expressed stood for a world, he said, of human "service" that "can be fashioned . . .

by the humans who inhabit it." The opening text in Sinclair's book was, of course, "The Man with the Hoe."[71]

Just three months before his death, Jack London was finally to declare to a World Peace Foundation director, John L. Jenkins, that he had been a lifelong "intellectual opponent of David Starr Jordan." Charmian recalled Jack implying as much three years earlier in 1913 when he and his Sonoma neighbors were embroiled in a lawsuit over water rights. Jack reportedly testified that he thought it "nothing" to face off against professors, including David Starr Jordan.[72]

London's path had split from Jordan's in yet another profound way. In childhood both were farm boys in fields cultivated one continent apart from each other, from Jack's California to Jordan's upstate New York. Both left the farm, Jordan never again to return to agriculture once the acreage of the Leland Stanford estate was reworked in Spanish mission architecture for the new university. To Jack London, however, the farm beckoned and brought new challenges. "Quite the farmer just now," he quipped to his admiring literary critic Fannie K. Hamilton in December 1909. Lightheartedly he joked that no sooner was he back home from the *Snark* adventure than his colts had kicked and thrown him. His Beauty Ranch, however, was no joking matter. As Jack knew, the United States was deep into a severe farm crisis. Feeding a growing population was proving to be a gravely worrisome proposition. Leading agricultural experts were concerned. The food supply for the twentieth century was at risk. Jack London had to be involved. To make a bold statement as a farmer-rancher, he needed serious acreage and the funds to purchase ample land for crops and livestock. He needed cash, and fast. Once again he had a fight on his hands.[73]

5 The Rancher, the Wheat King, and "Farmers of Forty Centuries"

I am that sort of farmer, who, after delving in all the books to satisfy his quest for economic wisdom, returns to the soil as the source and foundation of all economics.
—Jack London to Gaddis Smith, October 31, 1916

May 1910 found Jack London seriously short of cash. The *Snark* was up for sale in Sydney but not yet sold, and suddenly Jack needed money, and fast. The old Kohler & Frohling Ranch that abutted his property in Glen Ellen was on the market. If he bought it, his Beauty Ranch would expand to nearly one thousand acres. He appealed to his New York editor for a quick cash advance. "Dear Mr. Brett," he explained, "I am buying seven hundred acres of land . . . giving me miles of frontage on three big creeks, and some magnificent mountain land, to say nothing of timber." Reminding his editor that he always "delivered the goods," Jack worked up to a blazing one-sentence paragraph: "What I need and must have in my hands by June 1, is five thousand ($5,000) Dollars." Thirteen days later, on May 18, having heard nothing from Gotham, he fired off a telegram: "I SIMPLY MUST HAVE THAT FIVE THOUSAND. PLEASE TELEGRAPH ME."[1]

Editor George Brett's check for the full amount arrived a week later as an advance on novels and collections of stories for Macmillan. By June, Jack London's commitment to farming on a grander scale was legalized in the new purchase of seven hundred acres that nearly quintupled the size of his ranch. Surveying its acreage and mindful of his predecessors, Jack asked himself whether he could succeed where others had flatly failed. The question was deadly serious, for heroic measures were required to meet London's ambitious goal—that Beauty Ranch become a model of sustainable farming on a sound business basis. If he succeeded, the effort would be recorded in his fiction and educate the US public on the urgent need for reform in America's farm fields, pastures, and barns. Success, that is, would mean popular new novels to awaken the American public to the present national crisis of agriculture—agriculture so ruinous that it threatened the future food supply of the nation. The success of a sustainable Beauty Ranch, at the same time, would show the progressive way forward in explicit detail. London's challenge became his vow: "By using my head, my judgment, and all the latest knowledge in the matter of farming, I have pledged myself, my manhood, my fortune, my books and all I possess to this undertaking."[2]

Ranching overtook Jack London. It began innocently with a search for a rural retreat. Purchasing the irregular diamond-shaped Hill Ranch in Glen Ellen in July 1905, Jack had expected a "sweet domain" of "Californian timber and shrubbery" in Sonoma, the Native American name for the Valley of the Moon. An original seven-thousand-dollar cash transaction had given the famous author 130 acres and only coincidentally, as he then believed, the farm's "several horses, a couple of cows, mountain wagon, harnesses, plows, harrows," together with "colts, calves, pigeons, chickens, turkeys . . . hay."[3]

At first Jack resisted farming the land. In the midst of a divorce from his first wife, Bess, he was considering remarriage to Charmian Kittredge and simply wanted "a quiet place in the country to write and loaf in." "The only cleared ground on the [Hill Ranch] place," Jack explained to pal Cloudesley Johns, "will be used for a couple of riding horses, a couple of farm horses, & a couple of cows." The sale of leftover hay would be "like finding money." Rest and relaxation were the keynotes. His statement to Cloudesley was emphatic: "I'm not going ranching."[4]

But events conspired to propel London in a radically different direction. When he took the deed to the 130-acre Hill Ranch on July 6, 1905, Jack became the owner of a working farm. As such, he became heir to a monumental legislative act of the US Congress. The Morrill Land Grant Act of 1862 provided federal aid to public colleges of "agricultural and mechanic arts," each state receiving thirty thousand acres of public land per representative and senator. The so-called "land-grant colleges" soon became centers of the new scientific agriculture. In 1868, the Board of Regents of the University of California had understood its first duty to be the establishment of the College of Agriculture on the very Berkeley campus where Jack London studied for a term in 1896, when he was twenty. The Berkeley campus was the first land-grant college in California and the site of the first state-run Agricultural Experiment Station.[5]

For Jack, Berkeley was memorable for studies in social science and the humanities. Besides, farming stirred his grim boyhood memories of the "monotony of life and labor" in the "primitive countryside," with its "sweating plowman," "plodding horses," and immigrant foreign "country peasants." When he fled the farm furrow for the fo'c'sle on the seal-hunting schooner *Sophia Sutherland* in 1893, Jack believed he'd forever swapped the "monotonous" farm for the "wild life in the wild man-world" with "chesty, man-grown men."[6]

His sea bag nonetheless held two novels that tugged like harness lines to rein him toward farm life. Translated into English and widely circulated and well respected in America, Gustave Flaubert's *Madame Bovary* (1857) and Lyof (Leo) Tolstoy's *Anna Karenina* (1877) gave US readers vicarious visits to France and Russia even as they offered gripping accounts of jealousy, frustration, family tensions, money troubles—and the throbbing carnal lusts of the title characters, Emma Bovary and Anna Karenina.[7]

But what surely caught London off guard in both novels was the very world he sought to escape: agriculture. True, a landmark novel of his boyhood, *Signa*, lavishly described the rural hill country of Italy, the "natural richness of the soil," the "priceless . . . mountain-fed brook," and the slope that "glowed golden with corn" and produced the finest olives "on the whole mountain-side." *Madame Bovary*, however, mirrored the monotony of farm life as Jack knew it. Reading by "dim light of the swinging sea-lamp" amid the "sea-boots, oilskins," and other gear of crewmen in his bunk in the "sour and musty" fo'c'sle, London found a relentlessly dreary inventory of stables, cart horses, plows, and granaries, plus an oration on the glories of agriculture—all depressing to the romantically ambitious Emma Bovary and surely reinforcing young London's decision to flee the soil for the sea.[8]

If he expected *Anna Karenina* to provide an escape from livestock and farm fields, however, Jack was in for a surprise, for agriculture was as sanctified in Tolstoy's novel as it was maligned in Flaubert. A major character in the novel, Konstantin Levin (a stand-in for Tolstoy), is a large landowner whose progressive farming techniques are highlighted throughout. With the birthright of an aristocrat, the university-educated Levin is by no means the rustic "savage" of the Muscovites' coy censure. When Levin says, "I live in the country as I always have, and busy myself with farming," readers understand his life of commitment to social progress and scientific, progressive agriculture. A sportsman who enjoys hunting game birds, he also studies rural economics ("agronomic science"). His passions include cattle pens, a farm pond, manure-based fertilizer, and trees to shelter livestock from the wind. And Tolstoy underscores his experimental ingenuity in designing a special drying room for wheat—all the while readers are alternately caught up in the intrigues and jealousies of the family and friends of Anna Karenina and given bird's-eye views of a Moscow evening dress ball, current fashions, teas, formal dinners, travels by train, and a horse race that is a highlight of the social season, not to mention the overwrought affair of the title character and her lover.[9]

Whatever Jack London's reaction as he read *Anna Karenina* on the *Sophia Sutherland* voyage, he could not take leave of Levin and his farm, for Tolstoy continually amplified his story. By the concluding pages Levin enjoys family life and the rewards of his "horses with their neatly cropped tails," his "heavy-fleeced sheep," and the "Holland cow" that is central to his selective breeding program. Levin personally inspects every animal in his barnyard, cares deeply for forest management, and saddles up to ride to his arable acreage to plan each new season's field crops, which include clover, oats, corn, wheat and potatoes—all cultivated "without exhausting the soil."[10]

What did Jack London make of all this? No journal, letter, or diary records his impressions, though hindsight offers clues. In the pages of *Anna Karenina*, Jack London found a fictionalized Russian version of the American "Big Man" of his own ambition. Levin was the surrogate for a world-famous Russian count whose major novel was focused on farming. Not just any farming, but advanced techniques that nourished and replenished the soil and fed a population year-round in a punishing climate.

London also faced the galactic contrast between Levin's acreage and the leased fields that little Johnny (Jack) London's stepfather tilled with help from him and stepsister Eliza. The Londons struggled and toiled. Tolstoy's Levin, on the contrary, enjoys the services of a housekeeper, a farm manager, a cowboy, milkmaids, three carpenters responsible for equipment maintenance and repair, and a cadre of laborers to sow and scythe the crops. A whole new system of agriculture was suddenly opened to view.

The first hint of Tolstoy's legacy in Beauty Ranch is Jack's comment to Cloudesley, in 1905, that he planned to find a "hired man" to care for the horses and also, London said, to milk the cows and tend the vegetable plots and thus spare him and Charmian the dairy and greengrocer bills.[11]

Jack London did nothing by halves. Once farming gripped him, he grew determined to own the "distant hills" and to secure an ample supply of water. Steadily he bought adjacent ranches: the La Motte in 1908; the Caroline Kohler and Fish ranches in 1909; and then the seven-hundred-acre Kohler & Frohling, followed by the K&F Winery buildings in 1911 and the Freund Ranch in 1913. Neither his ranch guests nor the admiring readers of his fiction ever guessed how many hundreds of agricultural documents he pored over in search of the best hoes, wood-saws, water troughs, fencing, and hitching posts. Rejecting gasoline-powered tractors in favor of draft horses (probably because the cacophonous engines reminded him too much of the factories where he'd toiled as a boy), London nonetheless sought data on these machines, just as he informed himself about the chemical fertilizers that he banned from Beauty Ranch in favor of the organic green manures that nourished his fields.

Farm infrastructure preoccupied him too. Beauty Ranch needed roadways and a sewage system, and he ordered a pamphlet from a St. Louis septic disposal firm and another on a rock crusher for roadway gravel. His keen interest in cement and concrete for farm structures and materials resulted in the twin concrete silos that remain standing on his Beauty Ranch property in the twenty-first century.[12]

Water, too, was a vital concern. Irrigation and drainage were basics for a successful ranch, and correct piping and channeling were crucial in all seasons, wet or dry. London's ranch library had the US Department of Agriculture (USDA) pamphlets *Practical Irrigation for Beginners in Irrigation* (1906), *How to Build Small Irrigation Ditches* (1902), and *Drainage of Farm Lands* (1904). These USDA Bulletins represented, to London, the triumph of expertise, which was always an article of his faith. Their target audience was not the amateur gardener, but the farmer whose economic well-being—indeed, survival—depended on wise decisions about crops, soil, and livestock.[13]

All of which became Jack London's preoccupation. He amassed a library on alfalfa silage, on Hereford cattle, on the production of hay and ground cover crops, on feeds and beehives. No fans of his stories of the South Seas or the Klondike could guess how closely he monitored his stock, the sheep, the Angora goats, the beef and dairy cattle, the horses and pigs. Or the field crops of oats and barley and rows of berries, or the orchard trees he planted, which bore pears, apples, avocados, and plums for his prune crop.

He experimented. One crop required arid conditions, another aqueous. His desert cactus garden flourished, but the spineless cactus that seemed so promising as livestock feed proved to be nutritionally worthless. He let the cactus remain as a garden ornament and perhaps as a joke.[14]

An aqueous experiment, however, proved highly successful in a trial that held great promise, London was convinced, for the American future. He followed the advice of F. H. King's *Farmers of Forty Centuries or Permanent Agriculture in China, Korea, and Japan* (1911) and thus reached beyond the USDA advisories. King's book, he was convinced, offered Americans critical lessons for farming in a future that must embrace the past. "To anyone who studies the agricultural methods of the Far East," the agronomist King wrote, "it is evident that these people, centuries ago, came to appreciate the value of water in crop production as no other nations have." The East Asians' "rare wisdom," King went on to say, "combined both irrigation and dry farming methods to an extent and with an intensity far beyond anything our people have ever dreamed." King calculated that products from East Asian farms fed a population of some 500 million from acreage that was "smaller than the improved farm lands of the United States"—a population six times that of the United States fed on one-sixth the farm acreage, and continuously for forty centuries![15]

Farmers of Forty Centuries awakened Jack's memories of the terraced farmlands he'd seen in Korea and Japan in his sailing days on the *Sophia Sutherland* and on the Manchurian peninsula while covering the Russo-Japanese War. His collection of war photographs showed Korean "mosaic landscapes" with "terracing and irrigation of arable fields," all a sharp contrast to the farmlands that Jack London knew in Northern California. He determined to adapt the Asian farm to Beauty Ranch. Gripped by the work of the gadfly American agronomist King, Jack terraced and irrigated the hilliest terrain of Beauty Ranch.[16]

From the beginning, however, Jack London followed the example of Tolstoy's farmer in *Anna Karenina*. He delegated the daily work of the ranch to men on his payroll. As with Tolstoy's Levin, it was now *Mister* London who was master of Beauty Ranch in Glen Ellen, California. It was *Mister* London who ultimately supervised his thirty workers, read the farm journals and agricultural weeklies, jotted pencil notations on yellow slips from his "scribble-pads," and pinned them to the articles he carefully filed. It was *Mister* London who kept close watch on the progress of his crops and animals, *Mister* London who noticed that a jammed gate needed repairing, that a "strange cow" had wandered into his pasture, that costly equipment was exposed to "unexpected rain."[17]

London also had the invaluable assistance of—really, a partnership with—Eliza Shepard, his stepsister who had separated from her husband and came to live at Beauty Ranch as a full-time manager. London's many penciled notes to himself and to Eliza are a farmer's diary of bright hopes and caveats, but the business of farming was primary. "Eliza," he wrote, "I cannot impress on you too strongly the absolute, imperative need of farm accounts, Farm book-keeping." Every farm feature, from a silo to the earmarks on livestock, was cause for cost consideration as London's flood of memos cascaded to Eliza. ("Eliza my compliments on the silo figures. . . . Next year we'll see if we can do it more cheaply. . . . Eliza—tell me about the rock crusher. . . . Give me figures on sand & gravel haul? . . . Eliza Have you the figures for cost of making concrete blocks for silo? . . . Eliza, Don't you think this tattooing . . . will prove certainly cheaper. . . . It will not mar pig's ears. . . . Eliza Can you give me a full report on cows performance for past few months, along with your own conclusions and judgments on the various cows' performance.") Farming was a business—so said leading voices, such as the Kansas journalist William Allen White, who proclaimed that "the successful farmer of this generation must be a business man first." A prominent dean of a college of agriculture underscored the point in 1908: "The person who is not a good business man cannot be a good farmer."[18]

It was to his stepsister that London laid out the campaign plan in yet another penciled note:

> Eliza:—Note what I'm driving at in this farm of ours.
> (1) To grow food
> (2) To reap the profit of this food by returning 90% of it to the soil, and, (b) to turn the last 10% of it into the best pork, beef & horse, to sell same for another profit.[19]

Eliza Shepard's ranch oversight gave her stepbrother latitude for vagabonding. Just as Tolstoy's Levin traveled at intervals, so Jack London left Beauty Ranch when business took him to Los Angeles or to the East Coast. Or when he needed to get away to the inland waters of the San Francisco Bay, where he sailed for weeks at a time with Charmian or friends or by himself on his thirty-foot yawl, *Roamer*. Or to explore Northern California and Oregon on a camping sojourn with Charmian, as when he hitched a four-horse team to his Studebaker wagon in the summer of 1910. His best-known voyage, of course, took him half a world away from the ranch, when he sailed the Pacific in 1907 on the *Snark*, and it is striking to find his memos of ranch advice and reflection written from the middle of the Pacific Ocean.

By the 1910s, London indeed had turned Beauty Ranch into a flourishing agricultural experiment station and model for American agriculture. Through trial and error, he brought dead soil to life without chemical fertilizers. By then he owned fourteen hundred productive acres of orchard fruits, vegetables, and purebred livestock. His finances were ever on the edge because he not only supported and expanded the ranch with its thirty employees, but also shouldered the financial responsibility for his ex-wife, Bess, and daughters, Joan and Becky, plus his mother and former nanny Mammy Prentiss. Agriculturally, however, he'd succeeded. He had the know-how. His livestock was winning prizes at California county and state fairs, from his short-horn cattle to his Shire stallion, which was judged the 1912 grand champion at the California State Fair.

The moment was ripe for Jack London to publicize the lessons that Beauty Ranch held for US agriculture. In the meantime, the Londons' friends and Jack's business associates misunderstood the ranch. His editor saw it as a costly obsession. London's letters pleading for additional advances against royalties for farm expenditures convinced editor George Brett that the farm augured ill for his star author. The Londons' guests, for their part, enjoyed the ranch as a resort that offered horseback riding and swimming in a spring-fed, cleverly dammed pond. They might pause to commend Jack's savvy in buying an entire blacksmith shop from the village of Glen Ellen and installing it on the ranch for on-site repair of tools and equipment. Or they might admire Jack's prize five-thousand-dollar Shire stallion, named Neuadd Hillside, imported from England and "recognized as one of the leading breeds of draft horses" and "very like the Clydesdale" that a major US brewing company was to adopt for publicity purposes later in the century. The ranch guests might also compliment London on his ingeniously efficient and hygienic custom-designed piggery, humorously known as the Pig Palace. But recreation was the guests' focus, not crops or soil, much less the facts on how the Londons' pigs escaped the deadly hog cholera that decimated the swine on neighboring farms.[20]

Journalists who came to interview the celebrated author saw the ranch as a gentleman's farm and Jack London as playing his part in the currently popular Country Life or Back-to-the-Country movement. Its advocates were enthusiasts of rural ideals. "City people are becoming eager to secure farms and homes in the country," wrote one contemporary observer, "for there are many capable people in the crowded cities who . . . feel they could secure greater comfort and independence as farmers." Those who were "at the mercy of landlords and great industrial corporations" might also find new freedoms in rural spaces. The Country Life movement came to be regarded as a mix of agrarian-minded urbanites who were nostalgic for an imagined countryside, together with others who exploited idealized images of rural life in order to critique the industrial city. The movement reaped considerable publicity in 1908 when President Theodore Roosevelt appointed a national Commission on Country Life, its chairman the esteemed Cornell University horticulturist L. H. (Liberty Hyde) Bailey.[21]

Jack London, however, was no American country squire dabbling in farming. To him, Beauty Ranch was an essential part of the necessary revolution,

24. Plow horses at work at Beauty Ranch. Jack London collected the latest literature on gasoline-powered farm tractors but insisted on horsepower for his farm fields. (Henry E. Huntington Library, San Marino, California)

a ground-level effort to awaken America to the fact that its soils had been starved nearly to death over decades of misuse. Beauty Ranch, in sum, was meant to point the way to a future of sustainable farming—but in doing so, Jack must expose the egregious violations of the American soil in the distant and recent past.

Jack London's birth year, 1876, saw a huge mechanical thresher—the Monitor—operate in California's inland Colusa County. It was said to process over sixty-five hundred bushels of wheat daily, and its designer boasted that within "fifteen minutes" of cutting, "the wheat is in the sack." As far as Jack London knew when he first bought Sonoma farmland, an invention like the Monitor heralded a bright new day for an urbanizing, populous America that was desperate to fill its collective belly. The owner of the marvelous thresher—and the yet more ingenious models to come—was Hugh James Glenn (1823–83), the California "Wheat King," whom the newspapers compared to such Gilded Age titans as Cornelius Vanderbilt and Jay Gould, men who built business empires and whose names meant unsurpassed power and wealth.[22]

A late-midlife photograph shows the "erect . . . red-bearded" Glenn facing the camera in a dark suit, his wavy hair tonsured and brushed back over the ears, his slightly downturned mouth somewhat grim and set for capture by the lens and shutter. The Wheat King's eyes, however, are especially suggestive. Beneath thick dark brows they narrow in restless suspicion that was well warranted, for Glenn was murdered in February 1883, by a disgruntled employee who shotgunned him in the back of the head. In years to come, Jack London was to fire his own literary guns at the likes of Glenn, lest men like him return from the grave of history and once again haunt the country. First, however, London must fully grasp the dimensions of the wheat mogul's Gilded Age devastation of prime farmland.[23]

The Missouri-born Glenn had made his mark before Jack was born. A former medical doctor, cattle drover, Mexican War veteran, and gold rush forty-niner, Glenn bought land in Colusa County in 1867 at $1.60 per acre and launched what became the famous Glenn Ranch, his name synonymous with tens of thousands of acres of prime California agricultural land along the Sacramento River. "Always a busy man" who "seldom took any recreation," Glenn headquartered his operation in a rambling, multigabled hacienda at San Jacinto, itself "a bustling crossroad" with "a general store, school, blacksmith shops, post office, bunkhouses and a red light district that did a thriving business on Saturday and Sunday nights during the harvest." Venturing once, unsuccessfully, into politics in the 1879 California race for governor, he also built a family mansion in Oakland with "beautiful parlors" that featured Italian marble mantels, carved black walnut paneling, and the "choicest flowers." His daughter, one of three children, was married there in 1883.[24]

No absentee rancher, Glenn kept close watch on his wheat acreage and was known to "ride a mule eighteen hours a day when supervising his vast holdings." He oversaw seasonal armies of manual laborers driving "gang-plow" echelons of horses and mules by the hundreds, all in service to the gargantuan steam-powered machinery that cut, bound, threshed, and sacked wheat, then shipped it in unprecedented quantities to mills and markets in the United States and abroad. Managers and superintendents oversaw the operations, and bookkeepers calculated expenditures to a fraction of a cent. Aware that bad weather or grasshoppers (or varying global market prices) might cause a downturn in any given year, the bonanza farm owners and investors, many of them absentees, nonetheless counted on a good annual profit.[25]

By the 1870s Hugh Glenn ruled an empire of granaries, cattle ranches in Nevada and Oregon, a workforce of one thousand men, and eight hundred horses and mules, together with chartered grain ships and barges, markets

25. Hugh James Glenn, the California Wheat King who "mined" grain from his vast bonanza-farm acreage in the 1860s–1870s, just as he previously tried to mine gold as a forty-niner. (Charles Davis McCormish and Mrs. Rebecca T. Lambert, *History of Colusa and Glenn Counties, California*, 1914, p. 441)

in Liverpool, and some sixty-six thousand acres of prime wheat fields in California's Colusa County. From this "yellow sun-scorched land," amid "clouds of choking yellow dust," Hugh Glenn's operation produced 1 million bushels of wheat in 1880. His operation—and others like it in the Upper Midwest of Minnesota and the Dakotas—was called bonanza farming.[26]

As a prefix to "farming," the word "bonanza" sounded as expansive as America, with the Latin root for good (*bon*) amplified into an expression for prosperity and wealth. Admirers of Bret Harte's fiction of California found a panorama of the bonanza wheat fields in *Through the Santa Clara Wheat* (1873), a novella that opens with an "enormous wheat-field . . . stretching to the horizon line unbroken," a scene captured on canvas in California artist William Hahn's idyllic *Harvest Time* (1875), a painting reminiscent of the genre works of Winslow Homer.[27]

At first Jack London embraced the concept and celebrated the term. The New Yorker audience who attended his 1906 speech at the Grand Central Palace Exhibition Hall heard London praise the dazzling wheat production on a mechanized California "bonanza farm." He saw such farms in his mind's

26. Bonanza-farm harvest scene, 1876, depicting one of Hugh James Glenn's properties, a ten-thousand-acre farm. Within fifteen minutes of cutting, the ripe wheat was reportedly in the sack. (Engraving based on an oil painting, published in *Pacific Rural Press* 2 [1876]: 279)

eye from the fiction of his fellow novelist, the late Frank Norris, whose *The Octopus* (1901) featured California bonanza farmers, one of whom celebrates a "great ranch" that was "thick" with "wonderful wheat," all expressed in the term "bonanza."[28]

Norris's *The Octopus*, however, represented a scathing indictment of a wheat mogul who "guts" the land, works it "to death," never lets it rest or rotates crops, and at last finds the soil "exhausted." Indeed, Hugh Glenn's empire was eroding even as its emperor was crowned Wheat King. In yield per acre, Glenn's "vast wheat-crop—the true California gold" diminished annually by the mid-1870s. A former gold miner like Hugh Glenn would have known that his kind of agriculture was, as its name implied, analogous to the "*bonanza mines par excellence*" in the Utah Territory's Comstock lode of gold and silver ores. That is, bonanza farmers like Glenn were miners at heart. They were not nurturers of the earth but miners who plumbed it for riches, whether fuels or minerals or precious metals or crops. They were plunderers. Norris underscored this point. *The Octopus* indicted a bonanza wheat kingpin for the crime of believing that "he's still running his mine" and that "the same principles will apply to getting grain out of the earth as to getting gold."[29]

In case readers missed the point, Norris's narrator hammered it yet again. The bonanza operators "were not attached to the soil" but "worked their ranches as a quarter of a century before they had worked their mines. . . .

To get all there was out of the land, to squeeze it dry, to exhaust it, seemed their policy. When, at last, the land had worn out, would refuse to yield, they would invest their money in something else; by then, they would have made their fortunes. They did not care. 'After us, the deluge.'"[30]

Many readers of *The Octopus*, however, did miss this critical point, and initially Jack London was one of them. Like countless others, he was captivated by the struggle of the California wheat farmers against the monopolistic and strangling tentacles of the industrial railroad trust (i.e., the octopus). The plot of the novel was familiar from news reports of a notorious shootout in 1880 in Mussel Slough, an area near Fresno, California, where a group of homesteading wheat ranchers held conflicting claims. The prorailroad judge ruled in favor of the Southern Pacific, which sent a posse to oust the homesteaders. Seven men died in the gunfight that followed. In 1901 Jack London sided with the wheat growers in a glowing review of Norris's novel, which he described as the story of a titanic battle of "the tiller of the soil against the captain of industry."[31]

By the 1910s, however, rancher Jack London had made a whiplash turnabout. This type of "tiller of the soil," he realized, disguised the horrific fact of soil starvation. The Central Valley wheat lands were not cultivated, he understood, but bled and plundered. Now bonanza farms were waning everywhere in America. Investors had soured on their sinking crop yields, and foreign competition had depressed market prices. An explicit warning against them appeared in the compendious *Cyclopedia of American Agriculture* (1907–9), which coupled "*Bonanza farming*" with "*Soil exhaustion*," its entry citing the "extensive method of cultivation, the one-crop system, and the wastefulness of it, [which] tended to exhaust the soil very rapidly."[32]

To Jack London, the Hugh Glenns of the bonanza era must not be revered as legendary heroes of the past century. They must not rise again to devastate the nation's cropland. They must therefore be exposed as marauders, and their breed discredited for all time. Norris had said it first. His *The Octopus* gave the public insight into the bonanza farmers' mentality, their gold rush–era plundering extended to the farm fields. Readers, however, continued to misread *The Octopus*, seeing the railroad trust as the one and only "villain of the book." In the 1910s, Jack London landed a corrective follow-up punch. His novel *The Little Lady of the Big House* (1916) gave the public the specifics of the damage inflicted by bonanza kings like Glenn.[33]

London staged his critique through his protagonist's savage attack on the bonanza system. Early in the story, readers get a ringside seat at the young orphaned Dick Forrest's assault on his wealthy San Francisco guardians.

London deploys his favorite pugilistic terms: "Listen, guardians! Do you know what it is to hit your man . . . square in the jaw—and drop him cold?" London's "lusty and husky" young Forrest delivers the knockout punch of the new generation against the men of the gold rush era. "You picked up money like a lot of sailors shaking out nuggets from the grass roots in a virgin placer," charges Forrest. But "you were destructive. You were a bonanza farmer."[34]

London immediately spells out the ruinous practices embedded in the once-ebullient term, for his young hero flattens the bonanza generation in a verbal barrage: "You took forty thousand acres of the finest Sacramento Valley soil and you grew wheat on it year after year. You never dreamed of [crop] rotation. You burned your straw. You exhausted your humus. You plowed four inches and put a plow-sole like a cement sidewalk just four inches under the surface. You exhausted that film of four inches and now you can't get your seed back." The forty-niner bonanza farmers are soon down for the count, but London's Forrest hits them once again: "You've destroyed."[35]

One KO did not suffice. A crash course in good farming was urgently needed for the state of California and for all of America. By the 1910s Jack London understood that ravaged American farm soil could not be blamed solely on the bonanza system. Since colonial and pioneering days, he now knew, the farmers of America had unknowingly exhausted vast swaths of rich cropland, blindly assuming the soil to be an infinite resource.

Jack London plunged into farming with an urgency that approached zeal—and in terms quite new in the American experience. He was determined to alert the public to its peril. The stakes were high for him, higher still for the country at large. *The Little Lady of the Big House* KO'd bonanza farms, but in *The Valley of the Moon* (1912) Jack showed the US public how America farmed at its best, how its food supply could be secured for centuries. First, however, Jack faced the farm crisis that was manifest on his own acres.

Signing the deed to the first 130 acres of his Beauty Ranch property in 1905, London came face to face with decades of egregious neglect of the soil. Those who had first "toiled, and cleared, and planted" his acreage were nothing less than herculean, he knew, imagining them to be pioneering men who had "gazed with aching eyes, while they rested their labor-stiffened bodies" and finally "broke their hearts and their backs over this stubborn soil."[36]

Yet they, too, broke the soil, broke it in the worst way. Promoters of California ranching emphasized that Gold Rush days were a thing of the past, that "idlers" who think they can "pick gold from the streets in this land of gold" were no longer welcome. The lesson: "There is gold in the soil, and on top of the soil, but it can be had only by persistent labor." Labor, however, could be smart or stupid. Jack's neighboring farmers virtually boasted that depleted soil was proof of their diligent labor. One remarked, "You can't teach me anything about farming; I've worked three farms out." The crops first raised on Jack London's land were "meager" because the soil was "dead." London was heir to their "years and years of unintelligent farming" that left his land "all worn out."[37]

Farming in Sonoma, once London made the commitment, was a formidable undertaking against long odds. Descriptions of Sonoma farmland in the late 1800s boasted of "a good crop every year for twenty-seven years," but listings of farm properties for sale tell a different story. One farm was "not well kept up" and showed a "neglected appearance" because its owner was "absent the place." Another was advertised in boastfully negative terms as "not worn out," and still another was presented favorably precisely because no one had ever farmed it, thus preserving its "virgin richness." Looking back two generations from the 1920s, a Sonoma historian lamented the late-1800s coastal "overstocking" that led to wind erosion, with "disastrous results," and regretted that a once-flourishing "bonanza" potato crop in Sonoma, the Bodega Red, had nearly been driven to extinction. Having "ceased to produce well," it was now only memorialized in "old mounds that were potato field fence rows two generations ago."[38]

Jack London's acreage fit the description of these same farms. As his holdings reached some fourteen hundred acres, he quipped to editor George Brett, "The ground was so impoverished that an average of three farmers went bankrupt on each of the five ranches that I have run together, making a total of fifteen failures to make a living out of that particular soil." Aggressively buying properties, London defied the advice of the authoritative *Cyclopedia of American Agriculture*, which warned against buying a "worn-out farm." To bring it to a "high state of fertility . . . requires skill, takes time, and usually costs more than to buy good land in the beginning." A new farmer, went the advice, "usually has enough other problems without beginning with a serious handicap in the land itself."[39]

Beauty Ranch, Jack learned, was just one of countless US farms in much the same state of depletion coast to coast. Together they made a mockery of Thomas Jefferson's 1785 proclamation that "those who labor in the earth are the chosen people of God." They made a grisly joke of the beloved public image of farmers as stewards of the land, exemplars of the American work ethic, of intimate connection with the soil and the seasons, of self-sufficiency, independence, strength, stoicism, and honesty.[40]

In addition, American farms betrayed the ideal of the US Homestead Act of 1862, which was signed into law just fourteen years before London's birth. It had offered public land for sale for just $1.25 per acre, or, alternatively, a grant of 160 acres to settlers who occupied the land for five years. The law itself seemed ideally suited to the self-sufficient yeoman family farmer.

But the Homestead Act had attracted "a class of settlers who had nothing to lose and few qualifications for farm entrepreneurship." In their appetite for cheap land, they overreached, trying to "control more land than they could develop or operate." As a result, many farms were abandoned, while those in operation were "skewed toward the crops that required minimum capital and minimum labor." As the mid-twentieth-century historian Richard Hofstadter concluded, the farmers of America had "little attachment to land or locality" and made scant efforts to "acquaint themselves with the quality of their soil." "Imbued with the commercial spirit," they "failed to plan and manure and replenish," neglecting "diversification for the one-crop system and ready cash." Many of these farmers verified the prescient observation of Alexis de Tocqueville, who had remarked in 1840 that American farmers were not devotees of the soil but speculators. Carrying his "business-like qualities into agriculture," said the French traveler, the American "brings land into tillage in order to sell it again, and not to farm it."[41]

The seriousness of the farm crisis in the 1900s could not be overstated. Even the USDA now sounded the alarm in Farmers' Bulletins that were dispatched all over the country, including Beauty Ranch. *Renovation of Worn-Out Soils* (1906) pronounced the nation's arable cropland "greatly impaired," while *Waste Land and Wasted Land on Farms* (1916) featured a photograph of a gullied field and a caption scolding farmers for "bad tillage methods." The author, an experienced Washington State agronomist, traced two centuries of the exhaustion of abundant fertile soil from the Eastern Seaboard of the colonial era through the pioneering decades in the Midwest and West. His summary statement was stark: "Now we are confronted by the necessity of tilling soils whose ability to produce satisfactory crops has been greatly impaired."[42]

Not all influential voices were as frank. Jack had a 1906 article, "The Making of a Modern Farm," by Liberty Hyde Bailey, the esteemed dean of the College of Agriculture at Cornell University, a prolific author and the editor in chief of the magisterial four-volume *Cyclopedia of American Agriculture*. Bailey's article commended the modern farm family for its "good executive ability and the abiding quality that one finds in fine old farm families."[43]

Yet those "fine old farm families" left a legacy of damage and ruin that must be reversed, as London knew directly and personally. Once again, he turned to the novel as the optimal instrument of public instruction. Using the format of entertainment, he would expose America's disastrous history of farming and show the way forward. London seized an opportunity in the very popularity of the Country Life movement. In spring of 1911, he proposed a new book to George Brett: "I should like to begin a certain novel. . . . Its motif is *back to the land*." London outlined his plot featuring a young working-class man and woman struggling in a "large city." They would fall in love and marry amid "trials and tribulations." Facing "hard times," they would "start wandering penniless over the country of California" in "a magnificent, heroic, detailed pilgrimage" toward "the one and only spot" in which "they settle down to successful small-scale farming." This novel was to be a "love-story" throughout, "a big story, a true story," a "popular" story, and one in which London swore absolute and passionate belief in "every word."[44]

The new novel took its title from the Native American name "Sonoma," or *The Valley of the Moon*. Set in Oakland just after the San Francisco earthquake of 1906, it features a young woman laundry worker named Saxon whose long-deceased mother, London emphasizes, was a notable Anglo-Saxon poet and westering pioneer. Saxon's boyfriend, Billy Roberts, is an amateur prize-fighter and a brewery teamster, an occupation signaling a high level of skill to readers who routinely relied on horses both in the country and city and were well aware that the term "horsepower" literally referred to the power of these "living machines."[45]

The novel is anchored by the couple's love story, as London promised his editor, and its readers find lyrical scenes of their courtship and early marriage played out against harrowing episodes of tumultuous and violent local labor wars. Billy confides early on that horses fill his dreams, and when he drives the citified Saxon into the country for a picnic in a carriage with a team rented from a livery stable, she declares her desire "to live in the country." The storyline of urban turmoil and bloody brutality builds until, in desperation, Saxon sparks their rural pilgrimage into Southern and Northern California and into Oregon in search of the ideal farm site, where they can work the soil, raise livestock, and enjoy a better life. According to London's plan, that land proves to be Sonoma, the couple's farm—virtually identical to Beauty Ranch.[46]

London did not once hint to his New York editor that this novel was to be a tutorial on agriculture. His pointed messages in *The Valley of the Moon*, however, are as numerous as they are precise. Deep in the novel, when sympathetic readers are firmly committed to the couple and to the success of their quest, London at last presents the dark facts of America's ruinous farming past. In the voice of a California old-timer, London tells of the "abandoned farms by the tens of thousands" in New York, New Jersey, and New England. The desolation goes on, for "land-robbing and hogging" is now the norm "over the rest of the country—down in Texas, in Missouri, and Kansas, [and] out here in California." The lazy and sleazy "poor-white" tenant farmers have worsened the problem, for they "lease, clean out and gut a place in several years. . . . They skin the soil and move, skin the soil and move." Also censured are the bonanza farmers, who reaped a fortune but "put nothing back" and left the soil "almost desert."[47]

Fortunately, London shows, the one-crop "bonanza farms" have been mostly "broken up." The diversified "new farming" has arrived, and it features progressive "intensive cultivation." As London points out, "It isn't a case of having a lot of acres, but of how much [the farmers] can get out of one acre." (By 1909, in fact, the executors of the Glenn Ranch property were actually promoting the sales of irrigated ten- to thirty-acre tracts that were sectioned from Hugh Glenn's former wheat empire and were now advertised as prime soil for "the growth of citrus and deciduous fruits, vines, alfalfa and other products.")[48]

Irrigation, too, is a hallmark of progress. In a fruit orchard, readers see a "five-inch stream of sparkling water splashed into . . . [an] irrigation system and flowed away across the orchard through many laterals." Sparing readers more technics, London waxes poetic as a farmer beholds his "beloved water" and exclaims, "Isn't it beautiful? It's bud and fruit. It's blood and life. . . . Look what we're doing! Worked out land that ceased to grow wheat, and we turn the water on, treat the soil decently, and see our orchards!" London jabs at the bonanza era—"It makes a gold mine laughable."[49]

The Valley of the Moon also forced London's vexed views on racial identity to the surface. Early in the story, Saxon boasts of her namesake ancestry of the superior fighters with blue eyes and "yellow hair" who became the forebears both of the English and of "all the Americans that are real Americans." Billy's ancestry is a bit murky, but he vouches for himself as "American," and Saxon agrees that his name is "regular old American." The two bond over their shared ancestry of hearty pioneers who crossed the plains to reach California, and London makes much of their proud heritage, which includes heroic battles in the Civil War and Indian Wars. Both Saxon and Billy have resilience and verve they inherited from their illustrious white ancestors. (As Saxon exclaims, "We wouldn't be here today if it wasn't for the fighting spirit of our people before us.")[50]

Meanwhile, the novel spurns the Scandinavian immigrant as "awkward," the Irish as "crude," and the Chinese as "Chinks." The lovely Caucasian Saxon is proudly distinguished from the "Dagos and Japs and such" even as she briefly imagines "what her life would have been like had she been born a Chinese woman, or an Italian woman like those she saw . . . squat, ungainly and swarthy."[51]

The couple's pilgrimage, however, traces superior farming techniques precisely to those supposedly inferior racial groups. The Portuguese and Italians have arrived in America penniless but have worked hard, learned the customs of the country, saved every cent, and bought the farmland that "they will love and care for and conserve." The "miserable immigrant . . . Adriatic Slavs" from Dalmatia who began American life as fieldworkers now own the orchards that produce delicious crisp apples sold on the world market.[52]

East Asians, too, are on the rise in American farmlands. The Chinese immigrant "Coolie" who first "peddled vegetables in a couple of baskets slung on a stick" has now become "Sing Kee—the Potato King of Stockton." And Saxon's (and Billy's) "Japs" provide another lesson, for the terraced hillsides of Japanese farms offer an important lesson in land use. One advanced young American farmer explains that he traveled abroad "to see how the old countries farmed" and learned the Japanese secret of turning the steep and seemingly useless hillsides into productive terraces. "Take a hill so steep you couldn't drive a horse up it," he says. "No bother to [the Japanese]. . . . They terraced it—a stone wall, and good masonry . . . walls and terraces . . . straight up into the air . . . for four or five feet of soil they could grow things on." The Japanese, he adds, have monopolized certain fruit crops in California.[53]

In the Sacramento River delta, the pilgrim couple find themselves surrounded by farmworkers from every corner of the planet—"Chinese, Japanese, Italians, Portuguese, Swiss, Hindus, Koreans, Norwegians, Danes, French, Armenians, Slavs, almost every nationality save Americans." London was deeply ambivalent, indeed disturbed, about this polyglot mixture of racial groups that he considered aliens. He punctuated the novel with hymns to the pioneering white ancestry. But he also faced material facts. In 1910, he had recognized the inferior performance of the white boxer in the heavyweight prizefighting championship between the "Great White Hope," Jim Jeffries, and the black Jack Johnson. Jeffries was defeated because the black

27. Jack London on horseback at his Beauty Ranch. (Henry E. Huntington Library, San Marino, California)

boxer was better, and London said so. He went on the record then, just as he did now on the topic of the farm fields. *The Valley of the Moon* frankly acknowledged the glaring deficiencies of white American farmers past and present. American whites had farmed carelessly, greedily, ignorantly, and destructively—and continued to do so. Many were too stubborn to change their ways. Others, equally guilty, defaulted as they became absentees who sold off their heritage of precious farmland to "the foreigners."[54]

Billy and Saxon represent the hope that the lineage of the hearty white pioneers will revive and ultimately prevail. Their Sonoma ranch replicates Beauty Ranch, an agricultural polestar for America's future. In the meantime, the larger agricultural bounty of the state was being reaped by its smartest and most devoted farmers, the foreign immigrants.

The Valley of the Moon was not London's final word. The country's long-term farm crisis, he was convinced, could not be solved solely by creating smaller farms that relied on traditional methods from Europe or East Asia. Nor did the solution lie, in his view, in single-crop (monocrop) production, no matter how many bushels of apples were harvested by the Dalmatians or pecks of potatoes by the Chinese. London was convinced that many more Saxons and Billys were needed to farm on the model of Beauty Ranch. But he also envisioned a new, postbonanza concept of large-scale organic American farming.

Once again, he produced a novel that provided a lesson plan for the country. Published in the last year of London's life, *The Little Lady of the Big House* (1916) denounced the old bonanza-farm era but also renewed and promoted the idea of supersized agriculture. Best known for the fatal love triangle of its three main characters, two powerful men and a strong woman ironically termed the "little lady," the novel propels its readers through a saga of male rivalry and jealousy that climaxes melodramatically in a suicide. Its opening chapters, however, instill the agricultural ideas that were promoted in the United States and its territories during the decades of London's own lifetime under the aegis of the 1862 and 1890 Morrill Acts and the 1887 Hatch Act, which provided federal funds for the establishment of agricultural experiment stations in the states.

Readers of *The Little Lady of the Big House* can presuppose the wisdom of London's landowner-protagonist, Dick Forrest. In the early scene, we watch the young Dick KO the older gold rush generation for its bonanza-farm destruction of the soil. In the same scene, young Dick vows that within fifteen years he'll start a ranch that will have far more acreage than the old bonanza farm, but will feature the highest level of agricultural expertise known the world over. Specialists in "agricultural chemistry," in "livestock breeding," in "farm management" will be sought to tutor and advise this wealthy, willful young upstart and visionary. His youthful ambition is clear: to upstage the bonanza generation by farming productively and profitably—and organically—on acreage more vast than any ever imagined by the bonanza-era forty-niners. Young Forrest quips irreverently about a "post-graduate year in cow college," but relies on the expertise centered in the colleges of agriculture in the Morrill land-grant schools, and the novel names the Universities of California and Nebraska to validate the point.[55]

London delayed his agricultural messages until late in *The Valley of the Moon*, but he front-loaded them in *The Little Lady of the Big House*. Readers would soon enough get caught up in the love triangle between two men and the "little lady." First, however, comes Jack London's panorama of the new megafarm of the future, for the opening pages confirm that Dick Forrest has indeed fulfilled his vow. Forrest is now a Big Man nationally and internationally, and his Big House mansion is Jack London's memorial tribute to his own architect-designed Beauty Ranch mansion, the redwood and volcanic rock Wolf House, which was destroyed by fire in August 1913 when workmen's oily rags reached the combustion point shortly before he and Charmian were scheduled to move in. London planned to rebuild, but meanwhile the image of Wolf House was inset in the novel. The first scenes of *The Little Lady of the*

Big House show the agricultural triumph of the forty-year-old Forrest as he awakes to begin a typical day on his farm property of 250,000 acres.

Dressed by his valet in a quasi-military outfit featuring spurs and a trooperlike "Baden-Powell hat," Forrest can be seen as a Jack London writ large, a man of 180 pounds, his body bearing the scars of lifelong physical adventures and trials, and his face remarkably similar to London's, with full features and a ready smile. Forrest's livestock and croplands, however, make a case for farming on a scale that vastly exceeds Beauty Ranch, the Glenn holdings, or anything seen in the bonanza days of the northern plains Red River Valley.[56]

The Forrest operation is a model of modern efficiency made possible by the latest technological "paraphernalia of business," including the telegraph and telephone, and Dictaphones for voice recording. Dynamos help generate electricity for lighting and refrigeration, and the property includes a "sea of buildings with batteries of silos," together with "a paint-shop, a wagon-shop, a plumbing-shop, a carpenter-shop." An expert horseman, Forrest operates with a fleet of gasoline-powered tractors and several automobiles that drive along roadways smooth as "flowing ribbon[s] of silk." His prime purebred livestock is in demand for markets worldwide, from the Duroc hogs to the Shropshire sheep, Shire draft horses, and Angora goats. His executive staff includes foremen, department heads, a veterinarian, and several managers (a horse manager, a pasture expert) and on down to the Basque herders and the field hands. The estate includes one feature that London hoped to see on Beauty Ranch one day, a village with comfortable housing for the workers' families and a school for their children.[57]

Though the Forrest estate sounds like a cross between Beauty Ranch and a mega–bonanza farm, it was nonetheless crucial that London differentiate it from both of them. Its sheer scale far exceeds London's Sonoma operation, and its business plan and farming techniques provide a sharp contrast to the former Glenn bonanza operation. Forrest is the quintessential progressive new farmer, schooled in scientific agricultural expertise as he oversees a quarter million divided and subdivided acres. He says, "I believe the West and the world must come to intensive farming. . . . I've divided the five thousand acres into twenty-acre holdings. I believe each twenty acres should support, comfortably, not only a family, but pay at least six per cent." Through Forrest, London argues for diversified crops, crop rotation, and the intensive cultivation he understood from King's *Farmers of Forty Centuries*. He argues, in addition, for an equitable profit-sharing plan to protect farm employees from becoming "two-legged work beasties."[58]

Over and against the bonanza-era marauding of the soil, London's Forrest cultivates his quarter million acres with careful, intelligent stewardship. The plowing is itself a lyrical ballad as the Shire mares draw the plows "back and forth across, contour-plowing, turning the green sod of the hillsides to the rich dark brown of humus-filled earth so organic and friable that it would almost melt by gravity into fine-particled seed-bed." Such soil, London insists, is the result of "improvements on that quarter of a million acres, from drain-tiled meadows to dredge-drained tule swamps, from good roads to developed water-rights, from farm buildings to the Big House itself." It is all emphatically measured monetarily in a huge value-added sum that London intimates but deliberately refuses to specify, lest the outside world's fluctuating currency values demean and devalue his message—that thanks to modern agricultural expertise, the farm can grow to vast size while utilizing the best farm practices on the globe.[59]

Jack London's own biases are projected into *The Little Lady of the Big House*, starting with Dick Forrest's lineage as a robust white Anglo male. The vast farm operation at the highest level of expertise thus rests in the hands of the powerful, patriarchal white man. He holds the reins—and the electrical master switch, the deed, the payroll, and so on. But to London, such proprietorship held other distinct advantages. The business of large-scale farming was to be invested with the passion of personal stewardship of the land. No absentee owners were to be involved, no corporate arrangement, no stockholders, and no symbiotic relationships between the farmer and the producers of chemical soil additives.

London was surely disappointed in the poor sales of *The Little Lady of the Big House* (just over twenty-three thousand copies), and by 1916 his health was also a major worry. As his life drew to a close, however, London dispatched one last bulletin to the young farmers- and ranch-managers-in-training who were then studying at Davis, the University of California's farm campus, located east of Berkeley in the Central Valley ranchland. For the school publication, the *University Farm Agricola*, London accepted the 1916 invitation to be an outside contributor. He opened with a question and its answer: "The future of California as an agricultural state? There is no question about its future greatness if we give the land a chance."[60]

London then landed his one-two punch of the bold, revolutionary idea he knew none of the young farmers would hear from their professors or find in their textbooks. "The Chinese have farmed for forty centuries without using commercial fertilizer," he announced, adding his personal testimonial: "I am rebuilding worn-out hillside lands that were worked out and destroyed by our wasteful California pioneer farmers. I am not using commercial fertilizer."[61]

Then came his core conviction: "I believe the soil is our one indestructible asset"—though indestructible only with proper care according to the techniques that he listed, the animal and green manures and cover crops, the crop rotation, the "proper tillage and drainage." Then his sworn affidavit: "I am getting results which the Chinese have demonstrated for forty centuries." At last this exhortation: "We are just beginning to farm in the United States. The Chinese knew the how but not the why. We know the why, but we're dreadfully slow getting round to the how." He closed with this: "I'm for California and its latent possibilities." It was a cheer and a toast to the future that was the motor of his life journey.[62]

Being *for* California also meant promoting the Golden State in other areas of social and political well-being. As of 1912, Jack saw another opportunity to press for progressive, even revolutionary reform in a new novel that would transmit an urgent message on behalf of social change. Not that he was letting go of farm-related materials for the new book. Ranching in Glen Ellen and extolling the life of Beauty Ranch in *The Valley of the Moon*, he planned to tap his knowledge of soils and irrigation for the new project. His avid interest in major events in United States and world history over millennia would also come into play, as would the current public fascination with New Thought and the paranormal mentalism that was later known as psychic communication. Also in the mix was his horror at the US judicial and prison system, which punished "workmen," putting them in "stripes in San Quentin" and often damning these "labor men" to decades-long imprisonment for petty thievery. By 1914, Jack promoted the new book to a *Cosmopolitan* editor as a "paean" of "love, adventure, romance, and life everlasting," a surefire formula for robust sales. His words were deliberately bracing, for the new book was to take the public on a journey to Renaissance France, to the Nevada Territory, to East Asia, to the Holy Land—and to abhorrent conditions inside US prison walls.[63]

Few knew the gnarled history of the new book, how many of London's attempts to launch a crime novel had failed—and how the self-interest of an ex-convict held this new book hostage. Few, that is, were aware that a former outlaw once serving a life sentence in San Quentin kept Jack London hamstrung until one autumn evening in Oakland in 1912, when the former convict finally gave Jack London permission to use his name and his story for a novel that pulsed with cries for prison reform.

6 In That Prison, Things Unbelievable and Monstrous

The stir, or the pen, as they call it in convict argot, is a training school for philosophy.
—Jack London, *The Star Rover*, 1915

Dining at his favorite Oakland restaurant, the elegant Saddle Rock Café, Jack London was a welcome and frequent guest as the year 1912 drew toward a close. His fans, including some Saddle Rock diners, knew the celebrated author had been absent from California for much of the year. With his wife, he'd spent several snowy winter weeks in New York City and then, in February, boarded the merchant sailing ship *Dirago* on a voyage that rounded Cape Horn, circumnavigating two continents from Baltimore to Seattle. Jack and the stylish Charmian London returned to their Glen Ellen home in August, although they were seen regularly in and around San Francisco and Oakland enjoying the theater, the opera, and dining with friends.

Dinner at the Saddle Rock this autumn evening of 1912 sealed a business deal. After much deliberation, hesitation, and delay, Jack's companion, Edward Morrell, finally consented to allow Jack London to use his actual name and his life story as the basis of a new novel. It was a moment to celebrate. Startled guests at nearby tables saw a high-spirited Jack suddenly bolt from his chair and dash around the table, his plate of seared duck and goblet of *Liebfraumilch* wine momentarily forgotten. Diners saw him embrace the slender, steel-gray eyed Morrell and heard Jack exclaim, "Gosh, Ed, do you know what this means to me?"[1]

Morrell knew. A former San Joaquin Valley gang member and ex-con who frequently lectured on the need for prison reform, he had become something of a minor celebrity in the San Francisco Bay area. Many of London's readers might have flinched, nonetheless, at the prospect of a novel that would take them inside prison walls for an exposé of the horrors of life behind bars in California's notorious San Quentin and Folsom prisons. Socially and politically, a more depressing topic could hardly be imagined. What's more, Jack London was not known to be a prison reform advocate, although his picaresque autobiographical *The Road* (1907) included two grim chapters on the raffish young Jack's month-long imprisonment in upstate New York. London had wedged that episode amid chapters on cross-country adventuring in the book whose very title, *The Road*, linked him to America's buoyant "road" literature of Walt Whitman, Mark Twain, and numerous others.

Provocative issues that swirled about the criminal justice system in the 1910s nonetheless continued to tug at London, moving him to plan a novel that would challenge and upend public assumptions about crime and imprisonment. Those who believed that the brutal treatment of convicts was a deterrent to crime were soon to hear otherwise from Jack London. Those who regarded imprisoned convicts as "a pack of wild animals or an aggregation of desperate thugs," as one prison reformer put it, were to be thoroughly disabused of that notion. Those who trusted authorities' official reports of inmates treated with wholesome discipline were to hear a different story, of sadism and homocide.[2]

Also, those who believed that the death penalty was imposed solely on individuals who committed heinous crimes would find their assumptions shattered. Jack London's novel—to be published in 1915 as *The Star Rover* in the United States and as *The Jacket* in England—would raise the stakes of reform by exposing the death-dealing torments inflicted by public officials on persons whom one reformer called "the caged and voiceless."[3]

London well understood, however, that his readers expected and deserved to be entertained. Thrilling adventures and love stories were hallmarks of his fiction. Until recently, a prison novel that met these criteria had not seemed possible, not even for Jack London. With Ed Morrell's story in his hands, however, that was about to change.

When Edward Morrell made his way to the Londons' Beauty Ranch in 1911 as a "sojourner" and "houseguest," he came with a ready-made plot for the novel Jack had long yearned to write. The new novel came knocking at London's very door, for Morrell's biography was the perfect storyline for London's long-deferred crime and prison novel. Morrell's life was the stuff of surefire best-selling fiction. The Pennsylvania-born Ed Morrell (b. 1869[?]) told Jack and Charmian how had been convicted of grand larceny in Southern California in 1891, serving two years in San Quentin before being rearrested in 1894 as a member of a band of train robbers, the Outlaws, who fled to the mountains with money stolen from Southern Pacific trains. A romance with a lawman's daughter ended in a dustup with the Fresno police chief. Morrell took the chief's pistol, an incident that brought a second conviction for robbery and a life sentence that sent him to Folsom Prison and its "devil's cauldron" of a granite quarry, "where boiled the tortured souls of the State's condemned."[4]

Singled out as a troublemaker and transferred to San Quentin as a desperado, Morrell was sentenced in 1899 to spend the rest of his life in solitary confinement when another prisoner falsely accused him of hiding smuggled guns in the prison to foment an armed rebellion and breakout. Five years later, a new warden, John Tompkins, reviewed the record of this "Incorrigible" and saw nothing to warrant the draconian punishment. He selected Morrell to be the head trusty, a sort of sergeant-major among prisoners, and four years later in 1908 the sentence of the former "Incorrigible" was commuted by the acting governor of California, a former state prison director who had taken a liking to head trusty Ed Morrell.[5]

The former outlaw and inmate now provided all the elements of a Jack London adventure novel to be freighted with a serious underlying message urging prison reform. Negotiation between the two men began, each seeing advantages in collaboration. For Morrell, the lure was high visibility and potential earning power, for the famous Jack London was a sure path to national and international publicity and financial gain, or so he thought. For his part, Jack got an intact storyline, including the vivid mental image of the depths of Morrell's suffering in prison. From another inmate's published account he knew that Ed Morrell had been nearly at death's door from years in solitary confinement, his skin "yellow," his joints and limbs "horribly emaciated," his vision dimmed from the perpetual darkness and his voice atrophied to a thin whisper. Having entered the prison at 165 pounds, he was down to "about 95" and looked stricken by "famine," like "a human creature who had been through hell." Jack took notes for his novel, planning his fictionalized account of the former prisoner's rehabilitation. (Jack jotted in his notes: "Follow Morrell's story closely, to his own emergence, and regaining of health, and going after scalps of men who injured him in prison.") Having struggled unsuccessfully for years to develop a crime and prison novel, Jack saw Morrell as a godsend. It was as though a drought had ended and the rains had come.[6]

The topic of prison and crime were so deeply embedded in London's psyche that acquaintances might have predicted a prison novel as a matter of course in his fiction. His stepfather, John London, had worked in Oakland as a deputized night watchman in the last years of his life, with his wages

28. Edward Morrell, prison reformer and former San Quentin and Folsom convict who hoped an alliance with Jack London would secure his fame and fortune. (Henry E. Huntington Library, San Marino, California)

paid on a bounty system. From their Garfield Grammar School days together, Jack's friend Frank Atherton remembered that "young gangsters . . . sought to vent their spite" on young Jack because their friends or relatives had been "arrested by Mr. London."[7]

The rugged coastal waters that Jack London later sailed as an oyster pirate and as a recreational boater also kept him mindful of crime and punishment, for the San Quentin State Penitentiary was a stark material fact of the San Francisco Bay, the vast gray walls of "this colony of crime" looming beyond the shoreline waves that dashed against the rocky coast. The teenage Jack memorably remarked, "If I'm caught taking the oysters, I suppose I'll have to serve time." When that fate befell a number of his former fellow pirates, Jack told Atherton, "If I had stayed with that gang much longer, I'd probably be where some of them are today, in San Quentin." (A photograph pasted into one of Jack and Charmian's albums shows Jack in a rowboat on the San Francisco Bay waters, the undated picture captioned "Near San Quentin.")[8]

At that time, it is doubtful that the teenage Jack knew much about California's first state penitentiary, which opened in 1851 under a private contract and was, according to one historian, "woven into the major themes of California's political history," including racial and ethnic conflict and a public resistance to taxation. The prison at first held convicts in the San Francisco Bay waters on a double-masted brigantine. A permanent land site was selected at Point Quentin, but cost overruns and insufficient outlays of public funds for construction, staffing, operation, and maintenance prompted charges of graft and incompetence in the following years, as did several well-publicized escapes. The terms of the state contracts for privatized management, for buildings, and for the leasing of convict labor were so highly controversial that political careers were ruined. Yet the prison population grew. By 1878, the San Quentin State Prison "was overflowing with more than 1,400 inmates," and it was hoped that the new second "branch" prison on the American River at Folsom (near Sacramento) would become a "reformatory" when it opened in 1880 and would afford each prisoner a private cell.[9]

Two theories of incarceration were in play in the planning and operation of California state prisons by 1876, the year of Jack London's birth. Both were imported from the East. The older system had begun in 1818 at the Auburn penitentiary in upstate New York. According to historian Shelley Bookspan, "The theories of California prison policymakers throughout the nineteenth century" were based on the Auburn plan. It allowed inmates to work together in the prison factories or workshops and to have meals together but otherwise required "an intimidating regimen of silence" that was meant to promote meditation and prevent fraternization.[10]

The early 1870s, however, saw a movement known as the New Penology, also imported from the East, notably at the state prison at Elmira, New York. Whereas the Auburn system prescribed "hard labor, solitary confinement, and silence once and for all," as Bookspan points out, the New Penology advocated a rationalized system "aimed at returning the convict to society as a productive citizen." Emphasizing rehabilitation, the New Penology promoted the separation of first offenders and youths from hardened criminals, together with the possibility of reduced sentences earned by good behavior. The New Penology also introduced the concept of parole.[11]

In California, however, the New Penology did not replace the Auburn system. One California prison commissioner warned in 1871 that "the granite quarries in the deep canyon above Folsom—with the confined limits, and with the intense heat prevailing there in the summer, might, perhaps, answer as a place for the *punishment* of a limited number of the more hardened and robust convicts." The statement was prescient. As Bookspan remarks, San Quentin represented the "greater influence" of the New Penology, while "Folsom bore some resemblance to the hard labor, hard discipline characteristic of the Auburn style."[12]

Jack London had no inkling whether his month-long imprisonment in upstate New York in 1894 was endured under the regime of the New Penology or the Auburn system. Readers of his *The Road* (1907) were equally oblivious when encountering two dark chapters, "Pinched" and "The Pen," both detailing the now-famous author's youthful imprisonment when he rode the rails cross-country at eighteen years of age and was arrested for vagrancy at Niagara Falls. Tried without benefit of counsel, he was sentenced summarily to thirty days in the Erie County Penitentiary. "All that I had done was to walk along their sidewalk and gaze at their picayune waterfall," London wrote. "And what crime was there in that?" "I'd show them," he vowed, "when I got out."[13]

In a larger sense of those words, he never "got out," for the experience was traumatic. Handcuffed in a chain-gang procession, his head shaved and his clothing confiscated, London donned the requisite prison stripes and faced the prospect of a month at hard labor on a diet of bread and foul water that was passed off as coffee at dawn and soup at midday. His dwelling, he found, was a cell block teeming with vermin and riddled with graft and violence. "Our hall," he wrote, was "filled with the ruck and the filth, the scum and dregs of society—hereditary inefficients, degenerates, wrecks, lunatics, addled intelligences, epileptics, monsters, weaklings, in short, a very nightmare of humanity." Escape was out of the question, for "along the tops of the walls marched guards with repeating rifles," and rumors spread of "machine-guns in the sentry-towers."[14]

The boxcars and hobo camps of London's tramping, plus his prior crewing on the seal-hunting *Sophia Sutherland*, were a prep school of sorts for the Erie County Penitentiary. In this volatile mix, survival was everything. Proclaiming himself to be adaptively "fluid," London eagerly partnered with a prison-savvy "pal" who showed him the ropes of prison life. ("We became pretty chummy, and my heart bounded when he cautioned me to follow his lead. He called me 'Jack,' and I called him 'Jack.'")[15]

Confident of the younger sidekick's friendship, the older "Pal 'Jack'" somehow arranged for "Sailor Jack" London to be a privileged trusty or "hall-man," one of thirteen quasi-manager prisoners charged with maintaining order in the cell block, for it was understood that only in "extremity" were the guards to be summoned. As London wrote, "Here were thirteen beasts of us over half another thousand beasts, . . . and it was up to us thirteen there to rule. It was impossible . . . to rule by kindness. We ruled by fear." With a ratio of "thirteen against five hundred," Jack wielded his authority with "a broom-handle, end-on, in the face." He explained, "We would not permit the slightest infraction of rules, the slightest insolence. If we did, we were lost." His self-justification was this: "When one is on the hot lava of hell, he cannot pick and choose his path."[16]

White-collar crime flourished too, Jack emphasized, mainly as extortionist trafficking in tobacco and bread. He called it scaled-down capitalism and freely acknowledged his own complicity: "Oh, we were wolves, believe me—just like the fellows who do business in Wall Street."[17]

London also witnessed extremes of cruelty that resounded ever afterward: "I saw with my own eyes, there in that prison, things unbelievable and monstrous." Hanging over every prisoner, including the hall-men, was the threat of solitary confinement in the stygian blackness of the "dungeon." Jack recalled the relentless taunting that drove one man insane, while brute force crushed another who was pushed down five flights of steel stairs, stood naked and bleeding, screamed "in terror and pain and heartbreak," and then "collapsed in a heap, unconscious"—all for trying to "stand for his rights."[18]

London could only broach, obliquely, the "'unprintable' and 'unthinkable'" acts that he witnessed. No innocent, "no spring chicken in the ways of the world," he hints that what he saw in the penitentiary far exceeded his deepest knowledge of "the awful abysses of human degradation." The "bit of man-handling" that he termed "one of the very minor unprintable horrors of the Erie County Pen" was most probably gang rape. His own relationship with his prison veteran "pal" may well have slid from the fraternal to the obligatory sexual. As he said, "When one is on the hot lava of hell, he cannot pick and choose his path."[19]

Readers of *The Road* got glimpses of the modern-day prison as a reprise of what London termed the "Middle Ages," but he knew the literary market would not tolerate a more graphic picture than the one he had drawn. "I do but skim lightly and facetiously the surface of things as I there saw them," he insisted. He was mindful of magazine editors' repeated warnings against submitting fiction that throbbed with "too much 'meat,'" especially for the multitude of "lady readers" (this from editor Roland Phillips at *Cosmopolitan*). Nor could London's closest friend and sometime editorial adviser, the poet George Sterling, bring himself to respond to Jack's account of imprisonment in *The Road*. "Your 'tramp' proofs came right along," Sterling wrote in September 1907. "It's awfully interesting stuff; but somehow I wish you'd never written it. I can't dissociate a tramp from an evil smell."[20]

Jack London, however, lived with the "meat," the "evil smell," and every other carnal and spiritual outrage that he had seen and breathed and which, for the sake of his survival in prison, he had done nothing to stop or prohibit. The unearthly "scream" of the naked bleeding prisoner who collapsed at the bottom of the stairwell taught a lesson that every prisoner learned. London's month at the Erie County Pen became a touchstone for indelible moments that flared ever afterward in his writing. Taking notes in the wretched East End of London in 1902 for the exposé that became *The People of the Abyss*, Jack profiled a homeless shelter that was "too much like prison" and England itself as a "prison from which there was no hope of escape." Held overnight in shelter, he felt he had spent the night "in the army or in prison."[21]

Producing crime fiction, however, proved nearly impossible for London no matter how hard he tried. A perennial stock-in-trade for writers of popular fiction, the genre was a winner with the magazine- and book-buying public. It tantalized and beckoned London, and he kept up with its literature. His library held volumes of Arthur Conan Doyle and Edgar Allan Poe, whose Baltimore gravesite Jack visited with Charmian one rainy afternoon in February 1912. He also owned Nathaniel Hawthorne's son Julian's edited miscellany, *The Lock and Key Library: Classic Mystery and Detective Stories* (1909). Eager to write salable crime fiction, he culled newspapers and magazines for story ideas, and he clipped and filed accounts of spectacular crimes for possible reworking into fiction, among the possibilities "Some Clever Swindles"; "Poisoned Brother for Insurance"; and "Look Out for the Crook with Knockout Drops." One library volume was particularly promising, the former prosecutor Arthur Train's *True Stories of Crime* (1912), which was chock-full of lively accounts of forgery and various swindles, including inheritance claims to Central Park, Fifth Avenue mansions, and Texas coal mines. London also bought plot outlines from a struggling young writer, Sinclair Lewis, who sold him "The Common-Sense Jail," in which a tough-on-crime judge is taught a humbling lesson when he is arrested and jailed for a night.[22]

Eager to join the ranks of crime fiction writers, London sketched this plot: "Large situation: to a woman who is held up by desperate young fellow, in her own house—she is beautiful, etc. Fellow's first robbery. She persuades him. He throws gun down on table. Then somebody, (the butler) . . . comes in. she passes revolver to him and has him hold robber while she telephones police. Wind-up—when police take him away. He turned his head as he went out and called her a name unspeakable & vile." London, however, abandoned this story, filed it under "Notes for Crime Stories," then ventured to another outline for a novel, "A Prison Study," in a scrawl that is legible in key phrases: "San Quentin execution," "A man, falsely convicted . . . spends fifteen years in San Quentin," "woman who had sent him to prison. . . . He is railroaded, sentenced to long term. . . . When he gets out, he discovers her . . . a great lady. . . . In the end, maybe she kills him."[23]

These notes too were dispatched, null and void, to London's files, the plots no match for his bone-deep knowledge of the realities of prison and the egregious injustices of the criminal justice system. In the popular marketplace, boilerplate crime stories could flourish in the *Police Gazette* and the genteel detective novels of Mary Roberts Rinehart, but they would not originate from the pen of Jack London.

He could not let go. As if priming himself for a crime novel debut, as if determined to overcome writer's block on the topic, he kept abreast of literature on crime and incarceration. He gathered books that approached crime and prison from the vantage points of history, sociology, psychology, and the legal system. The "tools" of London's "trade," as he called his library, included English translations of the German Paul Nitsche and Karl Wilmanns's *History of Prison Psychoses*, the Russian Leonid Andreyev's *Seven Who Were Hanged*, and the Italian Enrico Ferri's *Criminal Sociology*.[24]

These titles all grappled with questions of criminal behavior and its origins, with the etiology of criminals' minds, and with the societal dysfunction that fostered criminal conduct—from police brutality to prison conditions that drove inmates insane or to suicide. London scoured them all. Some were academic, as in Nitsche and Wilmanns's statement on "transient psychotic disturbances which apparently arise from hypnagogic hallucinations." Elsewhere, the terms could be crystal clear, as in Jack's favorite undercover journalist, Josiah Flynt, whom some knew to be the nephew of the women's temperance leader Frances Willard. The lucid Flynt identified the slum as the spawning ground for the "professional criminal" ("The best-born lad in the world can go wrong if forced to live in this corrupt environment").[25]

London pasted the books with his signature wolf bookplate as if to hasten the day when he too could find his way to a crime novel. Meanwhile, he underscored and bracketed numerous passages, including Ferri's classification of "five categories" of criminals: "criminal madmen, born criminals, criminals by contracted habits, occasional criminals, and criminals of passion." The corporal punishment of transgressors, Jack learned from his books, was woefully consistent across continents from one century to the next. From *Curious Punishments of Bygone Days*, he learned of "whipping" with "a knotted cord" in the 1600s, a practice continued in the present in a Russian Siberian prison with a knotted "thong" of stout rawhide. The dungeon, a dreaded place in the Erie County Penitentiary during Jack's incarceration, was equally feared, he learned, in England's Wandsworth Prison: "It was solid black, a darkness to be felt, a darkness that seemed to press into your very eyes."[26]

These lines corroborated his prison memories but inspired no fiction, even as Jack hired parolees from San Quentin to work as farmhands at Beauty Ranch. Charmian reflected that sailing their boat *Roamer* in sight of San Quentin made Jack "eager to give a chance to those unfortunate enough to have come inside the forbidding gray battlements." Not that he was naive about potential problems. "Of course, you will have to watch this man," he advised his stepsister and farm manager Eliza as the two worked out bunk and board arrangements for a new ex-prisoner. "We won't board our 'paroled' men with our regular men," he decided, but at least one parolee, a Mr. Stryker, dined with the Londons at midday in February 1911, engaging Charmian in an "interesting time & talk."[27]

The reading public, meanwhile, got a spate of other authors' prison novels, and London dutifully added their titles to his library, each one a bid for prison reform. The British C. Vernon-Harcourt's *Bolts and Bars* (1905) offered a fictional first-person "tour" of the "barbarism at present in vogue" inside English prisons, while *An Eye for an Eye* (1905), by the celebrated American attorney Clarence Darrow, fictionalized an 1897 murder case in Chicago.

Darrow's novel featured an honest US workman who finds himself jobless, penniless, and hectored incessantly by his shrewish wife, whom he strikes in a deranged but fatal moment—and now awaits hanging for her murder with no possible appeal on grounds of mitigating circumstances.

Still other novels joined in a reformist ensemble. In the numerically titled *9009*, Jack's journalist friend Jimmy Hopper weighed in with coauthored prison fiction whose preface promised readers "a simple, clear, compressed story . . . which shows how Society creates a Monster." In addition, Jack's acquaintance, the journalist and attorney Brand Whitlock (a protégé of Clarence Darrow), turned to fiction in *The Turn of the Balance* (1907) to expose the class-based divide in the punishment of felonies. Whitlock's readers met a bank embezzler from an affluent family who evades prosecution, while the embezzler's working-class counterpart, a troubled Spanish-American War veteran, is executed in the electric chair when convicted of murder.[28]

These novels countered the propaganda that assured the public of the fair-minded civic integrity of the penal system. Readers of the September 1899 issue of the *Overland Monthly*, for instance, found one of the first Yukon stories of the refreshing new writer Jack London—but also saw a laudatory article on the management of California's State Penitentiary at Folsom. Though the facility housed "the most desperate criminals to be found within the prisons of this country," the *Overland Monthly* reported, these "violators" were nonetheless said to be "punished without unnecessary hardship or abuse." The magazine's readers were assured that the warden was "a gentleman of long experience in the management of criminals."[29]

Biennial reports of the State Prison Directors of the State of California similarly abounded with affirmative statements and numerical data from the officials at San Quentin and Folsom Prisons—from the warden, the clerk, the turnkey, the captains of the guard and of the yard, of the distribution department (responsible for supplies), and of the resident physician and the chaplain. The officials' facts and figures were meant to quell public anxieties and doubts about the expenditure of public money, emphasizing fiduciary care and expertise in the custodianship of criminals.

One report of 1896–1909 included two topics of keenest interest to Jack London. His "work beast" stints as a laborer and mill hand in younger days made him hyperalert to the signature industries at San Quentin and Folsom. Because the latter was situated on the roiling, raging American River, its masses of granite lent themselves to quarrying; the inmates crushed hundreds of thousands of tons of rock, mainly for county and municipal road-

29. Granite quarried in intense summer heat by prisoners in stripes at Folsom Prison. (San Francisco History Center, San Francisco Public Library)

ways, the proceeds supporting the prison. One ex-inmate recalled that "each striped creature" lived and toiled in a "crypt of stone." Jack could identify with the work site as a "crypt."[30]

Closer to his life was San Quentin's major prison industry—jute milling, the very industry in which he had toiled in Oakland for ten cents per hour at his mother's insistence. The irony was palpable. The San Quentin mill, with its quota of grain bags, twine, and rope, was a life-script he had escaped, fleeing both its mind-numbing monotony and the perils recalled by one former San Quentin inmate: "Scarcely a Saturday passes without some man, frequently two or three, being caught in the machinery and losing fingers and limbs."[31]

Jack had already covered these topics in fiction. His story "The Apostate" made its statement about jute mill toil, and his novel *Martin Eden* sent the public a message about physical injury from naked industrial machinery. He needed something new. And on the literary side, Oscar Wilde set a high standard in *The Ballad of Reading Gaol* (1896), with its clear-cut lines: "We sewed the sacks, we broke the stones, / We turned the dusty drill / . . . But in the heart of every man / Terror was lying still." Jack's copy of the *Ballad* was pasted with his wolf bookplate, as were other of Wilde's books in his library. A Jack London prison novel must not fall short of Wilde's stylistic power. Jack London did not yet see his way clear to the crime or prison novel he was determined to write.[32]

Events under way on the West Coast, however, were to prove auspicious for Jack's prison novel. In 1899, just as he began to make a name for himself as a promising writer of exotic Yukon fiction, Bay Area reporters were beginning to show interest in certain notorious San Quentin prisoners, those whose red flannel uniform shirts marked them as "Incorrigibles." That May, the *San Francisco Examiner Magazine* ran a feature titled "The Red Shirt Men of San Quentin," followed in July by a *San Francisco Chronicle* exposé of conditions endured by these "Incorrigibles." "In the Cell of Silence," the *Chronicle* piece, reported that seven convicts were "entombed alive in narrow cages," a veritable "hell on earth." These articles found their way into Jack London's files.[33]

So did the next round of press reports of prison horrors and investigations by elected officials of the California legislature. In February 1903, the year *The Call of the Wild* was published, California state senator Edward J. Tyrrell and his colleagues inquired into conditions at Folsom and San Quentin. On February 19, the *San Francisco Examiner* headlined: "Prison Cruelty Recalls Stories of Horrible Tortures of Middle Ages," with an inset story promising that the legislature would "Take Action." Similar scandals erupted once again in 1913, when the *San Francisco Bulletin* announced, "Legislators Hear True Story of Cruelties at San Quentin." These included affidavits from prisoners who cited suffocatingly bad air in "the hole" (with air holes measuring three-eighths of an inch at the bottom of steel double doors), together with open waste buckets and chloride of lime, which, when dampened, produced acidic vapors deliberately released to scald prisoners' nasal passages and throats.[34]

Other forms of prison torture were coming to light. Punishments could be brutal for such infractions as "assaulting an officer," "disobedience," general crookedness," "vulgarity," "bed not made before breakfast," "hands in pockets," "gazing around room," "refusal to eat crust," or, in one case, glaring at or "dog-eyeing" a guard. Whippings and beatings, supposedly of bygone days, were still practiced, as was the exile to the stone-floored dungeon (or "hole") for indeterminate periods, with bread and water the once-per-day fare. Likewise, solitary confinement was a torment of isolation seemingly without end. Another punishment was trussing, or manacling, in which "the prisoner is strung up by the wrists in a dark cell and thus left hanging, like

30. Prisoner "triced" by "bull ring" on orders from prison officials. Note that the feet barely touch the floor. (From the Prison Reform League, *Crime and Criminals*, 1910)

a carcass of beef." A variation was tricing, in which a prisoner's wrists were handcuffed behind his back, a rope tied to the cuffs, and the man hoisted up until the tips of his toes barely touched the floor. (One former Folsom prisoner remarked that tricing was not "satisfactory" to officials because men lost consciousness and thus ceased to suffer.) In yet another torture, "the derrick," a handcuffed prisoner was raised with his feet above his head and left dangling. One further punitive tactic, dubbed the "hummingbird," involved chaining a prisoner in a shallow tank of water and administering electric shocks until his muscles knotted and he fainted from pain.[35]

By 1900, one form of torture exceeded all others in its cunning and its devastation, for the straitjacket had migrated from mental institutions to prisons. What's more, the device had metamorphosed from a restraint protecting mental patients from self-injury into a torturous form of human bondage. The fear it aroused and the damage it wreaked was lifelong, and sometimes fatal. On the decree of a warden or some other official, any convict was ripe for a turn in the jacket, which struck terror and incited hatred to the depths of a prisoner's very being.

It was the straitjacket Ed Morrell had endured in prison that lighted the Promethean torch for Jack London's prison novel, which was published in England, we recall, as *The Jacket*. When he learned that the warden had repeatedly ordered Morrell to be straitjacketed to force him to confess to the location of guns allegedly smuggled into the prison, Jack realized the straitjacket would be fundamental for his prison novel.

First, however, he had much to learn about a device that was likened to the shape of a coffin lid, with "heavy metal eyelets one inch apart for the purpose of lacing the sack or jacket tightly around the body." While such restraints as shackles and handcuffs were common public knowledge, a veil of ignorance surrounded the prison straitjacket and its use, prompting prison reformers of the early 1900s to offer full descriptions, several of which Jack London gathered in his files and his library. One memoir, "San Quentin as I Knew It," insisted that "the public should know exactly what the straitjacket is and how it works." The author, Colonel Griffith J. Griffith, was an expert in the matter. During two years in San Quentin for assault with a deadly weapon (1904–6), he found the jacket to be "in constant use, scarce a day without two or three victims." Jack penciled a note, "Read Griffith's book," and this is what he found:

> It is a canvas overcoat, reaching from the head to the knees, in which the victim is tightly laced. Inside it are sleeves so placed that the arms are pinned over the floating ribs. If, through carelessness or vindictiveness on the part of the officer administering the punishment, the jacket is laced too tightly, or if the confinement is continued any great length of time, permanent deformity, paralysis or serious internal derangement will result. The natural excretions of the body are much affected and the circulation of the blood is impeded, which, as any doctor will tell you, causes great anguish and often excruciating pains to the head. In Folsom not long ago a prisoner died after he had been in the jacket half an hour.

From other former prisoners' accounts, Jack learned the specifics of the torment of the jacket. Cinched tightly by the burliest of guards, often with the aid of a stout rod to act as a screw, the victim "could scarcely breathe," and his hands and feet would "die," becoming "cold and inanimate." Once released, "the victim could not stand, but was obliged to grovel and wriggle on the floor," sometimes suffering "paralysis." Some men died.[36]

The newspapers, once again, reported California's legislative investigations and proclaimed the straitjacket the most sinister of torments in the state's prisons. "Assemblymen Probing Use of the Straitjacket in San Quentin

31. By order of prison officials, a penitentiary inmate is immobilized in the straitjacket, often a source of disability or death. (From the Prison Reform League, *Crime and Criminals*, 1910)

Prison," bannered the *San Francisco Examiner* in February 1903, the same month headlining: "Warden of Folsom Prison Tells How Instrument of Torture Was Introduced to Him." The *Examiner* reprinted a letter written by the San Quentin warden, Martin Aguirre, to his Folsom counterpart, advising that "as a rule" he kept men laced in the jacket "50–60 hours, and sometimes even as long as four days." Aguirre kept a supply of jackets, he said, in small, medium, and large sizes, adding that he deliberately fed the jacketed prisoners well and gave them all the water they wanted to drink, "for the more they eat and drink the harder the punishment is to endure." "Strait-Jackets Must Go from Prison," concluded the newspaper, reporting that the visiting delegation of the California Senate and Assembly now recommended that "strait-jacketing be abolished," convinced by the prisoners' testimony that it was "horrible."[37]

"Horrible," but not yet a relic of the past, as Jack learned when he read a report in the *California Assembly Daily Journal* of April 22, 1913. One full decade from the "Strait-Jackets Must Go" mandate of 1903, Jack London learned that the jacket still awaited inmates for whom, according to the government report, "every other possible means has proven ineffective to bring about proper observance of prison rules and governance." In 1914, a member of the California Assembly assured Jack in a letter that the straitjacket "and other cruel punishments" were now prohibited by law.[38]

Jack doubted that the law coincided with the reality, and he said so a few months later to a correspondent. "I have gone through prisons with the stripes on me," he wrote. "I have, as a trusty, shown visitors around (and I knew darned well what to show them and what not to show them)." The jacket especially weighed on him. So robust in movement around the wide world, so free to come and go at will on land and sea, he had once suffered the human cage of a prison cell. The complete and utter bondage of the strait-jacket, however, signaled an entirely different order of confining torment, an exponential intensification of human depravity and subjugation. Charmian stated that her husband did not believe in prison reform. As most people understood the term, she was correct. The jacket, however, was a clarion call to social change, and Jack a warrior for its abolition.[39]

The fight was joined by Progressive Era reform groups across the country, and London kept track of their efforts. His library included *Crime and Criminals* (1910), an indictment of the prison system published by the Prison Reform League. He also had the recent *Report of Commission on Prison Reform* by a working group comprising two state governors, a former Chicago Municipal Court judge, the Oklahoma commissioner of charities and corrections, and wardens and ex-wardens from prisons in Kansas, North Dakota, and Colorado. Their efforts merged with initiatives mounted by former prisoners who spoke out and published their own explosive accounts of imprisonment and of the failure of the criminal justice system and the urgent need for change. The prison memoirists, like the novelists and journalists, were speaking truth to power—to the public and elected officials. Their titles included J. Wess Moore's *Glimpse of Prison Life*, Jack Black's *The Big Break at Folsom*, Donald Lowrie's *My Life in Prison*, and Colonel Griffith J. Griffith's "San Quentin as I Knew It," together with an anonymous ex-convict's *Life in Sing Sing* under the pseudonym Number 1500.

At last Jack London conceived of a prison novel of his own to floodlight the horrors of the straitjacket, and not a moment too soon, for the term was appearing in the colorful slang that Americans relished. One popular US magazine cited school teachers' tendencies to "strait-jacket our speech," and another saw government restrictions putting "the national life into a strait-jacket." In a letter to Jack, his close friend George Sterling dismissed a mutual acquaintance as "bred in the classic strait-jacket."[40]

Perhaps Jack felt a slight chill at the poet's blithe use of a terrifying term. Perhaps he sensed the word was losing its shock value. Normalized as slang, the jacket was also striking a chord with the public far beyond the prison walls. Even as investigators exposed the straitjacket as crippling and fatal in the prisons, the US public was becoming fascinated by a spectacle that moved the jacket from the prison floodlight to the footlights of the theater. That is, the straitjacket had become a device for public entertainment. As London prepared his high-powered condemnation of the prison straitjacket, the renowned Harry Houdini was mesmerizing audiences coast to coast with spectacular feats of escape from shackles, chains, and the very straitjacket that Jack London vowed to make an American taboo.

Like London, Harry Houdini was a prime example of American self-fashioning. The son of a struggling rabbi who immigrated from Budapest to the United States with his wife and children, Ehrich Weiss (b. 1874) grew up first in Wisconsin, then in New York City tenements on the Upper West and East Sides. One of six children, the boy who renamed himself Harry Houdini was schooled in the Talmudic tradition, worked odd jobs to help his family, and, though he was slight of build, became passionate about sports, especially boxing and running. By his teen years, Erich had developed an interest in magic tricks, performed a few small shows, and changed his name to Houdini. As his biographer Kenneth Silverman writes, "Visitors to the 1893 World's Columbian Exposition in Chicago could sample Aunt Jemima pancake mix, ogle belly-dancing-great Little Egypt," and, "in the sideshow on the mile-long midway, they might also see nineteen-year-old Erich Weiss performing as Harry Houdini—one-half of a magic act called 'The Brothers Houdini.'" The brother act broke up, and in 1894 the five-foot-six Ehrich—now Harry—married a song-and-dance performer, the petite Bess Rahner, a Brooklyn brunette who partnered with him in a husband-and-wife act called simply "The Houdinis."[41]

With Bess as his assistant, the couple performed at dime museums, the indoor sideshows that occupied the lowest rungs of the entertainment industry. At twenty-one years of age, the ambitious Harry became part owner of a seedy burlesque show that toured the US Northeast, its income barely meeting expenses. He and Bess had developed a stunt, Metamorphosis, that involved "disappearance" from a locked and chained trunk. Adding handcuffing to the trick in 1895, he also undertook a personal body-building regimen, increasing his strength and muscle mass until he gained the strongman physique that had become fashionable. Visiting police stations while touring in New England, Harry garnered local publicity by allowing himself to be locked in multiple sets of handcuffs, withdrawing into another room, and emerging in seconds with the cuffs unlocked and dangling. The trick, at that time, did nothing to boost the show business fortunes of Harry and Bess, and they struggled for four additional years in financially shaky troupes of variety actors and circus performers. Then, in 1899, according to Silverman, "Harry's career skyrocketed. In fourteen dizzying months he became a star of American entertainment."[42]

The breakthrough came in spring of 1899, in a beer hall in St. Paul, Minnesota, when a visiting theater manager dared Harry to escape some handcuffs. He did so—and was promptly offered a contract to perform in high-quality vaudeville shows in the Orpheum theater chain throughout the United States and Canada. Onstage in majestic venues in major cities, Harry performed sleight-of-hand tricks with cards and needles. He also escaped from handcuffs and leg-irons, often inviting policemen onstage to fetter him. In July, accused in the *San Francisco Examiner* of concealing keys and thus of mere trickery, Houdini went to the city's police station to show his skill by performing nude. Examined by a surgeon for hidden keys, wires, or lock picks, his mouth taped and his clothing removed, he was shackled at the wrists and ankles, carried "buck naked" into a closet, and emerged in five minutes free of all constraints. Though nude stage performances before family audiences were out of the question, Houdini added police-station exhibitions to his tour because they generated publicity.[43]

Then came the straitjacket. In San Francisco in the summer of 1899, virtually in sight of San Quentin prison, Houdini asked the superintendent of the local " 'Insane Ward' " to lace him into a straitjacket, a restraint that had become controversial in medical reform circles as an archaic and even cruel restraint for mental patients. As Silverman recounts, "Harry freed himself in San Francisco and repeated the feat in Los Angeles three days later, walking into the city receiving hospital and . . . asking to see 'the best strait-jacket you have in the place.' " Laced and buckled into the jacket, he asked to be left alone for about ten minutes and emerged, freed, "with the straitjacket draped over his arm. 'It was a hard one,' he reportedly said, 'but I did it.' "[44]

Houdini's escape from the jacket depended on its cut and the tightness (or looseness) of the lacing, as Silverman explains. But audiences were not pondering the tailoring of the jacket or Houdini's wriggle room when, mouths open and aghast, they witnessed his escape from the straitjacket in subsequent stage performances. Adds Silverman, "With its note of sadism and overtone of social controversy, the Straitjacket Escape became a mainstay of 'The Houdinis.' " And the mainstay evolved, ever more spectacular as Houdini mastered the escape in full view of the audience and, later on, while suspended upside down from upper floors of tall buildings while thousands watched, breathless, from streets below.

Prison reform advocates, including Jack London, kept their own counsel about the uses of prison restraints and torture devices for theatrical entertainment. Their qualms were not voiced in print or in public forums. As Houdini became a household word, his tremendous popularity blocked such critique. If the straitjacket was trivialized as it was dramatized, its horrific prison usage was fenced off from entertainment. Houdini's Straitjacket Escape nonetheless raised the stakes for a reformer whose mission to curb prison torture was made that much more challenging.

In one major respect, however, the temper of the times proved as propitious for Jack London as for Harry Houdini. The spiritualist movement that had drawn London's mother, Flora, to a career of séances proved foundational for magicians, whose feats of legerdemain seemed genuinely otherworldly. The first escape artists, Silverman remarks, were the spiritualist mediums, succeeded in turn by magicians of unparalleled ability to enthrall a public that was avid to believe in the transcendence of the soul. Harry Houdini's career was shaped and furthered by the spiritualist strain in American culture. Surprisingly, so was *The Star Rover*, Jack London's prison novel. Once again, the former San Quentin and Folsom prisoner Ed Morrell had a crucial part to play.[45]

Jack initially valued Morrell's story for its ready-made action plot—including the former prisoner's torture in the straitjacket while at San Quentin. Morrell's incarceration had been theater of the absurd, with death a likely final act, and the jacket was a major element in his story. Charmian recalled Jack "fairly frothing over the straitjacket scars Morrell had been revealing."[46]

Just at the launch, however, London abruptly abandoned that plot, that novel. In nautical terms, he came about and steered a new course, as if he sensed that Ed Morrell's history might drive him to the straits of biography and lash him to his subject. Morrell, for his part, overplayed his hand, mistaking Jack and Charmian's hospitality for close friendship. In his mind, a partnership with Jack was in the offing, with coauthored books and perhaps a vaudeville lecture tour featuring Jack London and Ed Morrell onstage together coast to coast. The former prisoner joked about becoming a nuisance in the London household ("So as usual be prepared for me to pester to a finish"), and he thought nothing of suddenly announcing his arrival at Beauty Ranch to claim Jack's attention ("Dear Jack—I am going to give a run up Sunday. . . . I feel it is important that I have a chat with you"). Jack and Charmian were polite but guarded. Charmian herself lunched with Morrell at the Saddle Rock, but she and Jack came to understand that the former prisoner was an opportunist, a hustler. In the pages of *The Star Rover* he was to find himself shrunk to a minor character—but not before he serendipitously provided Jack with the key to the new novel.[47]

In addition to the straitjacket, that is, Morrell offered Jack a few offhand remarks that proved to be crucial to the long-delayed and radically new prison novel. Aware that Jack London took "little stock in things occult," the former San Quentin prisoner suggested that his novel might nonetheless benefit from some "speculation in this matter," based on Morrell's own "personal experiences." Morrell's casual suggestion, that is, provided Jack's eureka moment.[48]

While in prison, Morrell reported hearing an "occult" hypnotic "Voice," and Morrell's "occult" became Jack London's passport to a novel that broke the bounds of time and space while giving him free rein to rage against the US prison system. The straitjacketed prisoner's reported episodes of suspended animation or, if one will, of trances or astral projection were well timed to the current vogue of the New Thought or mentalism that also benefited Houdini. It cloaked pop psychology with science to produce statements of this sort: "A thought from the brain of one person travels on . . . until it is taken up by the brain or brains that are in harmony with the mind from which it is sent." London could find this and similar sentiments in his copy of *The Law of Mentalism* (1902), and he pitched his idea for *The Star Rover* to an editor as "accessible stuff . . . for all the New Thought folks." Morrell's experience of the "occult" became the gateway to London's experimental novel, which ranged through time and space with virtuosic élan even as it exposed the straitjacket as a barbaric holdover from a feudal mentality.[49]

Though Jack miniaturized Morrell's life story, its "occult" element kindled his imagination like sunlight beamed through a lens. Repelled from boyhood by his mother Flora's otherworldly séances, he now pivoted eagerly to Morrell's claim of paranormal power, for he saw its strategic brilliance for his fiction. As a child working in the Pennsylvania coal mines, he learned, Morrell had frequent déjà vu moments of "visualizing. . . . strange yet familiar" scenes he felt he surely "must have lived" in other times. Cinched in the straitjacket in San Quentin, Morrell felt "inspiration" from the same sorts of pictorial images that were accompanied repeatedly by a "Voice" from the "occult" that urged him to take control of his condition. His pain eased, he said, and his future unrolled before him, auguring his release. "I had got in touch with the Truth," he said, "through that wonderful Voice." Enduring countless jacketings, Morrell was convinced that he survived and prevailed from the strength of what the historian Kenneth Lamott terms "an autohypnotic technique."[50]

The "occult" did double duty for London. It propelled his long-delayed prison novel and solved a knotty problem of coordinating fictions that did not easily fit in the same mix. Always a wide-ranging reader and enthusiast of tales of the long ago and far away, London stocked his library with titles encompassing millennia, crossing continents, and beamed from pole to pole. He toyed with the notion of short stories gathered from "a number of diverse places." He also pondered a series of novels ranging from biblical times to the Middle Ages and into the eighteenth and nineteenth centuries and spanning the globe. With unbounded admiration for Jesus of Nazareth, London had long planned a "Christ novel," and he also gathered several volumes on the history and culture of Korea and considered developing a story set on that East Asian peninsula. Enjoying amateur fencing as a sport second only to boxing, he pondered a story highlighting swordplay and set in Renaissance France, when swordsmanship was at its height. He also owned, read closely, and underscored passages in Josiah Gibbs's *Mountain Meadows Massacre*, an account of a notorious episode in 1857 in which a wagon train of California-bound pioneers from Arkansas were gunned down in their meadow encampment in southern Utah by a zealous Mormon sect calling itself the Nauvoo Legion. All these ideas for fiction ran across centuries, across social class, across fame and obscurity, across cultures and places. They jostled in London's mind. To win lucrative advance publication contracts, he must persuade editors that these projects would cohere as an assemblage. He saw no way—that is, until he saw the opportunity for his prison novel flashing in plain sight in Morrell's account of the "occult."[51]

The "Voice" that guided Morrell's astral projections gave London a literary design of extraordinary power for his prison novel. He would reprise the time-travel frameworks that were so winning in his *Before Adam* and *The Iron Heel* and which succeeded in a cluster of notable novels—in Edward Bellamy's *Looking Backward*, in H. G. Wells's *Time Machine*, and in Mark Twain's *Connecticut Yankee at King Arthur's Court*. Beyond time travel was reincarnation, which was a mainstay of Rudyard Kipling's "Finest Story in the World" and Edwin Lester Arnold's *Phra the Phoenician*.

Time travel and reincarnation permitted freewheeling fictions that London could wrangle into a unified sequence of episodes in a picaresque time-travel novel. His narrator—a prisoner protagonist—could appear and reappear in protean identities in different epochs worldwide. A male prisoner tortured in the straitjacket in San Quentin, he could mentally and spiritually escape to travel in time and be reincarnated as a peasant, as an aristocrat, a Viking, and a member of the Korean royal imperial court. He could fall in love with a Korean noblewoman or a Jewish beauty in Jerusalem. He could be an eighteenth-century shipwrecked sailor and an eleven-year-old boy named Jesse Fancher, the son of the leader of pioneers who were doomed in the Mountain Meadow massacre. Time travel and reincarnation—the "occult"—were the guiding, unifying principle. Among readers of *The Star Rover*, the believers would believe, and others would suspend their disbelief. No reader, however, would doubt the sadistic brutality of the straitjacket.

The psychology of the reading public, as London well knew, must be taken into account. Ardent prison reformers were relatively few in the Progressive Era, and prison was hardly an enticing topic for the middle and upper middle classes in their lushly upholstered sitting rooms and sun parlors. To succeed, *The Star Rover*'s urgent message of prison reform must be woven with a warp and woof of thrilling, captivating tales. Immersing its readers in San Quentin prison from the outset, the novel must be brutally frank about excruciating conditions—yet give its audience a series of between-acts escapes in the form of captivating stories from early modern France to Scandinavia to Korea and Jerusalem and the American West. Readers could decide for themselves whether the prison scenes of straitjacketing were secondary to the tales, or the tales themselves paramount. It was a split decision, the two titles balanced fifty-fifty: *The Star Rover* in the United States, and in England *The Jacket*. The straitjacket, however, was the hardest hard fact in both versions, never for one moment to be doubted or dismissed as fiction.

"All my life I have had an awareness of other times and places. I have been aware of other persons in me." Thus begins *The Star Rover*. With an outline from Ed Morrell, the spotlight beams on a protagonist whom London conjures, a figure named Darrell Standing who claims to be reincarnated and adds time-travel voyaging to his life experience: "Not only did I range the world, but I ranged time." As a Minnesota farm boy, readers learn, Darrell Standing first experienced his occult powers, which he renews as a forty-four-year-old Folsom prisoner awaiting execution for murder. Eight years in San Quentin and now on Murderers' Row in Folsom, Darrell reflects on his past as a professor of agronomics in the College of Agriculture at the University of California at Berkeley. His bona fides include expertise in soils and irrigation and in the popular efficiency movement that was sweeping the nation in the 1910s, promoting the triumph of efficiency over waste in every realm of life, from the industrial shop floor to the home kitchen. The movement was especially attractive to the American bourgeoisie, and London keyed Darrell's professional status to this target audience, which could exert political pressure for prison reform.[52]

Darrell, we learn, was first sentenced to life in prison for killing a university colleague, the truth of which he admits. His death sentence, however, has been imposed for "assault and battery," specifically for merely bloodying the nose of a prison guard in a scuffle. If readers think this a fictional stretch, London points to the California statutes: "It is law, and as law it will be found in the criminal statutes." *The Star Rover*, set in 1913, anticipates the conclusion at which Darrell Standing will be hanged in accordance with this law (as, in fact, was Jacob Oppenheimer, known as "the Prison Tiger," whose memoir Jack also had on file).[53]

The bizarre law was worth a chapter in itself, but London's focus was prison torture—or tortures, plural. Darrell presents an inventory and indictment of what Jack witnessed in the Erie County Penitentiary and otherwise tallied from his research. The straitjacket was the apex of cruelty, but other demonic devices were not to be slighted. "I was given the dungeon and the starvation of light and food," Darrell says. "I was spread-eagled, and thumbed-up, and privily beaten by the stupid guards" wielding "pick-handles—a handy tool for the 'disciplining' of a helpless man." In freezing winter, fire hoses were turned on him and others. "We had no blankets in the dungeons," he explains, describing the "jeering and cursing" guards who "played the fierce streams on us, dungeon by dungeon, until our bruised flesh was battered all anew by the violence with which the water smote us." In solitary, Darrell "gamed with flies," mentally played chess, or conversed with his knuckles. Other prisoners went insane or committed suicide.[54]

Such torments often originated with gossip and lies that were fed to prison officials by informant stool pigeons. In *The Star Rover* London followed Morrell's lead among the prison memoirists who raged against the network of inmate spies who poisoned the woeful atmosphere with suspicion and distrust. Snitching on fellow inmates to gain, say, better food or an early release, the stool pigeons were themselves instruments of torture, since they brought officials' wrath upon the bodies and spirits of men they fingered as culprits. Worse, they invented infractions and trafficked in lies, false accusations against inmates whose only defense was denial of the trumped-up charges. Just as Ed Morrell was betrayed by a lying "stoolie" who swore that Morrell knew the whereabouts of guns stashed somewhere in San Quentin, so in *The Star Rover* Darrell Standing's "red wrath" is reserved for the self-serving, lying inmate whose double-cross has doomed him to the worst years of his foreshortened life. (To heighten drama, London swapped dynamite for the allegedly hidden guns in Morrell's account, since guns were too mundane to raise 1910s Americans' gooseflesh, while dynamite was as horrifying as nuclear terrorism became for later generations.) Just as the guns in Morrell's story were mythical, so was the dynamite sequestered in San Quentin in *The Star Rover*. Tortured in the straitjacket, Darrell Standing can only plead ignorance that is mistaken for stubbornness and, by some, for stoic endurance.[55]

Years pass before the fictionalized Ed Morrell appears to help Darrell revive his occult powers, at which point readers face the end result of a human being held legally in solitary confinement and tortured by straitjacket for years. As if London imaginatively cloned prisoner Ed Morrell for the novel, his Darrell is a wraith of "eighty-seven pounds," his hair and beard uncut for five years, his voice thinned to a whisper, his skin like parchment, his eyesight damaged from years of near total darkness, and his body "one mass of bruise and misery." He can no longer walk without aid, and he and the warden both know that, for him, "it looks like curtains."[56]

In an adjacent cell, however, the fictional Ed Morrell has made acquaintance with Darrell and invites him to join in the knuckle-rapping communication by which Morrell has long conversed with his fellow "Incorrigible," Jake Oppenheimer, a sort of cell-to-cell telegraphic code between the two "Incorrigibles." Letter by letter, they tap out words on the walls that separate them. Once Morrell has taught Darrell the code, he proceeds to tutor him in out-of-body star roving. "The trick is to die in the jacket," Morrell advises, that is, "to will yourself to die" in the awareness "that your body is one thing and your spirit is another thing." Morrell teaches a conscious deadening of the jacketed body from the toes up, then goes on to counsel that "when your body is all dead, . . . you just skin out and leave your body," for "stone walls and iron doors are to hold bodies in" but "can't hold the spirit in."[57]

London must persuade readers of the plausibility of the process. He invokes science as Darrell undergoes death-in-life and life-in-death. Soon enough, Darrell leaves "straitjacket hell" to vault the prison roof and tread "interstellar space," landing in Renaissance France, where he is reincarnated as the Count de Sainte-Maure, an expert swordsman who will duel triumphantly before succumbing to a "clownish" rapier blow to his head. No matter, for other stories of the reincarnated, time-traveling Darrell Standing will soon follow, as will the repeated horrific entr'acte scenes of jacketing in which Darrell smiles beatifically at the warden, whose frustration and outrage approach apoplexy with each denial of any knowledge of hidden dynamite.[58]

At the threshold of Morrell's tutelage and each new story, however, readers are called to a halt and refused permission to proceed until they hear the particulars of the straitjacket and absorb the impact of its horrifying message. "Have you ever seen canvas tarpaulins . . . with brass eyelets set in along the edges?" Darrell asks. He gives the jacket's shape and dimensions and offers an outline of the victim "face-downward" in a prone position, at which moment some readers' memories were surely jogged from newspaper revelations of goings-on a few years earlier at San Quentin and Folsom. Darrell describes the rope laced through the eyelets for the "'cinching,'" as some readers doubtless recalled the former Folsom prisoner Jack Black's widely published account of the jacket "like knives penetrating to my lungs." And as Darrell reports the "smothered groans" and "mad howling" of the jacketed prisoner, contemporary readers of *The Star Rover* probably remembered the jacket miseries detailed by Colonel Griffith in *Crime and Criminals*.[59]

These readers, however, were mainly residents of Northern California's Bay Area. Many could recall the horrifying, sensational publicity about prisons in their city newspapers in recent years. *The Star Rover*, however, took the issue to the entire nation, to the world. A star rover itself, the novel soared across the continent and the Atlantic to initiate a world public into the dark secrets of the US prisons. Those who failed to pay attention or refused to act to rid prisons of the straitjacket and other tortures could hear Jack London's censure in Darrell's tone, which drips with acid when he cites the "smug citizens who constitute the state, full of meat and sleep." London deeply believed that knowledge was power. Going forward, complacency or inertia was out of the question, or so London trusted. Reform and vigilance were imperative, lest the immediate and far future debase and scar itself with prisons that mocked the very notion of "civilization."[60]

The Star Rover arrived with British and US plaudits for London's "mysticism," his imaginative "tricks," and his literary achievement. As quality fiction, said one reviewer, *The Star Rover* ranked among London's "best." Another commended its "stirring adventures," while a third concluded that London "makes disbelief very difficult, and that is the highest compliment a reader can pay him."[61]

The novel's revelations about the prisons, the tortures, and the straitjacket were broadcast in high volume in nearly all reviews. Though one of them de-

32. Famous friends in the public eye, Harry Houdini and Jack London. (Henry E. Huntington Library, San Marino, California)

cried London's "vulgarity" and another his borderline "literary indecency," the consensus was voiced by a reviewer for the *Detroit Evening News*, who wrote, "Jack London has poured out another bucket of blood and human suffering" to tell "tales of horror that seem impossible but may have been sadly true." From late summer and well into autumn of 1915, the reviews cascaded from both sides of the Atlantic. The *Chicago Herald* cited "the crying need for prison reform in the United States—especially, perhaps, at San Quentin." "Terrible treatment meted out to 'lifers,' declared the *Pittsburgh Post*, "as in an investigation of San Quentin some years ago." "All too painfully realistic," declared the *Illustrated London News*. A "scathing indictment of the prison system," added the English *Sheffield Telegraph*. "Almost too horrible for the printed page," said the (British) *Nation*. Jack knew that, however many copies of the book were read and passed along to others, those who even saw just the reviews would learn the dire facts about conditions in America's prisons and perhaps join with the reform activists. In *The Star Rover*, his Progressive Era effort contributed to the cessation of corporal punishment in US prisons by the mid-1910s.[62]

A postscript is irresistible. *The Star Rover* jolted the public just as Jack and Charmian became friends of Harry and Bess Houdini in November 1915. The Londons saw the escape artist's matinee performance at the Oakland Orpheum, visited Harry backstage afterward, and took him to dinner at a favorite restaurant, doubtless the Saddle Rock Café, with its floral panels, heavy beams, and snowy napery. There is no record of the straitjacket surfacing in their conversation, though Jack and Harry found instant rapport. A few days later Houdini and Bess gave a Thanksgiving Day dinner for the Londons in their hotel suite. Photographs were taken of Jack and Harry and of the foursome together, and Charmian sent the Houdinis a copy of her *The Log of the* Snark with an inscription, hoping that "we may all gather in the Valley of the Moon some not far distant day."[63]

The Houdinis regretted that their travel schedule prevented them from seeing Jack and Charmian off for Hawaii on the *Matsonia* in mid-December when the Londons sailed for the pleasure of their beloved Hawaiian Islands, but, more important, for Jack's health, which was failing. The truth was, he was in a fight against his body. His kidneys were beginning to shut down. He had more to say and more to write. Within a year, however, Charmian was called upon to confirm the reports the Houdinis heard in Columbus, Ohio, reports that prompted their Western Union telegram demanding to know whether the "shocking" new reports of Jack's death were "founded on fact." At that moment—November 23, 1916—Charmian was responding to a flurry of such telegrams and hastening replies to family, to friends, and to the world at large.[64]

Afterword

UNFINISHED BUSINESS

I would rather be ashes than dust. I would rather that my spark should burn out in a brilliant blaze than it should be stifled by dry rot.
—Jack London, quoted by Ernest J. Hopkins, *San Francisco Bulletin*, December 2, 1916

In November 1916, Jack London was busy planning a luncheon with his daughters in Oakland at the Saddle Rock Café and a trip to New York to negotiate a new book deal. The winter rains were in the offing and the spring sea fogs months away when he spurred his horse, Fritz, into the high hills of Beauty Ranch on the afternoon of November 21, 1916. Sick and bedridden for days this autumn, he was exhilarated to be in the open air. Savoring the moment, he dismounted to finger the rich soil and view the abundant springs of the property that adjoined his ranch. "I may buy it," he would announce to Charmian the minute he got back to the cottage. "I could develop the springs, and that would mean better crops, bigger and better cattle and horses, more life."[1]

This evening he planned to fling caution "to the four winds" and feast on his favorite seared duck instead of the vegetable dishes Charmian was serving these days for his health. Doctors had warned that his life would be shortened by the mercury-laced medicine, corrosive sublimate, that he'd slathered on his infected arms and legs in the Solomon Islands eight years ago on the *Snark* voyage. (The human body, he might not have known, cannot expel mercury, a lethal element.) A strict vegetarian diet was advised, though London was "naturally a meat-eater." He'd cheated death countless times in every quarter of the globe, and the film crew that came to Beauty Ranch a few days ago had posed him crouching with his rifle like a hunter. Duck season was open, and tonight it would be canvasback or mallard.[2]

High in the saddle for the ride home, it is not likely that London paused to look back on his life's work, though Beauty Ranch served as the base camp for reconnaissance—and for scouting the ongoing progress of the necessary revolution in domestic and global affairs from politics to popular culture. This year, for instance, the celebrated tenor Enrico Caruso recorded "O sole mio" for the Victor Talking Machine Company, but the Londons had long enjoyed phonograph recordings of opera in the evenings at the ranch, as they had in the South Seas voyage on the *Snark*. As for sport, 1916 was the year when women were first permitted to attend prizefights, but London's female readers got advance ringside seats a decade earlier in his novella *The Game*. This fall, London surely heard fellow members of the San Francisco Bohemian Club extol the wonders of the city's Market Street "Path of Gold," with its colonnade of hundreds of thirty-three-foot-high electric light pillars. This was the very Market Street that London walked in the aftermath of the San Francisco earthquake of 1906, when he was first on the scene to report and photograph the devastation for a national magazine.

In addition, Jack supported the US commitment to conservation, advanced at this moment with America's newest national park, in the archipelago of Hawaii. He and Charmian had explored the Islands' volcanic sites on foot and horseback, and Jack's lush descriptions in print piqued public interest in the Paradise of the Pacific. August 1916, saw the official dedication of Volcanoes National Park, located on the Big Island of Hawaii just as Jack and Charmian sailed home from their most recent visit to the Islands.

A major social experiment was under way in the United States, and once again Jack was on the forefront. New Year's Day 1916 marked the advent of a nationwide ban on alcoholic beverages, which several states now outlawed, giving Americans a foretaste of the United States of Prohibition. London's wrenching autobiography of 1913, *John Barleycorn*, exposed the ruinous "long sickness" of alcoholism. Knowing that addiction to brewed and distilled alcohol crushed individuals and families, he urged the banishment of the saloon to "the pages of history," where hindsight, he hoped, would put it on par with "bull-baiting and the burning of witches." A fond hope, that, though addictive substances were to bedevil America well into the far future.[3]

Other unfinished business roiled here at home. Chronic labor strife consumed newspaper columns and the pages of London's fiction as well, from his "South of the Slot" and "The Dream of Debs" to the strike scenes in the earlier chapters of *The Valley of the Moon*. This November of 1916, a fatal shootout between police and unionists of the IWW (International workers of the World) in Everett, Washington was to become known as the Everett Massacre, but London's readers already saw "an I.W.W. riot" referenced in his recent novel, *The Little Lady of the Big House*. The capital-versus-labor wars seemed nowhere near resolution in this second decade of the twentieth century. They were unfinished business.[4]

So too was the warfare of nations, external and internal. The Mexican Revolution flared into US public attention in 1913, but two years earlier in 1911 Jack London alerted the public to the turmoil erupting south of the US border. Cloaked as a prizefighting story, London's "The Mexican" explained the populist revolt against the thirty-one-year dictatorship of the brutal Mexican militarist Porfirio Díaz. The regime long showered favors on foreign "gringo" investors while leaving Mexico, as critics charged, a "mother to foreigners and a stepmother to her own children."[5]

To London, war and war reporting were both finished and unfinished business up to the present moment. Turmoil on the US-Mexican border called him to the front in 1914, when *Collier's* magazine published the first of his seven dispatches on the US skirmish in and bombardment and occupation of coastal Vera Cruz, Mexico. By then the Mexican Revolution had splayed into a half-dozen rivalrous warring factions. When US interests were thought to be threatened by Mexico's turmoil, London stepped up to report on the expedition of the "blue jackets" of the US Navy and Marine Corps. Just as he derided the "Korean Pack-ponies" as racial inferiors in his Russo-Japanese War correspondence, so Jack's dispatches from Vera Cruz contrasted the Mexican "sorry soldier Indians" to the superior American military. His condescension was not unusual. In 1914, one of President Woodrow Wilson's emissaries to Mexico, a politician named John Lind, described the Mexicans as "more like children than men," while US Senator Henry Cabot Lodge dismissed Mexican governance in domestic terms as an "unruly household."[6]

As in the Russo-Japanese War a decade earlier, Jack highlighted the incongruities in Vera Cruz. The peaceful "sapphire sea" and "azure sky" of the Gulf of Mexico was shadowed by a convoy of "ominous" naval destroyers, and all the while American women breakfasted on "cool arcaded sidewalks of hotels bordering the Plaza." American patriotism ran high, Jack had reported, and soon enough he chronicled the US bombardment of Mexico's Naval School and its aftermath of "bloodstained cots and pillows," "broken parapets," "burst floors, rent ceilings," and "masses of fallen masonry." The continuing carnage was horrendous, from "a high-velocity American bullet" that shattered a man's leg to the obliteration of useful and pleasant "things the toil of men has made"—all from "the hot breath of war," the very "efficiency of twentieth century war machinery." War, London knew, turned "well-tailored, well-mannered, courteous men" into ferocious "raw savages." What's more, modern warfare showed how the primitive "arrowheads and spear points" had evolved into "battleships, submarines, aerial bombs, torpedoes," and other lethal "wonderful up-to-date machine contrivances."[7]

In any case, as London emphasized, war was profoundly wasteful and illogical. The notion of human "right and justice" pursued by a ravaging "steel-jacketed bullet" was deeply incomprehensible to any "rational, civilized man." Jack conceded nonetheless that those of "violent and disruptive" temperaments must be held in check, both individually and nationally, since a "world police force" and "a world court of arbitration" remained a "dream" in reserve for the future. For the present, nations must maintain their "war machinery and know how to handle it."[8]

The statement was never truer than in the present year, 1916, when war boiled in Europe. The Germans, as London understood it, were the imperial aggressors carving earthly space "in the way of war." As a German nationalist phrase went: "*Heute Deutschland, morgen die ganze Welt*" (Today Germany, tomorrow the whole world). London found no comfort in the distance afforded by the Atlantic Ocean and the North American continent. From his outpost in California he closely monitored the war's events, and letters from 1915 show Jack London firmly on the Allied side. Loathing war's mandatory barbarism, he justified it according to the urgency of the moment: "I believe that the present war is a war between civilization and barbarism, between democracy and oligarchy."[9]

To London, "oligarchy" and "barbarism" were the modern-day furies wreaking havoc on humankind. His prescient political novel *The Iron Heel* had dramatized the catastrophic destruction of modern civilization by corporate oligarchs who wield despotic power in a future American police state where the public cowers and dissidents are silenced or killed off. London knew to his very marrow that unchecked oligarchy could become civilization's headstone. As for barbarism, he saw it rampant in US prisons and in every city and town in America. It was displayed daily in the cruel disregard for the men, women, and children whose lives were sacrificed to factories, mines, mills, foundries, smelters, and sweatshops and who toiled for pennies while their bodies spent themselves into the bankruptcy of muscle, bone, and brain. Over some two decades his fiction and nonfiction documented the state of this modern barbarity and the imperative of revolutionary reform. The socialism that London relied on to arrest and correct its evils remained the bedrock of his faith, though he had recently resigned from the party, fed up with its dithering and internal strife.

War or no, corporate Big Business was still growing at an ever-faster and unnerving clip in the United States. Such industries as steel, petroleum, mining, manufacturing, telecommunications, and the railroads had become "commercial leviathans," in the words of twentieth-century historian Roland Marchand, whose study of the rise of corporate public relations prompted the historian to ask how these "leviathans" related to American families, religious institutions, communities, and the nation itself. Marchand's findings verified Jack London's prediction that the "assets, influence, and geographic reach" of giant corporations "might surpass those of one of the states and even challenge those of the entire nation." To quell social anxiety and win over public opinion, Big Business increasingly sought the services of advertisers and public relations experts who developed, in Marchand's term, corporate "fables" that were shaped around the notion of the compassionate corporation and its "soul." Public relations now flourished, and its founder, Ivy Ledbetter Lee, was in high demand, persuading the public that the nation's economic well-being required only the slightest government regulation of the railroads and other industries—and assuring Americans that a mining company's major stockholders, the Senior and Junior John D. Rockefeller, were entirely innocent of the deaths of twenty striking coal miners and their relatives in Colorado's infamous Ludlow Massacre of 1914. Managing the image of the titans of business and finance and shaping corporate brands in terms of fabulist beneficence now constituted a recognized and profitable profession.[10]

From the other side, however, Progressive ideas were percolating in the two major political parties and in public policy and practice. The municipal ownership and regulation of public utilities, such as water, had become the norm from the nineteenth-century debates, their advocates including the socialists as well as the enlightened civic leaders of major US cities, both committed to the public good. One of London's first publications, an 1896 letter to the *Oakland Times*, had urged that a public city water system replace the costly battles of two commercial water companies with their rate wars and sabotage of one another's facilities.

Other Progressive and socialist plans were swirling in the 1910s. A work-related pension for retirees was high on the list. So was financial support for orphans and for the disabled—with both groups' needs measurable in 1913, a year that recorded "some 700,000 job-related injuries that required at least four weeks' disability" and "some 25,000 factory fatalities." (The adult workers' deaths, of course, left a generation of children orphaned.) Also in play were ideas on maximal hours for the standard workweek, on a national minimum wage, on extra pay for overtime work, and on a prohibition of child labor. In the main, socialists' proposals reached an audience of cohorts in partisan publications such as *Wilshire's* magazine and the *International Socialist Review*. Progressives turned to *The Survey* or *Charities* to launch their ideas in essays beamed to like-minded colleagues and to sympathetic journalists who might spread the word in the popular press. From time to time Jack London's work appeared in *Wilshire's* or the *International Socialist Review*.[11]

London knew, however, that Americans needed a hands-on vision of the Progressive future and enough time to weigh and savor its advantages. Public support needed to build—and to be built. For the sake of the future, he bundled Progressive ideas for the wider public in "Goliah," a short story that appeared in *The Bookman* in 1910.

"Goliah" largely reprised Edward Bellamy's socialist *Looking Backward—2000–1887*, the wildly popular utopian novel which London much admired and which inspired the formation of some 160 Nationalist Clubs dedicated to remaking the economy and society by nationalizing industry. The Bellamyite movement had petered out by the late 1800s when Jack London began his literary rise, but the young author's newfound stardom sparked a twentieth-century recharge of Bellamy's socialist agenda. Set in 1924, "Goliah" lays bare the dark grip of the Big Business oligarchy as pitted against an enlightened potentate Goliah (a Goliath), the agent of revolutionary progress. The Golden Rule of the story is the pursuit of earthly happiness, for Goliah decrees that "laughter" must supplant the industrial-age "slaughter" by warmongering corporate chieftains and their political minions. National "leading figures" are summoned to this potentate's offshore yacht, including "bankers, railway lords, captains of industry, and Supreme Court justices," together with "Congress and the Senate." Under duress, all consent to bend their efforts to the new equitable social order (the captains of industry, for instance, henceforth putting executive skills to work "for the good of society"). Under Goliah's rule the swords are beaten into plowshares—the metal of modern "war vessels" turned into "useful appliances for the arts of peace."[12]

Social reform in "Goliah" is swift and immediate. Child labor is abolished, women factory workers sent homeward, and sweatshops shut down. Food and shelter are "well nigh automatic," and the national workday is set at eight hours. The age of retirement with pensions is established at fifty years of age but scheduled to decrease as the 1920s proceed (this in 1910, when average US life expectancy hovered at around fifty-three years). From the far future "Goliah" registers social progress from the mid-1920s into the 1930s: "The minimum working age went up from sixteen years to eighteen years. The eight-hours day became a seven-hour day, and in a few months the national working day was reduced to five hours."[13]

"Goliah" was London's fictional prospectus for the social legislation enacted in the 1930s United States. Among other Progressives, London helped set the stage for laws enacted and popularized over decades despite periodic attacks by political opponents. The Social Security Act of 1935 included a pension fund for retirees, together with a federal-state unemployment program and a commitment to public assistance for dependent children and the disabled. The Fair Labor Standards Act of 1938 introduced an eight-hour workday, a forty-hour workweek, a mandatory national minimum wage, and a guaranteed "time-and-a-half" wage for overtime work. Children under the age of sixteen were prohibited from work, as were those under eighteen in certain categories of hazardous jobs.

London's "Goliah" and other writings helped lay the groundwork, in turn, for the post–World War II era, when reforms advanced in "Goliah" were once again proposed by leading social theorists, including C. Wright Mills and the Harvard University sociologist David Riesman and by such influential political figures as Daniel Patrick Moynihan and even President Richard Nixon, who in 1969 proposed a federal minimum income for a decent material standard of living for all families. Projecting a modern world of labor-saving automation, Jack London had foreseen the end of domestic drudgery and of industrial workers' "barbarously filthy and slavish lives." Foregrounding the post–World War II social theorists, he predicted that tedious, repetitive work would soon disappear in a new era of unprecedented leisure. The "leisure and joy" and "higher standard of living" forecast in "Goliah" were reprised in Riesman's postwar prediction that stultifying factory work would soon vanish. The American "gospel of work," said Mills, "would soon be "replaced . . . by a leisure ethic." So as in "Goliah," in which solar energy has supplanted the tonnage of coal by "miners slaving out their lives in the bowels of the earth," the new postwar age was expected to define itself by flourishing arts, athletics, and the higher life of the mind and spirit. By the twenty-first century, computer-driven robotics and other labor-saving automation exceeded the vision of London and of the post–World War II theorists, though the era of enlightened leisure remained elusive. It too was unfinished business.[14]

In a letter to the British publisher Hughes Massie in 1915, London swore his willingness "to fight and die with England." Rather than "be the Emperor of Germany," he said, he'd "far rather be a dead man."[15]

Death stalked Jack London on this late November afternoon of 1916 even

33. The fenced volcanic rock that marks Jack London's grave. (Jack London California State Park; photograph by William Tichi)

as it scythed thousands of men in the prime of their lives on the front in Europe. London always saw himself on frontlines and on the canvas, where he fought round upon round. Like all prizefighters, he battled time and his own body. The boxer's legs go first, it is said, and then the reflexes, and finally the drive. Jack London was in the ring to the last, his punch thrusting straight and true through the twentieth century and into the twenty-first. Much of the business of society remained unfinished when, on the night of November 22, Charmian warned her husband, "You are *tired*, perilously tired, tired almost to death." Death claimed the forty-year-old Jack London that night, November 22, 1916. His ashes are interred, as he wished, beneath a volcanic boulder on his Beauty Ranch property, which is now the Jack London California State Park, in Sonoma, the Valley of the Moon.[16]

NOTES

ABBREVIATIONS

AC Anderson Collection (private collection of documents and artifacts emphasizing Jack London in Sonoma)

CKL Charmian Kittredge London

CSS Jack London, *Complete Short Stories*

HL Henry E. Huntington Library, San Marino, California (Jack London Collection and other holdings referenced by call marks in endnotes)

JL Jack London

JACK LONDON, AMERICAN PUBLIC INTELLECTUAL

1. CKL, *The Book of Jack London*, 2:108 ("red sweater," "lurid . . . conflagration"). *Jack London at Yale*, 6 ("shocked . . . measure," "the sons . . . order").

2. CKL, *The Book of Jack London*, 2:109 ("million . . . marble"). *Jack London at Yale*, 7 ("bombarded," "dodgers"); 12 ("combed . . . forehead"; "black . . . pumps"). CKL, *The Book of Jack London*, 2:109 ("a clear . . . hall").

3. *Jack London at Yale*, 15 ("I speak . . . socialism," "a science . . . human," "to get . . . to-day," "is . . . alive").

4. JL, *Revolution*, 28–29 ("Why are . . . fed"); 26 ("Why . . . alone"); 31 ("This is . . . class"); 32 ("The capitalist . . . it," "The capitalist . . . it"). JL, "Things Alive," in *The Portable Jack London*, 483 ("awakening . . . men," "a healthier . . . things").

5. *Jack London at Yale*, 6 ("literary").

6. See Posner, *Public Intellectuals*.

7. JL, "What Life Means to Me," in *No Mentor but Myself*, 94 ("set . . . rocking," "crowbar . . . career").

8. Labor, preface to Walker, *Jack London and the Klondike*, 6 ("this . . . professional").

9. Sinclair, *Mammonart*, 9 ("true . . . reality").

10. Quoted in Shi, *Facing Facts*, 212 ("savage realists"). Howells quoted ibid., 213 ("the American . . . toil" "vulgar . . . people"). Ibid., 215 ("Readers . . . underclass").

11. Lawson, "Twain, Class, and the Gilded Age," in *The Cambridge History of the American Novel*, 366 ("a growing . . . personnel," "white-collar," "between . . . barons"). Dreiser quoted in Shi, *Facing Facts*, 213 ("little . . . property"). Lawson, "Twain, Class, and the Gilded Age," 366 ("more . . . itself," "needing . . . entertained," "in . . . information").

12. Increase Mather quoted in Tichi, "Thespis and the Carnall Hypocrite," 101 ("vain romances"). Thomas Jefferson to Nathaniel Burwell, March 4, 1818, in *The Harper American Literature*, 1:535 ("mass of trash"). For extended discussions of the influence of fiction on US sociopolitical history, see Reynolds, *Mightier Than the Sword*, and Sicherman, *Well-Read Lives*.

CHAPTER 1

1. JL, *John Barleycorn*, 34 ("splendid constitution," "stomach . . . scrap-iron"), 27 ("learned how to fight"). Finn Frolich quoted in Kershaw, *Jack London*, 98 ("brain . . . minute"). Atherton, "Jack London in Boyhood Adventures," 15 ("power . . . unlimited"), 154 ("endowed . . . spirit"; "invincible"). Anna Strunsky quoted in CKL, *The Book of Jack London*, 1:321 ("Napoleon . . . Pen"). Emerson, "Napoleon; or, the Man of the World," *Essays and Poems*, 615 ("wrought . . . language"). On Emerson's valuation of Napoleon, see Tichi, *Embodiment of a Nation*, 37–40.

2. Stasz, *Jack London's Women*, 8 ("powerful-looking man"), 9 ("the most . . . man"), 10 ("Flora . . . Music"). Joan London, *Jack London and His Times*, 152 ("hordes . . . enlighteners," "roamed . . . public").

3. Stasz, *Jack London's Women*, 14 ("In . . . son").

4. *1876: A Centennial Exhibition*, 82 ("Krupp's . . . machine"), 177 ("other . . . empires," "37 . . . colonies").

5. Ibid., 165 ("an attractive . . . press," "a steam . . . stove"). Bayard Taylor quoted ibid., 177 ("not . . . instruction").

6. Howells, 1876, quoted in http://eng.mu.edu/corliss/gc_engine.html ("the national . . . steel"), accessed by Tichi in 2009. Joaquin Miller quoted in Rydell, *All the World's a Fair*. 35 ("all . . . West," "American's . . . here," "Great . . . growth").

7. CKL, *The Book of Jack London*, 1:36 ("Just Beyond"). Georgia Loring Bamford, *The Mystery of Jack London* 52 ("squalor . . . type"). Kershaw, *Jack London*, 15 ("poverty . . . Chinese").

8. JL, *John Barleycorn*, 25 ("delicious dainties," "strange . . . home-table"), 50 ("never . . . children," "insisted . . . see," "awful . . . things").

9. JL, *John Barleycorn*, 157 ("to . . . mind," "the glory . . . passion"), 26–27 ("I read . . . playing"). Atherton, "Jack London in Boyhood Adventures," 31 ("soiled . . . use").

10. Georgia Loring Bamford, *The Mystery of Jack London*, 49 ("forest . . . Japanese"). Ramé, *Signa*, 512 ("a little . . . back"). JL, "Five Factors of Literary Success," in *The Portable Jack London*, 512 ("all . . . dare it").

11. JL quoted in Kershaw, *Jack London*, 31 ("great success"). JL, *John Barleycorn*, 114 ("I still . . . boy"). For Jack London's work history, see Labor, *Jack London: An American Life*, 32–33, 61–62.

12. Atherton, "Jack London in Boyhood Adventures," 143 ("I'm striving . . . night"). Joan London, *Jack London and His Times*, 130 ("preparing . . . physics," "To . . . months").

13. For a full account, see Walker, *Jack London and the Klondike*.

14. JL to Cloudesley Johns, June 12, 1899, *Letters*, 1:83 ("I am . . . style," "not found").

15. JL to Mabel Applegarth, February 28, 1899, *Letters*, 1:50 ("You know . . . galore").

16. JL, *John Barleycorn*, 135 ("made . . . Atlantic"). Flora London's encouragement of Jack's writing is detailed in Labor, *Jack London: An American Life*, 59–61.

17. JL to Cloudesley Johns, February 22, 1899, *Letters*, 1:48 ("cottonball"). JL to Fannie K. Hamilton, July 15, 1906, *Letters*, 2:589 ("I swim . . . bout"). JL to George Brett, January 28, 1907, *Letters*, 2:666 ("on the mend").

18. CKL, *The Book of Jack London*, 2:262 ("so . . . beauty"). For a thorough analysis of London's complex relations with his first wife and his daughters, see Stasz, *Jack London's Women*.

19. George Sterling to JL, September 12, 1907 ("the recognition . . . you," "discomfort") (HL JL19062). Atherton, "Jack London in Boyhood Adventures," 161 ("utter despondency," "suicide"). CKL, *The Book of Jack London*, 2:29 ("nerve-racked look," "haunted . . . fever," "very . . . silence."). JL, *John Barleycorn*, 9 ("white logic. . . . soul sickness"). JL, *Martin Eden*, 482 ("falling . . . stairway," "darkness").

20. For discussion of homoerotic attraction between London and George Sterling, see Haley, *Wolf*, 194–95. JL to Ninetta Eames, April 3, 1900, *Letters*, 1:178 ("I shall . . . listed"); JL to CKL, September 30, 1903 ("I have . . . clean").

21. JL quoted by CKL, *The Book of Jack London*, 2:232 ("There *may* . . . follow").

22. *1876: A Centennial Exhibition*, 77 ("Red Man"), 143 ("Old . . . Band"). JL, *John Barleycorn*, 15 ("pride," "old . . . stock").

23. JL, "Mauki," *CSS*, 2:1532 ("plum-black"). Jordan, *The Human Harvest*, 54 ("the survival . . . race-progress," "the survival . . . nations"). Burbank, *Luther Burbank, His Methods and Discoveries and Their Practical Application*, 5:7–8 ("unsuspected . . . tendencies"); 12 ("a new . . . potatoes," "races . . . plums"); 8:14 ("races . . . corn"), 143 ("races . . . cane").

24. James (Jimmy) Hopper quoted in Kershaw, *Jack London*, 23 ("bigness," "dominating quality"). Georgia Loring Bamford, *The Mystery of Jack London*, 30 ("Merely . . . world"), 24 ("super-egoist"). CKL, *The Book of Jack London*, 2:221 ("all . . . battlefield"); 2:5 ("playing . . . way"); 1:211 ("full . . . plans"); 2:264 ("All . . . way"). JL to Anna Strunsky, February 11, 1900, *Letters*, 1:156 ("I love . . . fellows").

25. *1876: A Centennial Exhibition*, 23 ("big . . . powerful"). JL quoted in CKL, *The Book of Jack London*, 2:208 ("money's . . . buy"). JL, "The Material Side of Authorship," 1900, repr. *The Occident* 70.4 (December 1916): 141–42 ("compensation of living," "porterhouse," "cream," "saddle horses, bicycles, and automobiles; cameras, shot guns," tents, cash).

26. CKL, *The Book of Jack London*, 1:162 ("sympathy . . . understanding"). JL, *John Barleycorn*, 121 ("work beast"). JL quoted in CKL, *The Book of Jack London*, 2:20 ("looking . . . unemployed"), 41 ("degrading"). *1876*, 122 ("excellence . . . economy"). JL quoted in Atherton, "Jack London in Boyhood Adventures," 134 ("damned drudgery," "slave"). *Teaching of Buddha*, 132 ("The body . . . feels").

27. JL to Anna Strunsky, February 11, 1902, *Letters*, 1:280 ("I do . . . us").

28. JL quoted in CKL, *The Book of Jack London*, 2:341 ("Big Interests"). Morris, *The Tycoons*, 12 ("fierce . . . talent," "personified . . . caste"), 14 ("cut . . . way"). JL to Philo M. Buck, July 19, 1913, *Letters*, 2:1210 ("The captains . . . live in," "The men who

. . . the world"). See also CKL, *The Book of Jack London*, 2:234: "Jack was always sharp-set to study the enormous achievements of the human in harnessing force."

29. See JL quoted in CKL, *The Book of Jack London*, 2:57: "The superman cannot be successful in modern life. The superman is anti-social in his tendencies, and in these days of our complex society and sociology he cannot be successful in his hostile aloofness. Hence the unpopularity of the financial superman like Rockefeller; he acts like an irritant in the social body." JL to George P. Brett, June 20, 1905, *Letters*, 1:493 ("house," "misdeeds"). JL, "The Scab," *Novels and Social Writings*, 1126 ("buying . . . legislatures," "virtuously wrathful," "the dangerous . . . legislation," "tens . . . factories," "take . . . contracts," "starvation wages," "knowing . . . hunger").

30. Herring, *From Colony to Superpower*, 316 ("in a smashing . . . expansionism"). *American Heritage History of the Confident Years*, 323 ("electrified," "overwhelming victory," "the hero . . . hour"). JL to Edward Applegarth, September 13, 1898, *Letters*, 1:12 ("stroke . . . monarchy" "industrial . . . democracy"). JL to Cloudesley Johns, May 28, 1899, *Letters*, 1:80 ("God . . . Bay), 168 ("countenance . . . religion," "superstition," "to fly . . . devils").

31. Le Gallienne quoted in CKL, *The Book of Jack London*, 2:291 ("'the whole . . . soul'"). JL to Cloudesley Johns, December 10, 1900, *Letters*, 1:223 ("peace lovers," "war . . . past," "the forty . . . ordered," "the people . . . States," "stamped . . .'98"); December 22, 1900 ("control . . . South"). See JL quoted in CKL, *The Book of Jack London*, 2:294: "We're a long way from universal disarmament. The most peaceful nation to-day is likely to run up against some other nation that does not want peace. It would look as if we shall need armies for a weary time to come, to enforce the idea of peace."

32. JL quoted in CKL, *The Book of Jack London*, 2:266 ("in the great . . . age"). JL to Geddes Smith, October 31, 1916, *Letters*, 3:1600 ("return to the soil").

33. JL quoted in CKL, *The Book of Jack London*, 1:219 ("the slippery . . . labor"). JL to Cloudesley Johns, December 22, 1900, *Letters*, 1:226 ("economic . . . conditions"). JL, "What Life Means to Me," in *No Mentor but Myself*, 94 ("house . . . live in," "Some . . . alive").

34. JL to Cloudesley Johns, March 15, 1900, *Letters*, 1:170 ("To work . . . blood"). See Shi, *Facing Facts*, for discussion of late nineteenth- and early twentieth-century US writers as "savage realists" (212–22). For an account of Theodore Roosevelt's accusation that London faked a wildlife scene in *White Fang*, see Labor, *Jack London: An American Life*, 251–52. For critique of London as self-mythologizer, see Starr, *Americans and the California Dream*, 210–38.

35. Crane quoted in Shi, *Facing Facts*, 225 ("Preaching . . . literature").

36. JL to Cloudesley Johns, June 16, 1900, *Letters*, 1:191–92 ("atmosphere," "who . . . overtime"). JL quoted in CKL, *The Book of Jack London*, 2:79 ("rough . . . man," "so much . . . alone").

37. JL to Elwyn Hoffman, January 4, 1902, *Letters*, 1:268 ("short . . . jolts"). Emerson, "Self Reliance," in *The Collected Works of Ralph Waldo Emerson*, 2:28 ("trust thyself"). JL quotes Jordan in CKL, *The Book of Jack London*, 2:46 ("*Will it . . . to it!*").

CHAPTER 2

1. *New York Tribune*, January 20, 1906 ("springlike"). JL, *The Road*, 152 ("scorching"). *New York Tribune*, January 20, 1906 ("red . . . ribbons"). JL, *Martin Eden*, 40 ("burning eyes"). CKL, *The Book of Jack London*, 2:221 ("all . . . ferocity").

2. "They All Wear Red to Hear Jack London," *New York Times*, January 20, 1906 ("hard . . . arms"). JL, *The Sea-Wolf*, 34 ("placid . . . existence"). "They All Wear Red to Hear Jack London" ("genuine . . . occasion"). Johns, "Who the Hell Is Cloudesley Johns?: An Autobiography," 232–33 ("crisp . . . speech") (HL HM42387).

3. See Morris, *The Tycoons*. See also Brands, *Colossus: The Triumph of Capitalism, 1865–1900* (2010). Veblen, *The Theory of the Leisure Class*, 373 ("outlawry," "barbarian temperament," "spectacular . . . fraud"), 223 ("pecuniary culture," "freedom . . . life"). Cloudesley Johns remarks in his unpublished autobiography, "Who the Hell Is Cloudsley Johns?," that he and London read one another passages from *The Theory of the Leisure Class* while sailing on London's boat *Spray* (294) (HL HM42387).

4. JL, "Revolution," in Raskin, *The Radical Jack London*, 145 ("organized . . . mankind"), 146 ("education . . . uplift"), 145–46 ("wherein . . . eat").

5. Ibid., 145 ("deplorably . . . horribly"), 145 ("all . . . miserably," "the bottom . . . descent," "The workers . . . revolt"). "They All Wear Red to Hear Jack London," *New York Times*, January 20, 1906 ("We . . . from you").

6. See Trachtenberg, *The Incorporation of America*.

7. Gorn, *The Manly Art*, 224 ("scientifically," "new kinetic," "in keeping . . . age"), 222 ("rewarded . . . counterpunching"). For JL's admiration of boxing, see Labor, *Jack London: An American Life*, 208–9.

8. Gorn, *The Manly Art*, 194 ("a burst . . . prowess"). Boddy, *Boxing*, 91–92 ("specified . . . umpires," "head . . . biting"), 92 ("Under . . . knockout"). See reprint of 1897 *Sears, Roebuck & Co. Catalogue*, 594.

9. Holmes quoted in Gorn, *The Manly Art*, 191 ("headship . . . command"). For discussion of social anxieties that fostered enthusiasm for boxing, see ibid., 179–206.

10. Joan London, *Jack London and His Times*, 127 ("suppleness . . . grace"). Naughton, *Heavy-Weight Champions*, preface [n.p.] ("noble art," "when stoutness . . . ring"). Allanson-Winn, *Boxing*, 15 ("inflict damage"). JL's library contained Naughton's and Allanson-Winn's books, together with the two-volume Henning, *Fights for the Championship: The Men and Their Times* (1903).

11. JL, *John Barleycorn*, 50 ("pinched . . . poverty"). JL, "How I Became a Socialist," in Raskin, *The Radical Jack London*, 126 ("Social Pit," "sailor-men . . . horses"). JL, *The Road*, 111 ("bedded . . . water"). JL, "How I Became a Socialist" ("the woman . . . gutter," "terror").

12. JL to J. H. Eustice, January 29, 1901, *Letters*, 1:238 ("equal . . . men," "equality . . . life," "simple justice").

13. Sumner, *What Social Classes Owe to Each Other*, 112–13 ("doctrine of liberty," "mind . . . business"). JL, *War of the Classes*, 10 ("Laissez faire . . . hindmost"). Jefferson, *The*

Declaration of Independence as Adopted by Congress, in *The Harper American Literature*, 1:524 ("a decent . . . mankind"). Lincoln, *Lincoln-Douglas Debates of 1858*, 64–65 ("public . . . fail," "without . . . succeed"). See JL to Frederick I. Bamford, March 7, 1905, *Letters*, 1:470 ("Yours . . . Revolution").

14. JL, *John Barleycorn*, 28 ("as boy-helper . . . ice-wagon"). Sumner, "The Philosophy of Strikes," *Harper's Weekly*, September 15, 1883 ("the body . . . opinion," "people . . . standing," "contradictory . . . society").

15. "Sailor Jack" was London's nickname as a railroad hobo. JL, *John Barleycorn*, 40 ("French Frank"), 43 ("Whisky Bob"), 48 ("reckless maniac," "with . . . Hercules").

16. Bryce, *The American Commonwealth*, 263 ("the chief . . . power"). Hadley, *The Education of the American Citizen*, 25 ("must . . . sentiment"), 28 ("all-powerful"). Ghent, *Our Benevolent Feudalism*, 122 ("public . . . ever"). Ross, *Social Control*, 94 ("guard . . . peace"), 95 ("The mills . . . promptly"), 102–3 ("leaders," "influencers," "rallying . . . opinion").

17. JL, "The Somnambulists," in *Revolution*, 24 ("a tangled . . . lies"). Ross, *Social Control*, 73 ("never . . . prospector," "law . . . well").

18. Ross, *Social Control*, 96 ("The public . . . memory," "mere . . . rage"), 99 ("frown . . . capricious," "its favor . . . fitful," "its pains . . . virtue"). Ghent, *Our Benevolent Feudalism*, 122 ("acquiescence . . . regime"), 123 ("The imaginations . . . reach," "he . . . inequitable," "blind fatuity").

19. Bryce, *The American Commonwealth*, 249 ("No event . . . soil," "the reader . . . already," "previous . . . interest"), 250 ("among all classes," "two . . . aversions," "two . . . catchwords," "thought," "sentiment").

20. Hendrick, "President Hadley, of Yale," 143 ("slight . . . figure," "fists . . . fashion," "nervous force"). In *Social Control* Ross pinpoints Hadley's fears, 89 ("admiration . . . derision"). Hadley, *The Education of the American Citizen*, 54 ("existence . . . society"), 58 ("unreasoning emotion"). Le Bon, *The Crowd*, 70–71 ("sentiments," "suggestion and contagion"), 87 ("responsibility," "reason").

21. JL, "How I Became a Socialist," in Raskin, *The Radical Jack London* ("I *shall* . . . do"). JL, *John Barleycorn*, 124 ("I was working . . . paradox").

22. Georgia Loring Bamford, *The Mystery of Jack London*, 70 ("a terrible . . . sword," "mental ideas," "eloquence . . . force"); 44–45 ("Revolutionary . . . Life"); 70 ("many . . . frightened," "arrested . . . punishment," "Jack . . . age"); 17 ("strong . . . rugged," "uncouth," "unbelievably shabby," "ruddy . . . sunburned," "disheveled hair"). JL to the Editor, *Oakland Times*, July 29, 1896, *Letters*, 1:3 ("assiduous reader," "failed . . . represented"), 4 ("small fry capitalists").

23. *The Socialism of Jesus*, 10 ("a working-class . . . own") (HL JLE2036).

24. Georgia Loring Bamford, *The Mystery of Jack London*, 80–82 ("Ruskin . . . others," "strongly . . . Marx"), 84 ("was . . . knowledge," "economics . . . sociology," "great . . . assimilation," "felt . . . humanity"). Frederick Irons Bamford, *The Passion of Socialism*, n.p. ("the noble . . . people," "free . . . economics," "the training . . . freedom") (HL JL374313).

25. Howe, *Socialism and America*, 4 ("most . . . voice," "spoke . . . accents," "both . . . Marxism," "a torrent . . . Chicago," "speakers country," "socialist . . . up," "the socialist . . . towns"), 17 ("clung . . . domination").

26. Gerald Stanley Lee, *The Voice of the Machines*, 4 ("omnipresent . . . intimate," "cogs . . . belts"), 7 ("Modern . . . them"). JL, *John Barleycorn*, 124 ("saw . . . around"); 160 ("watch[ed] . . . work," "the cogs . . . actions").

27. JL, "What Socialism Is," in Raskin, *The Radical Jack London*, 56–57 ("A socialist . . . name," "wishes . . . himself"), 57 ("family . . . State," "must . . . laws," "perhaps unwritten," "all . . . laws," "Socialism . . . thereof").

28. Ibid., 57 ("any . . . under," "better . . . Government"). James Bryce, *The American Commonwealth*, 444 ("general . . . government," "the tyranny . . . railroads").

29. JL, "tools," see Hamilton, *"The Tools of My Trade": Annotated Books in Jack London's Library*, 1–2. JL to Cloudesley Johns, June 7, 1899, *Letters*, 1:81 ("The time . . . past"). JL to Johns, December 12, *Letters*, 1:133 ("a socialist," "economic man," "definitely . . . utopian").

30. Rogers, *The American Newspaper*, 111 ("Reading . . . action").

31. Hunter, *Socialists at Work*, 362 ("a large . . . sympathetic," "exercised . . . universities").

32. JL to Cloudesley Johns, April [30], 1899, *Letters*, 1:71 ("How . . . growing!," "on . . . toes"). Bryce, *The American Commonwealth*, 262 ("ten . . . not," "leaven . . . convince"), 249 ("When . . . committed," "vanquished," "triumphed"). Wilson, *The State*, 632 ("revolt," "selfish . . . individualism," "distorted competition," "to seek . . . all").

33. "THE TRUST" reprinted in Tichi, *Civic Passions*, 189. For a summary of the 1886 Supreme Court ruling on Santa Clara County v. Southern Pacific Railroad, see Marchand, *Creating the Corporate Soul*, 7.

34. Marchand, *Creating the Corporate Soul*, 2 ("Many companies . . . it," "the traditional . . . corporations," "momentous . . . forces," "a crisis . . . corporations").

35. Goldman, *Two-Way Street*, 3 ("The greater . . . secret"). John D. Rockefeller quoted in Marchand, *Creating the Corporate Soul*, 9 ("Silence . . . golden").

36. Vanderbilt and Morgan quoted in Marchand, *Creating the Corporate Soul*, 9 ("The public . . . damned"; "I owe . . . nothing"). George F. Baer quoted in Goldman, *Public Relations and the Progressive Surge, 1898–1917*, 11 ("The Christian . . . man").

37. Newspaper reports and anonymous speaker quoted in Johns, "Who the Hell Is Cloudesley Johns?," 233 ("Divine . . . Baer," "if God . . . guilty") (HL HM42387).

38. JL to Cloudesley Johns, February 4, 1901, *Letters*, 1:239 ("I know . . . step," "I should . . . not").

39. Wisehart, "How Big Men Think and Act," 30 ("dark . . . frame"). Hiebert, *Courtier to the Crowd*, 15 ("lean . . . man").

40. Hiebert, *Courtier to the Crowd*, 39 ("contained . . . come," "a dismal . . . 'graft.'"). Ivy L. Lee, *The City for the People*, 79 ("good horses," "removal of snow").

41. JL, *John Barleycorn*, 27 ("reporters . . . judges"), 28 ("sought . . . grief"), 24

("bleak . . . Francisco," "heavy . . . wagons," "plodding horses"). J[ames] W. Lee, *The Making of a Man*, 78–79 ("Commerce . . . subserve").

42. Hiebert, *Courtier to the Crowd*, 20 ("the most . . . South," "absorbed . . . investments").

43. McCosh, *The Divine Government*, 422 ("hand . . . God," "wealth," "the powers . . . operation," "God . . . gifts"). See May, *Protestant Churches and Industrial America*, 53 ("God . . . makes them").

44. Carnegie, *The Gospel of Wealth*, 25 ("man of wealth," "set . . . living," "trust . . . community," "doing . . . themselves"); 19 ("Law of Competition"), 16 ("sometimes . . . individual," "best . . . department").

45. Hiebert, *Courtier to the Crowd*, 22 ("provided . . . ills"). JL, *John Barleycorn*, 188 ("through . . . works").

46. For repeated announcements of seasonal boxing instruction at Princeton, see *The Daily Princetonian*, February–April 1896–98. Hiebert, *Courtier to the Crowd*, 33 ("worked . . . ring," "The experience . . . life"). Gorn, *The Manly Art*, 251 ("boxers . . . prowess").

47. Ivy L. Lee quoted in Washburn, *Press Agentry*, 14 ("Seek . . . win").

48. Clarke, *These Days of Large Things*, vi ("a culture . . . size"). JL to Joan London, October 11, 1913, *Letters*, 3:1258–59 ("big people and little people," "big people," "live . . . act," "big things").

49. Bryce, *The American Commonwealth*, 250 ("does . . . grow," "is . . . made," "aspire . . . opinion"), 248 ("faint," "shapeless," "ordinary . . . fluid," "crystallize," "definiteness . . . strength"), 250 ("man . . . cars," "what . . . think it"). Ivy L. Lee quoted in Hiebert, *Courtier to the Crowd*, 73 ("the language . . . tobacco juice"). JL, "Wanted: A New Law of Development," in *War of the Classes*, 55 ("the common man"). Bryce, *The American Commonwealth*, 270 ("in developing . . . people").

50. Atherton, "Jack London in Boyhood Adventures," 21 ("a big . . . strap").

51. JL, "The Somnambulists," in *Revolution*, 24 ("wonderful . . . nerve"). See *Oakland Enquirer*, February 8, 1902 ("interval . . . humor"). See "How Competition Breeds Monopoly," *San Francisco Examiner*, November 17, 1901 ("industrial . . . corporations"). See *The Chautauquan*, July 1902 ("present-day thought"). See *The Advance*, December 9, 1902 ("breezy . . . comments"); January 25, 1902 ("interest . . . sociology"). See Mrs. Humphrey Ward, "Chat about Authors," American Press Association, January 3, 1902. See also P. H. McHenry, "Topical Touches in Jack London's New Stories," *San Jose Mercury*, July 1903 ("deep thinker," "a socialist . . . eccentricity") (HL Jack London Scrapbooks 1 and 2; microfilm Box 517).

52. *New York Sun*, December 28, 1903 ("If you . . . *Wolf*") (AC 2005.1.221). *Scribner's Magazine*, December 1903 ("Jack . . . *Century*") (AC 2012.1.12). *Metropolitan Magazine*, April 1905 ("Great New Story") (AC 2005.1.1045). *Pacific Monthly*, September 1908 ("His . . . Novel") (AC 2005.1.916). *Saturday Evening Post*, December 23, 1912 ("best . . . wrote") (AC 2008.2.10). *Appleton Evening Crescent*, October 2, 1911 ("A Great . . . Story") (AC 2005.1.232).

53. *Denver Daily News*, January 12, 1904 ("Jack . . . crisis") (AC 2005.1.243). *New York*

Herald, June 17, 1910 ("Jack . . . *Herald*") (AC 2005.1.265). *New York Tribune*, July 9, 1911 ("Jack . . . Diamond") (AC 2005.1.260). *San Francisco Examiner*, July 7, 1913 ("Author . . . Operation") (AC NP1913B). *San Francisco Examiner*, August 1, 1913 ("Jack London . . . comedy") (AC 2005.1.299). *New York Herald*, June 12, 1910 ("Literary . . . Errant") (AC 2010.2.45). For full discussion of celebrity-focused journalism from 1890, see Ponce de Leon, *Self-Exposure*.

54. Fannie K. Hamilton, "Jack London: An Interview" ("high . . . hills," "open-air . . . room," "high . . . hills," "genius," "literary giant," "face . . . animated," "boyish . . . friend," "radiates purpose") (HL Jack London Scrapbook 1, 1899–1901, Box 517 microfilm).

55. Rogers, *The American Newspaper*, 3 ("a . . . force"). See *Los Angeles Times*, December 5, 1915" ("no man . . . poor") (HL JL2944). See Hobart Van Zandt to JL, July 29, 1913 ("enemy . . . peace," "Ole Man Otis," "most awfully") (HL JL 2743). CKL, "*Times* nasty . . . insurrectionists" (CKL Diary HL JL225). Sinclair, *The Brass Check*, 341–45 ("a pestilential agitator," "literary anarchist," "joy"). CKL, *The Book of Jack London*, 2:110 ("brilliant . . . author," "neurasthenic," "socialist . . . London").

56. "Millionaire Divides His Profits with His Workers to Share Their Happiness," *San Francisco Examiner*, April 18, 1902 ("millionaire-socialist," "inevitable . . . ownership").

57. Ivy L. Lee quoted in Goldman, *Two-Way Street*, 7 ("The anthracite . . . operators," "realizing . . . information").

58. Ibid., 7–8 ("Declaration of Principles," "This is . . . bureau," "All . . . fact," "press . . . to know about").

59. Ibid., 8 ("Angry protests . . . century").

60. Ivy L. Lee, "The How and Why of Publicity," 52 ("story"), 53 ("produces . . . emotions").

61. JL, "The Question of the Maximum," in *War of the Classes*, 39 ("market-places," "dollars . . . exchanges").

62. Addams, "A Modern Lear."

63. Gorn, *The Manly Art*, 251 ("sketched . . . blood"). Sinclair, *The Brass Check*, 311 ("Poison Ivy"). JL, "Revolution," in Raskin, *The Radical Jack London*, 155 ("parasites").

64. Slayton Lyceum Bureau agent to JL ("The college . . . trip," "It will . . . royalties") (HL JL18510).

65. For a full discussion of London's tour for the Slayton bureau, see Zamen, *Standing Room Only*, 111–30.

66. CKL, *The Book of Jack London*, 2, 111 ("gliding homeward"), 112 ("slaughtering," "an unpleasant . . . sight," "intellectual . . . Oil").

67. Campton-Rickett, *The Vagabond in Literature*, 3 ("There are blood," "an insatiable doors," "with an ingrained . . . civilization," "natural revolutionaries").

CHAPTER 3

1. JL to Bailey Millard, February 18, 1906, *Letters*, 2:547 ("The keel . . . laid"). CKL, *The Book of Jack London*, 2:117 ("dare . . . yes," "Blessed Ranch"), 134 ("mountain," "life"), 120 ("two-seated . . . runabout").

2. JL, "Small-Boat Sailing," in *The Human Drift*, 25 ("sea-breeze," "howling northers," "hard . . . excitement"), 23 ("wood . . . sea").

3. In 1907 the records of Anderson & Cristofani, formerly H. P. Anderson and Andersons Ways, marine builders, categorized a craft named *Snark*, customer Jack London, as "recreational." JL, *The Cruise of the* Snark, 5 ("the trip . . . world," "personal achievement," "big . . . living").

4. George Sterling to JL, October 9, 1906 ("O Jack . . . ocean!") (HL JL19059). CKL, *The Book of Jack London*, 2:122 ("warm . . . tanks," "valley resorts"). JL, *The Cruise of the* Snark, 15 ("the achievement . . . feat," "successful . . . environment," "the more . . . accomplishment," "life . . . nostrils").

5. JL, "The Language of the Tribe," 119 ("read . . . War"). Elson, *Guardians of Tradition*, 332 ("aura . . . tragedy"). Charles Sumner, "War," in *McGuffey's Sixth Eclectic Reader*, 148 ("mangled," "spattering brains").

6. Atherton, "Boyhood Adventures with Jack London," 133 ("always . . . wars"). JL, "The Impossibility of War," *Overland Monthly*, 35 (March 1900), 278 ("war . . . possible").

7. JL to Cloudesley Johns, March 15, 1900, *Letters*, 1:172 ("Men . . . exterminated").

8. JL to Cloudesley Johns, July 29, 1899, *Letters*, 1:99–100 ("great," "minding the . . . world," "the force . . . of law," "it is . . . together, "Mother Country," "obligations . . . character," "Saxon").

9. JL, *The People of the Abyss*, 139–40 ("superb . . . power," "myriads," "whose . . . life"), 144 ("the pomp . . . power," "these men . . . harnessers"). Hobson, "The Economic Taproot of Imperialism," 251 ("needs . . . investment").

10. Hobsbawm, *The Age of Empire*, 297 ("84,000 . . . wounded"), 303 ("humiliating . . . power").

11. JL, "The Japanese-Russian War," in *Jack London Reports*, 27 ("ludicrous"), 29 ("coolies . . . cotton"), 64 ("hellish business," "the masts . . . ships").

12. Hurd, "The Modern Battle Ship," 746 ("tore open," "bump . . . mines," "$10,000,000 . . . Japan," "the frailest . . . evolved").

13. CKL, *The Book of Jack London*, 2:117 ("plans for . . . boat").

14. JL, *The Cruise of the* Snark, 6 ("We expect . . . Europe"), 7 ("We . . . work"). CKL, *The Book of Jack London*, 2:164 ("when Jack . . . enthusiasm," "the glamour . . . Romance," "the commonplace").

15. JL, *Jerry of the Islands*, 270–71 ("shriek," "by . . . explosion," "flying . . . iron").

16. Johnson, *Through the South Seas with Jack London*, 16 ("men . . . inclination," "lady companions").

17. JL, *The Cruise of the* Snark, 5 ("cyclones and tornadoes," "lightning . . . cloud-bursts," "rip-tides . . . eddies," "surfs . . . coasts"), 1 ("followed . . . bit").

18. Ibid. ("When . . . start?"). Slocum, *Sailing around the World in a Small Boat*, 9 ("to cruise . . . sea"). JL to Cloudesley Johns, March 7, 1899, *Letters*, 1:52 ("a storyteller," "essayist," "without equal," "turned . . . trash"). JL, *The Cruise of the* Snark, 1 ("inevitable . . . boats," "in a small . . . long").

19. JL, *The Cruise of the* Snark, 1 ("had . . . plant").

20. CKL, *The Log of the* Snark, vii ("Why wait?"). JL, *The Cruise of the* Snark, 1 ("When . . . start?").

21. JL to Martin Johnson, November [?] 1906, *Letters*, 2:632 ("after-thought," "could . . . boiling"), 632–33 ("plain cooking," "minimum . . . grease," "You will . . . cabin-boy," "a Japanese . . . lion," "hot weather").

22. Ibid., 633 ("All . . . crew," "There is . . . wheel," "moments . . . danger," "I will . . . sailor," "The same . . . will be," "shore-liberty," "lots . . . adventuring").

23. JL quoted in CKL, *The Log of the* Snark, vii ("yacht"). JL, "The House Beautiful," in *Revolution*, 73 ("seventy-horsepower . . . life-preservers," "great store-room," "food . . . things"). Johnson, *Through the South Seas with Jack London*, 5 ("It is . . . San Francisco," "We could . . . steamer").

24. JL, *The Cruise of the* Snark, 6–7 ("To make . . . comfortable," "large . . . cockpit," "sunk . . . deck"), 5 ("colossal menaces," "seas . . . death," "Titans . . . destruction,"), 7 ("[wheel]house . . . hold," "the fact . . . board").

25. JL to Bailey Millard, February 8, 1906, *Letters*, 2:549 ("marketable goods," "It is . . . goods," "No writer . . . action," "graphic, reportorial," "How much . . . me"). London sent similar letters to editors at *Collier's Weekly*, *McClure's Magazine*, *Outing*, and the *San Francisco Examiner*, and to his English literary agent, James B. Pinker.

26. CKL, *The Book of Jack London*, 2:117 ("butter . . . ripples"). JL, *The Cruise of the* Snark, 5 ("Here . . . I," "a little . . . I am," "a splinter . . . rifle").

27. JL, *The Cruise of the* Snark, 5 ("a sailor," "thread," "precarious way," "maze . . . Titans," "having . . . mast," "The bit . . . them," "It is . . . tempest").

28. CKL, *The Book of Jack London*, 2:119 ("trees . . . vines," "a hedge . . . hawthorne"). Winchester, *A Crack in the Edge of the World*, 240–41 ("Restless tonight," "Don't . . . why," "queer behavior").

29. CKL, *The Book of Jack London*, 2:124–25 ("flew . . . seconds," "crazily," "sharp undulations").

30. Ibid., 125 ("were . . . skittish"). JL, "The Story of an Eye-Witness," in *The Portable Jack London*, 486 ("the smoke . . . burning," "lurid . . . away"). CKL, *The Book of Jack London*, 2:127 ("started . . . hills," "one or . . . flames," "the muffled . . . conflagration," "I'll never . . . them").

31. CKL, *The Book of Jack London*, 2:129 ("frantic telegrams," "twenty-five . . . San Francisco"), 125–26 ("solid," "honest," "two-foot-thick . . . walls," "mere . . . rock," "the flimsiest . . . debris," "'Jerry-built,'" "hurt . . . voice," "turned . . . swindle"), 129–30 ("jumped," "scribbled sheets," "snatched . . . hand," "swiftly typed," "the best . . . thing," "Why . . . arrive?," "Must . . . immediately," "Holding . . . expense," "Must . . . number").

32. "JL, "The Story of an Eye-Witness," in *The Portable Jack London*, 487 ("humped . . . walls"), 486 ("factories . . . gone"), 487 ("dead calm," "doomed," "deserted," "vast conflagration," "crumbled," "proudest . . . ruins").

33. Ibid., 486 ("a modern . . . city," "perfect order," "courtesy"). JL, "Advancing Russians Nearing Japan's Army," in *Jack London Reports*, 41 ("perfect order").

34. JL, "The Story of an Eye-Witness," in *The Portable Jack London*, 489 ("two . . . watching"), 487 ("Wrapped . . . blankets," "homeless," "carried . . . treasures," "abandoned"). For London's photograph of the Russian Cossack, see JL, *Jack London, Photographer*, 102; for the family of Korean evacuees, see JL, *Jack London, Photographer*, 103. JL to CKL, March 9, 1904, *Letters*, 1:418 ("Household . . . backs"). JL, "Japanese Supplies Rushed to Front by Man and Beast," in *Jack London Reports*, 93 ("Houses . . . devastation"). JL, "The Story of an Eye-Witness," 487 ("Wrapped . . . blankets," "homeless"). JL, "Japanese Supplies Rushed to Front by Man and Beast," 93 ("Houses . . . devastation"). JL, "Give Battle to Retard Enemy," 99 ("set . . . houses"). JL, "The Story of an Eye-Witness," 490 ("Japanese . . . Negroes").

35. JL, "The Story of an Eye-Witness," 486 ("picket-lines . . . soldiers," "menace . . . bayonets"), 489 ("There was . . . water," "surrender . . . complete").

36. JL, "Dr. Moffett," in *Jack London Reports*, 89 ("the chaos . . . war"), 44 ("draught . . . packhorse"), 43 ("coolies"). JL, "Japanese Supplies Rushed to Front by Man and Beast" ("their . . . army"). JL, "Over the Pekin Road on the Way to the Yalu," 57 ("lacerated," "freezing mud," "across . . . mountains," "excruciating pain").

37. JL, "The Story of an Eye-Witness," in *The Portable Jack London*, 487–88 ("harnessed," "to a . . . wagon," "dragging . . . trunk," "The hills . . . steep," "and up . . . dragged," "Everywhere . . . women," "was to . . . moving," "Over these . . . night," "An enumeration . . . known"). JL, "Fighting at Long Range Described," in *Jack London Reports*, 103 ("death-dealing missiles").

38. Johnson, *Through the South Seas with Jack London*, 30 ("the trouble . . . sea-bath"), 21 ("beginning . . . ashes"), 15 ("soared skyward," "terrible tangle"). JL to George P. Brett, May 2, 1906, *Letters*, 2:573 ("THE PARTIALLY-BUILT . . . SAFE"). Johnson, *Through the South Seas with Jack London*, 15 ("spending . . . freely"). JL to Bailey Millard, May 16, 1906, *Letters*, 2:575 ("there ain't . . . hull," "iron . . . ribs," "not . . . boat," "not . . . finished," "I am . . . look").

39. CKL, *The Book of Jack London*, 2:130 ("treated"), 134 ("moonlight . . . games," "blowing . . . popular"), 137 (beads, "gay . . . ribbons").

40. JL to Victor Talking Machine Company, October 11, 1906, *Letters*, 2:618 ("Countless . . . receive"). Johnson, *Through the South Seas with Jack London*, 11 ("all manner . . . floor"). JL to George P. Brett, January 28, 1907, *Letters*, 2:665 ("I have . . . exercise").

41. Johnson, *Through the South Seas with Jack London*, 15–16 ("Nothing . . . right," "The *Snark* . . . trouble"). JL, *The Cruise of the* Snark, 11 ("Inconceivable and monstrous"). Lewis Carroll, *The Hunting of the Snark*, 1876 en.wikipedia.org/wiki/The Hunting of the Snark ("infinite humour," "the impossible . . . creature"), accessed by Tichi in 2011.

42. CKL, *The Book of Jack London*, 2:137 ("habit . . . ahead"). JL quoted bid. ("retrospect," "old . . . women," "The world . . . now").

43. JL to George P. Brett, May 2, 1906, *Letters*, 2:573 ("new . . . story," "I have . . . Adam").

44. JL, *Before Adam*, 11 ("Mid-Pleistocene"). Weisman, *Essays upon Heredity*, 1:72 ("the substance . . . properties").

45. JL, *Before Adam*, 17 ("half . . . ape"), 9 ("falling . . . dream," "racial memory").

46. Ibid., 19 ("aerial . . . flights"), 66 ("primitive catamaran").

47. Ibid., 30 ("so . . . eyes," "advertise . . . him," "giant," "was . . . ways").

48. Ibid., 111 ("We lived . . . presence," "increasing . . . territory," "had decided . . . ours," "It was . . . to us").

49. All quotations from *Cleveland Plain Dealer* reviews reproduced in unpaginated back pages of JL, *Jerry of the Islands*.

50. JL, *The Iron Heel*, 73 ("strength," "roar . . . guns").

51. *Indianapolis News* assessment reprinted in unpaginated back pages of JL, *Jerry of the Islands*. JL, *The Iron Heel*, 236, 239, 240 ("Mercenaries"), 230 ("cool . . . society," "snarling . . . clothes," "we . . . sliding by").

52. JL, *The Iron Heel*, 221 ("storm-centre," "city . . . blood"). Norris, *The Pit*, 57 ("Empire").

53. JL, *The Iron Heel*, 230 ("holes"), 228 ("a mass . . . death"), 229 ("Panic"), 232 ("torn away"), 230 ("pools . . . blood"), 232 ("rattle," "people . . . abyss," "snarling . . . growling"), 233 ("nothing . . . living"), 248 ("smouldering ruins"), 249 ("green country"), 251n ("execution").

54. CKL, *The Log of the Snark*, ix ("amethyst flood").

55. JL, *The Cruise of the Snark*, 38 ("thrill . . . pride").

56. Ibid., 21 ("leaked . . . badly," "to say . . . galley," "keep . . . afloat," "I have . . . pumping").

57. Ibid., 21 ("magnificent," "that cost . . . all," "snapped . . . macaroni," "heave-to," "bow-on . . . sea," "the most . . . vessel"). CKL, *The Log of the Snark*, 3 ("*mal de mer*"). JL, *The Cruise of the Snark*, 24 ("forgotten . . . youth," "the cook . . . bunks").

58. CKL, *The Log of the Snark*, 13 ("The sea . . . is"). JL, *The Cruise of the Snark*, 92 ("sternly . . . environment," "one . . . solitudes," "a disabled . . . rescue"). Johnson, *Through the South Seas with Jack London*, 150 ("Not . . . below"). CKL, *The Log of the Snark*, 75 ("water famine"). Johnson, *Through the South Seas with Jack London*, 150 ("put . . . key," "Our . . . No water!"). JL, *The Cruise of the Snark*, 97 ("I . . . life"), 98 ("bucketfuls . . . tubfulls," "heavy . . . rain").

59. JL, *The Cruise of the Snark*, 94 ("stark calm," "something . . . windward," "rose . . . heavens," "The *Snark* goes . . . in," "lonely . . . blackness," "After . . . blows"). CKL, *The Log of the Snark*, 176 ("dear . . . tub," "the old girl").

60. See JL, "The White Silence," *CSS*, 1:141–49. JL, "The Son of the Sun," *CSS*, 3:1895 ("crashing . . . cunning," "palm-tufted . . . deeps," "flower-garlanded . . . maids," "long pigs," "head-hunters . . . beast").

61. JL, "The Whale Tooth," CSS, 2:1492 ("chiefs . . . men"); "The Terrible Solomons," CSS, 2:1519 ("with a . . . heads"); CSS, 1:209 ("primordial . . . North"); "The Wife of a King," CSS, 1:289 ("red-tanned moosehide"); "Keesh, the Son of Keesh," CSS, 1:571 ("squirrel-skin"); "The Terrible Solomons," CSS, 2:1522 ("sported . . . cartridges"); "Yah! Yah! Yah!," CSS, 2:1549 ("This fella . . . trader").

62. Riedl and Tietze, *Jack London's Tales of Cannibals and Headhunters*, 9–10 ("blackbirding . . . conditions"). See also Labor, *Jack London: An American Life*, 284–88.

63. JL, "The Terrible Solomons," CSS, 2:1524 ("ammunition," "dynamite," "detonators"). JL to Churchill Williams, March 12, 1911, *Letters*, 2:990 ("David . . . tales," "the real . . . Seas").

64. JL quoted in CKL, *The Log of the* Snark, 178 ("'Funny . . . Mate-Woman?'"); CKL, *The Log of the* Snark ("hang . . . table," "little note-pads," "manuscript tablet"), 179 ("carry . . . time").

65. JL to Edward Applegarth, September 15, 1898, *Letters*, 1:12 ("the Yanko-Spanko War," "I was . . . it," "stroke . . . monarchy," "industrial . . . Socialism").

66. JL, "Feathers of the Sun," CSS, 3:2044 ("Japan . . . simultaneously," "got in . . . way," "The war . . . harbour," "there were . . . war").

67. JL, "A Son of the Sun," CSS, 3:1889–90 ("crumpled . . . paper," "an . . . warrant"). Hobson, *Imperialism*, 15 ("Great Britain . . . Pacific"). JL, "Mauki," CSS, 2:1532 ("plum-black"), 1539 ("ubiquitous . . . Company"). JL, *The Cruise of the* Snark, 203 ("punishment . . . murders," "encountered . . . villages").

68. Gooch, "Imperialism," in *The Heart of the Empire*, 310 ("hunger . . . or no," "England . . . United States," "joined . . . scramble," "over . . . territory," "England . . . 'encroaches,'" "The notion . . . apply").

69. JL, "The Inevitable White Man," CSS, 2:1557 ("German . . . Samoa"); "Yah! Yah! Yah!," CSS, 2:1546 ("German . . . Guinea," "German Solomons"); "The House of Mapuhi," CSS, 2:1387 ("French dollars," "francs"). CKL, *The Log of the* Snark, 173 ("Paris . . . Pacific"). JL, "The Chinago," CSS, 2:1406 ("English Company," "imported . . . coolies," "explosive . . . gabble," "virtues . . . law").

70. JL, "The Devils of Fuatino," CSS, 3:1937 ("We are . . . ago"). Hobson, *Imperialism*, 27 ("occupation," "a small . . . industry"), 11 ("attack . . . races," "bristles . . . resentment," "fostering . . . empires").

71. JL, "The Chinago," CSS, 2:1408 ("French devils"); "Mauki," CSS, 2:1534 ("Ferocious creatures"); "Yah! Yah! Yah!," 2:1551 ("hell"). JL, *The Cruise of the* Snark, 111 ("garden," "wilderness"), 113 ("life . . . away," "One . . . corruption").

72. JL, "The Whale Tooth," CSS, 2:1499 ("inevitable . . . stronghold"); "The Terrible Solomons," 1519 ("terrible Solomons," "fever . . . walk-about," "loathsome . . . abound," "many . . . men").

73. JL, *The Cruise of the* Snark, 48 ("wonderful . . . land").

74. Ibid., 47 ("awakened . . . Winkles," "it . . . dreaming," "azure," "emerald," "fell . . . beach," "green . . . upward," "jagged . . . clouds"), 47–48 ("It was . . . real," "Dream Harbor," "that . . . dreaming").

75. Ibid., 49 ("restless . . . sea"). Johnson, *Through the South Seas with Jack London*, 84 ("rich . . . grass").

76. JL, *The Cruise of the* Snark, 50 ("house . . . coolness," "a beautiful . . . sandals," "as though . . . always," "a nectar . . . poi"). For repetition of the term "Aloha Land," see ibid., 45–51.

77. Von Tempski, *Born in Paradise*, 198 ("heavy-set"), 210 ("leonine head"). CKL, *Jack London in Aloha-Land*, 144 ("keen . . . eyes," "quick . . . action"). Johnson, *Through the South Seas with Jack London*, 83 ("throng . . . reporters").

78. Thurston, "The Sandwich Islands: The Advantages of Annexation," 265 ("little . . . savages").

79. Liliuokalani, *Hawaii's Story by Hawaii's Queen*, 181 ("missionary party").

80. Ibid., 361 ("missionary oligarchy"), 191 ("strangers . . . soil"). Bird, *The Hawaiian Archipelago*, 245 ("the Hawaiians . . . away"). Bates, *Sandwich Island Notes*, 421 ("*decreasing* . . . year"). David Malo quoted in Daws, *Shoal of Time*, 106 ("Great Countries," "white-men," "eat"). Thurston, "The Sandwich Islands: The Advantages of Annexation," 277 ("prosperous . . . sky").

81. CKL, *Jack London in Aloha-Land*, 54 ("the seaside . . . world"), 64 ("salt . . . canopies," "steady . . . surf," "like babies"), 56 ("dip," "diving . . . breakers"), 28 ("lingered . . . Hawaii"). For references to the Londons' appreciation of the sights of the Islands, see CKL, *Jack London and Hawaii*, 94–97, 116–18, 127–28, 223–26, 197, 99.

82. Ellis, *Polynesian Researches*, 87 ("wore . . . gods"). Bates, *Sandwich Island Notes*, 109 ("burning torrent"), 398 ("a land . . . gods"), 419 ("first . . . Constitution," "consolidation . . . people"). Bird, *The Hawaiian Archipelago*, 5 ("the natives . . . cannibals," "savages," "on the . . . community"), 145 ("a nice . . . mats"), 192–93 ("canoes . . . tree," "shoot . . . rapidity," "spritsail").

83. Bird, *The Hawaiian Archipelago*, 94 ("wave . . . boards," "a tough . . . for"), 95 ("daring riders," "knelt . . . breakers").

84. JL, *The Cruise of the* Snark, 54 ("flying. . . . Mercury," "winged"), 53 ("royal . . . earth"), 57 ("tossed . . . breaker"), 59 ("smashing blows," "driven . . . blast"), 62 "supersensitive . . . skin," "sun-burned . . . Mercury").

85. CKL, *Jack London in Aloha-Land*, 94 ("the best . . . citizenship," "the wonderful . . . valleys").

86. Ibid., 160 ("good genius"), 144 ("hair . . . islands," "something . . . head," "savours . . . statesmanship").

87. Ibid., 166 ("Mr. Thurston," "lucky," "strange . . . chanting"), 134–35 ("Mr. Thurston," "old Hawaiian," "capital luncheon," "ideal," "good coffee"), 154 ("nooned . . . interested"), 160–61 ("Mr. and . . . big house"), 161 ("Mr. and Mrs. . . . anything"). Von Tempski, *Born in Paradise*, 198 ("moved . . . Hawaiians").

88. CKL, *Jack London in Aloha-Land*, 173 ("exhaustively," "Pacific Ocean," "in all . . . glory," "treasures . . . glass," "that fell . . . Kamehameha," "All this . . . Bishop").

89. Stone, *Yesterday in Hawaii*, 16 ("totaled . . . area," "three . . . corporations").

90. Ibid., 141 ("tame"), 156 ("jungle," "a mere bridge," "a . . . torrent").

91. Ibid., 137 ("a private-car . . . plantations"). Bates, *Sandwich Island Notes*, 318 ("several . . . plantations"). Bird, *The Hawaiian Archipelago*, 106–7 ("sugar," "the great interest," "a . . . Utopia," "disastrous speculation," "barely . . . water").

92. Takaki, *Pau Hana*, 69 ("obediently," "national pride"). Bird, *The Hawaiian Archipelago*, 247 ("Americans . . . class"). CKL, *Jack London in Aloha-Land*, 153 ("unpoetical," "unimaginative"). Gowan, *The Paradise of the Pacific*, 62–63 ("from miles . . . pipe").

93. CKL, *Jack London in Aloha Land*, 30 ("shining landscape").

94. Baldwin, *A Memoir of Henry Perrine Baldwin*, 38 ("The partners . . . Maui"), 44 ("dense . . . gulches").

95. Ibid., 38 ("plunged," "You have. . . . me"), 40–41 ("greatest obstacle," "the deep . . . Maliko," "the workmen . . . hand"), 41 ("Mr. Baldwin. . . . below," "shamed . . . manager," "did not . . . rope"), 47 ("Central . . . globe"). Jack London owned a copy of *A Memoir of Henry Perrine Baldwin* and sketched a possible story based on Baldwin's accident. See his "How Baldwin lost his arm in feeder of sugar-grinding mill" (HL JL771).

96. G. Waldo Browne, *The Paradise of the Pacific*, 196 ("Grim Molokai," "banished victims"), 202 ("fate," "melancholy").

97. CKL, *Jack London in Aloha-Land*, 92–93 ("that Jack . . . picture"). Engineer quoted by JL, *The Cruise of the* Snark, 68 ("chamber-of-horrors rot," "write . . . straight," "tell . . . really are").

98. JL, *The Cruise of the* Snark, 63 ("disgracefully . . . time"), 67 ("enjoys . . . Honolulu," "magnificent," "the blue . . . valleys," "are grassy . . . lepers," "fishing . . . lepers").

99. JL, *The Cruise of the* Snark, 73 ("*yellow*," "swiftly . . . earth"). Jeanne Reesman finds that London's ideas about race changed markedly as a result of his experience on Molokai. See her *Jack London's Racial Lives*, chap. 4.

100. CKL, *Our Hawaii*, 169 ("Mr. Lorrin . . . written").

101. CKL, *Jack London in Aloha-Land*, 175 ("New England . . . Dole"), 176 "holding . . . uprising," "'Can't . . . them?,'" "'Can't . . . done!'").

102. Blackman, *The Making of Hawaii*, 145 ("'child' . . . America"), 142 ("its free . . . government"); see acknowledgments for "Honourable S. B. Dole" and "Honourable L. A. Thurston."

103. CKL, *Jack London in Aloha-Land*, 42 ("high . . . West"), 214 ("the . . . element"), 78 ("imported . . . breeds"), 137 ("picturesque"). Kawakami, *Japanese Immigrant Clothing in Hawaii*, 110 ("protection . . . hair"), 117 ("the tiny . . . hand"). Dorrance and Morgan, *Sugar Islands*, 45 ("arduous . . . hand").

104. JL, "The House of Pride," *CSS*, 2:1347 ("statue . . . Building"); "Shin-Bones," 3:2391 ("Bishop Museum"); "The House of Pride, 1349 ("Taboo . . . poi-pounders," *ukulele*), 1348 ("*luna*"), 1349 ("*hula*"); "Good-bye, Jack," 2:1475 ("cow-boys, "Von Tempsky" [*sic*], "Haleakala Ranch"). See A. Grove Day's foreword to Westervelt, *Myths and Legends of Hawaii*, iii ("imaginative").

105. JL, "Koolau the Leper," *CSS*, 2:1442 ("hideously . . . distorted," "rotted"). JL to the Editor, *Honolulu Advertiser*, January 7, 1910, *Letters*, 2:859 ("sneak . . . bounder," "lion").

106. Daws, *Shoal of Time*, 210 ("native . . . Kauai," "fled . . . rifle," "He killed . . . leper"). JL, "Koulau the Leper," *CSS*," 2:1441 ("they," "came . . . lambs," "many . . . strong," "gracius . . . us," "to preach . . . God," "was . . . beginning," "they that . . . servants," "who had . . . everything," "all the . . . theirs," "any Kanaka. . . . plantations").

107. JL, "Koolau the Leper," *CSS*, 2:1445 ("sea of vegetation," "green . . . airplants," "bananas . . . mangoes," "*taro* . . . melons," "In . . . fruit").

108. Ibid., 1444 ("fierce . . . ti-plant," "a woman . . . love-call," "Timing . . . song," "love . . . movements," "earthly . . . paradise"), 1443 ("alien powers").

109. Ibid., 1443 ("Who . . . men?"). JL, "The House of Pride," *CSS*, 2:1347 ("zealous," "stepped . . . holdings," "enormous wealth," "schools . . . churches," "big . . . men,"), 1350 ("You . . . right").

110. JL, "The House of Pride," *CSS*, 2:1349 ("his . . . dancing," "cosmic . . . life").

111. Ibid., 1354 ("silhouetted . . . stars," "love-cry," "outrigger canoes," "reclining . . . lotus-eaters," "the voices . . . song").

112. CKL, *Jack London in Aloha Land*, 144 ("firm-lipped smile").

113. JL, "My Hawaiian Aloha," in CKL, *The New Hawaii*, 43 ("great . . . sociology"), 31 ("shanghaied . . . love"), 47 ("Pan-Pacific movement"), 26 ("With . . . sight," "*kamaaina*").

114. Ibid., 48 ("Hawaii . . . *well-to-do*").

115. East Hawaii Cane Planters' Association, *The Real Issue in Hawaii* (1915), n.p. ("strenuously," "longer . . . laborer," "to which . . . produce") (HL JLE2043).

116. Baker, "Wonderful Hawaii," 28 ("dominated . . . interests," "a vivid . . . country," "these great . . . corporations," "modern aristocracy").

117. JL, "My Hawaiian Aloha," in CKL, *The New Hawaii*, 39 ("invading . . . land"), 5 ("The *haoles* . . . Stripes," "white man . . . looter"), 49 ("the land . . . corporations").

118. Ibid., 50 ("Be . . . democratic," "medieval . . . methods"), 53 ("distinctly feudal"). For Baker's repeated pejorative uses of "feudal" or "feudalism," see his "Wonderful Hawaii," 206, 210, 330, 333, 334.

119. CKL, *Jack London in Aloha-Land*, 181 ("shady . . . landscape," "swinging . . . contemplated"), 234 ("could . . . under," "ached . . . eyes"), 216 ("is . . . teaching," "It is . . . body").

CHAPTER 4

1. JL to Alice Lyndon, July 29, 1909, *Letters*, 2:821 ("best," "ever written"). *Pacific Monthly* advertising circular ("Jack . . . novel") (HL JLE3184).

2. CKL, *The Book of Jack London*, 2:174 ("rusty leviathan"). JL to George Sterling, May 2, 1909, *Letters*, 2:800 ("boxing . . . now," "husky . . . Englishmen," "I get . . . condition").

3. Unattributed quotation in CKL, *The Book of Jack London*, 2:175 ("'who . . . kinsman'"), 177 ("a blanket . . . wool," "great canal," "shopped . . . stores"), 177 ("hailed . . . newspapers," "boarded . . . towns").

4. JL to George P. Brett, July 27, 1909, *Letters*, 2:819 ("remain . . . years," "I should weeks," "I can . . . them").

5. JL to Curtis, Brown & Massie, November 26, 1909, *Letters*, 2:842 ("lay . . . convalesce"); to Eliza Shepard, January 7, 1910, 861 ("I can't . . . time").

6. *Athenaeum*, October 21, 1908 ("young . . . hurry," "to turn . . . writing"). *Sunset Magazine*, January 11, 1908 ("coarse . . . cruel"). *Chicago Standard*, January 11, 1908 ("sordid," "altogether disreputable") (HL Jack London Scrapbook 3: 1903–1904, Box 517 [microfilm]). Note: Though the Scrapbooks are dated by year, the entries are not consistently chronological.

7. CKL quoted by Sinclair in introduction to *Martin Eden*, 12 ("sick . . . mentally").

8. Williamson, *Oakland, Jack London, and Me*, 8 ("a curiosity . . . poverty"). JL, "What Life Means to Me," in *No Mentor but Myself*, 92–93 ("hotels . . . steamer-chairs," "captains . . . industry," "beautifully . . . charities").

9. JL, "What Life Means to Me," in *No Mentor but Myself*, 87 ("crude . . . raw"), 88 ("men . . . gowns," "unselfishness . . . living"), 91 ("parlor"). JL, *John Barleycorn*, 159 ("It was . . . head"). Von Tempsky, *Born in Paradise*, 199 ("bond . . . outlawry").

10. Georgia Loring Bamford, *The Mystery of Jack London*, 17 ("neatly dressed," "short trousers," "wrinkled . . . ill-fitting," "long . . . baggy," "south . . . slot").

11. Ibid., 34 ("the most . . . people," "who were . . . state," "residential," "attractive . . . gardens").

12. Ibid., 52 ("domicile," "shack," "'cottage,'" "of an indescribable . . . character," "element . . . sanitation," "crevices . . . rags," "keep . . . weather"), 53 ("picturesque"), 54 ("It is . . . look," "civilization," "ferocious primitive").

13. Jordan, *The Days of a Man*, 1:460 ("venturesome soul," "repellant . . . brutal"), 41 ("distinct dislike"), 460 ("a stocky . . . strength," "decided individuality"). Jordan, *The Voice of the Scholar*, 2 ("a social ornament," "the . . . few"), 50 ("well-dressed feeling"), 14 ("educated oligarchy"). Jordan, *The Days of a Man*, 1:313 ("feudal").

14. JL to Cloudesley Johns, June 7, 1899, *Letters*, 1:82 ("The Anglo-Saxon . . . times"); to John M. Wright, September 7, 1915, 3:1498 ("Pantheon"). JL, *The Sea-Wolf*, 266 ("Do you . . . lives to it?," "a . . . hero").

15. Jordan, *The Voice of the Scholar*, 460–61 ("to read . . . stories," "manner . . . hearers," "master . . . English," "recognized masterpieces," "tales").

16. Ibid., 171 ("for more . . . America"), 143 ("business . . . combinations"), 158 ("voluntary cooperation").

17. Jordan, *The Days of a Man*, 1:247 ("the sad . . . South," "overwork," "abominable"), 96 ("wholly . . . minority," "the problem . . . time," "conciliation," "the Anglo-Saxon . . . play").

18. Markham quoted in Sullivan, *Our Times*, 236 ("sat . . . painting," "was . . .

peasant," "a symbol . . . oppression"). Markham's *The Man with the Hoe* is reprinted in Sullivan, 237–39, and the following terms are quoted from the poem: 237–38 ("brutal jaw," "slanted brow," "the world's . . . greed," "masters . . . lands," "brother . . . ox").

19. Sullivan, *Our Times*, 239 ("the Mississippi . . . Canada," "the newspapers . . . stories," "the clergy . . . study"). For postal card showing "The Edwin Markham Home," see HL JLP478 Album 40.

20. JL to Cloudesley Johns, April 22, 1899, *Letters*, 1:69 ("richly . . . boom"). London's review of Markham appeared in the *New York Journal*, December 28, 1901 ("warm . . . hope," "a noble . . . progress") (HL Jack London Scrapbook, 1:1899–1901 [microfilm]).

21. Sullivan, *Our Times*, 239–40 ("delivered . . . places"). JL to Cloudesley Johns, April [3], 1899, *Letters*, 1:72 ("a noble-looking . . . sixty").

22. Jordan, "The Man Who Was Left Behind," reprinted in *The Human Harvest*, 52 ("slave . . . labor"), 53 ("oppressed," "In dealing . . . to-day," "from . . . sympathy").

23. Jordon, *The Days of a Man*, 460 ("defiant . . . society").

24. JL, *The Call of the Wild*, 20 ("driving snow," "wind . . . knife"), 54 ("deep . . . sounding").

25. JL, "The Class Struggle," in *War of the Classes*, 7 ("class . . . power").

26. JL, *The Call of the Wild*, 17 ("suffered . . . hunger"), 39 ("on . . . legs," "dead-tiredness . . . toil"), 40 ("there was . . . upon," "got rid of"). See also Tavernier-Courbin, "*The Call of the Wild* and *The Jungle*."

27. Joan London, *Jack London and His Times*, 252 ("Reviewers . . . environment").

28. London's bound gathering included William S. Waudby, "Children of Labor," *Frank Leslie's* 55.6 (April 1903): 545–56; Lillian W. Betts, "Child Labor in Factories," *The Outlook*, n.d.: 637–42; Robert Hunter, "Child Labor: A Social Waste," *The Independent* (February 12, 1903): 375–79; Lillian W. Betts, "Child Labor in Shops and Homes," *The Outlook* (April 18, 1903): 921–27; Ernest Poole, "Waifs of the Streets," *McClure's* (May 1903): 40–48 (HL JLE1924).

29. Bunje, *Oakland Industries, 1848–1938*, 33 ("gradually . . . labor"). Preceding data on Pacific Jute Manufacturing from Bunje (typescript rare book: HL 372193).

30. JL, "The Apostate," *CSS*, 2:1115 ("the jute-twine"), 1124 ("a work-beast"), 1125 ("the shrieking . . . looms").

31. Ibid., 1119 ("well-built . . . exuberance"), 1129 ("and in . . . smiled").

32. The *Cosmopolitan* magazine series on captains of industry spanned 1902–14. See vol. 34 (May 1902) ("To-day . . . hero"). For London's file on captains of industry, see HL JLE1922.

33. Tarbell, *The History of the Standard Oil Company*, 2:284 ("We are . . . people," "Our boast . . . sanctified"). *Cosmopolitan* 34 (May 1902) ("he . . . hero").

34. Nasaw, *Andrew Carnegie*, 462 ("tainted money"). Rayner, *The Associates*, 13 ("a hard . . . shark"). Tarbell, *The History of the Standard Oil Company*, 1:94 ("the most . . . seen").

35. JL quoted in CKL, *The Book of Jack London*, 2:57 ("The superman . . . tendencies," "In these . . . social body"). Cashman, *America in the Gilded Age*, 61 ("It was . . . business").

36. Burns, *David Starr Jordan*, 14 ("the most . . . science"), 15 ("erratic," "unsound"), 17 ("unfit"). JL, "What Life Means to Me," in *No Mentor but Myself*, 91 ("broken . . . class").

37. JL, *The Sea-Wolf*, 73 ("Sissy"), 113 ("I was . . . Van Weyden," "Hump"), 86 ("feuds . . . grudges").

38. JL quoted in CKL, *The Book of Jack London*, 2:57 ("superman," "Rockefeller," "anti-social," "hostile aloofness," "an irritant . . . body," "He . . . successful").

39. Jack London, *The Sea-Wolf*, 76 ("to make . . . work"), 16 ("probably . . . chest," "strength", "primitive," "wild," "enlarged gorilla," "snake"), 163 ("extreme . . . savagery," "some . . . prey"), 160 ("This man . . . monster," "He is without . . . to do").

40. Ibid., 77 ("a man. . . . unmoral"), 114 ("a hell-ship," "moment's . . . peace," "to making . . . unlivable"), 51 ("heartlessly indifferent," "industrial organization").

41. JL to the Editor, *San Francisco Examiner*, June 14, 1906, *Letters*, 1:492 ("never . . . McLean," "wild exploits," "imaginative development"). See MacGillivray, *Captain Alex MacLean*, for an account of the commingling of MacLean with London's Wolf Larsen in lore and legend.

42. Jack London, *The Sea-Wolf*, 160 ("the role . . . weak," "remain . . . ignominy," "have . . . man," "The battle . . . strong").

43. Ibid., 218 ("There was . . . woman").

44. Ibid., 280 ("Lucifer . . . spirit"), 274 ("burned . . . darkness").

45. Ibid., 86 ("a state . . . equilibrium," "flame . . . grass").

46. Strong, "The Anglo-Saxon and the World's Future," in Tichi, *Life in the Iron Mills*, 247 ("peasant," "debauching . . . morals").

47. JL, *The People of the Abyss*, 75 ("white . . . rooms").

48. JL to Cloudesley Johns, February 17, 1908, *Letters*, 2:737 ("Have just . . . friends").

49. JL, *Martin Eden*, 47 ("a wild man").

50. Ibid., 45 ("frightening . . . forks," "bristled . . . perils," "battered . . . spoons," "sheath-knives . . . fingers"), 32 ("shame . . . uncouthly," "rolling gait," "such as . . . trap").

51. Ibid., 35 ("stokeholes . . . streets"), 55 ("volcano . . . stars," "sensuous nights," "a coral . . . surf," "love-calls," "who chanted . . . tomtoms"), 50 ("p-a-u"), 49 ("Pow!").

52. Ibid., 73 ("stale vegetables," "soapsuds"), 74 ("half-cooked . . . mush," "hard," "as she . . . coffin," "worked . . . died").

53. Ibid., 70 ("pretty . . . scarred," "the tips . . . winter," "swollen . . . beef," "she would . . . work," "the weakness . . . overwork").

54. Ibid., 70 ("soft," "the aristocracy . . . labor").

55. Ibid., 37 ("cheap"), 32 ("I guess . . . see me"), 32 ("keenly sensitive," "irresistibly . . . to beauty," "discipline," "the gift . . . sympathy," "understanding"), 33 ("yearning").

56. Ibid., 35 ("caste," "pale . . . creature," "spirit . . . goddess," "sublimated . . . the earth"), 52 ("a million miles," "a world . . . conquer").

57. Ibid., 40 ("peril," "wrong"), 42 ("intense virility"), 39 ("critical . . . mind"), 211 ("protégé . . . friend").

58. Ibid., 89 ("Karl Marx . . . Mill"), 90 ("He . . . know").

59. Ibid., 41 ("primly . . . dogmatic").

60. Ibid., 58 ("himself").

61. See Fisher, *Local History, Geography and Civic*, 17 ("delightful roads," "diversified manufacturing," "happy . . . thousands"). See also *Central California Illustrated*, 132 ("Here is . . . give," "bright . . . societies"). See, in addition, bird's-eye view Oakland Map (1900) (Library of Congress division of Geography and Maps, catalog no. 75693098).

62. JL, *Martin Eden*, 110 ("conservative . . . formed"), 106 ("beyond . . . plumb-line").

63. Ibid., 107 ("proprietary"), 106 ("rethumb . . . image"), 108 ("passion," "He had . . . at first," "at least . . . thousand," "He was . . . economical," "He wanted . . . livelihood"), 165 ("Mr. Butler . . . if you want to").

64. Ibid., 336 ("keen-flashing intellects"), 337 ("great . . . cents"), 240 ("discovered . . . training"), 314 ("an individualist"), 313 ("the masters . . . society"), 340 ("You worship . . . established").

65. Ibid., 123 ("Why . . . income?").

66. Atherton, "Jack London in Boyhood Adventures," 152 ("amidst . . . machinery," "Verily . . . robots," "had . . . slave").

67. JL, *Martin Eden*, 189 ("great . . . clothes"), 194 ("out on . . . steam"), 188 ("All . . . sleep"), 201 ("the maggots . . . intoxication").

68. Ibid., 208 ("Some day . . . it up"), 207 ("beast").

69. See JL to Fannie K. Hamilton, December 6, 1909, *Letters*, 2:847 ("He was . . . ergo, he died").

70. London's "The Other Animals," in *Revolution*, rebuts Roosevelt's 1907 claim of a faked encounter between a wolf-dog and a lynx in London's *White Fang*.

71. JL, introduction to *The Cry for Justice*, ed. Upton Sinclair, 3 ("the needs . . . world," "service," "can be . . . inhabit it").

72. JL to John L. Jenkins, August 23, 1916, *Letters*, 3:1567 ("intellectual . . . Jordan"). CKL, *The Book of Jack London*, 2:271 ("nothing," "David Starr Jordan").

73. JL to Fannie K. Hamilton, December 1909, *Letters*, 2:847 ("Quite . . . now").

CHAPTER 5

1. JL to George P. Brett, May 5, 1910, *Letters*, 2:888 ("Dear Mr. . . . Dollars"), 891 ("I MUST . . . ME").

2. JL quoted in Haughey and Johnson, *Jack London Ranch Album*, 17 ("By using . . . undertaking").

3. Gregory, *History of Sonoma County, California*, 3 ("sweet domain," "Californian . . . shrubbery"). JL to George F. Brett, June 7, 1905, *Letters*, 1:490–91 ("several . . . hay").

4. JL quoted by Bailey Millard, "Jack London's Valley of the Moon Ranch," 7 ("a quiet . . . loaf in"). JL to Cloudesley Johns, June 27, 1905, *Letters*, 1:495 ("The only . . . cows," "like . . . money," I'm not . . . ranching").

5. Tindall and Shi, *America: A Narrative History*, 671 ("agricultural . . . arts"). See also 694, 830.

6. JL, *John Barleycorn*, 22 ("monotony . . . labor"), 12 ("primitive countryside," "sweating plowman"), 19 ("plodding horses," "country peasants"), 88 ("monotonous," "wild . . . man-world," "chesty . . . men").

7. See Hendricks and Shepard, in *Jack London Reports*: "Aboard the Sophie Sutherland he [i.e., Jack London] read such books as *Madame Bovary* and *Anna Karenina*, which he managed to procure before he left Oakland" (ix).

8. Ramé, *Signa*, 209 ("natural . . . soil," "priceless . . . brook"), 211 ("glowed . . . corn," "on the . . . mountainside"). JL, *The Sea-Wolf*, 103 ("dim . . . sea-lamp," "sea-boots, oilskins," "sour and musty").

9. Tolstoy, *Anna Karenina*, 43 ("savage"), 90 ("I live . . . farming"), 162 ("agronomic science").

10. Ibid., 163–64 ("horses . . . tails," "heavy-fleeced sheep," "Holland cow"), 168 ("without . . . soil").

11. JL to Cloudesley Johns, June 27, 1905, *Letters*, 1:495 ("hired man").

12. For London's files on agricultural matters, see his Ranch Notes: HL JLE Boxes 582 and 583.

13. For these USDA Farmers' Bulletins nos. 358, 263, 158, see HL JLE2051. For an account of London's conflicts with neighbors over water rights, see Labor, *Jack London*, 367–68.

14. London also became seriously engaged in eucalyptus tree farming, which was promoted by the USDA and prominent agriculturalists, including the nation's foremost forester, Gifford Pinchot, as a fast-growing hardwood. London trusted that income from lucrative eucalyptus harvests would alleviate the need to produce short stories and give him time to focus his efforts on novels. He ordered sixty thousand eucalyptus trees and did not live to learn that they were worthless as a cash crop. His extensive research files on eucalyptus species can be found in HL JLE Box 582.

15. King, *Farmers of Forty Centuries*, 7 ("To anyone . . . nations have," "rare wisdom," "combined . . . dreamed"), 6 ("smaller . . . States"). For London's knowledge of King, see London's "Farmers of Forty Centuries" (HL JLE2664).

16. Berglund, "Satoyama, Traditional Landscape Farming in Japan, Compared to Scandanavia," 61 ("mosaic landscapes"), 62 ("terracing . . . fields"). See also Hiromi Kobori and Richard B. Primack, "Conservation for Satoyama, the Traditional

Landscape of Japan." JL's photographs of Korean farm scenes can be found in HL JLP439 (Albums 1–3); JLP442 (Albums 4, 7, 10); JLP450 (Album 12).

17. For JL's notations on "strange cow," "unexpected rain," and various repairs, see HL JLE2723 and JLE2734.

18. See HL JLE2654 ("Eliza, I cannot . . . book-keeping"); JLE2742 ("Eliza . . . cheaply"); JLE2735 ("Eliza . . . haul?"); JLE2742 ("Eliza . . . silo?"); JLE1625 ("Eliza . . . ears," "Eliza . . . performance"). William Allen White, "The Business of a Wheat Farm," 531 ("the successful . . . first"). Bailey, *The Principles of Agriculture*, 4:5 ("The person . . . farmer").

19. JL, "Eliza . . . another profit" (HL JLE2734).

20. Bailey, *Cyclopedia of American Agriculture*, 3:493 ("recognized . . . horses," "very . . . Clydesdale").

21. Bowsfield, *Wealth from the Soil*, 15 ("City people . . . farmers"). Campbell, *Christianity and the Social Order*, 210 ("at the mercy . . . corporations"). See also Danbom, *Born in the Country*, 167–75, and *The Resisted Revolution*.

22. Rogin, *The Introduction of Farm Machinery in Its Relation to the Productivity of Labor in the Agriculture of the United States during the Nineteenth Century*, 151 ("fifteen minutes," "the wheat . . . sack").

23. French, *Cattle Country of Peter French*, 17 ("erect . . . red-bearded"). See also Street, *Beasts of the Field*, 731.

24. *Breadbasket of the World*, n.p. ("Always . . . recreation," "bustling crossroad . . . harvest"). French, *Cattle Country of Peter French*, 101 ("beautiful parlors," "choicest flowers"). For a detailed account of the Glenn operation, see Street, *Beasts of the Field*, chaps. 9 and 10. See also Conlogue, *Working the Garden*, 25–61.

25. French, *Cattle Country of Peter French*, 105 ("ride . . . holdings").

26. Cummin, *Granite Crags*, 350 ("yellow . . . land," "clouds . . . dust").

27. Harte, *Through the Santa Clara Wheat*, 341 ("enormous . . . unbroken"). For a reproduction of Hahn's *Harvest Time*, see Skolnick, *Paintings of California*, 46–47.

28. JL, "Revolution," *The Radical Jack London*, 150 ("bonanza farm"). Norris, *The Octopus*, 615 ("great ranch," "thick," "wonderful wheat," "bonanza").

29. Norris, *The Octopus*, 28 ("guts," "to death," "exhausted"). Cummin, *Granite Crags*, 350 ("vast wheat . . . gold"). Norris, *The Octopus*, 298–99 ("he's still . . . mine," "the same . . . gold"). See DeQuille, *Bonanza Mining*, 480–81 ("*bonanza . . . excellence*").

30. Norris, *The Octopus*, 298–99 ("guts," "to death, "exhausted," "were . . . soil," "worked . . . deluge").

31. JL, "Review of *The Octopus*," in *No Mentor but Myself*, 36 ("the tiller . . . industry").

32. Bailey, *Cyclopedia of American Agriculture*, 4:124 ("*Bonanza farming*," "*Soil exhaustion*," "extensive . . . rapidly").

33. Pattee, *The New American Literature*, 45 ("villain . . . book").

34. JL, *The Little Lady of the Big House*, 40 ("Listen . . . cold"), 39 ("lusty . . . husky"), 40 ("you picked . . . farmer").

35. Ibid., 40 ("You . . . back," "You've destroyed").

36. JL, *John Barleycorn*, 191–92 ("toiled . . . planted," "gazed . . . bodies," "broke . . . soil").

37. Charles Sedgwick Aiken, *California Today*, 20 ("idlers," "pick . . . streets," "there is . . . labor"). Neighbor quoted in Millard, "Jack London's Valley of the Moon Ranch," 7 ("years . . . worn out"). JL to George P. Brett, September 21, 1914, *Letters*, 3:1369 ("meager," "dead"). Neighbor quoted in Haughey and Johnson, *Jack London Ranch Album*, 13 (You can't . . . out").

38. *History of Sonoma County, California*, 21 ("a good . . . years"). *Sonoma County Land Journal*, 6 ("not . . . kept up," "neglected appearance," "absent . . . place," "not . . . out," "virgin richness"). Tuomey, *History of Sonoma County, California*, 461 ("overstocking," "disastrous results," "bonanza," "ceased . . . well," "old mounds . . . ago").

39. JL to George P. Brett, October 7, 1914, *Letters*, 3:1378 ("the ground . . . soil"). Bailey, *Cyclopedia of American Agriculture*, 1:135 ("worn-out farm," "high state . . . beginning," "The new farmer . . . land itself").

40. Thomas Jefferson quoted by Hofstadter, *The Age of Reform*, 23 ("those who . . . God").

41. Le Duc, "History and Appraisal of U.S. Land Policy to 1862," 25–26 ("a class . . . entrepreneurship," "control . . . operate," "skewed . . . labor"). Hofstadter, *The Age of Reform*, 42–43 ("little . . . locality," "acquaint . . . soil," "Imbued . . . spirit," "failed . . . replenish," "neglected . . . cash"). De Tocqueville quoted in Hofstadter, *The Age of Reform*, 42 ("business-like . . . agriculture," "brings . . . farm it").

42. W. J. Spillman, *Renovation of Worn-Out Soils*, USDA Farmers' Bulletin 245:3 ("greatly impaired") (HL JLE2167). J. S. Ball, *Waste Land and Wasted Land on Farms*, 6 ("bad . . . methods"), 10 ("Now we . . . impaired") (HL JLE2658).

43. Bailey, "The Making of a Modern Farm," *Outlook*, August 25, 1906, 942 ("good . . . families") (HL JLE2665).

44. JL to George P. Brett, May 30, 1911, *Letters*, 2:1007–8 ("I should . . . *the land*," "large city," "trials and tribulations," "hard times," "start . . . farming," "love-story," "a big . . . story," "popular," "every word").

45. McShane and Tarr, *The Horse in the City*, 6 ("living machines").

46. JL, *The Valley of the Moon*, 69 ("to live . . . country").

47. Ibid., 347 ("abandoned . . . thousands"), 348 ("land-robbing . . . hogging," "over . . . California"), 148 ("poor-white," "lease . . . and move"), 370 ("put . . . back," "almost desert").

48. Ibid., 369 ("broken up"), 292 ("new farming," "intensive cultivation," "It isn't . . . acre"). *Relics of '49 Glenn Ranch*, n.p. ("the growth . . . products") (HL 389023).

49. JL, *The Valley of the Moon*, 369–70 ("five-inch . . . laterals," "beloved water," "Isn't . . . beautiful?," "It's bud and fruit . . . orchards!," "It makes . . . laughable").

50. Ibid., 17 ("yellow hair," "all . . . Americans," "American," "regular . . . American," "fighting spirit"), 85 ("'We wouldn't . . . before us'").

51. Ibid., 13 ("awkward"), 22 ("crude"), 339 ("Chinks"), 17 ("Dagos . . . and such"), 83–4 ("what her life . . . swarthy").

52. Ibid., 348–49 ("they will . . . conserve"), 292–93 ("miserable immigrant . . . Adriatic Slavs").

53. Ibid., 338 ("Coolie," "peddled . . . stick," "Sing Kee . . . Stockton"), 293 ("to see . . . farmed," "Take a hill . . . up it," "No bother . . . grow things on").

54. Ibid., 351 ("Chinese . . . Americans," "the foreigners").

55. JL, *The Little Lady of the Big House*, 40 ("start . . . world over"), 41 ("agricultural chemistry," "livestock breeding," "farm management," "post-graduate . . . college").

56. Ibid., 6 ("Baden-Powell").

57. Ibid., 8 ("paraphernalia . . . business"), 11 ("sea of . . . silos," "a paint-shop . . . carpenter-shop"), 9 ("flowing . . . silk").

58. Ibid., 60 ("I believe . . . per cent"), 70 ("two-legged . . . beasties").

59. Ibid., 10 ("back seed-bed"), 21–22 ("improvements . . . House itself").

60. JL, "The Future of California as an Agricultural State," n.p. ("The future . . . land a chance") (HL JLE78).

61. Ibid.

62. Ibid.

63. JL, *The Valley of the Moon*, 196 ("workmen"), 202 ("stripes . . . San Quentin," "labor men"). JL to Roland Phillips, March 26, 1914, *Letters*, 3:1315 ("paean," "love . . . everlasting").

CHAPTER 6

1. Morrell, *The Twenty-Fifth Man*, 368 ("Gosh . . . to me?").

2. Ruef, *Letter of A. Ruef to the Prison Directors* ("a pack . . . thugs").

3. Griffith, "San Quentin as I Knew It," 72 ("caged . . . voiceless").

4. Morrell, *The Twenty-Fifth Man*, 269 ("devil's cauldron," "where . . . condemned").

5. One unit at San Quentin held "Incorrigible" prisoners. For a précis of Morrell's career, see Lamott, *Chronicles of San Quentin*, 150–55.

6. Lowrie, *My Life in Prison*, 49 ("yellow," "horribly emaciated," "about 95," "famine"), 48 ("a human . . . hell"). JL's notes: ("Follow . . . prison") (HL JL1193).

7. Atherton, "Jack London in Boyhood Adventures," 47 ("young gangsters . . . spite," "arrested . . . London"). London's stepfather had explained to him that arrest and conviction required being caught "in the act of stealing" or with stolen goods and that youthful violators were often headed for a life of crime. So said the eleven-year-old Jack to Atherton in the case of one Red Kelly, who was swept off the Oakland streets in a patrol wagon as Jack explained to his friend, "If he's convicted of robbery I suppose they'll send him to the Reform School; then after he gets out . . . he'll start robbing banks, and wind up in the Penitentiary" (49).

8. Lowrie, *My Life in Prison*, 110 ("this colony . . . crime"). See Atherton, "Jack London in Boyhood Adventures," 127 ("If . . . time"), 132 ("If . . . San Quentin"). See also Atherton's recollection of Jack's rejoinder when he himself wished aloud for a

shotgun to blast "the dirty hound" of a farmer who chased the two twelve-year-olds from his peach orchard. Jack fired back, "And be sent to San Quentin for life or be hung for murder?" (91). "Near San Quentin" (HL JL52486-4 #10924). See Labor, *Jack London: An American Life* for an account of London viewing a hanging at San Quentin prison (159).

9. McAfee, "San Quentin: The Forgotten Issue of California's Political History in the 1850s," 235 ("woven . . . history"). Bookspan, *A Germ of Goodness*, 32 ("was . . . inmates"), 31 ("branch," "reformatory").

10. Bookspan, *A Germ of Goodness*, xiv ("the theories . . . century," "an intimidating . . . silence").

11. Ibid., 23 ("hard . . . all"), 22 ("aimed . . . citizen").

12. James Woodworth quoted ibid., 30–31 ("'granite . . . convicts'").

13. JL, *The Road*, 81 ("All . . . waterfall," "And . . . that," "I'd . . . out"). For an account of London at Niagara Falls, see Labor, *Jack London: An American Life* (75–76).

14. JL, *The Road*, 94 ("Our hall . . . humanity"), 80 ("along . . . rifles," "machine . . . sentry-towers").

15. Ibid., 73 ("fluid," "We became . . . 'Jack'").

16. Ibid., 88 ("extremity"), 89 ("Here . . . fear," "thirteen . . . hundred," "a broom . . . face," "We . . . lost"), 94 ("When . . . path").

17. Ibid., 87 ("Oh . . . Street"), 88. London explained that the "coin of the realm" was the tobacco rationed by officials to the prisoners each week, while the inmates' hunger drove the market for bread. The hall-men, London explained, "controlled the food supply of the population, and, just like our brother bandits outside, we made the people pay through the nose for it." "We were economic masters inside our hall," he admitted, and "quite similar to the economic masters of civilization." The "initiative and enterprise" of the cadre of hall-men, he remarked in thick irony, was "patterned" on those "outside the walls, who, on a larger scale, and under the respectable disguise of merchants, bankers, and captains of industry, did precisely what we were doing" (85–86).

18. Ibid., 82 ("I saw . . . monstrous"), 87 ("dungeon"), 90 ("in terror . . . heart-break," "collapsed . . . unconscious"), 91 ("stand . . . rights").

19. Ibid., 88–89 ("unprintable," "unthinkable," "no . . . world"), 88 ("a bit . . . handling," "one . . . Pen").

20. Ibid., 75 ("Middle Ages"), 89 ("I do . . . them"). Roland Phillips to JL ("too much 'meat,'" "lady readers") (HL 16529). George Sterling to JL, September 12, 1907 ("Your . . . smell") (HL 10962).

21. JL, *The People of the Abyss*, 82 ("too . . . prison"); 94 ("prison . . . escape"); 136 ("in the army . . . prison").

22. "Some Clever Swindles" (HL JL570). "Poisoned Brother for Insurance" (HL JLE594). "Look Out for the Crook with Knockout Drops" (HL JLE595). Lewis, "The Common-Sense Jail" (HL JL1456).

23. JL, "Large situation . . . unspeakable & vile" (HL JL570). JL, "Notes for Crime Stories . . . A Prison Study" ("San Quentin execution . . . she kills him") (HL JL1080).

24. Other titles in London's library included the British H. L. Adam's *The Story of Crime: From the Cradle to the Grave*, the Americans Robert G. Ingersoll's *Crimes against Criminals*, and G. Frank Lydson's *The Diseases of Society (The Vice and Crime Problem)*. In addition, he filed articles in the *American Magazine* (1912): "The Man in the Cage" and "An Ounce of Correction a Pound of Corruption." He saved newspaper clippings on the alleged "criminal class" and on the police interrogation technique termed "the third degree." See *San Francisco Examiner*, 1906, "The Criminal Class" and "The Third Degree" (HL JLE593). See also London's file: Julian Leavitt, "The Man in the Cage" and "An Ounce of Correction a Pound of Corruption," *American Magazine*, February and April 1912 (HL JL1193).

25. Nitsche and Wilmanns, *The History of Prison Psychoses*, 57 ("transient . . . hallucinations"). Flynt, *Notes of an Itinerant Policeman*, 34 ("professional criminal," "the best-born . . . environment").

26. Ferri, *Criminal Sociology*, 24–25 ("five categories," "criminal madmen, born criminals . . . of passion"). Earle, *Curious Punishments of Bygone Days*, 96 ("whipping"). Benjamin Howard, *Prisoners of Russia*, 196 ("thong"). Adam, *The Story of Crime*, 325 ("It was . . . eyes").

27. CKL, *The Book of Jack London*, 2:225–26 ("eager . . . battlements"). JL to Eliza Shepard ("We . . . men," "Of course . . . man") (HL JLE2724). CKL Diary for February 12, 1911 ("interesting . . . talk") (HL JL225). Such men as Stryker were those whom the system aspired to "elevate and reform," according to one state official report. Had Jack London served time in San Quentin as a young man, he would have been statistically a "reformed" sailor, or perhaps an "elevated" jute mill or cannery worker, for each prisoner's occupation was recorded by the San Quentin clerk, whose tally included cooks, laborers, carpenters, blacksmiths, barbers, teamsters, bookkeepers, firemen, salesmen, and sailors, in addition to a bellboy, a paperhanger, saddler, pugilist, and numerous others in trades and artisanship. See *Report to the State Board of Prison Directors of the State of California upon a Proposed Reformatory for Adult Offenders* (Sacramento, 1910), 6 ("elevate and reform").

28. Hopper and Bechdolt, *9009*, vii ("a simple . . . Monster").

29. Elderkin, "The State Prisons of California—Folsom," 257 ("the most . . . country"), 264 ("violators," "punished . . . abuse," "a gentleman . . . criminals").

30. Morrell, *The Twenty-Fifth Man*, 269 ("each . . . creature," "crypt of stone").

31. Lowrie, *My Life in Prison*, 39 ("Scarcely . . . limbs").

32. Wilde, *The Ballad of Reading Goal*, 4 ("We sewed . . . lying still").

33. See JL file of San Francisco newspaper reports of conditions in San Quentin prison (HL JL1192).

34. Ibid.

35. For the complete listing of these and other punishable infractions by prisoners,

see "Exhibit B," *Biennial Report of the State Board of Prison Directors for the State of California for . . . 1909–1910*, 88–89. See also Lowrie, *My Life in Prison*, 54 ("dog-eyeing").

36. *In the Matter of an Investigation Respecting Punishment and the Use of the Straitjacket at the State Prisons at Folsom and San Quentin Prisons*, by a Sub-Committee on Prisons and Reformatories of the Assembly, *Assembly Daily Journal*, April 22, 1913. Hon C. C. Young, Speaker of the Assembly, in chair, 50 ("heavy . . . body") (HL JL1193). Griffith, "San Quentin as I Knew It," 83 ("The public . . . works"), 82 ("It is a canvas overcoat . . . half an hour"). For JL's note on Griffith, see HL JL1456. Lowrie, *My Life in Prison*, 64 ("could . . . breathe," "die," "cold . . . inanimate," "the victim . . . floor," "paralysis").

37. For JL's files of *San Francisco Examiner* articles on prison conditions (February 13, 21, 24, 1903), see HL JL1192.

38. *In the Matter of an Investigation Respecting Punishment and the Use of the Straitjacket at the State Prisons at Folsom and San Quentin Prisons*, by a Sub-Committee on Prisons and Reformatories of the Assembly, *Assembly Daily Journal*, April 22, 1913. Hon. C. C. Young, Speaker of the Assembly, in chair, 50 ("every . . . governance") (HL JL1193).

39. JL to William Teichner, March 6, 1911, *Letters*, 2:990 ("I have . . . show them").

40. *The Compact Edition of the Oxford English Dictionary*, 2:3080 ("strait-jacket . . . speech," "the national . . . strait-jacket"). George Sterling to JL, May 25, 1906 ("bred . . . strait-jacket") (HL JL19047).

41. Silverman, *Houdini!!!*, 8 ("Visitors . . . 'Houdini'").

42. Ibid., 22 ("Harry's . . . entertainment").

43. Ibid., 27 ("buck naked").

44. Ibid., 28 ("Harry . . . 'it.'"). Houdini later gave a somewhat different account. See ibid., 28.

45. For discussion of spiritualist context, see Silverman, *Houdini!!!*, 36–44.

46. CKL, *The Book of Jack London*, 2:226 ("fairly . . . revealing").

47. Edward Morrell to JL [undated] ("so as . . . finish") (HL JL1914); Morrell to JL [undated] ("Dear Jack . . . chat with you") (HL JL15592). See CKL, diary entry, December 23, 1911 ("lunch Saddle Rock with Morrell and Lowrie") (HL JL225). See also JL, *Letters*, 3:1361, 1520.

48. Edward Morrell to JL, January 13, 1914 ("little . . . occult," "speculation . . . matter," "personal experiences") (HL JL15583).

49. Segno, *The Law of Mentalism*, 22–23 ("A thought . . . sent"). JL to Roland Phillips, March 26, 1914, *Letters*, 3:1315 ("accessible . . . folks").

50. Edward Morrell, "A Sketch of Ed Morrell's Life" (typescript), 2 ("visualizing familiar," "must . . . lived"), 5 ("voice"), 7 ("occult"), 15 ("I had . . . Voice") (HL JL1495). Lamott, *Chronicles of San Quentin*, 154 ("an autohypnotic technique").

51. CKL, *The Book of Jack London*, 2:218 ("a number . . . places," "Christ novel").

52. JL, *The Star Rover*, 3 ("All . . . me"), 5 ("Not . . . time").

53. Ibid., 25 ("assault . . . battery," "It is law . . . statutes").

54. Ibid., 8 ("I . . . food," "I was . . . guards"), 18 ("pick-handles . . . man"), 24 ("We . . . blankets," "jeering . . . us"), 35 ("gamed . . . flies," "knuckles").

55. Ibid., 5 ("red wrath").

56. Ibid., 24 ("eighty-seven pounds"), 56 ("it . . . curtains").

57. Ibid., 57 ("The trick . . . thing"), 58 ("to will . . . die," "that . . . thing," "when . . . body," "stone . . . in").

58. Ibid., 69 ("straitjacket hell"), 68 ("interstellar space"), 84 ("clownish").

59. Ibid., 64 ("cinching"). Jack Black, *The Big Break at Folsom* ("like . . . lungs") (HL 65406). JL, *The Star Rover*, 64 ("smothered groans," "mad howling").

60. Ibid., 18 ("smug . . . sleep").

61. *Pittsburgh Press*, November 6, 1915 ("mysticism"). *Philadelphia American*, October 23, 1915 ("tricks," "stirring adventures") (HL JL2941). *Pall Mall Gazette*, June 7, 1915 ("Best") (HL JL2944). *Country Life*, August 7, 1915 ("The author . . . him") (HL JL2942).

62. *Detroit Evening News*, November 6, 1915 ("Jack . . . true"); *New York Post*, November 6, 1915 ("vulgarity") (HL JL2944). *The Spectator*, August 28, 1915 ("indecency") (HL JL2942). *Illustrated London News*, 1915 ("All . . . realistic"); *Sheffield Telegraph*, 1915 ("Almost . . . page") (HL JL2942).

63. CKL quoted in Kenneth Silverman, *Houdini!!!*, 198 ("we may . . . day").

64. Houdini telegram, November 23, 1916 ("shocking," "founded . . . fact") (HL JL 7646–47).

AFTERWORD

1. Charmian recalled feelings of foreboding about Jack's health in November 1916. She'd seen "doom" in his eyes, she said, and a certain "*deadness*." See CKL, *The Book of Jack London* 2:377, 380.

2. Ibid., 2:380 ("I may . . . it," "I could . . . life"), 372 ("to . . . winds," "naturally . . . eater").

3. JL, *John Barleycorn*, 206 ("long sickness," "the pages . . . history," "bull-baiting . . . witches").

4. JL, *The Little Lady of the Big House*, 62 ("an . . . riot").

5. In "The Mexican," the "white-walled, water-power factories of Rio Blanco" represent the domination of Mexican land and mineral wealth by US and British corporations, and his prizefighter-revolutionist hero exposes the rationale behind the revolt: "He saw the six thousand workers, starved and wan, and the little children, seven and eight years of age, who toiled long shifts for ten cents a day." The adult workers, doomed by toxic chemicals or slow starvation, were "perambulating corpses." Surely some readers grasped the parallels to conditions in the United States and pondered the outlook for rebellion closer to home. See JL, "The Mexican," *CSS*, 3:1995 ("He saw . . . day," "perambulating corpses"). Critics quoted in George Herring, *From Colony to Superpower*, 390 ("mother . . . children").

6. One revolutionary Mexican faction was loyal to the revolutionary leader Francisco Madero, another to Porfirio Díaz in the hope of restoring power, and yet another to General Victoriana Huerta. Still others fought for the constitutionalist Venustiano Carranza, for the populist Emilio Zapata in the south, or for Francisco

"Pancho" Villa along the border in the north. JL, "Trip to Ping Yang," in *Jack London Reports*, 36 ("Korean Pack-Ponies"). John Lind quoted in George Herring, *From Colony to Superpower*, 392 ("More . . . men"); Henry Cabot Lodge (quoted), 393 ("unruly household").

7. JL, "With Funston's Men," in *Jack London Reports*, 138 ("sapphire sea," "azure sky," "ominous"), 140 ("cool . . . plaza"), 143 ("bloodstained . . . pillows," "broken parapets," "burst . . . ceilings," "masses . . . masonry," "such . . . machinery"), 157 ("a high . . . bullet," "things . . . made," "the hot . . . war"), 157 ("the efficient . . . machinery"); "The Red Game of War," in *Jack London Reports*, 128 ("well-tailored . . . savages," "arrowheads . . . points," "battleships . . . contrivances").

8. JL, "With Funston's Men," in *Jack London Reports*, 145 ("violent . . . disruptive"), 146 ("world . . . force," "a world . . . arbitration," "dream," "war . . . handle it").

9. JL to James D. Wilson, August 5, 1916, *Letters*, 3:1562: "It behooves a country or nation like the United States to maintain a reasonable preparedness for defense against any country or nation that at any time may go out upon the way of war to carve earth space for itself out of weaker and unprepared nations." German phrase quoted in Eric Hobsbawm, *The Age of Empire*, 319 ("*Heute . . . Welt*"). The present war directly impacted London. His income was diminished, and his offer to serve as war correspondent for *Collier's* magazine was not accepted. As battles raged on in European fields, woods, and trenches, London gathered and filed data in some 150 folders that he labeled "War." They included magazine articles, newspaper clippings, pamphlets, and official reports, most all of these documents favoring the Allies. The topics ranged from peace leagues to infantrymen's hand tools, war and socialism, military tactics, the "Prussian-ization" of Germany, and repeated summonses to America to enter the war on the Allied side. See "Prussia's Dream of Empire" ("Prussian-ization") (HL JLE1780). For London's "War" files, see HL JLE1676–1831. JL to John M. Wright, September 7, 1915, *Letters*, 3:1498 ("I believe . . . oligarchy").

10. Roland Marchand, *Creating the Corporate Soul*, 9 ("commercial leviathans," "assets . . . nation," "social legitimacy," "fables"). For an account of Ivy Lee's lobbying for the railroads and for the Rockefellers in the Ludlow Massacre involving the Colorado Fuel and Iron Company, see Hiebert, *Courtier to the Crowd*, 62–69, 97–108. See also *Encyclopedia of the American Left*, 440–41. See also Gitelman, *Legacy of the Ludlow Massacre*.

11. Tindall and Shi, *America*, 792 ("some . . . disability," "some . . . fatalities").

12. JL, "Goliah," *CSS*, 2:1211 ("war vessels," "useful . . . peace"), 1208 ("laughter," "slaughter"), 1212 ("leading figures," "bankers . . . justices"), 1216 ("Congress . . . Senate"), 1213 ("for . . . society").

13. Ibid., 1216 ("well . . . automatic"), 1214 ("the minimum . . . five").

14. Ibid., 1218 ("barbarously . . . lives," "leisure . . . joy," "higher . . . living"), 1216 ("miners . . . earth"). See Riesman, *The Lonely Crowd*, 262. Mills, *White Collar*, 236 ("the gospel . . . ethic"). JL to John M. Wright, September 7, 1915, *Letters*, 3:1498 ("a . . . pro-ally," "I believe . . . oligarchy," "to fight . . . England").

15. JL to Hughes Massie, October 13, 1915, *Letters*, 3:1507 ("to fight . . . England," "be . . . Germany," "far . . . man"). For an accurate account of the cause of Jack London's death and of arrangements for his funeral, see Labor, *Jack London: An American Life*, 379–84.

16. CKL, *The Book of Jack London*, 2:384 ("you are . . . to death").

BIBLIOGRAPHY

Adam, H[argrove] L[ee]. *The Story of Crime: From the Cradle to the Grave*. London: T. Werner Laurie, 1908.

Adams, Henry C. "What Is Publicity?" *North American Review* 175 (December 1902): 895–903.

Addams, Jane. "A Modern Lear." In *The Jane Addams Reader*, edited by Jean Elshtain, 163–76. New York: Basic Books, 2002.

Adler, Jacob. *Claus Spreckels: The Sugar King in Hawaii*. Honolulu: University of Hawaii Press, 1966.

Aiken, Charles Sedgwick, ed. *California Today*. San Francisco: California Promotion Committee of San Francisco, 1903.

Allanson-Winn, R. G. *Boxing*. London: A. D. Innes & Co., 1897.

Allen, Helena G. *The Betrayal of Liliuokalani, Last Queen of Hawaii*. Glendale, CA: Arthur H. Clark, 1982.

The American Heritage History of the Confident Years. New York: American Heritage Publishing Co., n.d.

Anderson, Lisa. "Justice to Ruth Morse: The Devolution of a Character in *Martin Eden*." *Call* 19.1–2 (2008): 11–14.

Andreyev, Leonid. *The Seven Who Were Hanged*. Translated by Herman Bernstein. New York: J. S. Ogilvie, 1909.

Armstrong, William N. *Around the World with a King*. New York: Frederick A. Stokes, 1904.

Arosteguy, Katie O'Donnell. " 'Things Men Must Do': Negotiating American Masculinity in Jack London's *The Valley of the Moon*." *Atenea* 28.1 (June 2008): 37–54.

Atherton, Frank Irving. "Jack London in Boyhood Adventures." *Jack London Journal* 4 (1997): 14–172.

Auerbach, Jonathan. " 'Congested Mails': Buck and Jack's 'Call.' " *American Literature* 67.1 (March 1996): 51–76.

———. *Male Call: Becoming Jack London*. Durham, NC: Duke University Press, 1996.

Bacchilega, Cristina. *Legendary Hawai'i and the Politics of Place: Tradition, Translation, and Tourism*. Philadelphia: University of Pennsylvania Press, 2007.

Bailey, L[iberty] H[yde]. *The Country-Life Movement*. New York: Macmillan, 1911.

———. *The Nature-Study Idea*. 1903. Reprint, New York: Macmillan, 1920.

———, ed. *The Cyclopedia of American Agriculture: A Popular Survey*. Vols. 1–4. New York: Macmillan, 1907–9.

———, ed. *The Principles of Agriculture: A Text-Book for Schools and Rural Societies*. New York: Macmillan, 1913.

Bain, David Howard. *Empire Express: Building the First Transcontinental Railroad*. New York: Viking, 1999.

Baker, Ray Stannard. "Wonderful Hawaii." *American Magazine* 73.6–8 (1911): 25–38, 201–14, 328–39.
Baldwin, Arthur D. *A Memoir of Henry Perrine Baldwin, 1842–1911*. Cleveland: Privately printed, 1915.
Baldwin, Charles W. *Geography of the Hawaiian Islands*. New York: American Book Co., 1908.
Bamford, Georgia Loring. *The Mystery of Jack London*. Oakland, CA: Georgia Loring Bamford, 1931.
Barltrop, Robert. *Jack London: The Man, the Writer, the Rebel*. London: Pluto, 1976.
Barmash, Isadore. *"Always Live Better Than Your Clients": The Fabulous Life and Times of Benjamin Sonnenberg, America's Greatest Publicist*. New York: Dodd, Mead, 1983.
Baskett, Sam S. "Mythic Dimensions of 'All Gold Canyon.'" *Jack London Journal* 2 (1995): 10–24.
———. "Sea Change in *The Sea-Wolf*." *American Literary Realism* 24.2 (Winter 1992): 5–22.
Bates, George Washington. *Sandwich Island Notes*. New York: Harper & Brothers, 1854.
Beisner, Robert L. *Twelve against Empire: The Anti-Imperialists, 1898–1900*. New York: McGraw-Hill, 1968.
Benedetto, Robert, ed. *The Hawaiian Journals of the New England Missionaries 1813–1894*. Honolulu: Hawaiian Mission Children's Society, 1982.
Berglund, Bjorn. "Satoyama, Traditional Farming Landscape in Japan, Compared to Scandinavia." *Japan Review* 20 (2008): 53–68.
"*Berkeley*: A Pioneering West Coast Ferryboat." *Mains'l Haul: A Journal of Pacific Maritime History* 40.2 (Spring 2004): 1–52.
Berkman, Alexander. *Prison Memoirs of an Anarchist*. New York: Mother Earth, 1912.
Berkove, Lawrence I. "*Before Adam* and *The Scarlet Plague*: Two Novels of Evolution by Jack London." *American Literary Naturalism* 2.1 (2007): 12–16.
———. "'The Captain of the Susan Drew': The Reworking of *The Sea-Wolf*." *Thalia* 17.1–2 (1997): 61–68.
———. "Jack London and Evolution: From Spencer to Huxley." *American Literary Realism* 36.3 (Spring 2004): 243–55.
———. "London's Developing Conceptions of Masculinity." *Jack London Journal* 3 (1996): 117–26.
———. "A Parallax Correction in London's 'The Unparalleled Invasion.'" *American Literary Realism* 24.2 (Winter 1992): 33–40.
———. "Thomas Stevens: London's Comic Agent of Evolutionary Criticism." *Thalia* 12.1–2 (1992): 15–24.
Berliner, Jonathan. "Jack London's Socialistic Social Darwinism." *American Literary Realism* 41.1 (Fall 2008): 62–78.
Biennial Report of the State Board of Prison Directors of the State of California for . . . 1909–1910. Sacramento: Superintendent of State Printing, 1910.

Bigelow, Poultney. "The Bonanza Farms of the West." *Atlantic Monthly* 45 (January 1880): 33–44.
Bird, Isabella. *The Hawaiian Archipelago: Six Months among the Palm Groves, Coral Reefs and Volcanoes of the Sandwich Islands*. 1875. Reprint, Cambridge: Picador, 1997.
Blackman, William Fremont. *The Making of Hawaii: A Study in Social Evolution*. New York: Macmillan, 1899.
Boddy, Kasia. *Boxing: A Cultural History*. London: Reaktion, 2009.
Bookspan, Shelley. *A Germ of Goodness: The California State Prison System, 1851–1944*. Lincoln: University of Nebraska Press, 1991.
Bowsfield, C. C. *Wealth from the Soil*. Chicago: Forbes, 1914.
Brace, Charles Loring. *The New West: California in 1867–1868*. New York: G. P. Putnam, 1869.
Bradley, James. *The Imperial Cruise: A Secret History of Empire and War*. New York: Little, Brown, 2009.
Brandt, Kenneth K. "Repudiating 'The Gladiatorial' Theory of Existence: Tom King's Ethical Development in Jack London's 'A Piece of Steak.'" *Aethlon* 20.2 (Spring 2003): 101–8.
Breadbasket of the World: California's Wheat-Growing Era, 1860–1890. San Francisco: Book Club of California, 1985.
Bremner, Robert H. *From the Depths: The Discovery of Poverty in the United States*. New York: New York University Press, 1958.
Briggs, Harold E. "Early Bonanza Farming in the Red River Valley of the North." *Agricultural History* 6.1 (January 1932): 26–37.
Briscoe, Erica. "*The Iron Heel*: How Not to Write a Popular Novel." *Jack London Journal* 5 (1998): 5–38.
Brooks, John Graham. *The Social Unrest: Studies in Labor and Socialist Movements*. New York: Macmillan, 1913.
Browne, G. Waldo. *The Paradise of the Pacific: The Hawaiian Islands*. Boston: Dana Estes, 1900.
Bruni, John P. "Performing the Perfect Dog: The Reconstruction of Gender in Jack London's *The Call of the Wild* and *White Fang*." In *Forces of Nature: Natural(-izing) Gender and Gender(-izing) Nature in the Discourses of Western Culture*, edited by Bernadette H. Hyner and Precious McKenzie, 174–209. Newcastle-upon-Tyne, UK: Cambridge Scholars, 2009.
Bryan, Ferald J. *Henry Grady or Tom Watson?: The Rhetorical Struggle for the New South, 1880–1890*. Macon, GA: Mercer University Press, 1994.
Bryce, James. *The American Commonwealth*. Vol. 2. 3rd ed., rev. New York: Macmillan, 1905.
Buhle, Paul. *Marxism in the United States: Remapping the History of the American Left*. London: Verso, 1987.
Burns, Edward McNall. *David Starr Jordan: Prophet of Freedom*. Stanford, CA: Stanford University Press, 1953.

Cameron, Effie, and D. E. Keane. *Plantation Days: Remembering Honolulu*. Kahului, HI: Maui Land & Pineapple Company, 1987.

Campbell, Donna. "Jack London's Allegorical Landscapes: 'The God of His Fathers,' 'The Priestly Prerogative,' and *The Valley of the Moon*." *Literature and Belief* 21.1–2 (2001): 59–75.

Campbell, R. J. *Christianity and the Social Order*. New York: Macmillan, 1907.

Capron, E. S. *History of California from Its Discovery to the Present Time*. Boston: John P. Jewett & Co., 1854.

Carnegie, Andrew. *Autobiography*. London: Constable & Co., 1920.

———. *The Gospel of Wealth*. 1900. Reprint, Cambridge, MA: Harvard University Press, 1962.

Cashman, Sean Dennis. *America in the Gilded Age*. 3rd ed. New York: New York University Press, 1993.

Cassuto, Leonard. "Chasing the Lost Signifier Down 'The Sun-Dog Trail.'" *Jack London Journal* 2 (1995): 64–72.

———. "Jack London's Class-Based Grotesque." In *Literature and the Grotesque*, edited by Michael J. Meyer, 113–28. Amsterdam: Rodopi, 1995.

Central California Illustrated. Los Angeles: California Publishing Co., 1900.

Chaney, George Leonard. *"Alo'ha!": A Hawaiian Salutation*. Boston: Roberts Brothers, 1888.

Chang, Young-Hee. "Korean Sources and References in Jack London's *The Star Rover*." *Call* 21.2 (2010): 10–14.

Chernow, Ron. *Titan: The Life of John D. Rockefeller*. New York: Vintage, 1999.

Chinen, Jon J. *The Great Mahele: Hawaii's Land Division of 1848*. Honolulu: University of Hawaii Press, 1958.

Christopher, Renny. "Rags to Riches to Suicide: Unhappy Narratives of Upward Mobility: *Martin Eden, Bread Givers, Delia's Song*, and *Hunger of Memory*." *College Literature* 29.4 (Fall 2002): 79–108.

Chu, Patricia E. "Dog and Dinosaur: The Modern Animal Story." *Mosaic* 40.1 (March 2007): 79–94.

Clarke, Michael Tavel. *These Days of Large Things: The Culture of Size in America, 1865–1930*. Ann Arbor: University of Michigan Press, 2007.

Clymer, Jeffory A. *America's Culture of Terrorism: Violence, Capitalism, and the Written Word*. Chapel Hill: University of North Carolina Press, 2003.

———. "'This Firm of Men-Killers': Jack London and the Business of Terrorism." *Modern Fiction Studies* 45.4 (Winter 1999): 905–31.

Coffin, C. C. "Dakota Wheat Fields." *Harper's New Monthly Magazine* 60.358 (March 1880): 529–35.

Coleman, McAllister. *Eugene V. Debs: A Man Unafraid*. New York: Greenberg, 1930.

The Colorado Labor Wars: Cripple Creek 1903–1904: A Centennial Celebration. Edited by Tim Blevins, Chris Nicholl, and Calvin P. Otto. Colorado Springs: Pike's Peak Library District, 2006.

Columbian Exposition Souvenir of Alameda County. Oakland, CA: Tribune Publishing, 1893.
Colusa County Annual and Directory. Colusa, CA: Addington & Green, 1876.
The Compact Edition of the Oxford English Dictionary. 2 vols. Oxford: Oxford University Press, 1971.
Compton-Rickett, Arthur. *The Vagabond in Literature*. London: J. M. Dent; New York: Dutton, 1906.
Conlogue, William. *Working in the Garden: American Writers and the Industrialization of Agriculture*. Chapel Hill: University of North Carolina Press, 2001.
Cummin, C. F. Gordon. *Granite Crags*. Edinburgh: Blackwell, 1884.
Cutlip, Scott M. *Public Relations History: From the 17th to the 20th Century*. Hillsdale, NJ: Lawrence Erlbaum, 1995.
Danbom, David B. *Born in the Country: A History of Rural America*. Baltimore: Johns Hopkins University Press, 1995.
———. *The Resisted Revolution: Urban America and the Industrialization of Agriculture*. Ames: Iowa State University Press, 1979.
Daniel, Cletus E. *Bitter Harvest: A History of California Farmworkers, 1870–1941*. Ithaca, NY: Cornell University Press, 1981.
Darrow, Clarence. *An Eye for an Eye*. New York: Duffield & Co., 1905.
Davis, Harold E. *Henry Grady's New South: Atlanta, a Brave and Beautiful City*. Tuscaloosa: University of Alabama Press, 1990.
Daws, Gavan. *Shoal of Time: A History of the Hawaiian Islands*. Honolulu: University of Hawaii Press, 1968.
Decaire, John. "The Boys' Books of Despair." *Southwest Review* 88.2–3 (2003): 277–90.
De Quille, Dan [William Wright]. *History of the Big Bonanza*. Hartford, CT: American Books, 1877.
Derrick, Scott. "Making a Heterosexual Man: Gender, Sexuality, and Narrative in the Fiction of Jack London." In *Rereading Jack London*, edited by Leonard Cassuto and Jeanne Campbell Reesman, 110–29. Stanford, CA: Stanford University Press, 1996.
Dilke, Charles. "The Naval Strength of Nations." *Cosmopolitan Magazine* 32 (February 1902): 349–57.
Dole, Richard, and Elizabeth Dole Porteus. *The Story of James Dole*. Waipahu, HI: Island Heritage, 2004.
Dooley, Patrick K. "Jack London's 'South of the Slot' and William James's 'The Divided Self and the Process of Its Unification.'" *Western American Literature* 41.1 (Spring 2006): 50–65.
———. "'The Strenuous Mood': William James' 'The Energies of Men' and Jack London's *The Sea Wolf*." *American Literary Realism* 34.1 (Fall 2001): 18–28.
Dorrance, William H., and Francis S. Morgan. *Sugar Islands: The 165-Year Story of Sugar in Hawaii*. Honolulu: Mutual, 2000.
Dow, William. "Down and Out in London and Orwell." *Symbiosis* 6.1 (April 2002): 69–94.

Drache, Hiram M. *The Day of the Bonanza: A History of Bonanza Farming in the Red River Valley of the North*. Fargo: North Dakota Institute for Regional Studies, 1964.

Duncan, Charles. "'Where Piggishness Flourishes': Contextualizing Strategies in Norris and London." *Frank Norris Studies* 14 (Autumn 1993): 1–6.

Earle, Alice Morse. *Curious Punishments of Bygone Days*. New York: Duffield & Co., 1907.

East Hawaii Sugar Planters' Association. *The Real Issue in Hawaii*. Hilo, HI, 1915.

Eastman, Crystal. *Work-Accidents and the Law*. New York: Charities Publication Committee, 1910.

Egbert, Donald Drew, and Stow Persons, eds. *Socialism and American Life*. 2 vols. Princeton, NJ: Princeton University Press, 1952.

Elderkin, P. B. "The State Prisons of California—Folsom." *Overland Monthly* 34.20 (September 1899): 257–64.

Ellis, Juniper. "'A Wreckage of Races' in Jack London's South Pacific." *Arizona Quarterly* 57.2 (Summer 2001): 57–75.

Ellis, William. *Polynesian Researches: Hawaii*. 1829. Reprint, London: Charles Tuttle, 1969.

Ellis, Wilson R., ed. *The Resources of San Joaquin County, California*. Stockton, CA, 1886.

Elson, Ruth Miller. *Guardians of Tradition: American Schoolbooks of the Nineteenth Century*. Lincoln: University of Nebraska Press, 1964.

Emerson, Ralph Waldo. "Napoleon: Man of the World." In *Emerson: Essays and Poems*, edited by Joel Porte, 727–45. New York: Library of America, 1996.

———. "Self-Reliance." In *The Collected Works of Ralph Waldo Emerson*, vol. 2: *Essays: First Series*, edited by Joseph Slater, 27–51. Cambridge, MA: Harvard University Press, 1980.

———. "The Young American." In *Emerson: Essays and Poems*, edited by Joel Porte, 213–30. New York: Library of America, 1996.

Emmert, Scott. "The Familiar Uncommon Spectator: Jack London's Female Watchers in *The Game* and *The Abysmal Brute*." *Journal of Sport Literature* 22.1 (2004): 137–46.

Encyclopedia of the American Left. Edited by Mari Jo Buhle, Paul Buhle, and Dan Georgakas. Urbana: University of Illinois Press, 1992.

Eposito, Anthony V. *The Ideology of the Socialist Party of America*. New York: Garland, 1997.

Feldman, Mark. "The Physics and Metaphysics of Caging: The Animal in Late-Nineteenth-Century American Culture." *Mosaic* 39.4 (December 2006): 161–80.

Ferri, Enrico. *Criminal Sociology*. New York: D. Appleton & Co., 1898.

Fineman, Daniel D. "Logic, Capital, and London's Naturalism in *The Call of the Wild*." *Excavatio* 11 (1998): 124–28.

Fisher, P. M. *Local History, Geography and Civics: Alameda County, California*. Oakland: N.p., 1902.

Fitch, John A. *The Steel Workers*. 1910. Reprint, Pittsburgh: University of Pittsburgh Press, 1989.

Fite, Gilbert C. *The Farmer's Frontier, 1865–1900*. New York: Holt, Rinehart, and Winston, 1966.

Fitzgerald, Deborah. *Every Farm a Factory: The Industrial Ideal in American Agriculture*. New Haven, CT: Yale University Press, 2005.
Flaubert, Gustave. *Madame Bovary*. 1867. Translated by Eleanor Marx Aveling. Reprint, London: W. W. Gibbings, 1892.
Flynt, Josiah. *Notes of an Itinerant Policeman*. Boston: L. C. Page, 1900.
Foner, Philip S. *Jack London: American Rebel*. 1947. Reprint, New York: Citadel, 1964.
Forbes, Cochran. *The Journals of Cochran Forbes, Missionary to Hawaii, 1831–1864*. Honolulu: Hawaiian Mission Children's Society, 1984.
French, Giles. *Cattle Country of Peter French*. Portland, OR: Binfords & Mort, 1964.
Furer, Andrew. "Jack London, Bernarr Macfadden, and the Crime of Weakness." *Jack London Journal* 5 (1998): 72–79.
———. "Jack London's New Woman: A Little Lady with a Big Stick." *Studies in American Fiction* 22.2 (Autumn 1994): 186–214.
Gair, Christopher. "'The Beautiful and True and Good': Culture, Race, and Nation in *The People of the Abyss*." *Symbiosis* 3.2 (October 1999): 131–42.
———. "From Naturalism to Nature: Freedom and Constraint in *The Star Rover*." *Jack London Journal* 2 (1995): 118–32.
———. "Gender and Genre: Nature, Naturalism, and Authority in *The Sea-Wolf*." *Studies in American Fiction* 22.2 (Autumn 1994): 131–47.
———. "Hegemony, Metaphor, and Structural Difference: The 'Strange' Dualism of 'South of the Slot.'" *Arizona Quarterly* 49.1 (Spring 1993): 73–97.
———. "London Calling: The Importance of Jack London to Contemporary Cultural Studies." *Works and Days* 11.2 (Fall 1993): 27–43.
———. "'A Tale, Like Anything Else': *Martin Eden* and the Literary Marketplace." *Essays in Literature* 19.2 (Fall 1992): 246–59.
———. "'The Way Our People Came': Citizenship, Capitalism and Racial Difference in *The Valley of the Moon*." *Studies in the Novel* 25.4 (Winter 1993): 418–35.
Garland, Hamlin. *A Son of the Middle Border*. 1914. Reprint, New York: Macmillan, 1925.
Gates, Paul W. "The Homestead Act Free Land Policy in Operation, 1862–1935." In *Land Use Policy and Problems in the United States*, edited by Howard W. Ottoson, 28–46. Lincoln: University of Nebraska Press, 1962.
Gatti, Susan Irvin. "Stone Hearths and Marble Babies: Jack London and the Domestic Ideal." *Jack London Journal* 3 (1996): 43–56.
Ghent, W[illiam] J[ames]. *Our Benevolent Feudalism*. New York: Macmillan, 1902.
Gibbs, Josiah F. *The Mountain Meadow Massacre*. Salt Lake City: Salt Lake Tribune Publishing Co., 1910.
Gitelman, Howard M. *Legacy of the Ludlow Massacre: A Chapter in American Industrial Relations*. Philadelphia: University of Pennsylvania Press, 1988.
Glass, Loren. "'Nobody's Renown': Plagiarism and Publicity in the Career of Jack London." *American Literature* 71.3 (September 1993): 529–49.
Go, Julian. *Patterns of Empire: The British and American Empires, 1688 to the Present*. Cambridge: Cambridge University Press, 2011.

Goldman, Eric F. *Public Relations and the Progressive Surge, 1898–1917*. New York: Foundation for Public Relations Research and Education, 1965.

———. *Two-Way Street: The Emergence of the Public Relations Counsel*. Boston: Bellman, 1948.

Gooch, G. P. "Imperialism." In *The Heart of the Empire: Discussions of Problems of Modern City Life in England*, edited by Bentley G. Gilbert, 308–97. London: T. Fisher Unwin, 1902.

Gorn, Elliott J. *The Manly Art: Bare-Knuckle Prize Fighting in America*. 1986. Reprint, Ithaca, NY: Cornell University Press, 1989.

Gowen, H. H. *The Paradise of the Pacific*. London: Skeffington & Son, 1892.

Green, Will S. *The History of Colusa County, California*. San Francisco: Elliott and Moore, 1880.

Greene, Ann Norton. *Horses at Work: Harnessing Power in Industrial America*. Cambridge, MA: Harvard University Press, 2008.

Gregory, Tom. *History of Sonoma County, California*. Los Angeles: Historic Record Co., 1911.

Griffis, William Elliot. *Corea: The Hermit Kingdom*. New York: Charles Scribner's Sons, 1902.

Griffith, Griffith J. "San Quentin as I Knew It." In *Crime and Criminals*, 55–93. Los Angeles: Prison Reform League, 1910.

Hackett, Alice Payne. *Seventy Years of Best Sellers, 1895–1965*. New York: L. L. Bowker, 1967.

Hadley, Arthur Twining. *Economics: An Account of the Relations between Private Property and Public Welfare*. New York: G. P. Putnam's Sons, 1896.

———. *The Education of the American Citizen*. 1901. Reprint, Freeport, NY: Books for Libraries Press, 1969.

———. *Railroad Transportation: Its History and Its Laws*. New York: G. P. Putnam's Sons, 1885.

Haley, James L. *Wolf: The Lives of Jack London*. New York: Basic Books, 2010.

Hallahan, Kirk. "Ivy Lee and the Rockefellers' Response to the 1913–14 Colorado Coal Strike." *Journal of Public Relations Research* 14.4 (2002): 265–315.

Hamilton, Angus. *Korea*. New York: Charles Scribner's Sons, 1904.

Hamilton, David Mike, ed. *"The Tools of My Trade": The Annotated Books in Jack London's Library*. Seattle: University of Washington Press, 1986.

The Harper American Literature. Edited by Donald McQuade et al. Vol. 1. New York: Harper & Row, 1987.

Harte, Bret. *Through the Santa Clara Wheat*. 1872. Reprinted in *The Writings of Bret Harte*, vol. 6, 341–93. Boston: Houghton Mifflin, 1896.

Harvey, Anne-Marie. "Sons of the Son: Making White, Middle-Class Manhood in Jack London's David Grief Stories and the *Saturday Evening Post*." *American Studies* 39.3 (Fall 1998): 37–68.

Haughey, Homer L., and Connie Kale Johnson. *Jack London Homes Album*. Stockton, CA: Heritage, 1987.

———. *Jack London Ranch Album*. Stockton, CA: Heritage Publishing for the Valley of the Moon Natural History Association, 1985.

Hayes, Derek. *Historical Atlas of California*. Berkeley and Los Angeles: University of California Press, 2007.

Hayes, Kevin J. "How Jack London Read Joseph Conrad." *American Literary Realism* 30.2 (Winter 1998): 17–27.

Hendrick, Burton J. "President Hadley, of Yale." *World's Work* 28.2 (June 1914): 141–48.

Hensley, John R. "Eugenics and Social Darwinism in Stanley Waterloo's *The Story of Ab* and Jack London's *Before Adam*." *Studies in Popular Culture* 25.1 (October 2002): 22–37.

Herring, George C. *From Colony to Superpower: U.S. Foreign Relations since 1776*. New York: Oxford University Press, 2008.

Hiebert, Ray Eldon. *Courtier to the Crowd: The Story of Ivy Lee and the Development of Public Relations*. Ames: Iowa State University Press, 1966.

Hirsch, Adam J. *The Rise of the Penitentiary: Prisons and Punishment in Early California*. New Haven, CT: Yale University Press, 1992.

History of Sonoma County, California. San Francisco: Alley, Bowen, 1880.

Hittell, Theodore H. *History of California*. Vol. 3. San Francisco: N. J. Stone, 1898.

Hobsbawm, Eric. *The Age of Empire, 1875–1914*. 1987. Reprint, London: Abacus, 1994.

Hobson, J[ohn] A[ugustus]. "The Economic Taproot of Imperialism." *Social Democrat* 6.8 (August 15, 1902): 249–52.

———. *Imperialism: A Study*. 1902. Reprint, Ann Arbor: University of Michigan Press, 1965.

Hofstadter, Richard. *The Age of Reform: From Bryan to F.D.R.* New York: Vintage, 1955.

Holtz, William. "Jack London's First Biographer." *Western American Literature* 27.1 (Spring 1992): 24–36.

Hopper, James, and Fred R. Bechdolt. *9009*. New York: McClure, 1908.

Horwitz, Howard. "Primordial Stories: London and the Immateriality of Evolution." *Western Humanities Review* 50.4–51.1 (Winter 1996–Spring 1997): 337–43.

Howard, Benjamin. *Prisoners of Russia: A Personal Study of Convict Life in Sakhalin and Siberia*. New York: D. Appleton, 1902.

Howe, Irving. *Socialism and America*. 1977. Reprint, San Diego: Harcourt Brace Jovanovich, 1985.

Hunter, Robert. *Socialists at Work*. New York: Macmillan, 1908.

Hurd, Archibald S. "The Modern Battle-Ship." *Booklovers Magazine* 5.6 (June 1905): 745–59.

Illustrated History of Sonoma County, California. Chicago: Lewis, 1889.

Ingersoll, Robert G. *Crimes against Criminals*. New York: Roycrofters, 1906.

Jack London, Photographer. Edited by Jeanne Campbell Reesman, Sara S. Hodson, and Philip Adam. Athens: University of Georgia Press, 2010.

Jack London at Yale. Edited by State Secretary of the Socialist Party of Connecticut. Westwood, MA: Ariel Press, n.d.

Jack London in The Aegis. Edited by James Sisson III. Oakland, CA: Star Rover House, 1980.

Jack London Reports: War Correspondence, Sports Articles, and Miscellaneous Writings. Edited by King Hendricks and Irving Shepard. Garden City, NY: Doubleday, 1970.

Jacobi, Martin J. "Rhetoric and Fascism in Jack London's *The Iron Heel*, Sinclair Lewis's *It Can't Happen Here*, and Philip Roth's *The Plot against America*." *Philip Roth Studies* 6.1 (Spring 2010): 85–102.

Jelinek, Lawrence. *Harvest Empire: A History of California Agriculture*. San Francisco: Boyd & Fraser, 1953.

Joesting, Edward. *Kauai: The Separate Kingdom*. 1984. Reprint, Honolulu: University of Hawaii Press and Kauai Museum Association, 1987.

John, Richard R. *Network Nation: Inventing American Telecommunications*. Cambridge, MA: Harvard University Press, 2010.

Johnson, Martin. *Through the South Seas with Jack London*. New York: Dodd, Mead, 1913.

Johnston, Carolyn. *Jack London—An American Radical?* Westport, CT: Greenwood, 1984.

———. "The Myth of Androgyny in the Life and Works of Jack London." *Jack London Journal* 1 (1994): 159–67.

Jordan, David Starr. *The Call of the Twentieth Century: An Address to Young Men*. Boston: American Unitarian Association, 1904.

———. *The Care and Culture of Men*. San Francisco: Whitaker and Ray, 1903.

———. *The Days of a Man: Being Memories of a Naturalist, Teacher, and Minor Prophet of Democracy*. 2 vols. Yonkers-on-Hudson, NY: World Book Co., 1922.

———. *The Human Harvest: A Study of the Decay of Races through the Survival of the Unfit*. Boston: American Unitarian Society, 1907.

———. *The Philosophy of Hope*. San Francisco: Paul Elder & Co., 1902.

———. *The Strength of Being Clean: A Study of the Quest for Unearned Happiness*. Boston: L. C. Page, 1900.

Jowett, Garth S., and Victoria O'Donnell. *Propaganda and Persuasion*. 4th ed. Thousand Oaks, CA: Sage, 2006.

Juola, Patrick. "Becoming Jack London." *Journal of Quantitative Linguistics* 14.2–3 (August–December 2007): 145–47.

Kalakaua, [David]. *The Legends and Myths of Hawaii*. New York: Charles L. Webster, 1888.

Kasson, John F. *Houdini, Tarzan, and the Perfect Man*. New York: Hill and Wang, 2001.

Kawakami, Barbara F. *Japanese Immigrant Clothing in Hawaii, 1885–1941*. Honolulu: University of Hawaii Press, 1993.

Kent, Harold Winfield. *Charles Reed Bishop: Man of Hawaii*. Palo Alto, CA: Pacific Books, 1965.

Kershaw, Alex. *Jack London: A Life*. New York: HarperCollins, 1997.

Kersten, Andrew E. *Clarence Darrow: American Iconoclast*. New York: Hill and Wang, 2012.

Kersten, Holger. "The Erosion of the Ideal of the Heroic Explorer: Jack London's *The Cruise of the Snark*." In *Narratives of Exploration and Discovery: Essays in Honor of Konrad Gross*, edited by Wolfgang Kloss, 85–97. Trier, Germany: Wissenschaftlicher Verlag Trier, 2005.

Kim, Yung Min. "'A Patriarchal Grass House' of His Own: Jack London's *Martin Eden* and the Imperial Frontier." *American Literary Realism* 34.1 (Fall 2001): 1–17.

King, F[ranklin] H[iram]. *Farmers of Forty Centuries: Organic Farming in China, Korea, and Japan*. 1911. Reprint, Mineola, NY: Dover, 2004.

Kingman, Russ. *A Pictorial Biography of Jack London*. Zámecká, Czech Republic: Trialty for the Jack London Research Center, 1979.

Kipnis, Ira. *The American Socialist Movement, 1897–1912*. New York: Columbia University Press, 1952.

Kobori, Hiromi, and Richard B. Primack. "Conservation for Satoyama, the Traditional Landscape of Japan." *Arnoldia* 62.4 (2003): 2–10.

Koebner, Richard, and Helmut Dan Schmidt. *Imperialism: The Story and Significance of a Political Word, 1840–1960*. London: Cambridge University Press, 1965.

Kratzke, Peter. "Jack London's Optimistic View of the Law: A Reading of *The Son of the Wolf*." *Studies in Short Fiction* 32.1 (Winter 1995): 67–74.

Kropotkin, P[etr]. *Fields, Factories and Workshops*. New York: G. P. Putnam's Sons, 1911.

Kurisu, Yasushi. *Sugar Town: Hawaiian Plantation Days Remembered*. Honolulu: Watermark, 1995.

Labor, Earle. "The Archetypal Woman as 'Martyr to Truth': Jack London's 'Samuel.'" *American Literary Realism* 24.2 (Winter 1902): 25–32.

———. *Jack London: An American Life*. New York: Farrar, Straus and Giroux, 2013.

———. "Jack London's Pacific World." In *Critical Essays on Jack London*, edited by Jacqueline Tavernier-Courbin, 114–30. Boston: G. K. Hall, 1983.

———, ed. *The Portable Jack London*. New York: Penguin, 1995.

Labor, Earle, Robert C. Leitz III, and I. Milo Shepard, eds. *The Complete Short Stories of Jack London*. 3 vols. Stanford, CA: Stanford University Press, 1993.

———, eds. *The Letters of Jack London*. 3 vols. Stanford, CA: Stanford University Press, 1988.

Lamott, Kenneth. *Chronicles of San Quentin*. New York: David McKay, 1960.

Lawson, Andrew. "Twain, Class, and the Gilded Age." In *The Cambridge History of the American Novel*, edited by Leonard Cassuto, Clare Eby, and Benjamin Reiss, 365–79. Cambridge: Cambridge University Press, 2011.

Le Bon, Gustave. *The Crowd*. 1895. Reprint, New Brunswick, NJ: Transaction, 1995.

Le Duc, Thomas. "History and Appraisal of U.S. Land Policy to 1862." In *Land Use Policy and Problems in the United States*, edited by Howard. W. Ottoson, 3–27. Lincoln: University of Nebraska Press, 1963.

Lee, Gerald Stanley. *The Voice of the Machines: An Introduction to the Twentieth Century*. Northampton, MA: Mt. Tom, 1906.

Lee, Ivy Ledbetter. *The City for the People! The Best Administration New York Ever Had*. 2nd ed. New York: Committee on Press and Literature of the Citizens Union, 1903.
———. "Enemies of Publicity." *Electric Railway Journal* 49 (March 31, 1917): 599–600.
———. "The How and Why of Publicity." *Electric Railway Journal* (July 4, 1917): 52–53.
———. *Human Nature and Railroads*. 1915. Reprint, Charleston: Bibliobazaar, n.d.
———. "An Open and Above-Board 'Trust.'" *Moody's Magazine* 4 (July 1907): 158–64.
———. "The Problem of International Propaganda: A New Technique Necessary in Developing Understanding between Nations." Address by Ivy Lee, London, July 3, 1934.
———. *Railway Progress in the United States*. London: B. F. Stevens & Brown, 1912.
———. "Savings Banks." *World's Work* 4 (September 1902): 2488–90.
Lee, J[ames] W. *The Making of a Man*. 1892. Reprint, Chicago: Revell, 1899.
Leffingwell, Randy. *The American Barn*. 1991. Reprint, St. Paul, MN: N.p., 2003.
Lewis, Austin. *The Rise of the American Proletarian*. Chicago: H. Kerr & Co., 1907.
Liliuokalani. *Hawaii's Story by Hawaii's Queen*. 1898. Reprint, Rutland, VT: Charles E. Tuttle, 1964.
Lincoln-Douglas Debates of 1858. Edited by Robert W. Johannsen. New York: Oxford University Press, 1965.
Lindquist, Barbara. "Jack London, Aesthetic Theory, and Nineteenth-Century Popular Science." *Western American Literature* 32.2 (Summer 1997): 99–114.
Link, Eric Carl. "The Five Deaths of Wolf Larsen." *Studies in American Naturalism* 5.2 (Winter 2010): 151–63.
London, Charmian Kittredge. *The Book of Jack London*. 2 vols. 1921. Reprint, Kessinger, n.d.
———. *Jack London and Hawaii: The Adventures of Charmian and Jack London in Hawaii*. 1918. Reprint, Coventry, UK: Trotamundas, 2008.
———. *Jack London in Aloha Land*. 1917. Reprint. London: Kegan Paul, 2002.
———. *The Log of the Snark*. New York: Macmillan, 1917.
———. *The New Hawaii*. Rev. ed. London: Mills and Boon, 1923.
———. *Our Hawaii*. New York: Macmillan, 1922.
London, Jack. *The Abysmal Brute*. 1911. Reprint, Lincoln: University of Nebraska Press, 2000.
———. *Adventure*. New York: Grosset & Dunlap, 1911.
———. *Before Adam*. 1906–7. Reprint, London: Hesperus, 2004.
———. *The Complete Short Stories of Jack London*. Edited by Earle Labor, Robert C. Leitz III, and I. Milo Shepard. 3 vols. Palo Alto, CA: Stanford University Press, 1993.
———. *The Cruise of the Snark*. 1913. Reprint, Washington, DC: National Geographic, 2003.
———. *The Game*. 1905. Reprint. Lincoln: University of Nebraska Press, 2001.
———. "The House Beautiful." http://www.readbookonline.net/read/298/8657/.
———. *The Human Drift*. 1917. Reprint, Charleston: Bibliobazaar, 2006.

———. "The Impossibility of War." *Overland Monthly* 35 (March 1900): 278–82.
———. *The Iron Heel*. 1908. Reprint, New York: Penguin, 2006.
———. *Jack London: Novels and Social Writings*. New York: Library of America, 1982.
———. *Jack London's Tales of Cannibals and Headhunters*. Edited by Gary Riedl and Thomas R. Tietze. Albuquerque: University of New Mexico Press, 2006.
———. *Jerry of the Islands*. New York: Macmillan, 1917.
———. *John Barleycorn*. 1913. Reprint, New York: Modern Library, 2001.
———. "The Language of the Tribe." *Mid-Pacific Magazine* 10.2 (August 1915): 117–20.
———. *The Letters of Jack London*. Edited by Earle Labor, Robert C. Leitz III, and I. Milo Shepard. 3 vols. Stanford, CA: Stanford University Press, 1988.
———. *The Little Lady of the Big House*. 1916. Reprint, Teddington, UK: Echo, n.d.
———. *Martin Eden*. 1909. Reprint, New York: Penguin, 1984.
———. *Michael, Brother of Jerry*. 1917. Reprint, N.p.: Quiet Vision, n.d.
———. "My Hawaiian Aloha." 1916. Reprinted in Charmian K. London, *Our Hawaii*, 1–33. New York: Macmillan, 1922.
———. *No Mentor but Myself: Jack London on Writing and Writers*. Edited by Dale L. Walker and Jeanne Campbell Reesman. 2nd ed. Stanford, CA: Stanford University Press, 1999.
———. *Novels and Selected Writings*. New York: Library of America, 1982.
———. *The People of the Abyss*. 1903. Reprint, New York: Lawrence Hill, 1993.
———. *The Portable Jack London*. Edited by Earle Labor. New York: Penguin, 1994.
———. *Revolution and Other Essays*. London: Mills and Boon, 1910.
———. *The Road*. 1907–8. Reprint, New Brunswick, NJ: Rutgers University Press, 2006.
———. *The Sea-Wolf*. 1904. Reprint, New York: Modern Library, 2000.
———. *The Star Rover*. 1915. Reprint, New York: Modern Library, 2003.
———. "Things Alive." 1906. In *The Portable Jack London*, edited by Earle Labor, 483–85. New York: Penguin, 1994.
———. *The Valley of the Moon*. 1913. Reprint, Berkeley and Los Angeles: University of California Press, 1998.
———. *The War of the Classes*. 1905. Reprint, New York: Echo, 2009.
———. "What Life Means to Me." *Cosmopolitan* 40 (November 1905): 526–30.
London, Joan. *Jack London and His Times*. New York: Book League of America, 1939.
Lopez, Debbie L. "'Invisible Anthropophagi' and Asymmetrical Conclusions in London's Naturalist's Tale: 'The Red One.'" *Excavatio* 17.1–2 (2002): 374–402.
———. "*The Sea-Wolf*'s Romantic Illusions Lost." *Excavatio* 19.1 (2004): 348–57.
Lowrie, Donald. *My Life in Prison*. 1912. Reprint, Memphis: General Books, 2012.
Lukas, J. Anthony. *Big Trouble: A Murder in a Small Western Town Sets Off a Struggle for the Soul of America*. New York: Simon & Schuster, 1997.
Lundquist, James. *Jack London: Adventures, Ideas, and Fiction*. New York: Unger, 1987.
Luther Burbank: His Methods and Discoveries and Their Practical Application. Edited by John Whitson, Robert John, and Henry Smith. 12 vols. New York: Luther Burbank, 1914.

MacGillivray, Don. *Captain Alex MacLean: Jack London's Sea Wolf.* Vancouver: University of British Columbia Press, 2008.

Malo, David. *Hawaiian Antiquities (Mo'olelo Hawai'i).* Translated by Nathaniel B. Emerson. 2nd ed. 1903. Reprint, Honolulu: Bishop Museum Press, 1951.

Mandell, Nikki. *The Corporation as Family: The Gendering of Corporate Welfare, 1890–1930.* Chapel Hill: University of North Carolina Press, 2002.

Marchand, Roland. *Creating the Corporate Soul: The Rise of Public Relations and Corporate Imagery in American Big Business.* Berkeley and Los Angeles: University of California Press, 1998.

Markham, Edwin. "The Hoe-Man in the Making." *Cosmopolitan Magazine* 41.6 (October 1906): 567–74.

Marovitz, Sanford E. "The Double Bind: Leprosy in Two Hawaiian Tales by Jack London." *Eureka Studies in Teaching Short Fiction* 9.2 (Spring 2009): 160–66.

Martin, Everett Dean. *The Behavior of Crowds.* New York: Harper & Brothers, 1920.

May, Henry. *Protestant Churches and Industrial America.* 1949. Reprint, New York: Octagon, 1977.

McAfee, Ward M. "A History of Convict Labor in California." *Southern California Quarterly* 72.1 (Spring 1990): 19–40.

———. "San Quentin: The Forgotten Issue of California's Political History in the 1850s." *Southern California Quarterly* 72.3 (Fall 1990): 235–54.

McClelland, J. S. *The Crowd and the Mob from Plato to Canetti.* London: Unwin Hyman, 1989.

McClintock, James I. *Jack London's Strong Truths.* East Lansing: Michigan State University Press, 1997.

McComish, Charles Davis, and Rebecca T. Lambert. *History of Colusa and Glenn Counties.* Los Angeles: Historic Record Company, 1918.

McCosh, James. *The Divine Government.* New York: Charles Scribner's Sons, 1890.

———. *The Emotions.* New York: Charles Scribner's Sons, 1880.

McElrath, Joseph R., and Jesse S. Crisler. *Frank Norris: A Life.* Urbana: University of Illinois Press, 2006.

McGuffey's Sixth Eclectic Reader. 1879. Reprint, New York: Wiley, n.d.

McShane, Clay, and Joel A. Tarr. *The Horse in the City: Living Machines in the Nineteenth Century.* Baltimore: Johns Hopkins University Press, 2007.

Metraux, Daniel A. "Jack London's Critical Role as a Student of East Asian Affairs." *Call* 19.1–2 (2008): 7–13.

Millard, Bailey. "Jack London's Valley of the Moon Ranch." *Orchard and Farm* (October 1916): 7–8.

Mills, C. Wright. *White Collar: The American Middle Classes.* 1951. Reprint, New York: Oxford University Press, 1977.

Mitchell, J. Lawrence. "Jack London and Boxing." *American Literary Realism* 36.3 (Spring 2004): 225–42.

Mitchell, Lee Clark. "'And Rescue Us from Ourselves': Becoming Someone in Jack London's *The Sea-Wolf.*" *American Literature* 70.2 (June 1998): 317–35.
Miyamoto, Ted T. *Talk Story: Growing Up on a Sugar Plantation.* Fullerton: Institute of Gerontology, California State University for the Nikkei Writers Guild, 2010.
Moore, J. Wess. *Glimpse of Prison Life.* Gardena, CA: Institute Press, c. 1910.
Moran, Kathleen. "Jack London Tells His Wife, 'I'll Never Write a Word about It.'" In *A New Literary History of America*, edited by Greil Marcus and Werner Sollers, 503–7. Cambridge, MA: Harvard University Press, 2009.
Morrell, Ed[ward]. *The Twenty-Fifth Man.* Montclair, NJ: N.p., 1924.
Morris, Charles R. *The Tycoons: How Andrew Carnegie, John D. Rockefeller, Jay Gould, and J. P. Morgan Invented the American Supereconomy.* New York: Holt, 2006.
Mott, Frank Luther. *Golden Multitudes: The Story of Best Sellers in the United States.* New York: Macmillan, 1947.
———. *A History of American Magazines.* Vol. 4. Cambridge, MA: Harvard University Press, 1957.
———. *A History of American Magazines.* Vol. 5. Cambridge, MA: Harvard University Press, 1968.
Mullins, Joseph G. *Hawaiian Journey: An Illustrated Narrative of the History of the Islands.* Rev. ed. Honolulu: Mutual, 1978.
Murphy, Gretchen. *Shadowing the White Man's Burden: U.S. Imperialism and the Problem of the Color Line.* New York: New York University Press, 2010.
Nasaw, David. *Andrew Carnegie.* New York: Penguin, 2006.
Naughton, W. W. *Heavy-Weight Champions.* Milwaukee: Riverside, 1910.
Nelson, Richard Alan. *A Chronology of Propaganda in the United States.* Westport, CT: Greenwood, 1996.
Nitsche, Paul, and Karl Wilmanns. *The History of Prison Psychoses.* New York: Journal of Nervous and Mental Disease Publishing Company, 1912.
Nordhoff, Charles. *California: For Health, Pleasure, and Residence.* 1875. Reprint, New York: Harper & Bros., 1882.
———. *Northern California, Oregon, and the Sandwich Islands.* New York: Harper & Bros., 1875.
Norris, Frank. *The Octopus.* 1901. Reprint, New York: Penguin, 1994.
———. *The Pit.* 1902. Reprint, New York: Penguin, 1994.
Nuernberg, Susan M., ed. *The Critical Response to Jack London.* Westport, CT: Greenwood, 1995.
———. "New York City, Social Progress and the Crowd: Jack London's 'Telic Action and Collective Stupidity.'" *American Literary Realism* 40.1 (Fall 2007): 83–88.
Number 1500 [pseud.]. *Life in Sing Sing.* Indianapolis: Bobbs-Merrill, 1904.
O'Connor, Richard. *Jack London: A Biography.* Boston: Little, Brown, 1964.
O'Donnell, Katie Arosteguy. "'Things Men Must Do': Negotiating American Masculinity in Jack London's *The Valley of the Moon.*" *Atenea* 28.1 (June 2008): 37–54.

Okihiro, Gary Y. *Island World: A History of Hawai'i and the United States*. Berkeley and Los Angeles: University of California Press, 2008.

———. *Pineapple Culture: A History of the Tropical and Temperate Zones*. Berkeley and Los Angeles: University of California Press, 2009.

Okun, Peter T. "John Barleycorn's Body." *Arizona Quarterly* 52.2 (Summer 1996): 63–86.

Olmsted, Alan S., and Paul Rhode. "An Overview of California Agricultural Mechanization." *Agricultural History* 62.3 (Summer 1988): 86–112.

Ouida. See Ramé, Marie Louise.

Paris, Leslie. *Children's Nature: The Rise of the American Summer Camp*. New York: New York University Press, 2008.

Parish, Wayne W. "Ivy Lee, 'Family Physician to Big Business.'" *Literary Digest* 117 (June 9, 1934): 30.

Pattee, Fred Lewis. *The New American Literature, 1890–1930*. New York: Century, 1930.

Pease, Donald. "*Martin Eden* and the Limits of the Aesthetic Experience." *boundary 2* 25.1 (Spring 1998): 139–60.

Peluso, Robert. "Gazing at Royalty: Jack London's *The People of the Abyss* and the Emergence of American Imperialism." In *Rereading Jack London*, edited by Leonard Cassuto and Jeanne Campbell Reesman. Stanford, CA: Stanford University Press, 1996.

Petersen, Per Serritslev. "Jack London's Dialectical Philosophy between Nietzsche's Radical Nihilism and Jules de Gaultier's Boverysme." *Partial Answers: Journal of Literature and the History of Ideas* 9.1 (January 2011): 65–77.

———. "Jack London's Medusa of Truth." *Philosophy and Literature* 26.1 (April 2002): 43–56.

Pfaelzer, Jean. *Driven Out: The Forgotten War against Chinese Americans*. Berkeley: University of California Press, 2007.

Phillips, Lawrence. "The Indignity of Labor: Jack London's *Adventure* and Plantation Labor in the Solomon Islands." *Jack London Journal* 6 (1999): 175–205.

Pizer, Donald. "Jack London's 'To Build a Fire': How Not to Read Naturalist Fiction." *Philosophy and Literature* 34.1 (April 2010): 218–27.

Ponce de Leon, Charles L. *Self-Exposure: Human-Interest Journalism and the Emergence of Celebrity in America, 1890–1940*. Chapel Hill: University of North Carolina Press, 2002.

Posner, Richard. *Public Intellectuals: A Study in Decline*. Cambridge, MA: Harvard University Press, 2003.

Post, Robert, ed. *1876: A Centennial Exhibition*. Washington, DC: National Museum of History and Technology, Smithsonian Institution, 1976.

Powers, Stephen. "The California Ranch." *Atlantic Monthly*, June 1875, 684–96.

The Prison Reform League. *Crime and Criminals*. Los Angeles: Prison Reform League Publishing, 1910.

Programme of the Three Days' Celebration in Honor of the Arrival of Admiral Dewey. New York: Joseph Koehler, 1898.

Ramé, Marie Louise. *Signa*. London: Chatto and Windus, 1876.
Raney, David. "'No Ties Except Those of Blood': Class, Race, and Jack London's American Plague." *Papers on Language and Literature* 39.4 (Fall 2003): 390–430.
Raskin, Jonah, ed. *The Radical Jack London: Writings on War and Revolution*. Berkeley and Los Angeles: University of California Press, 2008.
Raucher, Alan R. *Public Relations and Business, 1900–1929*. Baltimore: Johns Hopkins University Press, 1968.
Rayner, Richard. *The Associates: Four Capitalists Who Created California*. New York: W. W. Norton, 2008.
Reesman, Jeanne Campbell. "The Call of Jack London: Earle Labor on Jack London Studies." *Studies in American Naturalism* 5.1 (Summer 2010): 21–36.
———. "Irony and Feminism in *The Little Lady of the Big House*." *Thalia* 12.1–2 (1992): 33–46.
———. *Jack London's Racial Lives: A Critical Biography*. Athens: University of Georgia Press, 2009.
———. "Jack London–Kama'aina." *Jack London Newsletter* 18.3 (September–December 1985): 71–76.
———. "Jack London's New Woman in a New World: Saxon Brown Roberts' Journey into the Valley of the Moon." *American Literary Realism* 24.2 (Winter 1992): 40–54.
———. "Marching with 'the Censor': The Japanese Army and Jack London, Author." *Jack London Journal* 6 (1999): 135–74.
———. "The Problem of Knowledge in Jack London's 'The Water Baby.'" *Western American Literature* 23 (1988): 201–15.
———. "Revisiting *Adventure*: Jack London in the Solomon Islands." *Excavatio: Emile Zola and Naturalism* 17.1–2 (2002): 385–93.
———. "Rough Justice in Jack London's 'Mauki.'" *Studies in American Naturalism* 1.1–2 (Summer–Winter 2006): 42–69.
———. "Socialism and Race in the Works of Jack London." *Excavatio* 13 (2000): 264–75.
Reesman, Jeanne Campbell, and Leonard Cassuto, eds. *Rereading Jack London*. Stanford, CA: Stanford University Press, 1996.
Reesman, Jeanne Campbell, and Sara S. Hodson, eds. *Jack London: One Hundred Years a Writer*. San Marino: Huntington Library Press, 2002.
Reesman, Jeanne Campbell, Sara S. Hodson, and Philip Adam, eds. *Jack London, Photographer*. Athens: University of Georgia Press, 2010.
Reesman, Jeanne Campbell, and Earle Labor. *Jack London*. Rev. ed. New York: Twayne, 1994.
Reesman, Jeanne Campbell, and Dale L. Walker, eds. *"No Mentor but Myself": Jack London on Writing and Writers*. Rev. and exp. ed. Stanford, CA: Stanford University Press, 1999.
Renza, Louis. "Edgar Allan Poe, Henry James, and Jack London: A Private Correspondence." *boundary 2* 27.2 (Summer 2000): 83–111.

Report and Proceedings of the Senate Committee Appointed to Investigate the Police Department of the City of New York. Vols. 1–5. Albany, NY: N.p., 1895.

Report to the State Board of Prison Directors of the State of California upon a Proposed Reformatory for Adult Offenders. Sacramento: Superintendent of State Printing, 1910.

Reuf, A. *Letter of A. Reuf to the Prison Directors*. San Francisco: California Prison Commission, 1911.

Reynolds, David. *Mightier Than the Sword: Uncle Tom's Cabin and the Battle for America*. New York: W. W. Norton, 2011.

Riedl, Gary, and Thomas R. Tietze, eds. *Jack London's Tales of Cannibals and Headhunters*. Albuquerque: University of New Mexico Press, 2006.

———. "Misinterpreting the Unreadable: Jack London's 'The Chinago' and 'The Whale Tooth.'" *Studies in Short Fiction* 34.4 (Fall 1997): 507–18.

Riesman, David, with Nathan Glazer and Reul Denny. *The Lonely Crowd*. 1950. Reprint, New Haven, CT: Yale University Press, 1969.

Rikoon, J. Sanford. *Threshing in the Midwest: A Study of Technological Change*. Bloomington: Indiana University Press, 1988.

Rivers, Kenneth. "Infinite Identities, Endless Environments: Jack London's *The Star Rover*." *Lamar Journal of the Humanities* 23.2 (1997): 21–33.

Roberts, Ian F. "Un/Civil Discourse: Jack London's Representation of the City." *Excavatio* 13 (2000): 143–48.

Robillard, Douglas. "Anna Strunsky and Jack London." *Essays in Arts and Sciences* 30 (October 2001): 17–31.

Rogers, James Edward. *The American Newspaper*. Chicago: University of Chicago Press, 1909.

Rogers, Justus H. *Colusa County, Its History Traced from a State of Nature through the Early Period of Settlement and Development to the Present Day*. Orland, CA: N.p., 1891.

Rogin, Leo. *The Introduction of Farm Machinery in Its Relation to the Productivity of Labor in the Agriculture of the United States during the Nineteenth Century*. Berkeley: University of California Press, 1931.

Roosevelt, Theodore. "Admiral Dewey." *McClure's Magazine* (October 1899): 57–62.

Ross, Edward Alsworth. *Social Control: A Survey of the Foundations of Order*. 1901. Reprint, Cleveland: Case Western Reserve University Press, 1969.

Royce, Josiah. *California from the Conquest in 1846 to the Second Vigilance Committee in San Francisco*. 1886. Reprint, New York: Knopf, 1948.

Ruef, A. *Letter of A. Ruef to the Prison Directors*. San Francisco: California Prison Commission, 1911.

Ruh, Adam, and Gary Scharnhorst. "Fifteen Minutes on Socialism with Jack London: A Recovered Interview." *Studies in American Naturalism* 2.1 (Summer 2007): 66–77.

Salvatore, Nick. *Eugene V. Debs: Citizen and Socialist*. Urbana: University of Illinois Press, 1982.

Sattler, Peter R. "Jack London and the Art of Waste Management." *Jack London Journal* 2 (1995): 73–80.

Schulten, Susan. *The Geographical Imagination in America, 1880–1950*. Chicago: University of Chicago Press, 2001.

Scott, Irving M. "Hydraulic Mining Illustrated." *Overland Monthly* 12.4 (December 1888): 576–85.

Sears, Roebuck and Co. Catalogue. 1897. Reprint, Philadelphia: Chelsea House, 1968.

Segno, A. Victor. *The Law of Mentalism*. Los Angeles: American Institute of Mentalism, 1902.

Seltzer, Mark. "The Love Master." In *Engendering Men: The Question of Male Feminist Criticism*, edited by Joseph Boone and Michael Caddon, 140–58. London: Routledge, 1990.

Shaheen, Aaron. "The Competing Narratives of Modernity in Jack London's *The Iron Heel*." *American Literary Realism* 41.1 (Fall 2008): 35–51.

Shannon, David A. *The Socialist Party of America*. New York: Macmillan, 1955.

Shannon, Fred A. *The Farmer's Last Frontier: Agriculture, 1860–1897*. 1945. Reprint, Armonk, NY: M. E. Sharpe, 1973.

Shaw, Pringle. *Rambling in California*. Toronto: James Bain, 1854.

Shi, David E. *Facing Facts: Realism in American Thought and Culture, 1850–1920*. New York: Oxford University Press, 1995.

Shillingsburg, Miriam J. "Jack London's Boxing Stories: Parables for Youth." *Eureka Studies in Teaching Short Fiction* 5.1 (2004): 7–15.

Shor, Francis. "*The Iron Heel*'s Marginal(ized) Utopia." *Extrapolation* 35.3 (Fall 1994): 211–29.

Sicherman, Barbara. *Well-Read Lives: How Books Inspired a Generation of American Women*. Chapel Hill: University of North Carolina Press, 2010.

Silverman, Kenneth. *Houdini!!!: The Career of Ehrich Weiss*. 1996. Reprint, New York: Harper, 1997.

Simpson, Mark. "Travel's Disciples." *Canadian Review of American Studies* 26.2 (Spring 1996): 83–115.

Sinclair, Upton. *The Brass Check: A Study of American Journalism*. 1928. Reprint, Urbana: University of Illinois Press, 2003.

———, ed. *The Cry for Justice: An Anthology of the Literature of Social Protest*. New York and Pasadena, CA: Upton Sinclair, 1915.

———. *Mammonart: An Essay in Economic Interpretation*. 1925. Reprint, Westport, CT: Hyperion, 1975.

Skolnick, Arnold, ed. *Paintings of California*. Berkeley and Los Angeles: University of California Press, 1997.

Slocum, Joshua. *Sailing around the World in a Small Boat*. 1900. Reprint, London: London Reprint Society, 1949.

Smith, Jane S. *The Garden of Invention: Luther Burbank and the Business of Breeding Plants*. New York: Penguin, 2009.

The Socialism of Jesus. New York: Collectivist Society, n.d.

Songs to Fan the Flames of Discontent. Spokane, WA: Industrial Worker, n.d.

Sonoma County, California: Its Resources and Advantages. Sonoma, CA: County Board of Supervisors, 1889.

Sonoma County Land Journal . . . Description of Properties for Sale and Exchange. August 1, 1883. Santa Rosa, CA: C. M. Peterson.

Standiford, Edward. *The Pattern of California History*. San Francisco: Canfield, 1975.

Stanley, Leo Leonidas. *Twenty Years at San Quentin*. Privately printed, 1933.

Stasz, Clarice. *American Dreamers: Charmian and Jack London*. New York: St. Martin's, 1988.

———. "Charmian London, Eliza Shepard, and the Jack London Biographers: Misjudgments, Misunderstandings, and Malice." *Jack London Journal* 5 (1998): 219–40.

———. "Jack London's Delayed Discovery of Fatherhood." *Jack London Journal* 5 (1996): 146–68.

———. *Jack London's Women*. Amherst: University of Massachusetts Press, 2001.

———. "Sarcasm, Irony, and Social Darwinism in Jack London's *Adventure*." *Thalia* 12.1–2 (1992): 83–90.

Stein, Richard L. "London's Londons: Photographing Poverty in *The People of the Abyss*." *Nineteenth-Century Contexts* 22.4 (2001): 587–629.

Stiles, T. J. *The First Tycoon: The Epic Life of Cornelius Vanderbilt*. New York: Knopf, 2009.

Stone, Scott C. S. *Yesterday in Hawaii: A Voyage through Time*. Waipahu, HI: Island Heritage, 2010.

Street, Richard Steven. *Beasts of the Field: A Narrative History of California Farmworkers*. Palo Alto, CA: Stanford University Press, 2004.

Streeter, John Williams. *The Fat of the Land: The Story of an American Farm*. New York: Grosset and Dunlap, 1904.

Sullivan, Mark. *Our Times: America Finding Itself*. 1927. Reprint, New York: Charles Scribner's Sons, 1971.

Sumner, William Graham. "The Philosophy of Strikes." *Harper's Weekly* 23 (September 15, 1883): 536.

———. *What Social Classes Owe to Each Other*. New York: Harper, 1883.

Sundeen, Mark. "The Man Who Would Be Jack London: Wrestling (and Driving Around) with the Legacy of the Most Widely Read American in the World." *Believer* 4.6 (August 2006): 27–37.

Supplement to 1876: A Centennial Exhibition. Washington, DC: National Museum of History and Technology, Smithsonian Institution, 1976.

Swafford, Kevin R. "Resounding the Abyss: The Politics of Narration in Jack London's *The People of the Abyss*." *Journal of Popular Culture* 39.6 (October 2006): 838–60.

Sweeney, Michael S. "'Delays and Vexation': Jack London and the Russo-Japanese War." *Journalism and Mass Communication Quarterly* 75.3 (Autumn 1998): 548–59.

Swift, John N. "Jack London's 'The Unparalleled Invasion': Germ Warfare, Eugenics, and Cultural Hygiene." *American Literary Realism* 35.1 (Fall 2002): 59–71.

Takaki, Ronald. *Pau Hana: Plantation Life and Labor in Hawaii, 1835–1920*. Honolulu: University of Hawaii Press, 1983.

Tarbell, Ida M. *The History of the Standard Oil Company*. 1902–4. Reprint, 2 vols., New York: McClure, Phillips, 1905.
Tarde, Gabriel. *On Communication and Social Influence*. 1899. Reprint, Chicago: University of Chicago Press, 1969.
Tavernier-Courbin, Jacqueline. "Bessie: The First Mrs. Jack London." *Jack London Journal* 5 (1998): 168–218.
———. "A Californian Blend of Naturalism and Romanticism: Frank Norris and Jack London." *Excavatio* 8 (1996): 118–28.
———. "*The Call of the Wild* and *The Jungle*: Jack London's and Upton Sinclair's Animal and Human Jungles." In *The Cambridge Companion to American Realism and Naturalism: Howells to London*, edited by Donald Pizer, 236–62. Cambridge: Cambridge University Press, 1995.
———. "A Controversial Female Trickster in Jack London's 'The Wit of Porportuk.'" *Thalia* 14.1–2 (1998): 42–49.
———, ed. *Critical Essays on Jack London*. Boston: G. K. Hall, 1983.
———. "A Daughter's Last Message." *Thalia* 12.1–2 (1992): 91–100.
———. "Jack London: 'A Pretty Good Correspondent.'" *Thalia* 12.1–2 (1992): 101–10.
———. "A Romantic Novel." *Jack London Journal* 1 (1994): 215–30.
———. "Social Myth as Parody in Jack London's Northern Tales." *Thalia* 9.2 (Fall–Winter 1987): 3–14.
———. "To Love or Not to Love? Jack London and Anna Strunsky's *The Kempton-Wace Letters*." *Symbiosis* 1.2 (October 1997): 255–74.
Taylor, Bayard. *Eldorado, or Adventures in the Path of Empire*. 2 vols. New York: George P. Putnam, 1850.
Teaching of Buddha. Tokyo: Bukkyo Dendo Kyokai, 1966.
Ten Bruggencate, Jan K. *Hawaii's Pineapple Century: A History of the Crowded Fruit in the Hawaiian Islands*. Honolulu: Mutual, 2004.
Theisen, Kay M. "Realism as Represented in 'South of the Slot,' Naturalism as Represented in 'To Build a Fire': Critical Thinking and Pedagogy." *Eureka Studies in Teaching Short Fiction* 5.2 (Spring 2005): 99–107.
Thompson, Robert A. *Historical and Descriptive Sketch of Sonoma County, California*. Philadelphia: L. H. Everts, 1877.
Thrum, Thomas G., ed. *Hawaiian Almanac and Annual for 1907*. Honolulu: Thrum, 1906.
———. *Hawaiian Almanac and Annual for 1908*. Honolulu: Thrum, 1907.
———. *Hawaiian Almanac and Annual for 1915*. Honolulu: Thrum, 1914.
———. *Hawaiian Almanac and Annual for 1916*. Honolulu: Thrum, 1915.
Thurston, Lorrin A. "The Sandwich Islands: The Advantages of Annexation." *North American Review* 156 (March 1893): 265–81.
Tichi, Cecelia. *Embodiment of a Nation: Human Form in American Places*. Cambridge, MA: Harvard University Press, 2001.
———. "Thespis and the Carnall Hypocrite: A Puritan Motive for Aversion to Drama." *Early American Literature* 4 (Winter 1970): 86–117.

———, ed. *Life in the Iron Mills*. Boston: Bedford St. Martins, 1998.

Tietze, Thomas R., and Gary Riedl. "'Saints in Slime': The Ironic Use of Racism in Jack London's *South Sea Tales*." *Thalia* 12.1–2 (1992): 59–66.

Tindall, George Brown, and David Shi. *America: A Narrative History*. 3rd ed. New York: W. W. Norton, 1992.

Tocqueville, Alexis [de]. *Democracy in America*. 1840. Reprint, New York: Vintage, 1990.

Tolstoi, Lyof N. *Anna Karenina*. Translated by Nathan Haskell Dole. New York: Thomas Crowell & Co., 1886.

Trachtenberg, Alan. *The Incorporation of America: Culture and Society in the Gilded Age*. New York: Hill and Wang, 1982.

Tuomey, Honoria. *History of Sonoma County, California*. Chicago: S. J. Clarke, 1926.

Train, Arthur. *True Stories of Crime*. New York: Charles Scribner's Sons, 1912.

Trimble, Paul C., and William Knorp. *Ferries of San Francisco Bay*. Charleston, SC: Arcadia, 2007.

Twain, Mark. *Mark Twain's Letters from Hawaii*. Edited by A. Grove Day. Honolulu: University of Hawaii Press, 1966.

Van Dillen, Lailee. "Becky London: The Quiet Survivor Talks about Her Father." *The Californian* 4.1 (January–February 1902): 34–39.

Veblen, Thorstein. *The Theory of the Leisure Class*. 1899. Reprint, New York: Penguin, 1979.

Vernon-Harcourt, F. C. *Bolts and Bars*. London: Digby, Long & Co., 1905.

Von Tempski, Armine. *Born in Paradise*. 1940. Reprint, New York: Hawthorne, 1968.

Walker, Franklin. *Jack London and the Klondike: The Genesis of an American Writer*. San Marino: Huntington Library Press, 1966.

Ward, Susan. "Jack London as a Western Writer." *Jack London Journal* 1 (1994): 26–42.

Washburn, Charles. *Press Agentry*. New York: National Library Press, 1937.

Weisman, August. *Essays upon Heredity and Kindred Biological Problems*. 2 vols. Oxford: Clarendon, 1891.

Westervelt, William D. *Myths and Legends of Hawaii*. 1913. Reprint, Honolulu: Mutual, 1987.

Whalen-Bridge, John. "Dual Perspectives in *The Iron Heel*." *Thalia* 12.1–2 (1992): 67–76.

———. "How to Read a Revolutionary Novel: *The Iron Heel*." *Jack London Journal* 5 (1998): 38–63.

White, Bruce. "Jack London on Elbert Hubbard: From 'Splendid Character' to Cad." *Jack London Journal* 3 (1996): 57–66.

White, Richard. *Railroaded: The Transcontinentals and the Making of Modern America*. New York: W. W. Norton, 2011.

White, William Allen. "The Business of a Wheat Farm." *Scribner's Magazine* 22.5 (November 1897): 531–48.

Whitlock, Brand. *The Turn of the Balance*. Indianapolis: Bobbs-Merrill, 1907.

Wilcox, Earl J. "A Naturalist in Search of His Subject: Jack London's *The People of the Abyss*." *Excavatio* 2 (Fall 1995): 116–23.

Wilde, Oscar. *The Ballad of Reading Goal*. New York: Brentano's, 1896.
———. *Children in Prison and Other Cruelties of Prison Life*. London: Murdoch & Co., 1898.
Williams, Jay. *Author under Sail: The Imagination of Jack London, 1893–1902*. Lincoln: University of Nebraska Press, 2014.
Williams, Tony. "London's Last Frontier: The Big House as Culture of Consumption." *Jack London Journal* 2 (1996): 156–74.
Williamson, Eric Miles. *Oakland, Jack London, and Me*. Huntsville: Texas Review Press, 2007.
Wilson, Christopher. *The Labor of Words: Literary Professionalism in the Progressive Era*. Athens: University of Georgia Press, 1985.
Wilson, Woodrow. *The State: Elements of Historical and Practical Politics*. Boston: D. C. Heath, 1907.
Winchester, Simon. *A Crack in the Edge of the World*. New York: HarperCollins, 2005.
Wisehart, M. K. "How Big Men Think and Act." *American Magazine* 108 (July 1929): 30–31, 125–27.
Wisniewski, Richard A. *The Rise and Fall of the Hawaiian Kingdom: A Pictorial History*. Honolulu: Pacific Basin Enterprises, 1979.
Woodward, Servanne. "Sympathy and Indifference as Opposing Principles in the Society of Jack London's *Son of the Wolf* (1900)." *Excavato* 2 (Fall 1993): 124–31.
———. "'The Wife of a King' from a Bergsonian Perspective." *Thalia* 12.1–2 (1992): 47–54.
Wright, Louise E. "Jack London's Knowledge of Thoreau." *Concord Saunterer* 14 (2006): 61–72.
———. "'Talk about Real Men': Jack London's Correspondence with Maurice Magnus." *Journal of Popular Culture* 40.2 (April 2007): 361–77.
Yamamoto, Michael T., Nina Yuriko (Ota) Sylva, and Karen N. Yamamoto, eds. *Waipahu . . . Recollections from a Sugar Plantation Community in Hawaii*. N.p.: N.p., 2005.
Zacks, Richard. *Island of Vice: Theodore Roosevelt's Quest to Clean Up Sin-Loving New York*. New York: Anchor, 2012.
Zamen, Mark. *Standing Room Only: Jack London's Controversial Career as a Public Speaker*. New York: Peter Lang, 1990.
———. "'The Storm of Applause': Jack London's Oratorical Career." *Jack London Journal* 1 (1994): 235–67.
Zarefsky, David. "'Public Sentiment Is Everything': Lincoln's View of Political Persuasion." *Journal of the Abraham Lincoln Association* 15.2 (Summer 1994): 23–42.

ACKNOWLEDGMENTS

For years I gestured toward Jack London as numerous critics do, listing his name in clusters of US writers and mining his work for short quotations. Then he came into sharp focus through the lens of his contemporaries, outstanding Progressive Era figures and investigative muckraking journalists. That is, London emerged as a major public intellectual spurring the country from the depredations of the Gilded Age and toward the Progressive Era—and worthy of a book on this very point. At first this project seemed straightforward from A to Z, which is to say that I began in the state of delusion familiar to many authors launching a new book.

So to a pilgrim's progress. *Jack London and the Fight for America's Future* owes its launch to Cindy Weinstein, who first saw that my early description was not for a book—but only a chapter—and urged expansion in whatever directions might become clear. Her generosity has continued, as has that of Thadious Davis and Teresa Goddu, all of whom supported my applications for two Andrew W. Mellon Fellowships at the Henry E. Huntington Library, which houses the voluminous Jack London Collection. Staffing the Huntington's Ahmanson reading room desk, Alisa Monheim and Jaeda Snow proved to be as efficient as they are genial, as is Gina Giang, who helped locate images. Making acquaintance with Jay Williams, who has been at work in the Jack London Collection, was a great gift. Completing the first volume of his *Author under Sail*, Jay generously provided pertinent facts that turn speculation into data. In due course Teresa and Amy S. Lang critiqued drafts of a new introductory chapter and offered invaluable editorial advice. Wendy Martin invited me to present a talk at Claremont Graduate University at which I introduced Jack London in the identity that is central to this book—as a foremost American public intellectual. Acquaintance with Darius Anderson led to an invitation to view and work in his "Jack London in Sonoma" trove of professionally catalogued manuscripts, artifacts, and memorabilia, a research effort that has significantly enriched this project. In addition, Darius provided lodgings in his sumptuous "Barn." I thank him and Sarah and also Tom and Eileen Anderson for their wondrous hospitality.

Readers of the enhanced ebook edition of *Jack London: A Writer's Fight for a Better America* owe a great deal to Rosemary Hanes of the Motion Picture and Television room of the Library of Congress. Rosemary guided me to the relevant 1910s footage that visually enlarges the issues raised in this book. Tia Reber and her colleagues at the Bishop Museum (Honolulu) also assisted in arranging archival motion picture film for inclusion here. Carol Dodge of the California Department of Parks and Recreation and Tjiska Vanwyck, the executive director of the Jack London State Park, have been most helpful. Readers also owe a debt of gratitude to Jamie Adams, the manager of information services in the Office of Information Technology for the Vanderbilt University College of Liberal Arts. Jamie edited and formatted all of the film footage and the Jack London digital slide show. Her work is a keystone of the enhanced ebook.

The semester-long academic leaves that enabled this project to advance were authorized by Vanderbilt University, and I thank the chair of the Department of English, Mark Schoenfield; the dean of the College of Arts and Science, Carolyn Dever; and Provost Richard McCarty. The administrative staff in the Department of English has assisted in numerous ways, from logistical to moral support, and I especially thank Janis L. May. The Vanderbilt University librarians have helped greatly, including the Interlibrary Loan Services officers Marilyn Pilley, David Hughett, and Rachel Adams, in addition to James E. Toplon, who helped find editions that were published and widely circulated in Jack London's era. The research assistance of doctoral candidate (and now professor) Benjamin Gradon and of Jonathan Thurston were most helpful, as were discussions of Jack London's fiction in Vanderbilt undergraduate courses and in the university's Master of Liberal Arts Studies (MLAS) program in the Graduate School. I thank Del Tinsley, J. T. Ellison, and J. B. Brooks for their encouragement in the BMW writers' group. In addition, I remain continuously appreciative of the William R. Kenan, Jr. Charitable Trust for underwriting my position.

Two figures have been lifelines for this project. Sara (Sue) Hodson, senior curator of manuscripts at the Huntington Library, served as my in-person *vademecum* to the collections, alerting me to particular invaluable holdings, from Jack London's formal files to his penciled notes on "scribble-pads." Lunch with Sue in the Huntington garden terrace became a treat, and her friendship continues to mean a great deal. From the East Coast, meanwhile, came the query of literary agent Deirdre Mullane, who represents authors of "crossover" books that might appeal both to scholars and to a wider public. Deirdre has been a cheerleader and guide for this project as well as an editor par excellence from earlier draft stages of the manuscript to the signing of the contract at the University of North Carolina Press under the auspices of Charles (Chuck) Grench, assistant director and senior editor at the press.

Paul Betz, managing editor of the press, guided the complex transition of this project from manuscript to book, for which I am most grateful. Christi Stanforth's superb copyediting contributed precision and, in a number of places, graceful phrasing.

Two outside UNC press reviewers of *Jack London and the Fight for America's Future* have provided crucial critiques. Their recommendations have prompted revision for structural unity and for argumentive focus. Their incisive readings, informed by expertise in US literary history as well as the Jack London oeuvre, have benefited this project tremendously. Each reviewer read the manuscript twice, first in its partial state and later upon completion. The extensive time committed to this work is a form of intellectual philanthropy for which I am most grateful.

Close to home, I have enjoyed the support of my daughters, Claire Grezemkovsky and Julia Harrison. As ever, Bill Tichi has been my first responder and editor, guardian of my well-being and confidant—my life's sine qua non.

INDEX

ENHANCED E-BOOK CREDITS

1. Jack London Portrait Gallery:

Jack London "bust" in three-quarters profile in shirt and tie (Library of Congress)

Jack London wearing soft cap (Henry E. Huntington Library)

Jack London bare-chested in boxing stance (Henry E. Huntington Library)

Jack London aboard *Snark* in South Seas wearing lava-lava alongside Charmian in sarong (Henry E. Huntington Library)

Bas-relief sculpture by Finn Frolich of Jack London's face in profile, 1914 (Henry E. Huntington Library)

Jack London day-of-issue first-class US postage stamp and cover (United States Postal Service)

Jack London in motion picture from *Martin Eden*, 1914 (Archival film and/or video materials from the collections of the Library of Congress, AFI/Douglas Wright Collection)

2. *Jeffries and Ruhlin prizefight at San Francisco, November 15, 1901* (Archival film and/or video materials from the collections of the Library of Congress, Paper Print Collection)
3. *San Francisco Earthquake and Fire*, 1906 (Archival film and/or video materials from the collections of the Library of Congress, "American Memory" project)
4. *Hawaiian Islands*, 1910s (Archival film and/or video materials from the collections of the Library of Congress, George Klein Collection)
5. Sugarcane Workers: *Hawaiian Islands, 1910s* (Archival film and/or video materials from the collections of the Library of Congress, George Klein Collection) and *Historical Highlights of Field Mechanization*, 1930 (Bishop Museum, Honolulu, Hawaii)
6. *Children of Eve, 1913* (Archival film and/or video materials from the collections of the Library of Congress, George Klein Collection)
7. Jack and Charmian London at Beauty Ranch, ca. 1915 (California Department of Parks and Recreation and Gaumont Film Company[Paris, France])
8. *Houdini Releases Himself from Strait Jacket While Suspended*, 1924 (Archival film and/or video materials from the collections of the Library of Congress, LC Purchase Collection)